Longitudinal Data Analysis

LONGITUDINAL DATA ANALYSIS

JAMES S. COLEMAN

Basic Books, Inc., Publishers   New York

A volume in the
Paul F. Lazarsfeld Lecture in Sociology Series,
published in collaboration with the
Institute for Advanced Studies in Vienna.

Library of Congress Cataloging in Publication Data

Coleman, James Samuel, 1926–
  Longitudinal data analysis.

  (Paul F. Lazarsfeld lecture in sociology series)
  References: p. 291
  Includes index.
  1. Sociology—Longitudinal studies. I. Title.
II. Series.
HM24.C6415   301   80–66309
ISBN 0–465–04224–4   AACR2

To My Sons

Thomas, John, Stephen, Daniel

Contents

Contents

Acknowledgments

I am grateful to the Institut für Höhere Studien in Vienna for making this book possible through its invitation to me to deliver the first Paul F. Lazarsfeld lectures in June 1979.

I am grateful as well to Andrew Walaszek, who did most of the programming for the LONGIT·CROSS program of chapter 2 and a large part of the programming for the LONGIT·PANEL and LONGIT·EVENTP programs.

Aage Sorenson and I had planned, some years ago, to collaborate on a book on longitudinal data analysis. Although this book is not the realization of our plans, it has been enriched by those plans and by our continuing discussions of these issues. In addition, my approach to these matters has been greatly enriched by the work of and discussions with Michael Hannan, Burton Singer, Seymour Spilerman, Arthur Stinchcombe, and Nancy Teema.

Preface

This book originated as a set of six lectures in Vienna in June 1979, in honor of Paul Lazarsfeld. The first lecture was held at the University of Vienna, where Lazarsfeld received his doctoral degree; the remaining five were held at the Institut für Höhere Studien, which Paul Lazarsfeld was instrumental in establishing in Vienna in the early 1960s. The lectures themselves have been expanded greatly and at points are highly technical. Before turning to the substance of the lectures, however, it is appropriate to indicate how their substance grows out of work by Paul Lazarsfeld, and even prior to that, to show briefly the intellectual development that culminated in Lazarsfeld's pursuit of this direction of work.

Paul Lazarsfeld both received his doctorate at the University of Vienna and made the shift from mathematics to social psychology here, in his work in the laboratory of Charlotte and Karl Bühler. He carried out his first social research in Vienna; some would argue that this work was more sociological, despite his presence in a psychology laboratory, than it was subsequently in America, where he was always in a sociology department. His first publication of any note was in 1933, reporting a study carried out in 1931 of Marienthal (a small industrial town near Vienna where a large fraction of the men were unemployed).[1] This research, which he carried out with Marie Jahoda and Hans Zeisel, is useful for what it tells us about Lazarsfeld's early orientation, both in methods and in substance.

What is most striking about the methods used in this study are their diversity and range, and particularly the mixture of qualitative and quantitative techniques. They included rich qualitative interviews, which obtained not only the respondent's current condition but also his life history. They included time budgets and money budgets, menus of households, measures of changes in subscriptions to a politically oriented newspaper, *Arbeiterzeitung*, and an entertainment-oriented newspaper, *Kleine Blatt* (the latter showing a lesser reduction in subscriptions, thus confirming the inference of loss of interest in politics), loss of membership in different kinds of organizations (leading

[1] Marienthal has since been absorbed into Gramatneusiedl.

to a similar inference), demographic information about the village, the health of children whose fathers were working and those whose fathers were not. They even measured the speed of walking of men (whose lives had been totally transformed by unemployment) and women (whose daily schedule, as they show elsewhere, was not greatly different than before). They showed that over half of the thirty-three men they observed walked at less than two miles per hour, while less than a quarter of women did. They observed, at the noontime peak of pedestrian traffic in Marienthal, sixty-eight men and thirty-two women walking the 300-meter stretch of the village's main street, and they counted the number of stops these pedestrians made. Fifty-seven percent of the men made three or more stops; only 9 percent of the women did.

The methods used in Marienthal exemplified the transformation of qualitative observations into quantitative measures. Lazarsfeld was always looking for a way to do this. Many observers on the main street of Marienthal in 1931 would gain a sense of slowness of life, the "weariness" of the community, as the authors termed it. But not many would discover how to translate these impressions into quantitative measures, such as the speed of walking or the number of stops made. And even fewer would have recognized the necessity for some kind of baseline for comparison, in this case provided by the women whose daily lives had not changed greatly.

Once Lazarsfeld came to America, his work became far more individualistic. His interests lay, as he often said, in the empirical analysis of action. He shaped the infant art of survey research into analysis of individual action in a social context. Panel analysis was an extension of this.

It could have gone otherwise in the hands of someone else; survey methods could have been used to characterize groups, organizations, communities, institutions. We should not forget that in the immediately preceding and even contemporary research in American sociology—the Lynds' *Middletown,* the large number of community and neighborhood studies that came from Robert E. Park's students, Lloyd Warner's and Hollingshead's studies of social stratification in American communities—in all this research, the community or some other social unit was the object of interest. Not so in Paul Lazarsfeld's work after *Marienthal.* Even when a community was the setting, as in the Sandusky *(The People's Choice)* and Elmira *(Voting)* studies of voting, or in the Decatur study *(Personal Influence),* the analysis was not of a community, but of individual decision making in a social context.

This direction of work Paul Lazarsfeld so impressed upon the discipline of sociology that most sociologists do it now, not just those in a "Lazarsfeld tradition" or a "Columbia tradition" or an "American tradition." As the continuing strength and vitality of that direction, and its extensive growth among European sociologists, attests, it is an important direction. In Lazarsfeld's own work, it probably came about through his immigration to America and the sudden exposure to á society with mass media: where closed communities like Marienthal had been pried open by the mass media, resulting in a vast amorphous society in which products seemed to be sold, attitudes seemed to be formed, and individual actions seemed to be shaped, no longer by *interpersonal* communication, but by *communication from the mass media* to atomistic individuals. Perhaps the most enduring substantive contribution of Lazarsfeld to sociology was to show that the process is not so simple, that interpersonal communication does play an important part, that there are opinion leaders and followers, that there is a two-step flow of communication.

In such a society, where the old structures were no longer so binding, encompassing, and powerful, the focus of interest must be on individual action. It cannot any longer be the community, treated as an inviolate unit, as a single actor. This does not mean, of course, that social structure is no longer important, but that it cannot be treated as fixed, and sociological analysis cannot be confined to fixed social units but must include both individuals and social structure. Lazarsfeld's principal ways of carrying out this analysis were survey analysis, where he made important analytical innovations, and panel analysis—that is, multiple interviews of the same persons—of which he was the principal initiator. With both these techniques he wanted to study empirically the determinants of action. For him, panel analysis carried the hope of answering causal questions that were obscured in a single survey, because a panel, by observing the same people at two or more points in time, could examine the sequence in which changes took place. It is this aspect of Lazarsfeld's work, this general aim, that I pursue in the chapters of this book.

It is no accident that I do so, for during my graduate training, this obsession of Lazarsfeld's to find the appropriate means, with panel data, to infer causation became an obsession of mine as well. Unlike Lazarsfeld, I came to believe that this could be done, not by constructing an index or a measure with useful statistical properties, but only by first establishing an explicit model of a process, and then using the panel data to infer parameters of that process.

The process that appeared appropriate for qualitative data as a starting point was a continuous-time, discrete-space Markov process. I developed the application of this model to survey panel data in *Introduction to Mathematical Sociology* (1964), and subsequently in other publications (particularly in Coleman, 1964b and 1968). More recently, biometricians attempting to measure the effect of various factors on survival rates (see Cox, 1972) and sociologists attempting to measure the effects of various factors on actions, such as marriage, divorce, and getting or losing a job (Tuma, Hannan, and Groeneveld, 1978; DiPrete, 1979), have applied the same model, and extensions of it. These new developments constitute a major change, for they use not panel data but continuous records of the times at which events occur. They constitute a considerable expansion in our capability of quantitative analysis of longitudinal data to make causal inferences. In addition, they make possible a unified approach to inference about causes of qualitative actions, whether the data are cross-sectional, panel data, or continuous records of events. The unifying element is the process assumed to be operative: a continuous-time, discrete-space stochastic process. It is this unifying character given to data analysis by the idea of a process that I emphasize in this book.

As it turns out, and as I discuss in the last section of chapter 5, developments in the analysis of times of events promise to bring more closely together than in the past the qualitative and quantitative orientations that characterized Paul Lazarsfeld's two methodological interests. He was not able to carry his observations of actions in Marienthal into quantitative analysis despite his ingenuity of measurement. That possibility was reserved for survey data on a sample of individuals, either cross-sectional or panel; and even that possibility was in part due to his inventiveness. What now begins to be possible is the use of quantitative methods in conjunction with observation of actions characterizing a single entity (an individual or a social system) over time or several such entities, similar to what has been called the "natural history" approach in sociology. It is fitting, then, that methods developed in part to address problems raised by Lazarsfeld in his quantitative capacity have begun to be capable of capturing some of the processes he studied in his qualitative capacity.

Longitudinal Data Analysis

Chapter 1

The Process,

the Model,

and Forms of Data

There is a broad class of processes in which an identifiable unit—which may be a person, an organization, a society, or whatever—changes from one of a set of mutually exclusive and exhaustive states to another. The process may be one in which persons change between a state of employment and a state of unemployment or between living in region A, B, C, or D of a country. Or it may be one in which societies change among different forms of government, or one in which organizations change between states of solvency and bankruptcy, or one in which children change in mood between being happy and sad. This class of processes gives rise to a variety of forms of data, some of which are familiar indeed, others less so.

I will give some examples of the kind of process I am describing and the problem of interest in each case. In each example, the model of the form I will introduce has been used to analyze the problem.

1. The process is movement between employment and unemployment,

two states that adult members of the labor force may find themselves in. The problem is discovering the causes of unemployment and employment (DiPrete, 1981).

2. The process is marriage and divorce. The problem is discovering what factors lead to divorce, and in particular, whether the existence of a guaranteed annual income affects the process (Hannan, Tuma, and Groeneveld, 1978).

3. The process is change of governments in societies where the possible forms are (a) traditional monarchy, (b) military dictatorship, (c) one-party state, (d) two-or-more-party state, (e) colony. The problem is to discover the effects of various characteristics of the societies on the form of government and the movement from one form to another (Hannan and Carroll, 1981).

4. The process is a choice of attending or not attending college. The problem is what factors affect this choice, and how those factors change over the years in secondary school (McDill and Coleman, 1963).

5. The process is purchasing one brand of consumer nondurable or another. The problem is discovering how entry of a new brand into the market affects choices and what the long-range effect will be (Coleman, 1964b).

6. The process is dying. The problem is determining whether a heart transplant affected the process, and also, how the process is affected by other variables such as age and previous surgery (Crowley and Hu, 1977).

As these examples indicate, a prominent area of application is the changes that persons undergo or the choices they make as they pass through life. Some of these changes are irreversible, such as passing through puberty, and others are reversible, such as ownership of a particular make of car. There have been two major research methods used to study these processes: the intensive examination of one or a few persons over a considerable span of time, and surveys of large samples of persons either at one time only, or with repeated interviews—two, three, or several times. The first method may be described as the *case study of life histories,* while the second is a *cross-sectional survey* (if limited to one interview) or a *panel survey* (if it uses repeated interviews). When inferences about causes are drawn from a cross-sectional survey, the method can be roughly termed *comparative statics* (though in methods of statistical analysis applied to cross-sectional samples, the techniques are not often described that way).

In principle it is possible to combine the two methods and follow a sample of persons over a span of time. Only recently, however, has this combination of intensive and extensive methods been pursued. In sociological research, Nancy Tuma and Michael Hannan, in publications referred to above, are principally responsible for introduction of this approach. It is apparent, when one sees the kind of richness of insight which case histories provide and the precision, conclusiveness, and scope which sample surveys provide, that methods which combine these virtues can be extraordinarily valuable for social science. Such methods have begun to be developed, and a few bodies of data appropriate to them have been collected and subjected to analysis (including the examples referred to above with publication dates 1977 and after). Thus it becomes possible to give some sense of just what can be done with these methods, and that is what I will attempt to do here.

The goals of the work that I will describe are to infer causation, a task that is at best difficult with cross-sectional data, but is often seen as greatly facilitated with longitudinal data. The general approach will be (1) to begin with the idea of a process, (2) to attempt to lay out a mathematical model that mirrors this process, and then (3) given particular kinds of data, to transform the mathematical model into a statistical model for estimating parameters of the process. In general the goal will not be one of testing hypotheses but rather one of estimating parameters in a mathematical model designed to mirror a substantive process.

There is a distinct difference between the way I am proceeding and a more common way of proceeding in the analysis of data in social science. The more common way can be termed *statistical data analysis,* in which the method of statistical analysis is designed for a particular form of data, and, in effect, determined by that data form. For example, there are a number of statistical techniques designed for analysis of cross-classifications of categorical data: logit analysis, probit analysis, loglinear methods, linear probability models, partitioning of chi-square, and others. These models of statistical analysis are used to lead to causal inferences about the effects of various factors on location in such a tabulation. And behind the causal inference lies some kind of model or theory about the way the effects take place. But the substantive process that generates the data is distinctly secondary to the statistical model and the data. A hint of this can be seen in the small and somewhat ancillary role that *change* plays in these statistical models, despite the fact that any causal process that generated the data necessarily involved change.

The approach I will outline in these chapters is somewhat different. The mathematical model is what may be termed a *model of the process.* The form of statistical analysis will be derived from, and subordinate to, the model of the process. As I will show in later chapters, a model of the same process can give rise to several different forms of statistical analysis, depending on the kind of data generated by the data-collecting method. Perhaps another way of putting the difference is to recognize that for analyzing problems of the sort that I have described earlier, there are two processes involved; one is the internal process within the unit of interest that results in its being in a given state. This is what I have called the substantive process. The second is the process by which data are generated, a process that is determined by the method of data collection. I am suggesting that the form of statistical analysis cannot depend only on the second, data-generating process, but must depend as well on the substantive process.

This orientation, although it may invite ready assent, leads to data analyses quite different from some of those in current use. By using the idea of a common underlying process, parameters with identical dimensional meaning for the effect of independent variables on action may be recovered from analysis of cross-sectional data, panel data, and continuous records of events or acts. And the model for data analysis differs depending on the form of data. For example, as I will indicate in subsequent chapters, the process in one of its forms implies use of a logit or loglinear data-analysis model for cross-sectional data, but a *different* data-analysis model for panel data, to recover the *same* parameters. Or, to put it differently, if there is a loglinear decomposition of the parameters of the *process*, this implies a loglinear form of data-analysis for cross-sectional data, but it implies a *different* form for panel data. This will also suggest why it is that the logit or loglinear model applied to analysis of two interdependent variables with panel data is curiously unable to identify separately the effects of each variable on the other. The model is, quite simply, misspecified (Fienberg, 1977, p. 105).

The three components of the present approach are, then, the substantive process, the data, and the formal model. To make clear just what I will cover in these chapters, I will describe the types of processes, the types of data, and the mathematical model.

1. THE PROCESSES

1.   The first aspect of the process is that changes occur between discrete states of a unit. For example, the unit is a person, the state is being employed or unemployed. Or the unit is a house, and the state is being occupied or unoccupied. Or the unit is a woman, and her state is the number of children to whom she has given birth. Or the unit is a nation, and the state is the form of government it has.

2.   Changes can occur at any point in time and are not constrained to predetermined time points.

3. Changes may be reversible or irreversible in different forms of the process.

4. Changes are not predetermined by the current state (though they may be affected by that state). For example, the process is not like that of certain primitive tribes, where a man may marry only a woman from a given segment of that tribe.

5. There are factors affecting this process, and analysis of the process should discover those effects.

6. In certain cases, the state that the unit is in is not fully observable, and the process of change among the unobservable states is also unobservable. For example, if the states are attitudes, there may be some unreliability in reporting.

2. THE FORM OF DATA

1. The most common form of data from which such causal inferences as described in (5) above are made is a single observation of many persons in a cross-sectional sample survey. The implicit mode of analysis is comparative statics. The usual form of data obtained is cross-classifications of occupancy in a given state and positions on other possibly causal factors. Most categorical data analysis is analysis of this form of data.

2. A less common form is two or more interviews or observations of many persons or other units at fixed intervals. It is the same persons or units that are reinterviewed or observed again. This is ordinarily termed a panel. The form of data is similar to that described for the cross-sectional sample survey, except that units are cross-classified according to the state at each observation. The information obtained concerns the state that each unit is in at each observation; there is no information about the number of events (that is, changes of state) between observations.

3. A third form of data is one or more observations on a sample of persons or other units with information about preceding changes, such as the number of changes in a specified period or the date of the last change. For example, the date of the last hospital visit is a question often asked in a questionnaire. This contrasts with what I have called *cross-sectional data* in that information is obtained about what happened during some time in the past. The data are ordinarily of the form of the number of things in a

fixed interval of time (for example, the number of absences in the last two weeks), or (as in the hospital visit question mentioned above) the amount of time for a fixed number of changes (for example, "the time since you last . . .").

4. More complete information is contained in the next form of data: a history of the sequence of states of the unit over a period of time. Here one knows the type of each event (for example, from state i to state j) and its position in the sequence but not the time at which the event occurred.

5. All of the preceding forms of data have contained a partial record of the history of events, ranging from merely the record of the current state to the history of the sequence of states. The final form of data is that complete record, including both the sequence of events and the time at which each event occurred. Common examples of such records are job histories, individuals' voting records, consumer diary panels that record purchases, administrative files in an office, dates of absence of a particular jobholder, and so on. Such records can be analyzed either for single individuals (or other units) or for sets of individuals.

With all forms of data described above, there is ordinarily additional information about factors other than the attribute of interest. The data are sometimes categorical, sometimes continuous variables; they are sometimes fixed characteristics of the unit, sometimes time-specific characteristics of the unit, and sometimes characteristics of a particular time, alike for all units.

3. THE MATHEMATICAL MODEL

For processes of the sort I have described above, the three critical elements in determining the class of mathematical models that is appropriate are the fact that units change between states, that the time of change is not fixed, and that the direction of change is not fixed by the current state occupied. This identifies the class of models as *discrete-state, continuous-time, stochastic* models. Models of this sort have been widely used in physical sciences to study radioactive decay, chemical reactions, Brownian motion, and other processes. They have begun to be used in the social sciences as well, in investigations of the sort described in the earlier examples.

This class of models remains very general, and I will place some further restrictions upon it, some of which will be subsequently relaxed. This indicates the general strategy I will pursue: to use a model that generally conforms to the idea one has of the substantive process, but to constrain the processes in ways that make possible estimation of parameters, although the assumptions implied by the constraints may not be met in reality. With this as a starting point, it then becomes possible to relax certain of the constraints (or to test the assumptions they imply) when richer data or more powerful estimating methods become available.

3.1. THE GENERAL MODEL

Continuous-time discrete-state stochastic processes are defined as follows: Let there be s states, indexed by i, $i = 1, 2, \ldots, s$.

The unit in question has a probability $p_1(t), \ldots, p_i(t), \ldots, p_s(t)$ of occupying state $1, \ldots, i, \ldots, s, \ldots, s$ at time t.

There is a transition rate at time t between some or all pairs of states, i and j, $q_{ij}(t)$. The transition rate is defined as the limit, as Δt approaches zero, of the ratio of the transition probability, $r_{ij}(t, t+\Delta t)$, to Δt:

$$q_{ij}(t) = \lim_{\Delta t \to 0} \frac{r_{ij}(t, t+\Delta t)}{\Delta t} \qquad i \neq j. \tag{1.1}$$

As this equation indicates, the dimension of $q_{ij}(t)$ is $1/t$ since the transition probability is dimensionless. It has a lower bound of zero if there is no direct transition from i to j and is unbounded above.

The process itself is defined by a system of differential equations, illustrated by the representative equation below:

$$\frac{dp_i(t)}{dt} = -p_i \sum q_{ij}(t) + \sum_{j \neq i} p_j(t)\, q_{ji}(t). \tag{1.2}$$

As equation (1.2) indicates, notation is simplified if $q_{ii}(t)$ is defined as $-\sum_{j \neq i} q_{ij}(t)$ so that equation (1.2) becomes

$$\frac{dp_i(t)}{dt} = \sum_{j=i}^{n} p_j(t)\, q_{ji}(t), \tag{1.3}$$

or in matrix notation

$$\mathbf{P}'(t) = \mathbf{P}(t)\, \mathbf{Q}(t) \tag{1.3a}$$

9

where $\mathbf{P}(t)$ is the row vector of state probabilities at time t, $\mathbf{P}'(t)$ is the first derivative of this vector with respect to t, and $\mathbf{Q}(t)$ is the matrix of transition rates $q_{ij}(t)$, with $q_{ii}(t)$ defined as indicated.

This model as it stands, for all but the richest forms of data, remains too general for use. At the same time, there is no place for the effects of other factors on the process. Both these problems may be alleviated by making $q_{ij}(t)$ no longer an explicit function of time, but rather a function of measured characteristics of the individual, some of which may vary with time. That is

$$q_{ij}(t) = f[x_1, \ldots, x_k, x_{k+1}(t), \ldots, x_n(t)] \tag{1.4}$$

By specifying the functional form that this dependence of q on other variables takes, it becomes possible to provide the framework for estimating the effects of other characteristics on change of state, and thus on the state of the individual.[1]

3.2. THE RESTRICTED MODEL

To begin with, however, I will jump back to the most restricted form of this model, in which there are only two states, movement only from one of them (such as from alive to dead), and with a transition rate that is constant over time and identical for all persons. Then by stages this model will be elaborated, with some of the restrictions removed. I will also refer loosely to data and observations to give a heuristic sense of the substantive meaning of different quantities. I will reserve serious discussion of parameter estimation until later.

A word of explanation is needed as to why I limit this restricted model to two states (and will continue to do so throughout much of the exposition) when categorical data, for which it is suited, are polytymous, not merely dichotomous. The reason has to do with the purpose of the whole enterprise. It can best be explained by recourse to analogy with causal models for continuous dependent variables. In those models, the effect of an independent variable on the dependent one is expressed by a single parameter, such as a regression coefficient. If we are to attempt to account for responses that are categorical, it is similarly natural and appropriate to think in terms of attributes, such

[1] In later analysis (chapters 5 and 6), I will reintroduce the possibility of direct dependence of q on time, following a strategy of Cox (1972), by assuming that $q_{ij}(t)$ is the product of two components, one independent of individual characteristics and dependent on time, able to vary freely with each point in time (Cox's *nuisance function*), and one dependent on individual characteristics but not directly on time.

as employment, and the effect of independent variables on the attribute, rather than on the *states* of the attribute.

Thus the purpose of the enterprise here is not to explain or account for a particular set of cross-tabulations, in which the variables may be dichotomous or polytymous. It is, rather, to account for behavior describable in terms of attributes (such as employment, marriage, childbearing, attitudes). Often, when these are given in polytymous form, the causal inferences are better expressed in terms of a dichotomy, one category versus all others. (For example, various studies of high school graduates are interested in the factors that lead to joining the military. The data *can* be presented as a polytymous response, distinguishing a variety of actions other than joining the military, rather than expressing the data as a dichotomy, joining the military versus all other actions. However, nothing is gained by doing so.

With richer forms of longitudinal data, and in some cases even with cross-sectional data, it is sometimes desirable also to have differing parameters for differing states, and at a later point I will reintroduce multistate models. But I explicitly refrain from doing so now, because the purpose of the enterprise is, as I have indicated, not to explain two-way or multiway tables, but to develop causal models for actions that take the form of all-or-none responses.

For purposes of exposition, I will first assume a process consisting of the transition from life to death. The model is

$p \equiv$ probability of being alive
$1 - p \equiv$ probability of being dead
$q \equiv$ transition rate from life to death, assumed alike for all and independent of time, with q defined by the process of equation (1.5) below:

$$\frac{dp}{dt} = -qp. \tag{1.5}$$

In accordance with equation (1.1), the relation between the transition probability in the analogous discrete-time process and the transition rate in this continuous-time process is

$$q = \lim_{\Delta t \to 0} \frac{r(\Delta t)}{\Delta t} \tag{1.6}$$

where $r(\Delta t)$ is the probability of dying in an increment of time Δt.

Equation (1.5) may be integrated to find q as a function of p at two time points, or p at a second time point as a function of p at the first and q.

Integrating,

$$\frac{p(t)}{p(0)} = e^{-qt} \tag{1.7}$$

or
$$p(t) = p(0)e^{-qt} \tag{1.8}$$

or
$$q = -\frac{1}{t} \log \frac{p(t)}{p(0)}. \tag{1.9}$$

Equation (1.6) shows the relation between q and r (Δt) as Δt becomes infinitesimally small. But from equation (1.8), we can see the relation for any Δt. The quantity $p(t)$ is the probability of still being alive at time t, as a function of the probability of being alive at time 0 and of q. The quantity $1 - p(t)$ is the probability of *not* being alive at time t, given that one was alive at time 0. This is precisely what $r(\Delta t)$ is. Or in terms of equation (1.8),

$$r(\Delta t) = 1 - e^{-q\Delta t}. \tag{1.10}$$

The derivation of equation (1.7) becomes useful when the data on a process consist of lengths of time an individual has been in a state. For example, if (to use a substantive example in which there is movement in both directions) state 1 is the state of being out of a hospital and state 0 is the state of being a patient in a hospital, then a survey might ask the question, "Did you become an inpatient in a hospital at any time in the past six months?" The proportion (of those who were not in the hospital six months ago) who answered no would be an estimate of $p(t)$ in equation (1.7).

Often it is not possible to obtain such information about events intervening between two time points, so we merely observe the proportion in a given state at time t, given occupancy (or nonoccupancy) of the state at time 0. In such a case, if there is a reverse process, then it must be included [where we now label the original q (to state 0) as q_0, and the new q (to state 1) as q_1]:

$$\frac{dp}{dt} = -pq_0 + (1 - p)q_1. \tag{1.11}$$

Integrating,

$$p(t) = p(0)e^{-(q_1 + q_0)t} + \frac{q_1}{q_1 + q_0}(1 - e^{-(q_1 + q_0)t}). \tag{1.12}$$

If, to continue the preceding hospital example, we observe that persons are out of the hospital (state 1) or in (state 0) at time 0, and out or in at a second survey at time t, then the proportion not in the hospital at time 0 is an estimate of $p(0)$, and the proportion not in at time t is $p(t)$. If it is the same persons who are observed at times 0 and t, in a panel, then the panel could be divided into two parts, one for which $p(0) = 1$, and one for which $p(0) = 0$. The proportion out of the hospital at time t could then be calculated separately for the two subsamples, as estimates of $p(t)$ in the two cases. At this point, however, I will not go into methods of estimation for q_{ij}'s, for we have not yet discussed causal structures, and it will turn out that this is not the best way of estimating the q_{ij}'s.

Equation (1.12) can be used also to show the equilibrium value of $p(t)$, that is, $p(\infty)$. For when $t \to \infty$, equation (1.12) becomes

$$p(\infty) = \frac{q_1}{q_1 + q_0} . \tag{1.12a}$$

Thus the equilibrium probability of being in state 1 of a two-state process is simply the transition rate into state 1 divided by the sum of the two transition rates.

Note that if, on the basis of two observations of a sample of persons, we estimate transition probabilities $r_{11}(t)$ and $r_{01}(t)$, we are estimating $p(t)$ in equation (1.12) under two different conditions, $p(0) = 1$ and $p(0) = 0$:

$$r_{11}(t) = e^{-(q_1 + q_0)t} + \frac{q_1}{q_1 + q_0}(1 - e^{-(q_1 + q_0)t}) \tag{1.13}$$

$$r_{01}(t) = \frac{q_1}{q_1 + q_0}(1 - e^{-(q_1 + q_0)t}) \tag{1.14}$$

It is useful also, for later reference, to give the more general solution for any number of states, though still maintaining the assumption of the restricted model that transition rates are constant over time and alike for all persons. If, as in equation (1.3a), $\mathbf{Q}$ $[=\mathbf{Q}(t)$ for all $t]$ is the matrix of transition rates, and $\mathbf{P}(t)$ is the row vector of state probabilities at time t, then the solution of equation (1.3a) is

$$\mathbf{P}(t) = \mathbf{P}(0)e^{\mathbf{Q}t} \tag{1.15}$$

where the scalar t multiplies each element of $\mathbf{Q}$, and $e^{\mathbf{Q}t}$ is defined as the infinite series analogous to that for e^x:

$$e^{Qt} = \mathbf{I} + \mathbf{Q}t + \frac{Q^2 t^2}{2!} + \frac{Q^3 t^3}{3!} + \cdots \qquad (1.16)$$

It is also the case that, following the definition of transition probabilities, the discrete-time Markov process which can be embedded[2] within the continuous-time process is related to $\mathbf{P}(0)$ and $\mathbf{P}(t)$ by

$$\mathbf{P}(t) = \mathbf{P}(0)\mathbf{R}(t) \qquad (1.17)$$

From equation (1.15) and (1.17), we get

$$\mathbf{R}(t) = e^{Qt} \qquad (1.18)$$

or, for a typical element,

$$r_{ij}(t) = \delta_{ij} + q_{ij}t + \frac{\Sigma q_{ik} q_{kj} t^2}{2!} + \frac{\Sigma\Sigma q_{ik} q_{kh} q_{hj} t^3}{3!} + \cdots \qquad (1.19)$$

Thus, in place of equation (1.14) for $r_{01}(t)$ in the two-state case, we could write:

$$r_{01}(t) = q_{01}t + \frac{\Sigma q_{0k} q_{k1} t^2}{2!} + \frac{\Sigma\Sigma q_{0k} q_{kh} q_{h1} t^3}{3!} + \cdots \qquad (1.20)$$

In the two-state case, some factoring from the infinite series will allow its expression as the simple equation (1.14); when the number of states is greater than two, this is no longer possible.

The relation between $\mathbf{R}(t)$ and $\mathbf{Q}t$ can also be expressed differently. In the matrix analogy of logarithms, equation (1.18) can be expressed as

$$\log \mathbf{R}(t) = \mathbf{Q}t \qquad (1.21)$$

where $\log \mathbf{R}(t)$ is defined as

$$\log \mathbf{R}(t) = [\mathbf{R}(t) - I] - \frac{1}{2}[\mathbf{R}(t) - I]^2 + \frac{1}{3}[\mathbf{R}(t) - I]^3 - \cdots \qquad (1.22)$$

[2] Note, however, that although every continuous-time process has an infinite number of discrete-time processes embedded within it, there are discrete-time Markov processes for which there are no corresponding continuous-time processes. For example, there is no continuous-time process corresponding to a discrete-time process of two states in which the probability at time $t + 1$ of being in state 1, given occupancy of state 1 at time t, is less than the probability of being in state 1, given occupancy of state 0 at time t.

This series expansion of $\mathbf{Q}t$ will be useful for later reference, just as the series expansion for $\mathbf{R}(t)$ given in equation (1.16) will be.

Another property of the model that may be useful when the process is observed continuously is the expected time of residence in state 1 (or state 0). If d_1 is the duration of a spell in state 1, the expected duration of the spell is given by equation (1.23):

$$E(d_1) = \int_0^\infty t q_0 p(t) \, dt \tag{1.23}$$

and substituting for $p(t)$ from equation (1.8),

$$= \int_0^\infty t q_0 p(0) e^{-q_0 t} \, dt \tag{1.24}$$

$$= \frac{1}{q_0} p(0).$$

Thus if a person were in state 1 at time 0 [that is, $p(0) = 1$], and the duration of time spent in that state until a change occurred were observed, say, by continuous observation, this duration would be an estimate of the inverse of the transition rate from the state. If a person spent two years out of the hospital before entering it again, the estimate of his transition rate to the hospital would be, in a dimension of 1/months, 1/24. Expressed in years, it would be 1/2. (Note that here we assume observation continuous until a change occurs. When "censoring" occurs, estimation is more difficult, as chapter 5 describes.)

Proceeding slightly differently, we can estimate the *half-life* of the process, that is, the time when we would expect exactly half the sample to have left the state, by reverting to equation (1.9) and solving for $t_{1/2}$

$$t_{1/2} = \frac{-\log(1/2)}{q_0}. \tag{1.25}$$

If everyone had a transition rate of 1/24 months to the hospital, equation (1.25) would show that after about 16.6 months, half of them would have entered the hospital. Or more generally, the time for any proportion to remain in state 1, t_p, is given by

$$t_p = \frac{-\log p}{q_0}. \tag{1.26}$$

15

As these last derivations suggest, times of residence in a state can be valuable information for use in estimating transition rates or their components.

Another derivation can be easily made when it can be assumed that the transition rate back to a state is so rapid that the move takes place instantaneously. If the event, for example, is being caught for speeding, and the states are *caught* (state 1) and *not caught* (state 0), we can assume that he spends effectively no time in the caught state (unless his license is suspended or he is put in jail). Then the probability of having been in state 1 (that is, caught) no times after time t is, (if we denote $p_n^*(t)$ as the probability of being caught n times):

$$p_0^*(t) = e^{-q_1 t}. \tag{1.27}$$

Then the probability of being caught exactly once and exactly at time τ between time 0 and t is the probability of not being caught from time 0 to τ ($e^{-q_1 \tau}$) multiplied by the probability of being caught at time τ (q_1) multiplied by the probability of not being caught again up to time t ($e^{-q_1(t-\tau)}$) or, taken together, $e^{-q_1 \tau} q_1 e^{-q_1(t-\tau)}$. The probability of being caught exactly once at *any* time during the period is the integral of that between 0 and t:

$$p_1^*(t) = \int_0^t e^{-q_1 \tau} q_1 e^{-q_1(t-\tau)} \, d\tau \tag{1.28}$$
$$= e^{-q_1 t} q_1 t.$$

Similarly, the calculation may be carried out for $p_2^*(t)$, and generally, for $p_n^*(t)$. It gives, for $p_n^*(t)$:

$$p_n^*(t) = \frac{e^{-q_1 t}(q_1 t)^n}{n!}, \tag{1.29}$$

which is just the Poisson distribution for Poisson parameter $q_1 t$, and with expected number of events $q_1 t$. Thus, if we observe that the average number of times caught in a given time period is $n(t)$, we can use this number to estimate the transition rate q_1, as $t/n(t)$.

Quite generally, we can think of three types of information that can aid in estimation of transition rates: *occupancy* of a state, which when summed over a sample gives a proportion [for example, proportions remaining in states, equation (1.8)], proportions having moved, or proportions found in state j at time t given residence in state i at time 0 [equations (1.13) and (1.14)], *numbers of events* (for example, the number of events in a given time period), and *times* (for example, times since last transition, time to next transition, time until a given fraction of the sample remains). The first of these is the least informative, and the last is the most informative. It provides a number for each individual that can take on any positive value, while occupancy at the individual level is always 0 or 1; to obtain a number that can take on a range of values between 0 and 1, information from a number of individuals must be aggregated. Unfortunately, however, it is the first of these types of information that is most often available.

I have attempted in this chapter to give a sense of the enterprise, the purpose behind the general approach. And I have tried to be persuasive in explaining that this approach is an important one for causal analysis of data about qualitative states, whether cross-sectional or longitudinal in form. Next, I have given the defining properties of both the general model and a severely restricted form of the model. Finally, I have given some derivations from the model, to indicate something about the variety of forms of data that can provide information about its parameters. I have left until the next chapter the question of how the idea of causation may be introduced into the model.

Before turning to the specific developments carried out in the succeeding chapters, it is useful to give an overview of what is treated in various parts of the book. Chapters 2, 3, 4, and 5 show how the model just described is applied to different forms of sociological data. Chapter 2 examines its use with cross-sectional data containing information about occupancy of states for a sample of individuals. Chapters 3 and 4 treat two-wave panel data on occupancy of states, that is, information on state occupancy for the same persons at two points in time. Chapter 3 deals with single attributes, while chapter 4 treats structural systems with two or more endogenous attributes. Chapter 5 treats another kind of information about the process, that is, information about events: the number of events since a given point in time, the length of time since the last event, and the record of the times at which events occur over a given period. As in the data on state occupancy, information on a number of individuals is assumed.

In the treatment involving state occupancy (chapters 2, 3, and 4), I will consider, with few exceptions, attributes which have only two states. The benefits of this simplification will become evident in those chapters. The exceptions consist of a short section on extension to polytymous dependent variables in chapter 2, section 7. In chapter 5, involving information about events, the question of the number of states is irrelevant; but in all parts of chapter 5 except section 6, only models treating a single kind of event at one time are examined.

In introducing causal ideas into the process described, as will be done in detail in chapter 2, cause enters through effects of other attributes or variables on the transition rate, q. Two different forms through which these effects may occur are treated, a linear decomposition of q, and a linear decomposition of the logarithm of q. I will refer to these as linear and exponential decompositions respectively. In both these decompositions, two cases are treated in the panel-data chapters (3 and 4): unrestricted parameters and restriction on the parameters so that effects of an independent variable toward state 0 are equal in magnitude and opposite in sign to the effects of that variable toward state 1. I will call these the unrestricted and restricted forms of the model respectively.

Table 1.1 shows the various forms of data and model and where they are treated in the book. A p is entered in the box if methods are fully developed in chapter 6 for estimating parameters of the model, and an e if methods are developed for estimating the standard errors of parameter estimates. A c is entered in the box if methods for estimation are incorporated into one of the computer programs.

TABLE 1.1

Forms of Data and Forms of Model

Form of Data	Form of Model			
	Linear		Exponential	
	Unrestricted	**Restricted**	**Unrestricted**	**Restricted**
Cross-Sectional Data	(linear probability model) 2.2 p, e, c	2.2 p, e, c	(multivariate logit model) 2.3 p, e, c	2.3 p, e, c
Panel Data: Constant Independent Variables	3.3 p, e, c	3.1 p, e, c	3.3 p, e, c	3.2 p, e, c
Panel Data: Nonconstant Independent Variables	3.6 p, e, c	3.4 p, e, c	3.5 p, e, c	3.5 p, e, c
Panel Data: Simultaneous Equations	4.5 p, e, c	4.5 p, e, c	4.5 p, e, c	4.5 p, e, c
Number of Events Since Point in Time	5.1 p, e		5.1 p, e	
Time Since Last Event	5.2 p, e		5.2 p, e	
Records of Events: Partial Likelihood	(does not exist)		5.3 p, e, c	
Records of Events: Maximum Likelihood	5.5 p, e, c		5.5 p, e, c	

As indicated in the table, the least complete work is carried out for numbers of events since a point in time, and for time since last event. Computer programs for the latter two forms of data were not developed because of the lesser importance of this kind of data.

Chapter 2

The Effects of Independent Variables: Cross-Sectional Data

If we have a model of the sort described in the first chapter, then this does not help greatly in a causal analysis, for Markov processes can be thought of as a stochastic extrapolation from the present into the future. As such, there is no notion of cause or of independent variables in a process. What is necessary is to conceive of the simple process described in the preceding chapter in such a way that the notion of cause enters naturally.

Consider the two-state two-directional process of the preceding chapter, but now assume there are two populations, each internally homogeneous but different from one another. For convenience, think of the action in question as that of being employed or being unemployed, and the two different populations as men and women.

If for men p is the probability of being employed, q_0 the transition rate to becoming unemployed, and q_1 the transition rate to becoming employed, the process is described by equation (2.1) below:

$$\frac{dp}{dt} = -pq_0 + (1 - p)q_1. \tag{2.1}$$

If for women p' is the probability of being employed, and q_j' the transition rates, the analogous equations are

$$\frac{dp'}{dt} = -p' q_0' + (1 - p')q_1'. \tag{2.2}$$

Now because q_1 and q_1' will in general differ for the two populations, as will q_0 and q_0', one can begin to think of sex as a causal factor in employment, and the causes as operating through the transition rates, q_j. We can think, in short, of the transition rates as decomposed into causal factors.

The usual notion of an attribute such as sex as a cause, or a determinant, of a status such as employment is a rather simple one, such as "men tend to be employed more than women." Without a detailed examination, this appears compatible with a situation in which q_1 is greater than q_1', (that is, the transition rate to employment is greater for men than women) or q_0' is greater than q_0 (the transition rate to unemployment is greater for women than men) or both. I will return to this correspondence between meaning and model in more detail later, but at this point it is sufficient to note that this seems compatible with the usual statements that are intended to express cause. The question, then, is how the qualitative statements of order relations among the q_j's can be further specified to give a measure of the effect of sex on employment. There are several approaches one can take to doing this. A first approach is to disavow any single simple expression of "effect of sex on employment" and instead specify the several different kinds of effects that can be manifested through variations in the transition rates:

1. Unemployed men come to be employed more rapidly than unemployed women: $q_1 > q_1'$.

2. Employed men have a lower rate of becoming unemployed than do women: $q_0' > q_0$.

3. Men tend to move into and out of employment less rapidly than do women: $q_1 < q_1'$, $q_0 < q_0'$.

Such an approach as this, while it shows the full detail of how men's and women's labor-force movements differ, is a cumbersome way of expressing causal relations; and it becomes especially so when there are several causal factors. For certain purposes, it is useful to know the full detail; but for many purposes, a single measure of effect is preferable.

A second approach is to attempt to discover the functional form through which one attribute affects another. That is, if $q_j = f(x_1, x_2, \ldots, x_n)$, where the x_k are independent attributes, an approach is to attempt to discover empirically the function f. This can, however, be a difficult task which distracts from the central task of getting some measure for the effects of the x_k. Again, for certain purposes it is valuable, but for many common research tasks it is a misdirected effort.

A third approach is to assume a relatively simple functional form of f, letting the form chosen depend partly on what seems to be empirically correct but partly on other criteria, such as computational simplicity and simplicity of interpretation. There are several functional forms with points to recommend them; I will discuss two of them in the text, and examine two others in the appendix to this chapter:

1. Linear decomposition of q_j, where q_{ji} is the transition rate (from state h) to state j for person i:

$$q_{ji} = \sum_{k=0}^{n} b_{kj} x_{ki} \tag{2.3}$$

where x_{ki} ($k = 0, 1, \ldots, n$) are values of dichotomous attributes with values 0 or 1, or continuous variables. [I will use the convention that $x_{0i} = 1$ for all persons i, so that b_{0j} is the constant in the linear decomposition of equation (2.3)]. The parameters b_{kj} are measures of the effect of x_{ki} on q_j. The transition rates in both directions are decomposed in this way. When the dependent status is dichotomous, as is assumed here, then in order to have a single measure for the effect of each independent attribute on the dependent one, some assumption is necessary about the relation of the coefficients for the transition rates in the two directions. If the states of the dependent attribute are 0 and 1, then the relationship between the coefficients for the two attributes when we have independent attributes $x_k = (0, 1)$ and continuous variables x_k, which can take on positive or negative values, are

$$q_{1i} = \sum_{k=0}^{n} b_k x_{ki} \tag{2.4}$$

$$q_{0i} = \sum_{k=0}^{n} c_k x_{ki} \tag{2.5}$$

where I will use the notation of b_k for effects on q_{1i} and c_k for effects on

21

q_{0i}. Furthermore, we now assume that $c_k = -b_k$ for all k from 1 to n. The constant terms, c_0 and b_0 are not assumed equal. With this decomposition, the case of a single independent attribute, as in the example of sex affecting employment, becomes, for men [substituting in equation (2.1)]:

$$\frac{dp}{dt} = -p(c_0 - b) + (1 - p)(b_0 + b)$$

and for women:

$$\frac{dp'}{dt} = -p' c_0 + (1 - p')b_0.$$

Generally, for a single independent attribute, the equations become

$$\frac{dp_i}{dt} = -p_i(c_0 - bx_i) + (1 - p_i)(b_0 + bx_i) \tag{2.6}$$
$$= -p_i(c_0 + b_0) + b_0 + bx_i,$$

where i indexes individual i. For a set of m independent dichotomous attributes, with individual i characterized by x_{ki} ($k = 1, \ldots, m$), $x_{ki} = 0$ or 1:

$$\frac{dp_i}{dt} = -p_i(c_0 + b_0) + b_0 + \sum_{k=1}^{m} b_k x_{ki}. \tag{2.7}$$

And if there are attributes and continuous variables, with the latter indexed from $m + 1$ to n, equation (2.7) remains the same except that the summation runs from 1 to n.

  2. Exponential linear decomposition of q_{1i}:

$$q_{1i} = e^{\sum b_k x_{ki}} \tag{2.8}$$

where x_k are values of dichotomous attributes and continuous variables. Again, where the destination state of the dichotomous attribute is 0, the transition rate is

$$q_{0i} = e^{\sum c_k x_{ki}} \tag{2.9}$$

as before using c_k for effects on q_{0i} to reduce the need for subscripts. Again,

22

it is assumed, in order to have a single measure of the effect of variable k, that $c_k = -b_k$ for $k = 1, \ldots, n$. For a single dichotomous independent attribute, the differential equation (2.1) becomes

$$q_1 = e^{b_0 + bx_i},$$

$$q_0 = e^{c_0 - bx_i}, \text{ and} \qquad (2.10)$$

$$\frac{dp_i}{dt} = -p_i(e^{b_0 + bx_i} + e^{c_0 - bx_i}) + e^{b_0 + bx_i}.$$

For the general case with independent attributes and continuous variables $k = 1, \ldots, n$, equation (2.9) becomes

$$\frac{dp_i}{dt} = -p_i(e^{b_0 + \sum\limits_{k=1}^{n} b_k x_{ki}} + e^{c_0 - \sum\limits_{k=1}^{n} b_k x_{ki}}) + e^{b_0 + \sum\limits_{k=1}^{n} b_k x_{ki}}. \qquad (2.11)$$

Later, the ratio of the transition rates, q_1/q_0, will turn out to be of some importance for the exponential linear decomposition. This ratio in the case of a single independent attribute is, from equations (2.8) and (2.9), and using the assumption that $c_k = -b_k$ for $k = 1, \ldots, n$:

$$\frac{q_{1i}}{q_{0i}} = e^{b_0 - c_0 + 2bx_i}. \qquad (2.12)$$

And for the general case with $k = 1, \ldots, n$ independent attributes and continuous variables the ratio is

$$\frac{q_{1i}}{q_{0i}} = e^{b_0 - c_0 + 2\sum\limits_{k=1}^{n} b_k x_{ki}}. \qquad (2.13)$$

The linear decomposition will have, as will be evident later, certain useful properties deriving from simplicity. It has, however, one serious defect: All transition rates must be nonnegative, while a linear sum has no such constraint. The exponential linear decomposition obeys the same constraints on the right-hand side of equation (2.8) as on the left. Consequently, it has more theoretical justification.

Assumptions about change in q_j with change in the independent variable underlying the two decompositions may be seen by differentiating q_j with respect to x_k, a continuous variable.

23

In the linear decomposition, differentiating equation (2.3) gives

$$\frac{dq_j}{dx_k} = b_{kj},$$ (2.14)

that is, the change in q_j per unit change in x_k is a constant, b_{kj} (or for q_0, $-b_k$). This shows how q_j may in principle take on a negative value.

Differentiating equation (2.8) for the exponential linear decomposition gives

$$\frac{dq_j}{dx_k} = b_{kj}e^{\sum b_{kj}x_k}$$ (2.15)

$$= b_{kj}q_j.$$

Equation (2.15) shows that the assumption about change in q with change in x for the exponential linear decomposition is an especially straightforward and appealing one, which can never take q_j below its lower bound of zero: q_j is increased or decreased by a constant fraction with increase in x_k.

A notational comment is useful here, for it will simplify notation throughout the chapters. I will often refer to the *row* vector $b_1, \ldots, b_n$ as **b**, and the *column* vector $x_{1i}, \ldots, x_{ni}$ as $\mathbf{x}_i$. This will allow writing $\mathbf{bx}_i$ rather than the more clumsy $\sum_{k=1}^{n} b_k x_{ki}$. At some points, the constant term [b_0 and $x_{0i}(\equiv 1)$] will be included within the sum of products, and to indicate that, I will write $c_0 + \mathbf{cx}_i$, or $b_0 + \mathbf{bx}_i$ as the case may be. Later, I will want to distinguish, as in equations (2.4) and (2.5), and (2.8) and (2.9), between effects in the two directions, that is c_k and b_k. Then I will designate the vectors **c** and **b**, respectively.

With this as the formulation of the basic model, the task now is to show how data of different types correspond to the parameters of the process. This task may be divided into two parts, for the estimation of parameters from data using efficient methods requires in most cases iterative techniques that obscure the relationship between parameters and data. The first task is merely to obtain a relationship between a quantity in the model that corresponds directly to the observed data and the parameters that are assumed to govern the process. The second task is to use this relationship to estimate the parameters. The first of these tasks I will carry out in the present chapter and chapters 3, 4, and 5. The second I will reserve for chapter 6, where maximum likelihood methods of estimation for all forms of data are presented. In a way it all began with probit models, for which it was necessary to use iterative methods to obtain maximum likelihood estimates. This has opened up a pandora's box, in which a linear relationship between data and parameters is an unusual and seldom-encountered case. The difficulties as well as opportunities are greatly compounded by the fact that the combination of powerful estimation methods with powerful computing capability means that it has become possible to use individual-level data with categorical dependent variables, just as is true with continuous dependent variables, and to discard the very idea of cross-tabulation, which in effect institutes grouping of data. The cost of this greater power is that the research analyst gains a less strong intuitive understanding of the way effects are manifested in data being analyzed.

Because of this difficulty I will present, for the first example, a simple lease-squares method of estimation for use with grouped (cross-tabulated) data and compare it to the maximum likelihood estimate that is also presented for the example. In subsequent examples, only the maximum likelihood estimate is used, despite the fact that the discussion of maximum likelihood estimation is reserved for chapter 6.

In the present chapter, I will consider only cross-sectional data, and in chapters 3, 4, and 5 I will proceed from this minimal information to increasingly rich forms of longitudinal information. This will have the additional virtue of providing a conceptual link between the parameters estimated in analysis with different forms of data: cross-sectional data, panel data consisting of two or more surveys of the same persons, and continuous records.

1. CROSS-SECTIONAL DATA

Ordinarily, methods for analyzing categorical cross-sectional data give little attention to the social or psychological process of which the data are a reflection. Often a *data-generating* process is postulated, a binomial or multinomial process in which each state has a given probability of occurrence on any observation. And sometimes attributes or variables are considered as *independent* or *explanatory*, on the one hand, and *dependent* or *response* attributes on the other. But in much statistical analysis, a model of the social or psychological generating process is absent. Here we take as that process a continuous-time stochastic process, and as the first approximation to reality, a stationary Markov process.

But if this is done, the question immediately arises: The notion of cause or explanatory variables in such a process is a notion of effects on the transition rates, the q_j's. How can this notion correspond to, or be translated into, a conception of cause that is reflected in purely static data?

The answer, of course, is that the transition rates leave their marks on static data. In particular, if transition rates in two systems differ, the equilibrium states of the two systems will in general be different. This point is extremely important, because ordinarily when we observe static data and want to make some inference about explanatory variables that account for the distribution among states, we make an assumption, implicit or explicit, that statistical equilibrium exists. If we make that assumption, then we can use the relationship between statistical equilibrium and the transition rates to provide information about the latter.

This is a general strategy. The particular way it works out in the case of the linear and exponential linear decomposition of q_j will be spelled out below.

First, we return to the basic two-state equation with two-directional flow, equation (2.1). Statistical equilibrium exists when $dp/dt = 0$, or

$$0 = -pq_0 + (1 - p)q_1. \tag{2.16}$$

If this is solved for p, we have

$$p = \frac{q_1}{q_1 + q_0}. \tag{2.17}$$

2. LINEAR DECOMPOSITION OF q_j'S: THE LINEAR PROBABILITY MODEL

When there is a linear decomposition of q_j, this becomes, for individual i, from equation (2.7):

$$\hat{p}_i = \frac{\sum_{k=0}^{n} b_k x_{ki}}{c_0 + b_0}. \tag{2.18}$$

With static cross-sectional data, all that can be observed is the proportion of persons in each state. None of the derivations of chapter 1 can be used, for those involve observations of proportions that have remained in the same state, proportions of those in a given state at one time found in a particular state at another time, or observations of times at which transitions are made or times at which given proportions remain in the state of origin.

Restricted to observations of p in equation (2.18), we can immediately see that nothing about the absolute values of transition rates can be learned from the data. This is intuitively apparent also, for static data, observed at statistical equilibrium, should certainly be unable to give any information about absolute rates of movement between states.

In equation (2.18), the right-hand side gives the probability of being in state 1 for a person i characterized by a given vector x_i of values of the n independent attributes and variables. For a person, the observed value of p must be 0 or 1; but for a subset of persons all characterized by the same values for the vector x_i, the observed proportion of persons in state 1 should approach p_i the larger the subset. This assumes, of course, that the vector b of b_k's could be estimated, so that the numerator and denominator of the right-hand side of equation (2.18) could be calculated.

This, of course, is taking as given what must be found. But we notice that the denominator of the right-hand side of equation (2.18) is the same for all persons in the sample, since it depends only on c_0 and b_0, the same for all persons. Thus, what can be done is to divide each term of the numerator by $c_0 + b_0$, a constant. If we denote $b_0 /(c_0 + b_0)$ by β_0, and $b_k/(c_0 + b_0)$ by β_k, then equation (2.18) becomes

$$p_i = \sum_{k=0}^{n} \beta_k x_{ki} . \tag{2.19}$$

Equation (2.19) becomes the fundamental equation for use in considering the linear decomposition of the q_j's. It may be noted that this is what has been termed in explanatory analysis of categorical data the *linear probability model*. In a subsequent section, I will discuss methods that have been developed for estimating the vector β, in particular, an iterative method for obtaining maximum likelihood estimates of β. It is useful to state here, however, something suggested by the form of equation (2.19). With methods for estimating parameters from individual observations, and with the minute individual variability in independent variables implied by use of many independent variables, some of which are continuous, the idea of contingency tables and categorical data analysis becomes somewhat outmoded. Such analysis involves essentially grouped data; and if there are methods for analyzing ungrouped data, the analysis of grouped data becomes only a special case.

27

Where methods for estimation from individual observations exist, traditional categorical data analysis is replaced by what could be termed *multivariate analysis with quantal response*. It has, in fact, been so termed by econometricians working primarily with multivariate probit and logit models.

3. EXPONENTIAL LINEAR DECOMPOSITION OF q_j'S: THE LOGIT MODEL

When the explanatory model is based on an exponential decomposition of q_j's, then it is useful to solve equation (2.16) for q_1/q_0 because of the simple form of equation (2.13):

$$\frac{p}{1-p} = \frac{q_1}{q_0}. \tag{2.20}$$

Taking the logarithm of both sides, and using equation (2.13), we have

$$\log \frac{p}{1-p} = b_0 - c_0 + 2 \sum_{k=1}^{n} b_k x_{ki}. \tag{2.21}$$

Note here that $b_0 - c_0$ is constant over all persons in the sample. If we denote this sum by the constant β_0, and define $\beta_k = 2b_k$ for $k - 1, \ldots, n$, we have for the exponential linear decomposition:

$$\log \frac{p}{1-p} = \sum_{k=0}^{n} \beta_k x_{ki}. \tag{2.22}$$

When p, the probability of occupancy of state 1, is expressed in terms of x_k, the result is the multivariate logistic equation:

$$p_i = \frac{1}{1 + e^{-\sum \beta_k x_{ki}}}. \tag{2.23}$$

It appears at first that in contradiction of what I indicated earlier, it is possible to estimate, from equation (2.22), the absolute values of transition rates.

But this is illusory, because each β_k essentially provides a term in a product which makes up q_1 or q_0 for a person with a given vector $\mathbf{x}_i$; but one term in that product, c_0 or b_0, is unidentified since the constant term β_0 contains only the difference $b_0 - c_0$.

As with the linear decomposition, which gives rise at statistical equilibrium to the linear probability model, the exponential linear decomposition gives rise to the multivariate logit model. Thus while it may not be surprising, in view of the form of decomposition of the q_{hj}'s, when this model of a dynamic process is assumed to be at statistical equilibrium, and cross-sectional data are used to estimate something about the q_{hj}'s, the results are two widely used methods for analysis of categorical data. (It should be mentioned parenthetically that whenever loglinear models are used for analysis of the effects of independent attributes on a dichotomous categorical response, they become identical to multivariate logit models restricted to categorical independent variables.)

As in the case of equation (2.19) with the linear decomposition, equation (2.22) becomes the basis for estimation of the vector β in the exponential linear decomposition. As in that case, it is possible to estimate β on the basis of individual observations rather than contingency tables or data grouped in other ways. There are, however, problems in doing so, because at the individual level $p = 0$ or 1 so that the left-hand side of equation (2.22) is $-\infty$ or ∞. Methods have been developed, however, for estimating β in the face of this problem. In chapter 6, I will present an iterative method that gives maximum likelihood estimates of β, along with estimates of the variance and a measure of goodness of fit.

I have not yet discussed interpretation of the values obtained for the β_k's, and how they can be given intuitive and understandable meaning. That will be done in the next section, where I raise this question for the q_j's as well.

4. RELATIONSHIP OF SIZE OF PARAMETERS TO EXPECTED EFFECTS ON PROPORTIONS

Nothing has been said so far concerning the relation of the size of parameters to the manifest (expected) effect on observed proportions. In the case of the linear decomposition, the parameters b_k constitute additions to the transition rates, and under the assumption of statistical equilibrium, the parameters

β_k that are estimated from the data are simply additions to the expected proportion in state 1. Thus no problem of interpretation arises about what the size of β_k means in the case of the linear probability model.

The matter is less simple for the exponential linear decomposition. Here the parameters b_k, when transformed to e^{bk}, are *multipliers* to the transition rates. But this does not translate directly to their effect on the expected proportions in state 1, since the proportions in state 1 are nonlinear functions of the transition rates.

Two simple transformations of the β_k's that are calculated from the exponential linear decomposition can help give a heuristic understanding of the meaning of a given value for β_k. For the first and most straightforward transformation, we ask this question:

a. What is the value of p corresponding to a given value of β_0 when $x_k = 0$ for $k = 1, \ldots, m?$

The answer to this question is given by setting $x_k = 0$ for $k \geq 1$ in equation (2.23).

$$p^* = \frac{1}{1 + e^{-\beta_0}} \, .$$

This gives the value of p when all independent variables x_k are zero. This corresponds to β_0 for the linear model, which gives the value of p in the linear model when all independent variables are zero.

When, however, there are interaction terms in the model, as in the second analysis of example 1 carried out in section 6, equation (2.23) must include the β_k's for those interaction terms that are one when the original variables $x, \ldots, x_n$ are zero. The general formulation is $p^* = 1/(1 + e^{-\beta_0 - \Sigma \beta_{i..k}})$, where the summation extends over all combinations of independent variables for which interaction effects are included.

b. By what factor does x_k amplify or depress the value of p when $x_k = 1$, relative to the value of p when $x_k = 0?$

The answer to this question may be found by examining the relation between $p\,(x_k = 0)$ and $p\,(x_k = 1)$, asking what quantity ϕ_k^* will satisfy the equation

$$\phi_k^* \frac{1}{1 + e^{-\sum\limits_{j \neq k} \beta_j x_j}} = \frac{1}{1 + e^{-\sum\limits_{j \neq k} \beta_j x_j - \beta_k}} \, , \quad \text{or} \quad \phi_k^* = \frac{1 + e^{-\sum\limits_{j \neq k} \beta_j x_j}}{1 + e^{-\sum\limits_{j \neq k} \beta_j x_j - \beta_k}} \, .$$

As it turns out, ϕ_k^* is a function of the values of the other independent variables or, to put it differently, a function of p. Consequently, it cannot be specified independently of p. One can, however, conceive of a standard value of ϕ_k^*, that is, the value of ϕ_k^* when, in the absence of variable k, $p = 0.5$. Solving for ϕ_k^* in this case gives a standard value, which may be labeled ϕ_k:

$$\phi_k = \frac{2}{1 + e^{-\beta_k}}. \tag{2.24}$$

The quantity ϕ_k thus shows the effect of variable k as a multiplier of p when $p = 0.5$. If ϕ_k is less than 1, variable k depresses p toward zero; if ϕ_k is greater than 1, variable k amplifies p toward one. Thus a positive effect of k is shown by $\phi_k > 1$, and a negative effect by $\phi_k < 1$.

For direct comparison of the parameters of the exponential decomposition and those of the linear decomposition, it may be of interest to ask a third question:

c.   What amount is added to p when $x_1 = 1$ if, when $x_1 = 0$, p is 0.5? The answer can be found simply. In the model,

$$p = \frac{1}{1 + e^{-(\beta_0 + \Sigma \beta_j x_j)}}$$

where the summation includes all variables other than the one in question. If when $x_k = 0$, we have $p = 0.5$, this means that

$$0.5 = \frac{1}{1 + e^{-(\beta_0 + \Sigma \beta_j x_j)}},$$

which can be solved to give $\beta_0 + \sum \beta_j x_j = 0$. Thus, if we define a transformation α_k of β_k such that

$$0.5 + \alpha_k = \frac{1}{1 + e^{-(0 + \beta_k)}},$$

and solve for α_k, we have the desired transformation:

$$\alpha_k = \frac{e^{\beta_k} - 1}{2(e^{\beta_k} + 1)}. \tag{2.25}$$

The meaning of α_k then is the effect of attribute k in increasing or decreasing p when p is at 0.5. If k is a continuous variable, α_k is the effect of k on

31

increasing or decreasing p when p is at 0.5. An example that illustrates the use of α_k is given in a later section.

In the maximum likelihood estimation procedures described in chapter 6, a standard deviation of β_k is calculated. It is useful to get some idea of what this implies for the variability of p^*, ϕ_k, and α_k, even though these are nonlinear transformations of β_0 and β_k. This can be done for p^* by finding the value of p^* corresponding to $\beta_k + \sigma_k$ and $\beta_k - \sigma_k$ (denoted p^{*+} and p^{*-}), then determining a variability for p^* as $\frac{1}{2}(|p^* - p^{*+}| + |p^* - p^{*-}|)$. Variabilities for the other two quantities may be found in the same way.

For some purposes, one might want to express the constant term, β_0, simply as β_0; for most purposes, however, it will be more useful to express it as p^*, that is $1/(1 - e^{\beta_0})$. The effects of independent variables may for various purposes be expressed as β_k, ϕ_k, or α_k. In the LONGIT·CROSS program listed in the appendix, β_k and α_k are calculated, along with standard deviations of the β_k's. In the examples presented in this chapter, p^* will be presented rather than β_0, a.d for effects of the independent variables β_k will be presented, as will α_k for comparison with the linear model.

5. INTERACTION EFFECTS

Until now, I have assumed that each of the independent variables acts independently to affect the dependent attribute. But if there are two dichotomous attributes as independent variables, then apart from the independent effects, there may be an interaction effect, that is, an effect that depends on the value of both variables. With two attributes, x_1 and x_2, one such interaction effect can be identified. This may be done by constructing a third attribute, x_{12}, orthogonal to the first two. With two dichotomous attributes as independent variables, there are four types of individuals characterized by their values on x_1 and x_2. The third attribute x_{12} can be created orthogonal to the first two. This allows the four types of individuals to be characterized according to three dimensions: their value of attribute 1, their value of attribute 2, and the sameness or difference in their values of attributes 1 and 2:

	x_1	x_2	x_{12}
Type 1	1	1	1
Type 2	1	0	0
Type 3	0	1	0
Type 4	0	0	1

If there are three independent attributes, all dichotomies, there are four possible interactions: between 1 and 2, between 1 and 3, between 2 and 3, and between 1, 2, and 3. As in the two-attribute case, new attributes may be constructed from the combinations of values on the original attributes, such that these attributes are mutually orthogonal and orthogonal to the original attributes. Higher-order interactions, $x_{ki...j}$ among dichotomous attributes can be found as the sum of two products: $x_{ki...j} = x_k x_{i...j} + (1 - x_k)(1 - x_{i...j})$ where $x_{i...j}$ is the interaction between attributes $i, \ldots, j$. The interaction term x_{123}, for example, may be calculated from x_1 and x_{23}, x_2 and x_{13}, or x_3 and x_{12}.

The four interactions for three independent attributes may be denoted x_{12}, x_{13}, x_{23}, and x_{123}. The classification of individuals on these attributes is carried out as shown below:

x_1	x_2	x_3	x_{12}	x_{13}	x_{23}	x_{123}
1	1	1	1	1	1	1
1	1	0	1	0	0	0
1	0	1	0	1	0	0
1	0	0	0	0	1	1
0	1	1	0	0	1	0
0	1	0	0	1	0	1
0	0	1	1	0	0	1
0	0	0	1	1	1	0

By such a process, new attributes may be constructed and introduced into the model for which effects are to be estimated. In carrying out the analysis, nothing more is required than specifying the values that these new attributes take for each individual in the sample. The estimation procedure remains unchanged, for the new attributes x_{jk} or x_{jkl} are no different in principle than the original attributes. It should be noted, however, that when all possible interactions have been introduced as explicit attributes, the model will fit the data perfectly, for the number of parameters estimated equals the number of degrees of freedom. For example, with two independent attributes, there are $2^2 = 4$ degrees of freedom (that is, four types of individuals) and four parameters when x_{12} is included: $\beta_0, \beta_1, \beta_2, \beta_{12}$. With three independent attributes, there are $2^3 = 8$ degrees of freedom (eight types of individuals) and eight parameters when x_{12}, x_{13}, x_{23}, and x_{123} are included: $\beta_0, \beta_1, \beta_2, \beta_3, \beta_{12}, \beta_{13}, \beta_{23}, \beta_{123}$.

An example illustrating introduction of interaction effects will be presented later in the chapter.

6. EXAMPLES

6.1. EXAMPLE

Survival of Seedlings: A first example will help illustrate a number of points despite the fact that it is not from social science. First, it will give an idea of the relation between results obtained by hand calculations in simple cases where they can be easily carried out, and the maximum likelihood estimates obtained by iterative methods. Second, it will give an idea of the difference between the exponential decomposition (the logit model) and the linear decomposition (the linear probability model) in a case which illustrates especially well the shortcomings of the latter. Third, the example will illustrate the transformation of the parameters in the exponential linear decomposition to give greater intuitive meaning to the parameters as measures of the size of the effect. Finally, the example can be used to illustrate interaction effects.

The example is one taken from Wakeley (1954) and analyzed by Bliss (1967) and Fienberg (1977, p. 77) for the logit model. It concerns the effects of winter planting of pine seedlings ½ inch too low or ½ inch too high on the mortality of the seedlings by the following fall. In this experiment, there are two types of seedlings, longleaf and slash seedlings, so there are two independent variables, depth and type. The data are shown in table 2.1.

TABLE 2.1
Survival of Seedlings

Depth	Longleaf			Slash		
	Dead	Alive	Total	Dead	Alive	Total
Too high	41	59	100	12	88	100
Too low	11	89	100	5	95	100
Totals	52	148	200	17	183	200

Inspection of the table indicates that slash pine seems to be more likely to stay alive, and that planting too low appears better for survival than planting too high. Analysis of the data, first by hand calculations using simple unweighted least squares, and then by the iterative maximum likelihood method outlined in chapter 6, shows whether these judgments are correct, and whether the results could have happened by chance. If depth is variable 1 (too high: $x_1 = 0$; too low: $x_1 = 1$), and type is variable 2 (longleaf: $x_2 = 0$; slash: $x_2 = 1$), and p is probability of being alive, we have the two models (where x_{1i} and x_{2i} take on values of 0 or 1).

Exponential linear decomposition [from equation (2.22)]:

34

$$p_i = \frac{1}{1 + e^{-(\beta_0 + \beta_1 x_{1i} + \beta_2 x_{2i})}}$$

$$\log \frac{p_i}{1 - p_i} = \beta_0 + \beta_1 x_{1i} + \beta_2 x_{2i}. \tag{2.26}$$

Linear decomposition [from equation (2.19)]:

$$p_i = \beta_0 + \beta_1 x_{1i} + \beta_2 x_{2i}. \tag{2.27}$$

Estimates for the β_k in the two cases may be made by using a simple unweighted least-squares method outlined in Coleman (1964a): If we call the left-hand side of equations (2.26) and (2.27) ρ_{ij}, where i and j refer to values of x_2 and x_1 respectively, the estimate is

$$\beta_1 = \tfrac{1}{2}(\rho_{11} - \rho_{10} + \rho_{01} - \rho_{00})$$
$$\beta_2 = \tfrac{1}{2}(\rho_{11} - \rho_{01} + \rho_{10} - \rho_{00})$$
$$\beta = \tfrac{1}{4}(3\rho_{00} + \rho_{01} + \rho_{10} - \rho_{11})$$

where ρ for the exponential linear decomposition is $\log p_i/(1 - p_i)$ and for the linear decomposition is p_i.

For the exponential linear decomposition, the calculations are

$$\beta_1 = \tfrac{1}{2}(2.944 - 1.992 + 2.091 - 0.364) = 1.339$$
$$\beta_2 = \tfrac{1}{2}(2.944 - 2.091 + 1.992 - 0.364) = 1.241$$
$$\beta_0 = \tfrac{1}{4}(3[.364] + 2.091 + 1.992 - 2.944) = 0.558$$

For the linear decomposition, the calculations are

$$\beta_1 = \tfrac{1}{2}(.95 - .88 + .89 - .59) = .185$$
$$\beta_2 = \tfrac{1}{2}(.95 - .89 + .88 - .59) = .175$$
$$\beta_0 = \tfrac{1}{4}(3[.59] + .89 + .88 - .95) = .648$$

The maximum likelihood estimates from the appended LONGIT·CROSS computer program can be compared with these, and the standard errors included as well, to give some sense of the possibility that the results could have occurred by chance if there were no relation of depth of planting or type of seedling to survival (that is, if β_1 or β_2 were zero). Table 2.2 below gives the comparisons, including the α transformations of the exponential parameters.

TABLE 2.2

Effects of Seedling Type and Planting Depth on Seedling Survival

| | Exponential | | | | Linear | | |
	Least Squares β	Maximum Likelihood β	s.e.	α	Least Squares β	Maximum Likelihood β	s.e.
Seedling Type	1.24	1.42	(.31)	.305	.175	.134	(.038)
Depth	1.34	1.50	(.32)	.318	.185	.148	(.038)
Constant (p*)	.636	.606			.648	.682	

The maximum likelihood estimates, compared with their standard errors, indicate that the effects of both the type of seedling and the depth of planting are strong and could hardly have happened by chance. Maximum likelihood estimates are over 3½ times their standard errors for the linear model, and over 4½ times their standard errors for the exponential (logit) model.[1] Slash pine survives much better than longleaf, and planting the seedling too deep is much better than planting it too shallowly.

A goodness of fit test was also calculated (as part of the LONGIT·CROSS program contained in the appendix) and it shows that for the logit model, $\chi_1^2 = 1.34$. This indicates that the two experimental variables explain the results very well, without necessity for introduction of an interaction term.

The values of α shown in table 2.2, calculated by equation (2.25), mean that if, for longleaf seedlings, the survival probability was 0.5, it would be $0.5 + 0.305 = 0.805$ for slash seedlings; and if, for seedlings planted ½ inch too high the survival probability was 0.5, it would be $0.5 + 0.318 = 0.818$ for seedlings planted ½ inch too low. These are directly comparable to the estimates for the linear probability model, which are to be interpreted as additions to p, in the presence of x_i. The much larger size of these transformed parameters (.318 versus .148, .305 versus .134), as compared to the parameters from the linear decomposition model, indicates its much better fit to the data as well as the fact that the estimated value of p when $x_1 = x_2 = 0$ is .682 rather than .5. We can use the parameters from table 2.2 to give the predicted proportions alive in each cell. These, calculated from the maximum likelihood estimates by equations (2.19) and (2.26), are given in table 2.3. The predicted proportions for the exponential model are identical to those calculated by Fienberg (1977, p. 77), who also obtained maximum likelihood estimates for the logit model using this example.

---

[1] The standard errors are calculated from the estimate of the covariance matrix, which is the inverse of the negative of the matrix of second derivatives of the log likelihood with respect to the parameters, the Fisher information matrix. This is discussed further in chapter 6.

TABLE 2.3

*Actual and Predicted Proportions
of Seedlings Alive, for Data
from Table 2.1*

	Data	Exponential (Logit)	Linear
Longleaf high	.59	.606	.682
Longleaf low	.89	.874	.830
Slash high	.88	.864	.816
Slash low	.95	.966	.965

The exponential or logit model gives predictions that are considerably closer to the data than are the predictions from the linear decomposition model, illustrating, as do the larger effects shown in table 2.2, the better fit of the exponential decomposition than the linear decomposition to these data.

Interaction Effect: In this example, the interaction effect discussed earlier in the chapter can be especially well illustrated. Since this is a case of two independent variables, there is one potential interaction effect, the interaction between type of seedling and depth of planting. With inclusion of the interaction effect, the model will fit the data exactly, since the numbers of parameters and number of degrees of freedom are equal. Table 2.4 shows the parameters when the interaction is introduced as a third independent variable.[2]

TABLE 2.4

*Effects of Seedling Type, Planting Depth, and Interaction
Between Them on Survival*

	Exponential			Linear	
	β	s.e.	α	β	s.e.
Seedling Type	1.241	(.335)	.276	.175	(.035)
Depth	1.339	(.335)	.292	.185	(.035)
Interaction	−.387	(.335)	−.096	−.115	(.035)
Constant* (p*)	.59			.59	

The analysis shows that for the linear model, the interaction between type of seedling and depth is a large one, three times its standard error and similar in size to the main effects. For the exponential model, however, the interaction effect is small and not significantly different from zero. This indicates that

[2] As indicated in the discussion of interaction effects, p^* is evaluated where the original variables (x_1, x_2) are zero. The interaction term x_{12} is one when $x_1 = x_2 = 0$, and thus p^* is obtained from $\beta_0 + \beta_{12}$. In this case, because all degrees of freedom have been exhausted, p^* necessarily equals the proportions alive in the longleaf shallow cell.

for these data the exponential model provides a more parsimonious explanation for the survival of seedlings than does the linear model.

6.2. EXAMPLE

Correct Racial Self-Identification of Young Children: In studying the development of racial identity in children, researchers have examined a number of responses of the children: to dolls of different colors [as for example in the famous Clark and Clark (1958) experiments cited in the U.S. Supreme Court school desegregation decision of 1954] and to themselves. In one such experiment, Porter (1971, pp. 116–117, table 16) asked black and white children of ages three, four, and five about their identity as whites or blacks (or as Negroes, using the term then current). Boys and girls were distinguished in the tabulations, as were children from middle-class, working-class, and lower-class families. The data as presented by Porter (which I have taken from Simon and Alstein, 1977, p. 121, table 5.10) are given in table 2.5.[3]

TABLE 2.5

Correctness of Racial Self-identification by Children of Different Ages, Sexes, Races, and Social Class Backgrounds

		Middle Class			Working Class			Lower Class		
		3 yrs.	4 yrs.	5 yrs.	3 yrs.	4 yrs.	5 yrs.	3 yrs.	4 yrs.	5 yrs.
					Boys					
White	Correct	1	8	10	0	4	7	0	2	4
	Incorrect	2	6	13	1	4	5	3	2	7
Black	Correct	1	2	4	2	9	7	0	6	3
	Incorrect	2	5	6	3	8	8	1	6	2
					Girls					
White	Correct	4	9	14	2	6	6	1	6	6
	Incorrect	4	12	6	1	5	3	0	6	4
Black	Correct	0	2	1	4	6	3	4	7	0
	Incorrect	4	16	3	7	18	4	3	7	6

The data are particularly difficult for analysis by inspection, and by some statistical methods, because there are so few cases per cell. There are 344 cases distributed among seventy-two cells, with six cells having zero entries. It is data of this sort that make a method of estimation which requires no grouping into cells at all, as does the maximum likelihood method outlined

[3] Two numbers in the table as published were inconsistent with the reported percentages, but those numbers were recovered from another table (table 5.8) using data from the same children.

in chapter 6, especially useful. Zero cells constitute no problem for the method, since in principle each case can have a different profile of independent variables.

It is difficult to get a sense by inspection of the effect of any of these variables. Using the computer program contained in the appendix, effects are found to be as shown in table 2.6.

TABLE 2.6

Effects of Race, Age, Social Class, and Sex on Correctness of Racial Self-identification

	Exponential			Linear	
	β	s.e.	α	β	s.e.
Race	−.653	(.230)	−.158	−.163	(.055)
Age	.155	(.168)	.039	.036	(.040)
Social Class	−.165	(.142)	−.041	−.044	(.034)
Sex	.072	(.226)	.018	.024	(.054)
Constant *(p*)*	.433			.450	

(Black = 1, white = 0; 3 yrs. = 3, 4 yrs. = 4, 5 yrs. = 5; middle class = 3, working class = 2, lower class = 1; boys = 1, girls = 0.)

The table shows that only race has an effect that is much larger than its standard error: The white children were about .16 more likely to give a correct racial self-identification than the black children. With both models, the coefficient is nearly three times its standard error. Older children are not significantly more likely to correctly identify themselves; the social-class difference is small and nonsignificant (and in the direction of less accuracy for children of higher-class backgrounds); and sex shows no significant difference.

The linear model in this case fits slightly better than the logit model: All the coefficients are slightly higher multiples (or fractions) of their standard errors than for the exponential model. This is apparent also in the slightly lower values of α from the exponential model compared to β from the linear model.

6.3. EXAMPLE

College Attendance by Moroccan Jews in Israel and France: With the emigration of Jews from the Arab world in the 1940s, 1950s, and 1960s, Moroccan Jews were faced with an alternative: to emigrate to Israel or to France. By the early 1970s many of those who had emigrated to Israel had begun to protest that they were subject to discrimination and were in fact doing less well than their counterparts who had emigrated to France. The Israel Ministry of Education, in response to the protests, commissioned research to discover the factual basis of these claims. In order to control for self-selection between Israel and France (it was contended, for example, that well-to-do Jews emigrated to France while the poor emigrated to Israel), the research design consisted of a sample of sixty-six pairs of brothers who had emigrated as adults, one of whom had emigrated to Israel and the other to France. For an additional comparison, eighty-two Rumanian Jews who had immigrated to Israel during the same period (between 1948 and 1967) were studied as well. The research was carried out by Inbar and Adler (1977). One claim of the Israeli Moroccans was that the educational system discriminated against their children, who were less likely to go on to college. Table 2.7 shows the number of children of the French and Israeli brothers and the Rumanians who were and were not admitted to college, controlled by age of the child at the time of the father's immigration. The latter variable is introduced because of evidence from earlier research that age at immigration is an important determinant of the likelihood of admission to a university in Israel.

TABLE 2.7

*College Admission by Country of Origin
and Destination and by Age at Immigration
for Jewish Immigrants**

Age at Immigration		Israeli Moroccans	French Moroccans	Rumanians
0–5	C	3	8	1
	$\bar{C}$	23	12	0
6–11	C	3	7	0
	$\bar{C}$	34	30	3
12–15	C	6	2	8
	$\bar{C}$	15	25	9
16+	C	4	5	5
	$\bar{C}$	17	17	3

* Data from Inbar and Adler, 1977, pp. 56, 57, tables 23, 24.

The small numbers of cases make inferences difficult and shaky. Disregarding age at immigration shows that 14 out of 29 Rumanians were admitted to a university, but only 22 out of 106 French Moroccans and 16 out of 105 Israeli Moroccans were admitted to a university.

This example illustrates a different facet of the models under discussion. In both the preceding examples, the independent variables were dichotomies (type of seedling, sex of child) or ordered classes (middle class, working class, lower class; age three, four, or five), which could be treated as continuous variables. Here it is desirable to treat one or both of the independent classifications as unordered classes. The authors suggest that the effect of age at immigration may be curvilinear, with immigration during elementary school years constituting a special handicap (see also Inbar, 1976).

The four age groups may be characterized by a set of three dummy variables:

$$x_1 = 1 \text{ for } 0\text{--}5, 0 \text{ for all others,}$$
$$x_2 = 1 \text{ for } 6\text{--}11, 0 \text{ for all others,}$$
$$x_3 = 1 \text{ for } 12\text{--}15, 0 \text{ for all others.}$$

The effect of each of these variables is an effect relative to the 16+ age group, which is the one excluded from characterization by a dummy variable.

Similarly, the three immigrant groups can be characterized by two dummy variables:

$$x_4 = 1 \text{ for French Moroccans, 0 for all others}$$
$$x_5 = 1 \text{ for Israeli Rumanians, 0 for all others.}$$

The observed effect of each of these two variables is an effect relative to the Israeli Moroccans, which is useful since this is the group of focal interest. However, as it happens, these two variables can be interpreted differently, with x_4 characterizing the country of destination (1 for France, 0 for Israel) and x_5 characterizing the country of origin (1 for Rumania, 0 for Morocco). The absence of the fourth logical category (Rumanian immigrants to France) is responsible for the dual interpretation. Thus any estimated effects of x_4 and x_5 are subject to this dual interpretation.

TABLE 2.8[a]

*Effects of Age at Immigration and Country of Origin
and Destination on University Admission*

	Exponential			Linear	
	β	s.e.	α	β	s.e.
Age 0–5 (relative to 16+)	.174	(.478)	.043	.018	(.087)
Age 6–11 (relative to 16+)	−.741	(.477)	−.177	−.100	(.071)
Age 12–15 (relative to 16+)	−.363	(.452)	−.090	−.044	(.078)
French Moroccans (relative to Israeli Moroccans)	.415	(.367)	.102	.055	(.051)
Rumanians (relative to Israeli Moroccans)	1.688	(.497)	.343	.322	(.103)
Constant (p^*)	.186			.196	
R^2	.086			.077	

[a] See Section 10 of this chapter for meaning of R^2.

Estimates of effects on university admissions are shown in table 2.8. The strongest effect shown by this analysis is the greater university admission of Rumanian immigrants to Israel (β more than three times its standard deviation in both models), though some other variables show smaller (and statistically nonsignificant) effects. The Moroccan Jews who immigrated to France appear to be slightly more likely than those who went to Israel to attend university, and there seems to be some indication of a similar age effect. The "vulnerable-age" hypothesis is that children who immigrate in early years of school (ages six through eleven in this analysis) are less likely to do well in school than those who immigrate earlier or later. Apart from the Rumanian effect, the largest effect in both models is a negative value for ages six through eleven, which is consistent with the vulnerable-age hypothesis. Altogether, however, the only large effect is the Rumanian effect. The comparison of the two models shows that the exponential decomposition does slightly better than the linear model.

6.4. EXAMPLE

Social Status in High School and Its Effect on College Plans: In a study of high school students' social status in the school (whether they were regarded by others in the school as members of the leading crowd), the effects of such status on changes in intentions to attend college over the four years of high school were studied (McDill and Coleman, 1963). The problem of interest was just how one's position in the high school social structure influences post–high school plans. The data on membership in the leading crowd as a freshman, and plans to attend college measured in the freshman year, are given in table 2.9.

TABLE 2.9

*Social Status in High School and Intentions
to Attend College Among High School
Freshman*

		Leading Crowd Membership (Social Status)	
		Member	Nonmember
College Plans	YES	85	206
	NO	59	252

Analysis of the data using the LONGIT·CROSS program to obtain maximum likelihood estimates of parameters gives results as shown in table 2.10.

TABLE 2.10

*Estimates of Effect of Social Status in High School on
Plans to Attend College for High School Freshmen*

	Exponential			Linear	
	β	s.e.	α	β	s.e.
Effect of social status	.57	(.19)	.139	.141	(.047)
Constant (p^*)	.45			.450	

The data show an effect that can be regarded as either strong or weak. According to both models, social status changes by about 0.14 the probability of attending college, which is not a large effect. But the observed relationship is not due to sampling error, because β is nearly three times its standard error for both models.

This example is not particularly illuminating in itself, but it will be useful for comparison with the models for panel data in the next chapter since there was a second observation of these same students as seniors.

7. LOGITS WITH POLYTYMOUS RESPONSES

For a dichotomous dependent attribute, equilibrium of the stochastic process under the exponential linear decomposition is identical to the multivariate logit model. We can ask a further question: Is the equilibrium of a multistate stochastic process identical to a multivariate logit model with polytymous responses? And if the answer is that it is not in general the same (as will turn out to be the case), is there a set of constraints that, imposed on the stochastic process, make it identical to the multivariate logit? If there are (as will turn out to be the case), then this will show what implicit assumptions about the response process lie behind the polytymous logit.

If there are s states for the dependent response, with $s > 2$, then if p_j is the probability of giving response j, the polytymous logit can be defined as

$$\frac{p_j}{p_h} = \frac{e^{\sum_k b_{kj} x_{ki}}}{e^{\sum_k b_{kh} x_{ki}}} = e^{\sum_k (b_{kj} - b_{kh}) x_{ki}}. \tag{2.28}$$

Alternatively, the logit for p_j may be defined as

$$p_j = \frac{e^{\sum_k b_{kj} x_{ki}}}{\sum_{h=1}^{s} e^{\sum_k b_{kh} x_{ki}}} . \tag{2.29}$$

In either case, there are $s - 1$ independent logits. The two definitions are equivalent, for dividing the logit for p_j in equation (2.29) by the logit for p_h gives the ratio shown in equation (2.28). The question, then, is whether this form would be given by the equilibrium of the stochastic process with exponential linear decomposition. At equilibrium, the equation for the rate of change of the probability of occupying state j is

$$\frac{dp_j}{dt} = 0 = -p_j \sum_{h \neq j} q_{jh} + \sum_{h \neq j} p_h q_{hj} \qquad \text{or,} \tag{2.30}$$

$$p_j = \frac{\sum_{h \neq j} p_h q_{hj}}{\sum_{h \neq j} q_{jh}} . \tag{2.31}$$

In general, the exponential decomposition of q_{hj} does not make equation (2.31) equal to equation (2.29). However, if we assume that the transition rate from each other state into j is the same, then the transition rate q_{hj} is independent of h and can be written $q_{.j}$. Making this substitution and employing a little algebra gives

$$p_j = \frac{q_{.j}}{\sum_{h=1}^{s} q_{.h}} . \tag{2.32}$$

Substituting for $q_{.j}$ the exponential linear decomposition gives an equation,

$$p_j = \frac{e^{\sum_k b_{kj} x_{ki}}}{\sum_{h=1}^{s} e^{\sum_k b_{kh} x_{ki}}}$$

which is identical to the polytymous logit of equation (2.29). This means that the polytymous logit is identical to the equilibrium state of a stochastic process of an especially simplified form: A process in which the transition rate q_{hj} into destination state j is independent of the origin state h, and this is true for every destination state j. Thus, if we wish to make this assumption for given data, the polytymous logit is the appropriate model of the response. If this assumption is not warranted, then the polytymous logit is an inappropriate model. Another way of seeing its inappropriateness is to note that in the general stochastic process without the assumption that q_{hj} is independent of h, there are $s(s-1)$ parameters b_{khj} for every independent variable k. With the removal of one degree of freedom because $\sum_{h=1}^{s} p_h = 1$, this leaves $s(s-1) - 1$ parameters. But there are only $s - 1$ parameters estimated for each independent variable in a multivariate logit. Thus some assumption of constraint on the transition rates is necessary to bring about this reduction, and the constraint that does so is the one specified above.[4]

The estimation of parameters for the polytymous logit, when this assumption is warranted, is carried out exactly as in the dichotomous case, except $s - 1$ times. Using equation (2.28) with the index h referring to the last state s, the logarithm of the equation gives a linear decomposition of $\log(p_j/p_s)$, with $b_{kj} - b_{ks}$ ($=\beta_{kj}$) as the parameters to be estimated.

8. A REINTERPRETATION OF THE PROCESS

In some kinds of actions that can be classified as in one of s states, the process under consideration may be a different one. In particular, there may be a set of s mutually exclusive and exhaustive actions (with $s \geq 2$) that a person may take in a one-way process. In such a case, there is no statistical equilibrium among the probabilities of being in each of the s states, but instead there is a process going to completion from an origin state into one of the s states. In this case, the process may be described by equation (2.33), where the origin state is state 0 and the destination states are states $1, \ldots, s$.

$$\frac{dp_0}{dt} = -p_0 \sum_{j=1}^{s} q_{0j}. \tag{2.33}$$

It is possible to solve for $p_j(t)$ or $p_j(\infty)$, where $p_j(t)$ is the probability of being in state j at time t. If what is under consideration is an action of

[4] Nancy Tuma (1981) shows that another process also generates a polytymous logit at equilibrium: a birth-death process with moves only to adjacent states in a single dimension.

type 1, . . . , s, and if the process is observed at a time before it has gone to completion, $p_j(t)$ is given by equation (2.34):

$$p_j(t) = \frac{q_{0j}}{\sum\limits_{h=1}^{s} q_{0h}} (1 - e^{\sum\limits_{h=1}^{s} q_{0h}})$$ (2.34)

and if the process has gone to completion, $p_j(\infty)$ is given by equation (2.35):

$$p_j(\infty) = \frac{q_{0j}}{\sum\limits_{h=1}^{s} q_{0h}} .$$ (2.35)

Both equations can be put in the form of

$$\frac{p_j}{\Sigma p_h} = \frac{q_{0j}}{\Sigma q_{0h}} .$$ (2.36)

If we renormalize to consider the probability of acting in direction j given that an action has been taken, this becomes

$$p_j = \frac{q_{0j}}{\Sigma q_{0h}} .$$ (2.37)

This reduces to equation (2.17) for $s = 2$, and s > 2 is equivalent to equation (2.32), developed for polytymous actions in the preceding section under the assumption that q_{hj} is independent of h.

Thus for cross-sectional data in which it is more reasonable to assume a one-way process that has gone all or part way to completion, the analysis of the present chapter remains valid when based on the fraction of the sample that has acted. But the underlying stochastic equation is different from the two-way process considered earlier.

9. WHAT IF STATISTICAL EQUILIBRIUM DOES NOT HOLD?

It is useful to examine what errors are made in estimation of β in equation (2.19) and β in equation (2.22) if the assumption of statistical equilibrium on the basis of which these equations are constructed is incorrect. If $dp/dt = g \neq 0$, there are three cases of interest: (1) g is a random variable, correlated with one or more of x_k; (2) g is a random variable, uncorrelated with any x_k; (3) g is a constant, identical over all individuals.

Instead of equation (2.16), we write

$$g = -pq_0 + (1-p)q_1. \tag{2.39}$$

Solving for p, we have

$$p = \frac{q_1 - g}{q_1 + q_0}. \tag{2.39}$$

For the linear decomposition of q_j's, if we let $g^* = g/(b_0 + c_0)$, we have, instead of equation (2.19):

$$p = \sum_{k=0}^{n} \beta_k x_k - g^*. \tag{2.40}$$

If g is a constant, the estimate of β_0 obtained from equation (2.19) will be an underestimate of the true β_0 by the amount g^* if g is positive, and an overestimate if g is negative. That is, if, instead of being at statistical equilibrium, p was below its equilibrium value (that is, g was positive), then the size of q_1 relative to q_0 is underestimated; but none of the coefficients of effect of the explanatory variables is misestimated.

If g is a random variable uncorrelated with any x_k and with a positive or negative mean, the same bias is introduced as indicated above, the size determined by the mean of g, $\bar{g}$. In addition, the existence of a nonzero variance for g reduces the explanatory power of the x_k's and increases the variance of the estimates of the β_k's, but it does not introduce a bias into these estimates.

Finally, in the worst case, if g is a random variable correlated with one or more of the x_k's, then there will be an underestimation of β_k for any x_k with which g is positively correlated, and there will be an overestimation of β_k for any x_k with which g is negatively correlated. (In substance this means that if p is below its equilibrium value for any subgroup, say males for some peculiar reason, and thus g is positive, or above its equilibrium value for the complement of that subgroup, say females, making g negative— or if both of these conditions are true—then a positive effect of being male on the dependent attribute would be underestimated, while a negative effect would be overestimated, that is, more highly negative.) In some cases, we might expect this worst case to occur.

For the exponential decomposition, the same qualitative statements about potential biases hold. In this case, equation (2.22) becomes

$$\log \frac{p}{1-p} = \sum_{k=0}^{n} b_k x_k + \log \left[1 - \frac{g(q_0 + q_1)}{q_0 q_1} \right]. \qquad (2.41)$$

If g is positive, then this new term is negative, while if g is negative, the new term is positive. From this, statements like those above for the linear decomposition follow.

These potential biases are of course not a function of the particular underlying processes assumed. Rather, they would exist, undiscoverable with cross-sectional data, whatever approach is taken to estimating effects of independent variables. With the attention drawn to these potential "cross-sectional biases," the model used here merely emphasizes the assumptions one makes when carrying out analysis of cross-sectional data.

10. STATISTICAL TESTS FOR THE MODEL AS A WHOLE

There are several kinds of statistical tests one might want to make for analyses of this sort. One, a descriptive statistic, is a measure of the combined strength of the explanatory variables in their effect on the response attribute. If their effect is small, the parameters expressing effects ($\beta_1, \ldots, \beta_s$, or with panel data $b_1, \ldots, b_s$ and $c_1, \ldots, c_s$) will be near zero and not statistically significant except in large samples, and the values of $\hat{p}_i$ estimated by the model will not vary greatly for different individuals. In linear regression, a statistic that shows this combined power is R, the multiple correlation between the independent variables and the dependent variable, or as it is more often used, R^2.

R^2 is ordinarily much smaller for dichotomous response variables than for the linear regression models where the response z_i is a continuous variable, for a dichotomous response must always be 0 or 1, and unless $\hat{p}_i$ is near 0 or 1, there will be deviations between z_i and $\hat{p}_i$. The equation for R^2 can be written by taking the definition of the multiple correlation as the zero-order correlation between the observed values and those predicted from the analysis:

$$R^2 = \frac{\{\Sigma(z_i - \bar{z})(p_i - \bar{p})\}^2}{\Sigma(z_i - \bar{z})^2 (p_i - \bar{p})^2}. \tag{2.42}$$

Since the mean of the predicted values p_i, which is denoted by $\bar{p}$, is equal to the mean of the observed responses z_i, denoted by $\bar{z}$, equation (2.42) can be written after some simplifications:

$$R^2 = \frac{(\Sigma z_i p_i - n\bar{z}\bar{p})^2}{(\Sigma z_i^2 - n\bar{z}^2)(\Sigma p_i^2 - n\bar{p}^2)}. \tag{2.43}$$

This statistic can be used to test the overall explanatory power of the variables in the model.

A second kind of statistic, the goodness of fit statistic, sometimes used with cross-tabulations, is very different from the statistic described above. The χ^2 goodness of fit statistic (to be described below) does not measure or test the statistical significance of the strength of the explanatory variables. It tests, rather, whether the *form* of the model is appropriate to the data. If there is a sizeable interaction effect, for example, with the linear decomposition, but not for the exponential decomposition (as in the case of the seedling survival example), then the χ^2 goodness of fit test would show a good fit (small value of χ^2) for the exponential decomposition, and a poor fit (large value of χ^2) for the linear decomposition. Thus a large value of χ^2 is a signal that either a different form of the model should be used, or that interaction terms are necessary. In contrast, a low value of R^2 indicates that different independent variables are necessary in order to account for the response. Thus the χ^2 goodness of fit test may show a very good fit, while R^2 is very small, showing that taken together the independent variables explain a small fraction of the variance in z_i.

The most common goodness of fit measure used is the Pearson χ^2 statistic for test of goodness of fit, which is

$$\chi^2 = \sum_{i=1}^{N} \frac{(n_i - \hat{n}_i)^2}{\hat{n}_i} \tag{2.44}$$

49

where

> n_i is the observed frequency in the cell,
> $\hat{n}_i$ is the predicted frequency in the cell,
> N is the number of cells.

In the case with a dichotomous response, like we have here, $\hat{n}_i$ is calculated as the product of the number of cases for a given configuration of the independent variables, and the probability of a positive or negative response for that configuration. For example, in the seedling example, there are 100 cases for longleaf seedlings planted too high. For the exponential decomposition, the probability of a positive response for longleaf seedlings planted too high is .606. Thus $\hat{n}_i$ is 60.6 for the "alive" cell with this configuration of independent variables. In Example 1 of this chapter, there are eight cells altogether, based on four experiments with $n_i = 100$ for each of the four. The observed values of n_i are, in each of the four experiments, 95, 5; 88, 12; 89, 11; and 59, 41. The corresponding predicted values, $\hat{n}_i$, are 96.6, 3.4; 86.4, 13.6; 87.4, 12.6; and 60.6, 39.4, for the exponential decomposition.

When the model fits the data, this statistic is asymptotically distributed as χ^2 with degrees of freedom equal to the number of independent observed values of $\hat{n}_i$, minus the number of parameters estimated. For example, with the seedling example, the exponential decomposition gives a χ^2 with 1 degree of freedom of 1.34, showing that deviations as large as those observed would have occurred by chance 24 times out of a hundred. However, the linear decomposition gives a χ^2 of 9.85, showing that deviations as large as those observed, if the model is correct, would have occurred less than one time out of a hundred. This indicates that either an interaction term, or a different model (e.g., the exponential decomposition) is necessary.

When cell values are very small, this statistic deviates from a χ^2 distribution, and in particular, when there is only one observation for each two cells, as occurs when each individual has a different vector of values on the independent variables, a condition which can occur in the analyses described in this book and carried out in the LONGIT computer program contained in the appendix, the statistic is no longer distributed even approximately as χ^2.

Thus, when the data to be analyzed are cross-tabulated into cells, and the numbers in a cell are sufficiently large (Fienberg, 1977, uses the rule of thumb that the total number of cases be at least ten times the number of cells), then the goodness of fit statistic may be used. The statistic, given by equation (2.44), is distributed as χ^2 with $m-n$ degrees of freedom, where m is the number of independent cell values and n is the number of parameters estimated. In the calculations of LONGIT·CROSS contained in the appendix and used for calculating the examples, the Pearson χ^2 statistic, given by equation (2.44) above, is used.

However, the method of maximum likelihood used in this book makes possible analysis of data at the individual level, in which each person may have different values of the independent variables. That is, if for individual i, there is the observation z_i (=1 or 0), and $z_i = f(x_{1i}, x_{2i}, \ldots, x_{ni}, e_i)$, each individual i may have a different profile of independent variables, x_{1i}, $x_{2i}, \ldots, x_{ni}$. This is one of the principal virtues and attractions of the methods outlined in this book. When data of this sort are analyzed, each individual is in effect in a separate cell, and the goodness of fit statistic cannot be used. In that case, the goodness of fit statistic begins to measure something else, that is the strength of the independent variables in accounting for the observed data. Thus the usual χ^2 goodness of fit statistics have meaning only when there are cells over which proportions can be calculated; for it is these proportions, not the observations of single individuals, which must be compared with predicted proportions.

In the computer program LONGIT·CROSS contained in the appendix, a Pearsonian χ^2 test of goodness of fit can be (optionally) carried out if the data are in the form of cross-tabulations and the number of independent observations is known. There is an option also for calculation of R^2, which does not require that the data be in the form of cross-tabulations.

APPENDIX 1: ALTERNATIVE DECOMPOSITIONS

Two other decompositions of transition rates should be mentioned, for each has some points to recommend it.

1. PRODUCTION FUNCTION

$$q_j = b_{0j} \prod_k x_{ki}^{b_{kj}}. \tag{A2.1}$$

This is equivalent to an exponential decomposition in logarithms of the independent variables:

$$q_j = e^{b_{0j} + \Sigma b_{kj} \log x_{ki}}. \tag{A2.2}$$

51

For the two transition rates q_1 and q_0, this becomes

$$q_1 = e^{b_0 + \Sigma b_k \log x_{ki}} \tag{A2.3}$$

$$q_0 = e^{c_0 + \Sigma c_k \log x_{ki}}. \tag{A2.4}$$

Here it is necessary when x_{ki} is a dichotomy to let it take on values other than 0 or 1. We may redefine x_{ki} to equal e^1 or e^0 in place of 1 or 0 in this case. For the continuous variables no change is necessary, so long as their values are greater than zero. We have as the ratio q_1/q_0,

$$\frac{q_1}{q_0} = e^{b_0 - c_0 + \sum_{k=1}^{n} (b_k - b_k) \log x_{ki}}. \tag{A2.5}$$

If we differentiate q_j with respect to x_{ki}, a continuous variable, we obtain, from equation (A2.1)

$$\frac{dq_j}{dx_k} = \frac{b_{kj}}{x_{ki}} q_j \tag{A2.6}$$

(with a change of sign if $q_j = q_0$ rather than q_1). This shows that the change in q_j per unit of x_{ki} is proportional to the value of q_j and inversely proportional to the value of x_{ki}. Thus, as x_{ki} becomes larger, a given absolute increase has less effect on q_j than when x_{ki} is smaller. The parameters b_k can in this case be considered elasticities of q_j with respect to x_{ki}.

2. A DIFFERENT EXPONENTIAL DECOMPOSITION

In the theory of reaction rates in chemistry, chemical states are characterized by their potential energy level. In order to make the transition between two states, the system must pass through a boundary state in which the potential energy level is higher than that which characterizes either state (see Glasstone, 1946, pp. 1087 ff). The chemical reaction rate that is formally analogous to the transition rates q_j in the present model is a function of the difference in potential energy between the activated state (the boundary) and the state of origin. Thus, if the potential energy level of state 1 is E_1, that of state 2 is E_2, and that of the boundary between them is E_{12} ($> E_1$, E_2), then the reaction rate k_{12} is $e^{-(E_{12} - E_1)/RT}$ and the rate k_{21} is $e^{-(E_{12} - E_2)/RT}$.

We may adopt this way of perceiving the structure underlying transition rates. If we do so, then each state is characterized by a quantity, say s_h for state h, and each boundary between states is characterized by a quantity s_{hj}, where $s_{hj} > s_h$ and $s_{hj} > s_j$. Then the decompositions of q_j and q_h are:

$$q_j = e^{-(s_{hj}-s_h)}$$

$$q_h = e^{-(s_{hj}-s_j)}$$

and dividing,

$$\frac{q_j}{q_h} = e^{s_h - s_j}.$$

Effects of independent attributes and variables on the transition rates can take the form of linear decomposition of s_h and s_j. Exactly the same form of decomposition will result here as in the exponential linear decomposition. Thus, in models with two states and a single dichotomous dependent attribute, this decomposition is indistinguishable from that one.

However, a different situation exists when there are two interdependent attributes. In this case, there are two parameters for the boundary, and four parameters for the states. If the parameters for the states are labeled s_0, s_1, s_2, s_3 for states 00, 01, 10, and 11 on the two attributes, then an effect on attribute 1 takes the form of a decomposition that makes s_2 differ from s_0 and s_3 differ from s_1. A positive effect of attribute 2 on attribute 1 makes $s_3 > s_1$ and $s_0 > s_2$. But also a positive effect of attribute 1 on attribute 2 makes $s_3 > s_2$ and $s_0 > s_1$. Thus, if we solve for the eight independent transition rates in the interdependent system, and then estimate the five independent parameters of the six (two boundary parameters and four state parameters, one of which is an arbitrary level), there is no way of estimating the amount of effect of x_1 on x_2 and x_2 on x_1. For if $s_3 > s_1$, s_2, and if $s_0 > s_1$, s_2, this tells us only the degree of consistency between the two. The conception of an effect of each on the other is not meaningful with this decomposition of the transition rates.

APPENDIX 2: USE OF THE LONGIT·CROSS PROGRAM

This program is designed for analysis of cross-sectional qualitative data in which there is one *response* variable, coded 0 or 1, and one or more *independent* variables, which may be either of the same form as the response variable (that is, taking on values of 0 or 1) or of any other form, such as an ordered set of categories that can be given values such as 1, 2, 4, 7, . . . , or a continuous variable.

Control Cards

To be read from unit 2, assumed to be read from cards or card-image records with blocksize 4560.

Card 1: The number of different data sets or problems to be analyzed on this run. This number appears with the units position in column 5. There is no limit to the number of problems per run.

Cards 2–5: They are repeated for each problem or data set. If data are read from cards on the same unit as the control cards, card 1 prefaces the entire run; cards 2–5 preface each data set.

Card 2: Position 5: The number of independent variables (min 1, max 19; can be increased by change in dimension statement).

Position 10 (units): The number of records to be read, where one record represents one individual for ungrouped data, or one cell for grouped or cross-tabulated data (min 4, max 2000).[5]

Position 15: 1 if only linear model

2 if only exponential model

3 if first linear, followed by exponential

Card 3: Position 5: 1 if input data are to be printed out, 0 otherwise.

Position 10: 1 if predicted proportions in state 1 are to be printed, 0 otherwise.

Position 15: 1 if a Pearson chi-square is to be calculated (only possible if data are from cross-tabulation and alternate records are cells that differ (1 or 0) on dependent variable); 0 otherwise.

Position 20: 1 if multiple R^2 is to be calculated; 0 otherwise.

Position 30 (decimal): The number of independent individuals represented by the data for the calculation of statistical tests. If this equals the sum of the weights, then this number can be deleted.

Card 4: This card contains the format specifications for the data. The conventions of Fortran format statements are used. For a *standard* format, reading from cards or card-image records, the deci-

---

[5] Dimensions can be larger than given in the program. Dimensions should be as large as necessary for the problem at hand, and no larger than machine capacity.

mal point for each of the variables described under *Input Data* below is in position 5, 10, . . . , 70. If there are more than fourteen total variables for each individual, two cards per individual are used. For this standard format, card 5 should read (14F5.0) in positions 3–10.

Input Data

To be read from unit 2, assumed to be read from cards or card-image records with blocksize 4560.

1. Data are read individual by individual (or for cross-tabulated data, cell by cell), in the following order:
   a. Value of the dependent attribute, having the value 0 or 1.
   b. Values of each of the independent attributes or variables.
   c. The weight of the individual. For a self-weighting sample, the weight is one. For a nonself-weighting sample, the weight is the sampling weight associated with the individual. For the case in which the record represents all individuals in a cell of a tabulation, the weight is the number of individuals in the cell if the sample is self-weighting, or the sum of the weights for individuals in the cell if it is not.
2. Data format is specified by the user on control card 4.

Alternate Options

By modifying the Read statement in the program, variables can be read in a different order (for reading from records in which the data appear in a different order).

By modifying the JCL statements, data may be read from different units, different length records, differently blocked. JCL must in any case be specific to the machine and the operating system.

Example of Control Cards, Data, and Output

The control cards, data, and output for the example in section 6.3 are presented with the appended program.

INPUT TO LONGIT.CROSS PROGRAM

(Example of Section 6.3)

```
   1
   5   24   3
   0    1    1    1
(10F4.0)
  0.  0.  0.  1.  0.  0. 23.
  1.  0.  0.  1.  0.  0.  3.
  0.  0.  0.  0.  1.  0. 34.
  1.  0.  0.  0.  1.  0.  3.
  0.  0.  0.  0.  0.  1. 15.
  1.  0.  0.  0.  0.  1.  6.
  0.  0.  0.  0.  0.  0. 17.
  1.  0.  0.  0.  0.  0.  4.
  0.  1.  0.  1.  0.  0. 12.
  1.  1.  0.  1.  0.  0.  8.
  0.  1.  0.  0.  1.  0. 30.
  1.  1.  0.  0.  1.  0.  7.
  0.  1.  0.  0.  0.  1. 25.
  1.  1.  0.  0.  0.  1.  2.
  0.  1.  0.  0.  0.  0. 17.
  1.  1.  0.  0.  0.  0.  5.
  0.  0.  1.  1.  0.  0.  0.
  1.  0.  1.  1.  0.  0.  1.
  0.  0.  1.  0.  1.  0.  3.
  1.  0.  1.  0.  1.  0.  0.
  0.  0.  1.  0.  0.  1.  9.
  1.  0.  1.  0.  0.  1.  8.
  0.  0.  1.  0.  0.  0.  3.
  1.  0.  1.  0.  0.  0.  5.
```

OUTPUT FROM LONGIT.CROSS PROGRAM

LONGIT.CROSS PROGRAM   12/7/80

```
   5   24   3
   0    1    1    1         0.
ITERATION CONVERGED AFTER STEP :    32
```

LINEAR MODEL

COVARIANCE MATRIX

0.00425	-0.00124	-0.00171	-0.00374	-0.00373	-0.00344
-0.00124	0.00264	0.00126	0.00019	0.00017	-0.00008
-0.00171	0.00126	0.01050	0.00106	0.00104	-0.00062
-0.00374	0.00019	0.00106	0.00749	0.00364	0.00348
-0.00373	0.00017	0.00104	0.00364	0.00501	0.00348
-0.00344	-0.00008	-0.00062	0.00348	0.00348	0.00610

B COEFFICIENTS AND STANDARD ERRORS

```
B( 0)=    0.1957      SE( 0)=    0.0652
B( 1)=    0.0552      SE( 1)=    0.0514
B( 2)=    0.3218      SE( 2)=    0.1025
B( 3)=    0.0180      SE( 3)=    0.0865
B( 4)=   -0.1004      SE( 4)=    0.0708
B( 5)=   -0.0443      SE( 5)=    0.0781
```

```
P-VECTOR :
                0.2137      0.2137      0.0952      0.0952      0.1513      0.1513
                0.1957      0.1957      0.2688      0.2688      0.1504      0.1504
                0.2065      0.2065      0.2508      0.2508      0.5354      0.5354
                0.4170      0.4170      0.4731      0.4731      0.5174      0.5174


GOODNESS OF FIT TEST
CHI SQUARE=        13.06     WITH    6   D. F.

MULTIPLE R-SQUARE =  0.077

ITERATION CONVERGED AFTER STEP :      6

LOGISTIC (EXPONENTIAL) MODEL


COVARIANCE MATRIX
        0.16029   -0.07764   -0.08837   -0.12117   -0.11179   -0.09617
       -0.07764    0.13497    0.08066    0.01163   -0.00065   -0.00566
       -0.08837    0.08066    0.24698    0.04345    0.02518   -0.03818
       -0.12117    0.01163    0.04345    0.22877    0.11141    0.09989
       -0.11179   -0.00065    0.02518    0.11141    0.22792    0.10232
       -0.09617   -0.00566   -0.03818    0.09989    0.10232    0.20448


    B COEFFICIENTS AND STANDARD ERRORS
    B( 0)=    -1.4746     SE( 0)=    0.4004     A( 0)=    -0.3138
    B( 1)=     0.4153     SE( 1)=    0.3674     A( 1)=     0.1024
    B( 2)=     1.6878     SE( 2)=    0.4970     A( 2)=     0.3439
    B( 3)=     0.1736     SE( 3)=    0.4783     A( 3)=     0.0433
    B( 4)=    -0.7410     SE( 4)=    0.4774     A( 4)=    -0.1772
    B( 5)=    -0.3625     SE( 5)=    0.4522     A( 5)=    -0.0897
P-VECTOR :
                0.2140      0.2140      0.0984      0.0984      0.1374      0.1374
                0.1862      0.1862      0.2920      0.2920      0.1418      0.1418
                0.1944      0.1944      0.2575      0.2575      0.5955      0.5955
                0.3710      0.3710      0.4627      0.4627      0.5531      0.5531


GOODNESS OF FIT TEST
CHI SQUARE=        23.60     WITH    6   D. F.

MULTIPLE R-SQUARE =  0.084


                        LONGIT.CROSS PROGRAM
1.      //LONGIT JOB (2ZB004,COL,Q,NORC),COLEMAN,RE=750K,
2.      // TE=YES,ID='LONGIT.CROSS',RO=NORC,Q=0
3.      // EXEC FORTXCLG
4.      //FORT.SYSIN DD *
5.      C
6.      C
7.      C
8.              INTEGER N,NS,I1,I,J,FLAG
9.              DIMENSION Z(2000),W(2000),X(20,2000),SS(20,20),P(2000),
10.            &B(20),BL(20),D(2000),WEIGHT(2000),R(20),C(20),FMT(18)
11.             DATA SUMA,BL/21*0.0/
12.             ISTEP=0
13.     C
14.     C       NS=NUMBER OF INDEPENDENT VARIABLES, N=NUMBER OF CELLS OR
```

57

```
15.    C      DISTINCT TYPES OF INDIVIDUALS AS READ IN ONE RECORD.
16.    C      FLAG=1 IF ONLY LINEAR MODEL, 2 IF ONLY LOGIT, 3 IF BOTH
17.    C
18.           WRITE(6,8893)
19.    8893 FORMAT(//1X'LONGIT.CROSS PROGRAM               12/7/80'/)
20.    C
21.           READ (2,8888)NJOBS
22.           WRITE(6,8888)NJOBS
23.           DO 3000 JQQ=1,NJOBS
24.           READ (2,8888)NS,N,FLAG
25.           WRITE(6,8888)NS,N,FLAG
26.           READ(2,8788)JW,NWP,NC,NR,CNUM
27.           WRITE(6,8788)JW,NWP,NC,NR,CNUM
28.    8788 FORMAT(4I5,F10.0)
29.    C
30.    C      JW=1 IF DATA ARE TO BE WRITTEN, NWP=1 IF PREDICTED PROPORTION
31.    C       IN EACH STATE IS TO BE WRITTEN.
32.    C      NC=1 FOR PEARSON CHISQUARE, NR=1 FOR MULTIPLE R-SQUARE.
33.    C      CNUM=EFFECTIVE NUMBER OF CASES FOR STATISTICAL TESTS. IF THIS
34.    C       EQUALS SUM OF WEIGHTS, LEAVE BLANK
35.    8888 FORMAT(3I5)
36.           TN=.0001*NS
37.           READ(2,8889)FMT
38.           NS=NS+1
39.           NSM=NS-1
40.           NSV=NS
41.    8889 FORMAT(18A4)
42.           DO 4008 I1=1,N
43.           READ(2,FMT,Z(I1),(X(J,I1),J=2,NS),W(I1)
44.    4008 IF(JW.EQ.1)WRITE(6,FMT)Z(I1),(X(J,I1),J=2,NS),W(I1)
45.           DO 4118 I1=1,N
46.           X(1,I1)=1.
47.           SUMA=SUMA+W(I1)
48.           IF(Z(I1).EQ.1) D(I1)=0.5
49.           IF(Z(I1).EQ.0) D(I1)=-0.5
50.    4118 CONTINUE
51.           DO 4009 I=1,N
52.           WEIGHT(I)=W(I)
53.    4009 P(I)=W(I)
54.    1000 IF(ISTEP.GE.100) GOTO 2000
55.    C
56.    C
57.           DO 5 I=1,NS
58.           DO 5 J=1,NS
59.       5 SS(I,J)=0.0
60.           DO 15 I1=1,N
61.           DO 15 I=1,NS
62.           DO 15 J=I,NS
63.           SS(I,J)=SS(I,J)+X(I,I1)*X(J,I1)*WEIGHT(I1)
64.      15 SS(J,I)=SS(I,J)
65.    C
66.    C
67.           CALL INVER(SS,NS)
68.
69.    C
70.           DO 35 I=1,NS
71.      35 R(I)=0
72.    C
73.           DO 40 IC=1,N
74.           IF(FLAG.NE.2)GOTO 136
75.           D(IC)=D(IC)*W(IC)
76.           GOTO 137
```

58

```
77.          136 D(IC)=D(IC)*P(IC)
78.          137 DO 45 J=1,NS
79.              C(J)=0.0
80.              DO 45 I1=1,NS
81.           45 C(J)=C(J)+SS(I1,J)*X(I1,IC)
82.              DO 40 I=1,NS
83.              C(I)=C(I)*D(IC)
84.           40 R(I)=R(I)+C(I)
85.    C
86.    C
87.              DO 81 I=1,NS
88.           81 B(I)=BL(I)+R(I)
89.
90.    C
91.              ISTEP=ISTEP+1
92.    C
93.              DIFR=0.
94.              DO 83 I=1,NS
95.              DIFR=DIFR +ABS(B(I)-BL(I))
96.           83 CONTINUE
97.              IF(DIFR.GE.TN) GOTO 89
98.              WRITE(6,88) ISTEP
99.           88 FORMAT(1H0,'ITERATION CONVERGED AFTER STEP : ',I5)
100.             IF(FLAG.EQ.2)GOTO 141
101.             WRITE(6,117)
102.         117 FORMAT(/1X,'LINEAR MODEL')
103.             GOTO 142
104.         141 WRITE(6,118)
105.         118 FORMAT(/1X,'LOGISTIC (EXPONENTIAL) MODEL')
106.         142 WRITE(6,115)
107.             DO 113 K=1,NS
108.         113 WRITE(6,110)(SS(K,J),J=1,NS)
109.         115 FORMAT(//1X,'COVARIANCE MATRIX')
110.         110 FORMAT(5X,8F10.5)
111.             WRITE(6,112)
112.             IF(FLAG.NE.2)GOTO 128
113.             DO 121 K=1,NS
114.             SS(K,K)=SQRT(SS(K,K))
115.             A=(EXP(B(K))-1.)/(2.*(EXP(B(K))+1.))
116.             K1=K-1
117.         121 WRITE(6,123)K1,B(K),K1,SS(K,K),K1,A
118.         123 FORMAT(5X,'B(',I2,')=',F10.4,5X,'SE(',I2,')=',F10.4,
119.            &5X,'A(',I2,')=',F10.4)
120.             GOTO 124
121.         128 DO 111 K=1,NS
122.             SS(K,K)=SQRT(SS(K,K))
123.             K1=K-1
124.         111 WRITE(6,122)K1,B(K),K1,SS(K,K)
125.         112 FORMAT(//5X,'B COEFFICIENTS AND STANDARD ERRORS')
126.         122 FORMAT(5X,'B(',I2,')=',F10.4,5X,'SE(',I2,')=',F10.4)
127.         124 DO 192 I=1,N
128.             P(I)=0.
129.             DO 191 J=1,NS
130.         191 P(I)=P(I)+B(J)*X(J,I)
131.             IF(FLAG.EQ.2) GOTO 4100
132.             IF(P(I).GT.1)P(I)=1
133.             IF(P(I).LT.0) P(I)=0
134.             GOTO 192
135.        4100 P(I)=1./(1+EXP(-P(I)))
136.         192 CONTINUE
137.             IF(NWP.EQ.1)WRITE(6,888)
138.         888 FORMAT(1H0,'P-VECTOR :')
```

```
139.            IF(NWP.EQ.1)WRITE(6,878)(P(I),I=1,N)
140.        878 FORMAT(12X,6F10.4)
141.            CALL TESTS(NC,NR,N,NSV,NS,CNUM,SUMA,P,Z,X,W)
142.            IF(FLAG.NE.3) GOTO 3000
143.        127 FLAG=2
144.            ISTEP=0
145.            DO 3003 I=1,NS
146.            B(I)=0.0
147.       3003 BL(I)=0.0
148.            SUMA=0.0
149.            GOTO 3
150.       3000 CONTINUE
151.            STOP
152.    C
153.         89 DO 2111 I=1,N
154.       2111 P(I)=0
155.            DO 90 I=1,NS
156.         90 BL(I)=B(I)
157.            DO 92 I=1,N
158.            DO 91 J=1,NS
159.         91 P(I)=P(I)+B(J)*X(J,I)
160.            IF(FLAG.EQ.2) GOTO 4000
161.            IF(P(I).GT.1)P(I)=1
162.            IF(P(I).LT.0) P(I)=0
163.            GOTO 4001
164.       4000 P(I)=1./(1+EXP(-P(I)))
165.       4001 D(I)=Z(I)-P(I)
166.            FACT=P(I)*(1-P(I))
167.            DUM=P(I)
168.            IF(FACT.LT..0291)FACT=0.0291
169.            IF(FLAG.EQ.2) GOTO 4003
170.            WEIGHT(I)=W(I)/FACT
171.            P(I)=WEIGHT(I)
172.            GOTO 92
173.       4003 WEIGHT(I)=W(I)*FACT
174.         92 CONTINUE
175.    C
176.    C
177.            GOTO 1000
178.    C
179.    C
180.       2000 WRITE(6,9991) ISTEP
181.       9991 FORMAT(1X,'ITERATION DID NOT CONVERGE IN ',I4,' STEPS ')
182.            IF(FLAG.EQ.3)GOTO 127
183.            GOTO 3000
184.            END
185.
186.
187.    C
188.            SUBROUTINE TESTS(NC,NR,N,NSV,NS,CNUM,SUMA,P,Z,X,W)
189.            DIMENSION P(2000),Z(2000),X(20,2000),W(2000)
190.            IF(CNUM.GT.0.)GOTO 19
191.            CNUM=SUMA
192.    C
193.    C       CALCULATION OF CHI SQUARE GOODNESS OF FIT TEST
194.         19 IF (NC.NE.1)GOTO 10
195.            NH=N/2
196.            NHH=NH-NSV
197.            CHI=0.
198.            DO 11 J=1,NH
199.            I=J*2-1
200.            I1=J*2
201.            IF(Z(I).EQ.1.)GOTO 13
```

```
202.            IT=I
203.            I=I1
204.            I1=IT
205.         13 CONTINUE
206.            DO 12 K=1,NS
207.            DIFR=X(K,I)-X(K,I1)
208.            IF(DIFR.NE.O.)GOTO 21
209.         12 CONTINUE
210.            WT=W(I)+W(I1)
211.         11 CHI=CHI +(CNUM/SUMA)*WT*((W(I)/WT -P(I))**2)/(P(I)*(1.-P(I)))
212.            WRITE(6,877)
213.            WRITE(6,879)CHI,NHH
214.        877 FORMAT(//1X,'GOODNESS OF FIT TEST')
215.        879 FORMAT(1X'CHI SQUARE=',F12.2,'    WITH',I4,'  D. F.')
216.     C
217.     C      CALCULATION OF R SQUARE
218.         10 IF(NR.NE.1)GOTO 14
219.            D2=0.
220.            DNUM=0.
221.            DENOM=0.
222.            DEN2=0.
223.            ZB=0.
224.            PB=0.
225.            WT=0.
226.            DO 36 I=1,N
227.            DNUM=DNUM +Z(I)*P(I)*W(I)
228.            DENOM=DENOM +Z(I)*Z(I)*W(I)
229.            DEN2=DEN2 +P(I)*P(I)*W(I)
230.            ZB=ZB +Z(I)*W(I)
231.            PB=PB +P(I)*W(I)
232.         36 WT=WT +W(I)
233.            ZBS=ZB*ZB/WT
234.            PBS=PB*PB/WT
235.            RSQ=(DNUM -ZB*PB/WT)**2/((DENOM -ZBS)*(DEN2 -PBS))
236.            WRITE(6,196)RSQ
237.        196 FORMAT(/1X,'MULTIPLE R-SQUARE =',F7.3/)
238.     C
239.         14 RETURN
240.         21 WRITE(6,4)I,I1
241.          4 FORMAT(1X,'DATA OUT OF ORDER FOR CHI SQUARE TEST, I=',2I6)
242.            GOTO 10
243.            END
244.     C
245.     C
246.            SUBROUTINE INVER(A,N)
247.     C
248.            DIMENSION A(20,20),INDEX(20,2),IPIVOT(20),PIVOT(20)
249.            COMMON PIVOT,INDEX,IPIVOT
250.            EQUIVALENCE (IROW,JROW),(ICOLUM,JCOLUM),(AMAX,T,SWAP)
251.     C
252.            DETERM=1.0
253.     C
254.            DO 20 J=1,N
255.         20 IPIVOT(J)=0
256.     C
257.            DO 550 I=1,N
258.            AMAX=0.0
259.     C
260.            DO 105 J=1,N
261.            IF(IPIVOT(J)-1) 60,105,60
262.     C
263.         60 DO 100 K=1,N
264.            IF(IPIVOT(K)-1) 80,100,740
```

61

```
265.    C
266.        80 IF(ABS(AMAX)-ABS(A(J,K))) 85,100,100
267.    C
268.        85 IROW=J
269.           ICOLUM=K
270.           AMAX=A(J,K)
271.    C
272.       100 CONTINUE
273.       105 CONTINUE
274.    C
275.           IPIVOT(ICOLUM)=IPIVOT(ICOLUM)+1
276.           IF(IROW-ICOLUM) 140,260,140
277.    C
278.       140 DETERM=-DETERM
279.    C
280.           DO 200 L=1,N
281.           SWAP=A(IROW,L)
282.           A(IROW,L)=A(ICOLUM,L)
283.       200 A(ICOLUM,L)=SWAP
284.    C
285.       260 INDEX(I,1)=IROW
286.           INDEX(I,2)=ICOLUM
287.           PIVOT(I)=A(ICOLUM,ICOLUM)
288.           DETERM=DETERM*PIVOT(I)
289.           A(ICOLUM,ICOLUM)=1.0
290.    C
291.           DO 350 L=1,N
292.           IF(PIVOT(I).NE.0) GOTO 349
293.           A(ICOLUM,L)=0.
294.           GOTO 350
295.       349 A(ICOLUM,L)=A(ICOLUM,L)/PIVOT(I)
296.       350 CONTINUE
297.    C
298.           DO 550 L1=1,N
299.           IF(L1-ICOLUM) 400,550,400
300.       400 T=A(L1,ICOLUM)
301.           A(L1,ICOLUM)=0.0
302.           DO 450 L=1,N
303.       450 A(L1,L)=A(L1,L)-A(ICOLUM,L)*T
304.    C
305.       550 CONTINUE
306.    C
307.           DO 710 I=1,N
308.           L=N+1-I
309.           IF(INDEX(L,1)-INDEX(L,2)) 630,710,630
310.       630 JROW=INDEX(L,1)
311.    C
312.           JCOLUM=INDEX(L,2)
313.    C
314.           DO 705 K=1,N
315.           SWAP=A(K,JROW)
316.           A(K,JROW)=A(K,JCOLUM)
317.           A(K,JCOLUM)=SWAP
318.       705 CONTINUE
319.    C
320.       710 CONTINUE
321.    C
322.       740 RETURN
323.           END
324.    //GO.FT02F001 DD UNIT=SYSDA,VOL=SER=NRES01,DISP=OLD,
325.    // DSN=$2ZB004.COL.CROSS.TST8,DCB=(RECFM=FB,LRECL=80,BLKSIZE=4560)
326.    //GO.FT06F001 DD SYSOUT=A,DCB=(RECFM=FB,BLKSIZE=133)
327.    //
?
```

Chapter 3

Panel Data

The next substantial increase in information about q_{ij} is provided by information from a panel of persons observed or interviewed at two points in time; at these times their state is observed or a response is obtained. There are unusual situations in which equation (1.12) can be used in conjunction with two different samples of persons from the same population at two times to obtain estimates of $p(0)$ and $p(t)$. These depend, however, on the system being out of statistical equilibrium and moving back toward equilibrium. Ordinarily, the assumptions necessary to employ such data are stronger than one would wish to make.

When there is a two-wave panel, then each individual is observed in state 1 or 0 at time 0 and state 1 or 0 at time t. Thus, if data are aggregated or grouped (as in a two-by-two table), the observations can be expressed as proportions of persons, given occupancy of state h at time 0, found in state j at time t. This is $r_{hj}(t) = n_{hj}(t)/n_h(0)$. If all persons were identical, $r_{hj}(t)$ could be used as an estimate of the transition probability, and equation (1.19) [or in the case of a two-state system, equation (1.13)] could be used to estimate the transition rates q_{hj}.

There are problems of identification of the underlying transition rates, the matrix $\mathbf{Q}$, from the matrix of observed transition probabilities $R(t)$. Such problems do not exist either with cross-sectional data (in which of course something less than $\mathbf{Q}$ is estimated) or with continuous records that supply information on events rather than states. These problems, which can be characterized generally as problems of *embeddability*, have been examined extensively by Singer and Spilerman (1976b). The question of embeddability is the question of whether an observed $\mathbf{R}$ matrix can be embedded in any continuous-time Markov process. Although it is true that there is some transition matrix $\mathbf{R}(t)$ for every matrix of transition rates $\mathbf{Q}$ and time t, the converse is not true: There does not exist a matrix $\mathbf{Q}$ with properties of transition rates $(q_{ii} \leq 0,\ q_{ij} \geq 0\ (i \neq j),\ q_{ii} = -\sum_j q_{ij}$, all q_{ij} real numbers) for each matrix of transition probabilities $\mathbf{R}(t)$.

The task of determining whether a matrix $\mathbf{R}(t)$ is embeddable in some matrix $\mathbf{Q}$ is the task that Singer and Spilerman address. In addition, DiPrete has developed a computer program for discovering the embeddability of a given observed matrix and the embeddability of its proximate neighbors (which differ from $\mathbf{R}(t)$ only by small fluctuations).[1]

Embeddability may fail to be present because the data are generated by a different process. For example, if the data in a two-state process are generated by a discrete-time process in which $p_{12} > p_{22}$, then the process has a fundamental periodicity, and it is not embeddable in any continuous-time process. In fact, for a two-state process, as Singer and Spilerman show, the condition for embeddability is exactly that this inequality does not hold. The inequality may alternatively be expressed as $p_{11} + p_{22} < 1$, or $p_{12} > p_{22}$. So long as this inequality does not hold, the data are embeddable in some continuous-time process.

Since the models to be discussed throughout most of this chapter result from two-state processes, I will not discuss the much more complex questions of embeddability in multistate models. Application of the simple criterion for embeddability in a two-state process (that $p_{11} + p_{22} \geq 1$) can be easily carried out for any data set by aggregating the data and calculating the 2×2 matrix of transition probabilities.

However, one question that remains unclear is the relation between embeddability and heterogeneity. That is, if the data are generated by processes that are Markovian, but with each individual i having his own transition matrix $\mathbf{Q}_i$, then it is not known that the same criterion for embeddability exists. That is, it is not known whether the observed transition matrix for the heterogenous aggregate will meet the criterion of $p_{ij} \leq p_{jj}$ if and only if the data could have been generated by some mixture of Markov processes. This of course is the question of interest here, because the models to be examined in this chapter allow for each individual to have his own transition matrix, dependent on his profile of independent variables.

[1] Inquiries about the program should be made to Professor Thomas DiPrete, NORC, University of Chicago.

My conjecture, in the absence of such a result, is that the same criterion does hold, and thus the criterion of embeddability in a two-state process for a single Markov process can be used for a mixture of processes. In addition, there is the question of convergence of computer programs designed to esti- mate these individual Q_i's through estimating effects of independent variables. Experience with use of the computer program LONGIT·PANEL suggests that nonconvergence of the computer program is equivalent to failure to meet the criterion of embeddability. It is true, of course, that if $p_{ij} = p_{jj} - \epsilon$, where ϵ is arbitrarily small, convergence would be arbitrarily lengthy.

This last point is relevant to another issue, the spacing of time points for the panel observations relative to the speed of the process. Even if data are generated by a Markov process, increasing the time period between observa- tions brings p_{ij} increasingly close to p_{jj}. Thus, small departures from a Markov process can have greater de-stabilizing effect on any estimation procedure if the panel waves are distant from one another. Too-distant observation points, given a true underlying Markov process, can have a similar effect in preventing embeddability, just as the nonexistence of an underlying Markov process does.

Although issues of embeddability are important, the criterion for a two- state process is a simple one. Its principal value in applications of the present models will be to account for (that is, to understand) failure of the convergence of computing algorithms for particular data sets.

The approach ordinarily taken to estimate q_{10} and q_{01} is not, however, the approach that will be taken here. For we do *not* make the assumption that transition rates are identical for all persons, but rather that they are functions of attributes and continuous variables characterizing persons, as given in equation (2.4) or equation (2.8). Consequently, what is desired is to establish some correspondence between observations and q_{hj}'s that allows use of individual-level data to estimate b_k's in the functions given in equation (2.4) or equation (2.8). As it turns out, and as might be anticipated from the cross-sectional analysis, this differs for the linear decomposition and the exponential linear decomposition.

There are various problems that are insoluble with cross-sectional data but that appear from the very outset soluble with panel data. Chief among these is the problem of causal inferences when no causal ordering can be specified a priori. With cross-sectional data, a parameter expressing the effect of attribute x on attribute y can be estimated only with the assumption that the observed relation between x and y is the result of changes in y that follow movement to a given state in x and not the reverse. With panel data some information about the sequence of states is available, and under certain conditions this information can aid in establishing the causal order.

More generally, if there is a system of attributes, all potentially affected by each of the others, panel data can be used to draw inferences about the parameters expressing effects in that system. A special case of this systemic problem is one that Lazarsfeld posed in the early 1940s; the problem of *mutual effects*. This problem arises when there are two activities, such as seeing an ad and buying the product advertised, and the effects of each activity on the other must be determined: Does seeing an ad for a product lead to buying it or does buying a product lead to paying attention to ads for it— or do both effects exist, or neither?

This information about causal ordering is in many cases the principal purpose of obtaining panel data rather than depending on cross-sectional data. For unless external information is available, such as the knowledge that some attributes, such as sex, are fixed, the causal inferences that are based on cross-sectional data are dependent on strong assumptions—assumptions that certain causal coefficients are zero.

Panel data cannot solve the causal ordering problem completely, as will be evident in what follows. A causal structure may be misspecified in ways that the panel information does not uncover. But the panel does constitute a great increment in information.

I will examine panel data and its usefulness for estimating q_{ij}'s in several steps. First, a single attribute will be taken as a dependent variable. Although this appears to assume a priori the causal ordering, it differs in a fundamental way from the comparable specification with cross-sectional data. Although there may be an initial correlation between y (the assumed dependent variable) and x (the assumed independent variable), a condition that would lead, with cross-sectional data, to the inference of an effect of x on y, no inference of an effect of x on y can be drawn unless there are *changes* in y between the two waves of the panel that are compatible with the assumption of an effect.

Beyond this narrowing of the problem I will begin with two restrictions, which will be relaxed subsequently. First is the assumption of equal effects with opposite signs for the two states of the dependent attribute, that is, $c_k = -b_k$ for $k \geq 1$. This assumption is necessary with cross-sectional data. With panel data it is not necessary, but parsimony sometimes makes it desirable. Second is the assumption that all independent variables are constant. Data for which this assumption is met allow somewhat simpler models and simpler calculations.

I will start with the most restricted model for both the linear decomposition and the exponential linear decomposition, and then I will move by stages to the less restricted models.

1. LINEAR DECOMPOSITION: EQUAL AND OPPOSITE EFFECTS AND CONSTANT INDEPENDENT VARIABLES

Equation (1.12) appears potentially useful in establishing a correspondence between observed data at the individual level and the q_{hj}'s. At the individual level, we may characterize the individual by a $p(0)$, which must be 0 or 1, and a $p(t)$, also 0 to 1. We may note also that because of the particular assumption made, c_k in the decomposition of q_0 equals $-b_k$ in the decomposition of q_1 for all $k \geq 1$, and the sum $q_0 + q_1$ is a constant over all persons. Thus $e^{-(q_0+q_1)t}$ can be written as a constant, a_1, and $(1 - e^{-(q_0+q_1)t})/(q_0 + q_1)$ can be written as a constant a_2, allowing equation (1.12) to be written as

$$p(t) = p(0)a_1 + q_1\,a_2. \tag{3.1}$$

And using the decomposition of q_1 given in equation (2.4),

$$p_i(t) = p_i(0)a_1 + a_2 \sum_{k=0}^{n} b_k x_{ki}. \tag{3.2}$$

If we rewrite $a_2 b_k$ as b_k^*, this has the form of a linear decomposition of a variable $p(t)$ that takes on the values 0 or 1. To simplify notation, we can define an attribute $x_{-1} = p(0)$, and relabel a_1 as b_{-1}^*. Doing this allows rewriting equation (3.2) as

$$p_i(t) = \sum_{k=-1}^{n} b_k^* x_{ki}. \tag{3.3}$$

This equation is formally identical to equation (2.19) used for estimating the values of β_k with cross-sectional data, differing only in that an additional attribute, x_{-1}, standing for the value of $p(0)$, is included.

There is, however, an important difference in this case, for the fact that $b_{-1}^* = e^{-(q_1+q_0)t}$ means that estimates of the absolute values of b_k can be obtained from the b_k^*. For

$$b_k = \frac{-t(1 - b_{-1}^*)b_k^*}{\log b_{-1}^*} \qquad (k = 0, 1, \ldots, n) \tag{3.4}$$

Equation (3.4) gives estimates of all components of q_1 and q_0 but c_0. The estimate of c_0 can be found by use of the equation

$$c_0 = q_0 + q_1 - b_0,$$

where $q_0 + q_1$ is estimated by $\dfrac{\log b_{-1}}{t}$ and b_0 is estimated in equation (3.4) as b_0.

The same weighted least-squares methods useful for the linear decomposition of cross-sectional data may be used here to estimate the b_k^* (see Grizzle, Starmer, and Koch, 1969).

However, although b_0, b_1, . . . , b, k and c_0 can be estimated in this way, a maximum likelihood method is described in chapter 6, and the maximum likelihood method is used in the LONGIT·PANEL computer program included as an appendix to this chapter. Although this estimation procedure requires iteration for solution, I suggest it here for general comparability with estimates in cases that are not amenable to the simpler estimation procedure, and because it gives direct estimates of the variances of all b_k and c_0.

1.1. EXAMPLE

Changes in Knowledge of a Political Issue: In a study of internal political processes in a trade union, Lipset et al. (1956) studied changes in union members' knowledge (in the International Typographical Union) about a campaign issue in the period preceding the campaign to elect union officials. They interviewed union members before the campaign period and restudied the same union members through a mail questionnaire in June, immediately after the election. They asked about the union political parties' positions on the Taft-Hartley Act and classified union members according to whether or not they correctly identified each party's position. Thus they could examine changes in knowledge of the parties' positions over the campaign. They also measured each member's *ideological sensitivity,* that is, the degree to which he described the union election in terms of values or issues rather than personalities or other things unrelated to issues. They reasoned that union members with high ideological sensitivity would increase their knowledge about issues over the period of the campaign more than those whose ideological sensitivity was low. Although ideological sensitivity was measured on an 8-point scale, it was reported only as high, medium, or low.[2] Table 3.1 shows the changes

---

[2] Because the independent variables for models discussed in this book can be continuous variables just as easily as ordered or unordered classes, the original scale, treated as a continuous variable, rather than the classification into three categories could have been used if it had been presented this way in the original publication.

in knowledge of the Progressive Party's position on Taft-Hartley for members with each of the three levels of ideological sensitivity.

TABLE 3.1

Changes in Knowledge of Progressive Party Position on the Taft-Hartley Act Among Union Members with Differing Levels of Ideological Sensitivity

		Ideological Sensitivity					
		High		Medium		Low	
January position→		Correct	Incorrect	Correct	Incorrect	Correct	Incorrect
June position {	Correct	42	8	41	31	6	12
	Incorrect	7	18	14	75	4	57

The table shows that the higher the level of ideological sensitivity, the more likely a union member was to retain correct knowledge of Taft-Hartley if he knew it in January, and the more likely he was to acquire correct knowledge if he did not have it in January.

Analysis of the data using the model described in the preceding section was carried out with the LONGIT·PANEL program, treating the three categories of independent variables as two independent attributes. Thus, $x_1 = 1$ for those high in ideological sensitivity, 0 otherwise, and $x_2 = 1$ for those medium in ideological sensitivity, 0 otherwise. The parameters b_1 and b_2 measure the effect of high or medium relative to low. Table 3.2 shows the estimates of effect.

TABLE 3.2

Estimates of Effect of Ideological Sensitivity on Knowledge of Progressive Position on Taft-Hartley

	Linear	
	b	s.e.
Transition rate toward correct when $x_1 = 0$	.241	(.063)
Transition rate toward incorrect when $x_1 = 0$	.502	(.116)
Effect of high sensitivity (relative to low) (b_1)	.275	(.113)
Effect of medium sensitivity (relative to low) (b_2)	.162	(.084)

$R^2 = .275$

The effect of high and medium sensitivity are, in accordance with the authors' reasoning, both positive, and the effect of high is greater than that of medium. Here, of course, we cannot examine the differential effects toward suppressing loss of knowledge and augmenting the loss, because the assumption that $c_k = -b_k$ means that b_1 and b_2 are averages of the two kinds of effects.

69

1.2. COMPARISON OF PARAMETERS WITH THOSE OBTAINED FROM CROSS-SECTIONAL DATA

Parameters estimated from panel data are not directly comparable to those estimated from cross-sectional data. Thus, even if a process is in statistical equilibrium, and data are obtained at two points in time, the β's calculated from the cross-sectional data at either wave will not be directly comparable to the b's calculated from the panel data. However, the derivations in chapter 2 show how the translation can be made. In the linear model β_k for the effects of attribute k is merely $b_k/(b_0 + c_0)$, where the b_k is calculated from the restricted model presented in the preceding section. In comparing the unrestricted model to be presented in a subsequent section, where effects in the two directions are free to differ, the β_k is the average of the effects in the two directions. The estimate of β_0 with cross-sectional data is comparable to $b_0/(b_0 + c_0)$.

In the exponential model, the correspondence is even more direct. From equations (2.21) and (2.22), β_k for the effect of variable k is simply $2b_k$, and β_0 is the difference $b_0 - c_0$.

Altogether, if we label the estimate of β_k from panel data β_k^*, then we have the following correspondence for the linear and exponential models.

	Linear Model		Exponential Model	
	Restricted	**Unrestricted**	**Restricted**	**Unrestricted**
For $k = 1, \ldots, n$: $\beta_k^* =$	$b_k/(b_0 + c_0)$	$(b_k - c_k)/2(b_0 + c_0)$	$2b_k$	$b_k - c_k$
For $k = 0$: $\beta_0^* =$	$b_0/(b_0 + c_0)$	$b_0/(b_0 + c_0)$	$b_0 - c_0$	$b_0 - c_0$

In subsequent tables for panel data, I will include β_k^* for the linear model. These values have another use as well, when compared with the analogous estimates of β_k from the cross-sectional data that constitutes the first or second wave of the panel. If the process is in statistical equilibrium, β_k from the cross-sectional data and β_k^* from the panel data will be the same within random error. If the effect of attribute k has not yet brought the dependent attribute into statistical equilibrium, then the estimate of β_k from the first wave will be less than that from the second, and both will be less than β_k^* from the panel data.[3]

Use of this calculation for the preceding example gives a value of β_0^* of .324. The estimated effect of high ideological sensitivity is .370, and that of medium sensitivity is .218.

[3] See section 9 (p. 87) on left censoring and distinguishing prior effects from current effects.

2. EXPONENTIAL LINEAR DECOMPOSITION

Inspection of equation (1.12), which was used for obtaining a correspondence between the b_k's and observed data in the linear decomposition model suggests that a somewhat different procedure must be used for the exponential decomposition. Of most importance is the fact that the sum of transition rates, $q_0 + q_1$, which is independent of the values of x_k in the linear composition, is not so in the exponential linear decomposition. This sum appears both in an exponent and a denominator in equation (1.12).

It is possible to simplify equation (1.12) if we write the equation separately for two subsets of the sample, S_0 consisting of all persons with $p(0) = 0$, and S_1 consisting of all persons with $p(0) = 1$. Then for the subset S_0, $p(t)$ is the transition probability $r_{01}(t)$. If we signal the fact that $q_1 + q_0$ is not independent of the values of x_k by affixing an asterisk to a as used in the preceding section so that

$$a_0^* = q_1 + q_0$$
$$a_1^* \quad e^{-(q_1 + q_0)t}$$
$$a_2^* = (1 - a_1^*)/a_0^* \, ,$$

then we may write, from equation (1.12),

$$r_{01}(t) = q_1 a_2^*. \tag{3.5}$$

Analogously, $r_{10}(t)$, the probability of being in state 0 at time t, given occupancy of state 1 at time 0, is $1 - p(t)$ for subset S_1, those persons with $p(0) = 1$. From equation (1.12) we can obtain

$$r_{10}(t) = q_0 a_2^* \tag{3.6}$$

Rewriting equation (3.5) and (3.6) gives

$$\frac{r_{01}(t)}{a_2^*} = q_1 \tag{3.7}$$

$$\frac{r_{10}(t)}{a_2^*} = q_0 \, . \tag{3.8}$$

And taking logarithms and writing q_j as an exponential linear function of b_k gives

$$\log \frac{r_{01i}(t)}{a_2^*} = b_0 + \sum_{k=1}^{n} b_k x_{ki} \tag{3.9}$$

$$\log \frac{r_{10i}(t)}{a_2^*} = c_0 - \sum_{k=1}^{n} b_k x_{ki} \cdot \tag{3.10}$$

This gives the probability $r_{hj}(t)$ of moving [in equation (3.9) from state 0, and in equation (3.10) from state 1] as a function of the vector of independent variables $\mathbf{x}$. This cannot be directly solved by least-squares techniques as before because the left-hand side not only contains a quantity that can be directly observed (that is, the observation on individual i who was in state h at time 0 is $z_{hji}(t) = 0$ or 1, and $z_{hji}(t) = r_{hji}(t) + \epsilon_i$, where ϵ_i is an error term with mean 0), but also through a_2^* it contains quantities, q_{hj}, that are to be estimated only after $\mathbf{b}$ is known. This suggests the use of a maximum likelihood method to arrive at an estimate iteratively. The method is described in chapter 6 and incorporated into the LONGIT·PANEL program contained in the appendix to the present chapter.

As with the logit model for cross-sectional data, the quantities b_k that are estimated for the exponential decomposition have less heuristic value than do those for the linear model. However, the parameters are easily put in a form that provides heuristic value. Because $q_1 = e^{\sum b_k x_k}$, the transition rate toward state 1 when all $x_k (k = 1, \ldots, m)$ are zero is $q_1 = e^{b_0}$.[4] Similarly, since $q_0 = e^{\sum c_k x_k}$, the transition rate away from state 1 when all independent attributes are zero is e^{c_0}.

The effects of independent attributes k, when expressed as e^{b_k}, can be interpreted as multipliers to the transition rate to state 1, so if e^{b_k} is greater than 1.0, the transition rate is estimated to be amplified by variable k, while if e^{b_k} is less than 1.0, the transition rate to state 1 is depressed by variable k. In the restricted model, where $c_k = -b_k$ for $k \geq 1$, the quantity e^{b_k} in addition constitutes an estimate of the depression of the transition rate q_0 to state 0 (if $e^{b_k} > 1.0$) when $x_k = 1$, or an amplification of q_0 (if $e^{b_k} < 1.0$).

In the unrestricted model, where c_k is not constrained to equal $-b_k$, then e^{c_k} is an estimate of the amplification of the transition rate q_0 to state 0 by variable k if $e^{c_k} > 1.0$ or the depression of q_0 if $e^{c_k} < 1.0$.

In the examples presented in this and the next chapter, I will report values of e^{b_k} and e^{c_k} for the exponential decomposition, as well as b_k and c_k, because of their greater heuristic value. What are reported as standard errors are the standard errors of b_k and c_k. The values of b_k, c_k, and standard errors are calculated in the LONGIT·PANEL program.

[4] When interaction terms are included, see the comments in chapter 2, footnote 2.

2.1. EXAMPLE

Effects of Social Status in High School on Intentions to Attend College: The example of effects of high school social status on college plans, which was introduced in the preceding chapter, can be reexamined here because the same students were restudied as seniors and again asked about college plans. The data at two points in time are shown in table 3.3.

TABLE 3.3

*Social Status in High School and Intentions to Attend College
as a High School Freshman and Senior*

		Leading Crowd Membership (Social Status)			
		Member		Nonmember	
Freshmen's College Plans→		Yes	No	Yes	No
Seniors' College Plans	Yes	63	18	137	49
	No	22	41	69	203

Comparing columns 1 and 3 shows that members of the leading crowd who do intend to go to college as freshmen are slightly more likely to maintain that intention than those who are not members. Comparing columns 2 and 4 shows that members who do not plan to attend are somewhat more likely than nonmembers to change their plans to attend. Table 3.4 shows the analysis with the exponential decomposition. (The linear decomposition is included alongside it for comparison.)

TABLE 3.4

Estimates of Effect of Social Status in High School on Plans to Attend College, Freshman and Senior Data

	Exponential			Linear		
	b	s.e.	e^b	b	s.e.	β^*
Transition rate toward college when $x_1 = 0$	−1.25	(.14)	.287	.283	(.041)	.367
Transition rate away from college when $x_1 = 0$	−.71	(.12)	.490	.488	(.057)	.633
Effect of social status on college plans	.34	(.16)	1.411	.131	(.062)	.170
R^2	.23			.23		

The estimates in table 3.4 show a positive effect (about twice the size of its standard error) of high school social status on college plans. The fit of the exponential model and the linear model are approximately the same as shown by the same values for R^2.

These results using panel data can be compared with the results from the cross-sectional data in chapter 2, tables 2.9 and 2.10. The values of β^* in table 3.4 for the linear model, calculated through the correspondence described in section 1.2 of this chapter, can be used for a direct comparison with the cross-sectional results in table 2.10. The constant of .450 in table 2.10 (that is, 45 percent of nonleading crowd members planning to attend college) compares with .367 here. This indicates that there was not statistical equilibrium, as assumed in the cross-sectional analysis, but a drift toward a lower level of college attendance. (The data in table 3.3 show this also: a total of ninety-one changed their plans and decided not to attend college, while only sixty-seven changed their plans in favor of attending college.)

The measure of the effect here ($\beta^* = .170$) compares with a slightly smaller measure there ($\beta = .141$). This means that the movement for and against attending college slightly strengthened the relationship in the senior year over what it was in the freshman year. This can also be seen in table 3.3 by the fact that among the nonmembers there is a much higher ratio of the number who abandon college plans to the number who acquire them than there is among the members of the leading crowd (69:49 compared to 22:18).

This example illustrates the comparability of the estimates of effect across types of data, and shows as well that the differences between the two sets of estimates can indicate how the behavior and the relationship between variables have changed over time.

To turn back to another example, that of table 3.1, comparison between the exponential and linear models is provided by table 3.5, which gives the parameter estimates for the exponential model. Comparing these with the linear model shows e^{b_0} and e^{c_0} for the exponential model close to the b^0 and c^0 of the linear model and a slightly less good fit of the exponential model than of the linear model.

TABLE 3.5

Exponential Model: Effects of Ideological Sensitivity Exponential on Knowledge of Issue (See Table 3.2)

	b	s.e.	e^b
Transition rate to knowledge when $x_1 = x_2 = 0$	−1.41	(.24)	0.244
Transition rate from knowledge when $x_1 = x_2 = 0$	−0.63	(.30)	0.532
Effect of high sensitivity (relative to low) (b_1)	0.76	(.30)	2.141
Effect of medium sensitivity (relative to low) (b_2)	0.48	(.25)	1.623

3. LINEAR DECOMPOSITION AND EXPONENTIAL LINEAR DECOMPOSITION: $c_k \neq -b_k$

The linear decomposition of q_{ij} allows a great simplification when we assume that $c_k = -b_k$ for all $k \geq 1$, because when this is so $q_1 + q_0$ is constant over all individuals. It is this fact that makes possible a simple correspondence between observed data and parameters of effect. In equation (3.3), the quantity *p(t)* (which is the probability of observing state 1 rather than 0 at time *t*) is linearly related to the independent variables x_{ki}.

However, in all circumstances for the exponential linear decomposition, and when $c_k \neq -b_k$ for the linear decomposition, this simplicity vanishes, for $q_1 + q_0$ [which appears both in an exponent and as a denominator in equation (3.2)] is no longer independent of x_i, no longer constant over all individuals.

To give some intuitive sense of the way estimation proceeds in this case, as well as in others in which the correspondence between observation and causal parameters is nonlinear, it is useful to sketch the outlines of the maximum likelihood estimation procedure described in chapter 6.

If $z_i(t)$ is the state of individual *i* at time *t* [$z_i(t) = 0$ or 1], and $p_i(t)$ from equation (1.12) is the probability that individual *i* is in state 1, then it is possible to write the likelihood of obtaining the particular set of $z_i(t)$ that is observed. This likelihood is a simple function of $z_i(t)$ and $p_i(t)$ [see chapter 6, equation (6.1)]. To maximize the likelihood with respect to each of the b_k and c_k, the derivative of the likelihood (or of the logarithm of the likelihood, which gives the same maximum and is easier to differentiate) with respect to each b_k and c_k is taken. This involves differentiating $p_i(t)$, and this is where equation (3.3) is used.

This differentiation results in $2n + 2$ equations, which in principle can be solved for the $2n + 2$ parameters, the vectors **b** and **c**. However, because these equations are nonlinear in **b** and **c**, it is necessary to solve the equations iteratively, using a standard method. The method is described in chapter 6 and involves calculating a cross-products matrix (much as is done in weighted linear regression) for each iteration. When there is convergence to a stable pair of vectors **b** and **c**, these are the maximum likelihood estimates.

3.1. EXAMPLE

Experiments in Mass Communication: In Hovland's World War II work testing the effects of mass communications (films and radio programs) on soldiers' attitudes, some experiments that were carried out illustrate well the difference between the restricted model and the unrestricted model. One of those experiments was a radio program intended to impress upon soldiers the likelihood of a long war with the Japanese. They were asked for their estimates of the length of the war before and after hearing the program. One would expect the effects of the program to be primarily in one direction, that is, toward saying a longer period. The data in table 3.6 show this.

TABLE 3.6

Estimates of the Length of the Pacific War*

		After			
		Experimental Group		Control Group	
		2 years or more	1½ years or less	2 years or more	1½ years or less
Before	2 years or more	72	5	53	12
	1½ years or less	48	80	9	107

* Data from C. I. Hovland, A. A. Lumsdaine, and F. D. S. Sheffield (1949).

Comparing the experimental and control groups, the program seems to have had a strong effect in leading those who had a low estimate to increase it, but much less of an effect on those who already had a high estimate. Use of the restricted and unrestricted linear models with these data give parameters as shown in table 3.7.

Table 3.7

Components of Transition Rates and Actual and Expected Proportions for Estimates of Length of the Pacific War (See Table 3.6) (Linear Model)[a]

	Restricted			Unrestricted		
	b	s.e.	β^*	b	s.e.	β^*
Transition rate toward longer war without program (b_0)	.125	(.037)	.268	.090	(.030)	.296
Transition rate toward shorter war without program (c_0)	.341	(.059)		.214	(.063)	
Program effect: increment to b_0	.282	(.055)	.604	.404	(.080)	.877
Program effect: increment to c_0				−.129	(.074)	
[a] R^2	.44			.45		

		Experimental		Control	
		Initial Estimate			
Proportion estimating 2 or more years		2+	1½−	2+	1½−
	Actual:	.935	.375	.815	.078
Predicted {	Restricted:	.952	.325	.727	.100
	Unrestricted:	.935	.375	.815	.078

The unrestricted model fits perfectly, of course, since there are four degrees of freedom and four parameters. But the interesting point is that the fit of the restricted model is not very good. With the unrestricted model the estimated increment to the transition rate toward a longer war is more than three times the estimated decrement to the transition rate toward a shorter war. The exponential model partly compensates for this difference because its effect parameters are multipliers. In the exponential model, the parameters of effect (multipliers e^{b_1} and e^{c_1}) for the unrestricted model, comparable to .404 and $-.129$ for the linear model, are 5.490 and .400. These imply that the program amplified the transition rate to a longer war by 5.49 times its original value and depressed the transition rate toward a shorter war by .40 of its previous value.

To give a further feel for comparison of the restricted and unrestricted models, it is useful to present the unrestricted version of an earlier example. In table 3.3, data were presented to show the effect of status in the high school social system on college plans, estimating only a single effect under the assumption that $c_1 = -b_1$. Using the same data, table 3.8 shows the estimates when this restriction is removed, with both the exponential and linear models.

Table 3.8

*Components of Transition Rates in College Plans
for High School Students: Unrestricted Model*[a]

	Exponential			Linear		
	b	s.e.	e^b	b	s.e.	β*
Transition rate to college when $x_1 = 0$	-1.28	(.15)	0.277	.277	(.043)	.367
Transition rate away from college when $x_1 = 0$	-0.74	(.13)	0.477	.477	(.062)	.633
Effect of social status in bringing about college plans	0.48	(.30)	1.723	.172	(.124)	.228
Effect of social status in maintaining college plans	0.22	(.27)	1.252	.096	(.110)	.178
[a] R^2	.23			.23		

When the restriction is removed the estimates of effects show that the effect toward acquiring college plans for those students who had no college plans is somewhat greater than the effect in maintaining college plans among those who already had them. However—and this illustrates a major reason for using the restricted model—the estimates of effect in the unrestricted model have standard errors that are roughly twice as large as for the restricted model, since estimates of two parameters are being made from data that were used in the restricted model for estimating only one. Thus, even though the estimate of effect toward acquiring college plans is larger than was the estimate of the combined effect in the restricted model, the standard deviation is so large that the estimate is no longer significant at the 5 percent level.

4. NONCONSTANT INDEPENDENT VARIABLES: LINEAR DECOMPOSITION WITH EQUAL AND OPPOSITE EFFECTS

In all the analysis of two-wave panels discussed so far, the independent variables have been assumed constant. If one or more of these variables is not constant, then the analysis becomes somewhat more complicated. The transition rates q_1 and q_0 become functions of time, and we have

$$\frac{dp(t)}{dt} = -p(t)q_0(t) + (1 - p(t))q_1(t). \tag{3.11}$$

This is a linear differential equation of the first order, and when solved is

$$p(t) = e^{-\int^\tau (q_0(\tau) + q_1(\tau))d\tau} \left\{ \int_o^t e^{\int^\tau [q_0(\theta) + q_1(\theta)]d\theta} q_1(\tau)d\tau + K \right\}. \tag{3.12}$$

If $q_0(t)$ and $q_1(t)$ are written in terms of $x_k(t)$, we have

$$q_0(t) = \sum_{k=0}^n c_k x_k(t),$$

and

$$q_1(t) = \sum_{k=0}^n b_k x_k(t),$$

so that $q_1(t) + q_0(t)$ becomes

$$b_0 + c_0 + \sum_{k=1}^n (b_k + c_k)x_k(t).$$

Then if, as assumed, $c_k = -b_k$ for $k \geq 1$, then $q_1(t) + q_0(t)$ is constant, equal to $b_0 + c_0$. I will, for simplicity of notation, denote this constant as a. This means that equation (3.12) may be simplified to give

$$p(t) = e^{-at} \left\{ \int_o^t e^{a\tau} \sum_{k=0}^n b_k x_k(\tau) d\tau + K \right\}. \tag{3.13}$$

Evaluating this at $t = 0$ gives $K = p(0)$, and equation (3.13) can be written as

$$p(t) = p(0) e^{-at} + \sum_{k=0}^n b_k e^{-at} \int_o^t e^{a\tau} x_k(\tau) d\tau, \tag{3.14}$$

where, as indicated earlier, $a = b_0 + c_0$, and by assumption $c_k = -b_k$ for $k \geq 1$, so that $q_1(t) + q_0(t) = a$, independent of x_k and of time.

There are two situations concerning change in the independent variables $x_k(\tau)$. In one we know the time path of change in $x_k(\tau)$, with x_k as an explicit function of τ. In that case, equation (3.14) can be integrated [if $x_k(\tau)$ is a sufficiently simple function of τ], giving $p(t)$ as a function of p_0, $x_k(0)$, and $x_k(t)$. Not much can be said in general about use of these equations to estimate the effect of x_k without knowing explicitly the functional form of $x_k(\tau)$.

The other case is more usual: We have observations on $x_k(0)$ and on $x_k(t)$, but we do not know the path of change in x_k between times 0 and t. Often in such a circumstance, we would assume, in the absence of other information, that x_k changes linearly between time 0 and time t [or in the case where $x_k(\tau)$ takes on only values of 0 and 1, that the probability of a change at any instant of time is constant, that is, the assumption of a stationary Markov process]. In this case, $x_k(\tau)$ in equation (3.14) becomes $x_k(0) + \dfrac{(x_k(t) - x_k(0))}{t} \tau$ and equation (3.14) becomes

$$p(t) = p(0)e^{-at} + \sum_{k=0}^n b_k x_k(0) \left(\frac{1 - e^{-at} - ate^{-at}}{a^2 t} \right)$$

$$+ \sum_{k=0}^n b_k x_k(t) \left(\frac{e^{-at} + at - 1}{a^2 t} \right). \tag{3.15}$$

This equation, like the equation for constant x_k, is linear in x_k: But now there are two vectors, $\mathbf{x}(0)$ and $\mathbf{x}(t)$. The sum of the coefficients of those vectors is, as might be expected, equal to the coefficients for x_k when $x_k(0) = x_k(t)$ for all k, that is, when x_k is constant over time:

$$b_k \left(\frac{1 - e^{-at} - ate^{-at}}{a^2 t} \right) + b_k \left(\frac{e^{-at} + at - 1}{a^2 t} \right) = \frac{b_k(1 - e^{-at})}{a}. \tag{3.16}$$

79

Note that in equation (3.15), $p(t)$ is a linear function of $x_k(0)$ and $x_k(t)$. Because this is so, it is possible to use a noniterative method for estimation, as described in Grizzle, Starmer, and Koch (1969). If this is done, however, it is desirable to express equation (3.14) in terms of $x_k(0)$ and Δx_k [$= x_k(t) - x_k(0)$] because of colinearity between $x_k(0)$ and $x_k(t)$ for these variables in which $x_k(t) \sim x_k(0)$. When this is done, equation (3.15) becomes

$$p(t) = p(0)e^{-at} + \sum b_k x_k(0) \left\{ \frac{1 - e^{-at}}{a} \right\}$$

$$+ \sum_{k=0}^{n} b_k \Delta x_k \left\{ \frac{e^{-at} + at - 1}{a^2 t} \right\}. \quad (3.17)$$

For purposes of consistency among different data forms, I will outline the maximum likelihood of **b** in chapter 6. This also allows us to generalize without great difficulty to the case in which it is not assumed that $c_k = -b_k$ for all $k \geq 1$.

We might ask just what bias, if any, is introduced into b_k if the process is one in which x_k does not change independently but is itself a function of the attribute taken as a dependent variable. That is, suppose the system is one in which one or more of x_k are endogenous, affected directly or indirectly by the dependent attribute. Such systems will be examined in more detail in the next chapter, but it is useful to raise the point here.

In such a circumstance, suppose the chance that the dependent variable changes at time t is p^*. Then before that change, the transition rate for x_k out of its existing state is q_{k0}, while after the change, the transition rate is q_{k1}. If $q_{k1} = q_{k0}$, then the assumption of a constant rate of change is valid. If not, then we must ask about the expected time that x_k will be subject to a transition rate of q_{k0}, and the time it will be subject to a rate of q_{k1}, or in another way account for the differences in a transition rate to which the independent variable x_k is subject at different times.

5. NONCONSTANT INDEPENDENT VARIABLES: EXPONENTIAL LINEAR DECOMPOSITION

In the exponential linear decomposition, the analysis of the preceding section carries through as far as equation (3.12). Beyond that point, however, matters become more difficult, because $q_0(t) + q_1(t)$ is no longer constant over all persons, nor constant over time. Thus, where we assume that x_k changes linearly between time 0 and t,

$$q_1(\tau) = \exp\left\{\sum b_k\left[x_{ki}(0) + \frac{\{x_{ki}(t) - x_{ki}(0)\}\tau}{t}\right]\right\}, \qquad (3.18)$$

and similarly for $q_0(\tau)$. The sum does not allow much simplification, despite the assumption that $c_k = -b_k$, because $q_0(\tau) + q_1(\tau)$ remains a function both of the x's and of time.

However, some progress may be made, for in equation (3.12), $q_0(\tau) + q_1(\tau)$ appear in terms of the form $\exp[\int(q_0(\tau) + q_1(\tau))d\tau]$, and these may be integrated. When $q_0(\tau)$ and $q_1(\tau)$ take the form given by equation (3.18), the integration gives

$$\int_0^t [q_1(\tau) + q_0(\tau)]d\tau = \alpha_0 t, \text{ where} \qquad (3.19)$$

$$\alpha_0 = \frac{e^{\sum b_k x_k(t)} - e^{\sum b_k x_{k0}(0)}}{\sum b_k[x_k(t) - x_k(0)]} + \frac{e^{\sum c_k x_k(t)} - e^{\sum c_k x_k(0)}}{\sum c_k[x_k(t) - x_k(0)]}. \qquad (3.20)$$

The equation for $p(t)$ can be written as follows, expressing $q_1(\tau)$ in terms of its components

$$p(t) = p(0)e^{-\alpha_0 t} + e^{-\alpha_0 t}\int_0^t e^{\alpha_0 \tau} e^{\sum b_k\{x_k(0) + [x_k(t) - x_k(0)]\tau/t\}} d\tau. \qquad (3.21)$$

Integrated, this gives

$$p(t) = p(0)e^{-\alpha_0 t} + \frac{q_1(t) - q_1(0)e^{-\alpha_0 t}}{\alpha_0 + \mathbf{b}\Delta\mathbf{x}/t}. \qquad (3.22)$$

In this equation $p(t)$ is obviously a very involved function of $\mathbf{x}(0)$ and $\mathbf{x}(t)$, which appear not only explicitly in equation (3.22), but are also hidden in α_0 [see equation (3.20)]. Iterative methods are necessary for estimation of $\mathbf{b}$ and $\mathbf{c}$, whether or not the assumption is made that $c_k = -b_k$ for $k \geq 1$. These are described in chapter 6.

6. NONCONSTANT INDEPENDENT VARIABLES: LINEAR DECOMPOSITION WITH EFFECTS DIFFERING IN DIFFERENT DIRECTIONS

Returning to equation (3.12), and evaluating the constant of integration K, we have, for the case where $q_1(\tau) + q_0(\tau)$ is no longer assumed to be constant over persons and time:

$$p(t) = e^{-\int_o^t [q_0(\tau) + q_1(\tau)]d\tau} \left\{ p(0) + \int_o^t e^{-\int_o^\tau [q_0(\theta) + q_1(\theta)]d\theta} q_1(\tau)d\tau \right\}. \quad (3.23)$$

It is first necessary to evaluate the integrals in the exponents. We have, under the assumption made earlier that $\mathbf{x}(\tau)$ changes linearly between time 0 and t:

$$\int_o^t [q_0(\tau) + q_1(\tau)]d\tau = \int_o^t \sum_{k=0}^n (b_k + c_k)\{x_k(0) \\ + [x_k(t) - x_k(0)]\tau/t\}d\tau = \alpha_2 t \quad (3.24)$$

where

$$\alpha_2 = \sum_{k=0}^n [b_k + c_k][x_k(t) + x_k(0)]/2. \quad (3.25)$$

Thus equation (3.23) becomes

$$p(t) = p(0)\, e^{-\alpha_2 t} + e^{-\alpha_2 t} \int_o^t e^{\alpha_2 \tau} q_1(\tau)d\tau .$$

This equation has the same form as equation (3.14), and thus the solution of the equation is just like equation (3.15), but with α_2 replacing a:

$$p(t) = p(0)\, e^{-\alpha_2 t} + \sum_{k=0}^n b_k x_k(0) \left\{ \frac{1 - e^{-\alpha_2 t} - \alpha_2 t e^{-\alpha_2 t}}{\alpha_2^2 t} \right\} \\ + \sum_{k=0}^n b_k x_k(t) \left\{ \frac{e^{-\alpha_2 t} + \alpha_2 t - 1}{\alpha_2^2 t} \right\} \quad (3.26)$$

In this equation $p(t)$ is again nonlinearly related to $\mathbf{x}(0)$ and $\mathbf{x}(t)$, for $\mathbf{x}(0) + \mathbf{x}(t)$ is hidden in α_2 [see equation (3.25)]. Thus, as in the case of the preceding section on the exponential linear decomposition, it becomes necessary to use iterative methods for solution. Maximum likelihood methods are described in chapter 6.

6.1. EXAMPLE

Effect of Social Status in High School on College Intentions: Social Status Measured at Two Points in Time: In a preceding example, status in the social system of the high school was found to have a positive and statistically significant effect on intentions to attend college. It was assumed that high school social status, that is, membership in the leading crowd, is constant over that period of time. But unlike some attributes such as sex or race, membership in a high school leading crowd is not constant over time. For example, of the 602 students whose membership in the leading crowd was shown in table 3.3, 123 had changed status between freshman and senior years. Thus, it is a misspecification to treat membership in the leading crowd as an attribute that remains unchanged over the high school years. It is closer to a correct specification to analyze the data by the methods described in the preceding section, where the independent variables are free to change over time and are assumed to change linearly between the two points of observation. This leaves aside for the present the question of whether in fact the "independent" variable, membership in the leading crowd, is independent of college plans. That is a question to be addressed in the next chapter. For the present, it appears reasonable to assume such independence.

Table 3.9 shows college plans among high school seniors classified by their plans as freshmen and their membership in the leading crowd as freshmen and seniors. Inspection of the table indicates that those who are members of the leading crowd as seniors are indeed more likely as seniors to have plans to attend college than are those who, like them, as freshmen had college plans and were in the leading crowd but, unlike them, are not leading-crowd members as seniors.

TABLE 3.9

Social Status in High School and College Plans in the Freshman and Senior Years

Freshman Membership in Leading Crowd →		Yes				No			
Senior Membership in Leading Crowd ⟶		Yes		No		Yes		No	
Freshman College Plans ⟶		Yes	No	Yes	No	Yes	No	Yes	No
Senior College Plans Yes		50	12	13	6	41	9	96	40
No		10	23	12	18	8	16	61	187

Analysis of the data using the methods of the preceding section, which assume equal probability of change in leading-crowd membership at each point in the high school years, gives the results shown in table 3.10, for both the linear and exponential models.

TABLE 3.10

Estimates of Effects of Social Status in High School, Measured as Freshman and Senior, on College Plans

	Exponential			Linear		
	b	s.e.	e^b	b	s.e.	β^*
Transition rate toward college when $x_1 = 0$	−1.35	(.22)	.260	.257	(.043)	.312
Transition rate away from college when $x_1 = 0$	−.56	(.14)	.573	.567	(.073)	.689
Effect of social status on acquiring college plans	.83	(.71)	2.298	.339	(.196)	.397
Effect of social status on maintaining college plans	.80	(.56)	2.232	.315	(.122)	.382

The results (with the linear model fitting slightly better than the exponential model) indicate considerably stronger effects than those found in either the restricted or the unrestricted models in which membership in the leading crowd was assumed constant over high school (for comparison, see tables 3.4 and 3.8). That is, among some students for whom leading-crowd membership did affect college plans, their change in leading-crowd membership during high school obscured this effect when membership was measured only at the freshman level. Such a result indicates that for estimation it is important not to assume constancy in independent variables that are subject to change. As indicated earlier, this of course leaves open the question of whether or not those variables themselves might be endogenous, affected by the very variables or attributes treated as dependent in the analysis. Such problems will be discussed in chapter 4.

7. PANEL ANALYSIS AND LAGGED REGRESSION ANALYSIS

At this point, a question may arise about the similarities and differences between the approach described here and the frequently used regression analysis with lagged values of the dependent variable as one of the independent variables in the regression equation. It can be shown that changes in continuous variables generated by linear differential equations result in the same relationship between $y(t)$ and $y(0)$, $x_1(0)$, . . . , $x_s(0)$, $x_1(t)$, . . . , $x_s(t)$ as exists for qualitative attributes under the restricted linear model.

Thus, particularly since lagged regression is often used for continuous variables (and also because it is sometimes used for dichotomous attributes taken over a unit such as a census tract, in which one observes $p(0)$ and $p(t)$ as proportions and uses $\log p(t)/[1-p(t)]$ as the dependent variable in the regression), it becomes germane to ask just how the more complicated analysis presented here relates to those analyses. More particularly, one can ask if the more complicated iterative maximum likelihood solutions are necessary in cases where lagged regression can be used. The iterative solutions are of course necessary when the observations are on individuals for which only the values of 0 or 1 are observed for the dependent attribute, but what about these other cases where lagged regression is a feasible alternative?

As is implicit in section 4 (linear decomposition with $c_k = -b_k$ for $k > 0$), the coefficients on $p(0)$, $x_k(0)$, and $x_k(t)$ are constant over individuals when certain assumptions are made. In the case of dichotomous attributes (or proportions) as dependent variables, there are two assumptions: The transition rate is a linear function of the independent variables, and for each variable, the effects in both directions are the same (that is, $c_k = -b_k$ for $k > 0$). Under these assumptions, the exponent in equation (3.15) is constant, and $p(t)$ is a linear function of the independent variables. In this case a lagged regression with $p(t)$ (not $\log p(t)/[1 - p(t)]$) as the dependent variable provides least-squares estimates that are compatible with the maximum likelihood estimates given here. These estimates, however, are not direct estimates of the parameters b_k that affect the transition rates, but they are estimates of b_k multiplied by a constant. In the case of constant independent variables, this constant is $(1 - e^{-at})/a$ for the independent variables other than the lagged value $p(0)$, for which the constant is e^{-at}. In the case of changing independent variables (assumed to change linearly between observation times 0 and t), the constant is $(1 - e^{-at} - ate^{-at})/a^2 t$ for $x_k(0)$, and $(e^{-at} + at - 1)/a^2 t$ for $x(t)$. Thus the parameters b_k, b_0, and c_0 can be recovered from the regression coefficients obtained in a least-squares regression. However, the results of this chapter give several implications for such analyses. A first implication is that even when the assumptions are not violated, one is losing information by using as independent variables *only* the values of the exogenous x_k at time 0 and not their values at time t, and is in fact inducing a bias in the estimation. For when the values $x_k(t)$ are included in the least-squares equation, the values of b_k recovered by this method will in general be different if the exogenous variables are not constant. Another implication is that when these variables are not constant, the least-squares method using $x_k(0)$ and $x_k(t)$ will give inefficient estimates since two estimates of each b_k are recovered, and some method must be found for combining these estimates.

More extensive implications arise when the assumptions are violated, either because $c_k \neq -b_k$ or because a different decomposition of q (such as the exponential decomposition) is appropriate. Nor is the latter problem overcome by taking $\log p(t)/[1 - p(t)]$ as the dependent variable, as inspection of equation (3.22) will show. Under these conditions, the least-squares lagged regression cannot recover the parameters for the dynamic process. All that can be said for such a procedure is that it generates *some* kind of parameters, though not parameters for any kind of well-defined process.

On the other hand, the least-squares lagged regression with a dependent variable that is some function of the $p(t)$ has virtues that derive from its faults. Because the parameters it estimates bear no relationship to any well-defined process, it can estimate those parameters for almost any data set with the required degrees of freedom. This is not true for the iterative maximum likelihood procedures contained in the LONGIT·PANEL program and described in chapter 6. Because the parameters estimated are parameters in a dynamic process, there are data sets for which the estimation procedure will not converge: those data sets that are excessively incompatible with the process for which the parameters are estimated, or data in which the observations are spaced too far apart relative to the speed of the process.

8. GENERALIZATIONS OF A PANEL

Up to this point, and in all the examples, the panel data consisted of individuals all observed or interviewed at the same interval of time. Ordinarily, panels or repeated observations on a sample do meet this condition, at least approximately. However, sometimes there are data in which individuals are observed at different intervals. For example, observations may take place at intervals that differ from person to person as a result of administrative contingencies or other factors.

When this irregularity occurs, it makes infeasible any form of estimation that depends upon grouped data of the sort that is presented in cross-tabulations. However, so long as we maintain the Markov assumption, this irregularity of observation does not disturb estimation procedures that are based on individual-level data. For just as $x_1, \ldots, x_n$ differs from person to person, the time interval may vary as well. The estimation procedures are unaffected, since each individual with a unique profile of $x_1, \ldots, x_n$ is taken as the unit of analysis. If time periods differ for persons otherwise alike in their profile of independent variables, a different definition of a unique individual, which includes the interval of observation as well as the values of the independent variables, is used. Estimation is unaffected since it does not depend in the first place on an assumption that the time period between observations is the same for all. If this time period differs for different persons, estimation *does* depend on the assumption that the rates governing the process are the same for differing time intervals, except as they vary as a function of changes in values of independent variables.

Thus, one virtue of the maximum likelihood methods of estimation described in chapter 6 and used for the examples of this chapter is that they do not depend on data that is so nicely grouped as the data shown in the examples. Individuals may have unique profiles of values of independent variables, and also may have unique time intervals between observations. The Markov assumptions are somewhat more binding in this case, because if rates do differ systematically over time [for example, decline with the length of time in the state, as is hypothesized by McGinnis (1968) in the use of Markov processes with geographic mobility data], then parameters b_k and c_k will be overestimated for individuals with longer observation intervals and underestimated for those with shorter intervals. However, if the Markov assumptions are met, then estimation can be carried out, despite the variability of intervals between observations.

9. LEFT CENSORING AND DISTINGUISHING PRIOR EFFECTS FROM CURRENT EFFECTS

In all the analyses of this chapter, $p(0)$ has been taken as given. This means that we take as given the initial distribution of responses, and estimate parameters which would maximize the likelihood of having observed $z_i(t)$ given $p_i(0)$ ($i = 1, \ldots, N$). Now let us suppose that the relation of $p(t)$ to the independent variables is identical to the relation of $p(0)$ to the independent variables, although there was change at the individual level. In other words, there is statistical equilibrium. Because of the identity of the cross-sectional and over-time models, the parameters b and c would, in such a circumstance, be compatible, through the correspondence described in section 1.2, with the parameters β which could be calculated using either the cross-sectional data at time 0 or that at time t. If, however, there is not statistical equilibrium, then the values of β calculated at times 0 and t would differ, and β^*, calculated from the values of b and c estimated with the panel data, would be still different.

Such a result means that the current effects of the independent variables, between times 0 and t, are different from those that occurred before time 0. A more direct way of discovering this, which gives separate estimates for the prior effects of the independent variables and the current effects, is to estimate parameters which maximize the likelihood not only of $p_i(t)$, but of $p_i(0)$ as well. The likelihood function in this case becomes, in place of equation (6.22),

$$\mathcal{L} = \prod_{i=1}^{N} p_i(0)^{z_i(0)}(1 - p_i(0))^{(1 - z_i(0))} p_i(t)^{z_i(t)}(1 - p_i(t))^{(1 - z_i(t))} \quad (3.27)$$

The quantity $p_i(0)$ is modeled as if it were at statistical equilibrium with either the exponential or linear decomposition, decomposing q_1 and q_0 in the ratio $q_1/(q_1 + q_0)$ $(= p(0))$ into parameters b and c, rather than the β of chapter 2. Then the quantity $p_i(t)$ is modeled by using for each independent variable k (including the constant term, $k = 0$), two parameters, b_k and b_{kt} (or in the unrestricted model, b_k, b_{kt}, c_k, c_{kt}). The first of these, b_k, or b_k and c_k, is the same parameter used in modeling $p(0)$, while the second, b_{kt}, or b_{kt} and c_{kt}, can be considered a parameter for an interaction term between the time period (denoted by t) and the independent variable.

The measure of the current effect of variable k on the response is $b_k + b_{kt}$, while the measure of the prior effect is b_k. If b_{kt} is positive (or in the unrestricted model, if b_{kt} is positive and c_{kt} is negative), then the current effect of the independent variable on the response is more positive than the prior effect; if b_{kt} is negative (or in the unrestricted model, b_{kt} negative and c_{kt} positive), then the current effect is less positive than the prior effect.

For use of this model in estimating parameters the first derivative of the log likelihood becomes (to invade briefly the domain of chapter 6)

$$\frac{\partial L}{\partial b_k} = \sum_{i=1}^{N} \frac{z_1(0) - p_i(0)}{p_i(0)(1 - p_i(0))} \frac{\partial p_i(0)}{\partial b_k} + \sum_{i=1}^{N} \frac{z_i(t) - p_i(t)}{p_i(t)(1 - p_i(t))} \frac{\partial p_i(t)}{\partial b_k}. \quad (3.28)$$

This leads to an iteration algorithm (using the notation of chapter 6, section 1.1) which is, in place of equation (6.8)

$$\mathbf{b}^{(v+1)} = b^{(v)} + (d_0^{(v)} \, w_0^{(v)} \, x_0^{*\,(v)tr} + d_t^{(v)} \, w_t^{(v)} \, x_t^{(v)tr})$$

$$(x_0^{*\,(v)} \, w_0^{(v)} \, x_0^{*\,(v)tr} + x_t^{*\,(v)} \, w_t^{(v)} \, x_t^{*\,(v)tr})^{-1} \qquad (3.29)$$

where $d_0^{(v)}$, $w_0^{(v)}$, $x_0^{*\,(v)}$, and $d_t^{(v)}$, $w_t^{(v)}$, $x_t^{*\,(v)}$ are the quantities $d^{(v)}$, $w^{(v)}$, and $x^{*(v)}$ given in chapter 6, section 1.1, defined for $p_i(0)$ and $p_i(t)$, respectively. It is important to note that $\partial p_i(0)/\partial b_k$ here is a derivative in terms of the original parameters b_k (and c_k), not the relative parameters β_k that were necessary to use for chapter 2. It is also important to note that the derivative of $p_i(t)$ with respect to b_k is more complicated in this case. Since $p_i(0)$ is no longer taken as given, the derivative of $p_i(0)$ with respect to b_k in the equation for $p_i(t)$ is no longer zero. Thus the equations for estimation of b become somewhat more complicated.

The approach discussed in this section also makes possible another non-trivial extension of the models of this chapter. This extension is to more than two waves, with an interaction term between each time period and each independent variable. If there are T time periods, denoted by t_0, t_1, t_2, . . . , t_T, then for independent variable k, there are $T + 1$ parameter values, b_k, b_{k1}, . . . , b_{kT}. The parameter b_{kj} is the interaction term for variable k at the time period beginning at t_{j-1} and ending at t_j. The total effect of k during that period is $b_k + b_{kj}$, the prior effect which was responsible for the distribution at time t_0 plus the period-specific component of the effect, b_{kj}. In such a case, equation (3.28) has $T + 1$ terms of the form that are found on the right-hand side of equation (3.28), and equation (3.29) is expanded accordingly.

Alternatively, with T time periods, one can follow a procedure which conditions upon the parameters estimated from use of equation (3.29) for the first two periods. After estimating b_k and b_{k1} for all k by use of equation (3.29), b_{k2} and successive period-specific parameters are estimated conditional upon b and b_1, by use of the procedures outlined in chapter 6, section 3 (for which the LONGIT·PANEL program can be used), taking $p_i(t_1)$ as the initial observation for estimating $b_{k(2)}$. The parameter $b_{k(2)}$ estimated by this procedure is an estimate of the total effect of k during the period t_1 to t_2. Thus the period-specific component, b_{k2}, is estimated as $b_{k2} = b_{k(2)} - b_k$. The same procedure is used for succeeding time periods, using $p_i(t_{j-1})$ as the initial observation in estimation of $b_{k(j)}$.

A second value of the treatment of left censoring outlined in this section is that the isolation of period-specific effects from prior effects can be useful in coping with response unreliability. In all the models of this book, responses are assumed to give the individual's state with perfect reliability (I have treated briefly the case of response unreliability in Coleman, 1968). If, however, there is no change in the individual's state, but only response unreliability, such that the relationship of the dependent response to the independent variables remains unchanged, estimation of the vector **b** by use of methods outlined in this chapter and implemented in the LONGIT·PANEL program will show effects b_k which would generate $p_i(t)$ [or $p_i(0)$] as the equilibrium distribution. Such "effects" are wholly spurious, created by the response unreliability. It is possible, by use of data from three or more waves, to determine the extent of this unreliability, though I will not pursue the matter here (see Coleman, 1968). But the point of importance here is that this unreliability of response will be captured by the parameters b_k by use of the methods described in this section, while the period-specific component, b_{kj} for period j, measures a true effect occurring during the period k, and acting to change the relation between independent variable k and the dependent response. All or a portion of b_k may be due to response unreliability; but b_{kj} is not.

10. TREND DATA IN LIEU OF PANEL DATA

Often, panel data do not exist, but trend data exist for independent samples of the same population taken at a number of time points. The models outlined in this chapter may be used for trend data, if the data can be cross-classified by the same independent variables at each of the time points. In such treatment, $z_i(0)$ and $z_i(t)$ are no longer zero or one for cell i in the cross-classification, but are some value between zero and one.[5] In general, trend data can be treated like panel data with loss of 2^m degrees of freedom, where m is the number of independent variables. This means that for the unrestricted model, at least three attributes, creating eight cells at each time period, must be used in the cross-classification in order to have sufficient degrees of freedom.

The model described in the preceding section, taking left-censoring effects into account and estimating a period-specific component of the effect of each independent variable for each period, appears especially promising for use with trend data. This would allow one to estimate for each of the attributes used in the cross-classification a parameter for its differential change at each time period. For such an analysis, at least three attributes are necessary in the cross-classification, because the number of parameters estimated by use

[5] See footnote on page 239 (chapter 6) for a modification necessary in the definition of the second derivative and in the computer program for such a case.

of equation (3.29) with the unrestricted model is $4m + 4$, where m is the number of independent variables, and the number of degrees of freedom given by the observations $z_i(0)$ and $z_i(t)$ is 2^{m+1}. If $2^{m+1} \geq 4m + 4$, and m is an integer, then m must be 3 or greater.

APPENDIX: USE OF THE LONGIT·PANEL PROGRAM

This program is designed to use panel data, with observations on individuals at two points in time, to estimate parameters of effect of qualitative attributes or continuous variables on a dichotomous response.

It is assumed that for each individual, data exist at two points in time for dependent response, so he can be classified either in state 0 or 1 at each time. He is also characterized, either at one time point or at both, by values of up to nine independent attributes or variables. If there is more than one individual with the same values on the dependent attribute at both times and on all independent variables (as is true, for example, for grouped data that are cross-classified into a tabulation), then all those with the same values can be read in a single record, with the number of individuals represented by that record being the *weight* for that record.

Control Cards

To be read from unit 2, assumed to be read from cards or card-image records with blocksize 4560.

Card 1: The number of different data sets or problems to be analyzed on this run. This number appears with the units position in column 5. There is no limit to the number of problems per run.

Cards 2–5: They are repeated for each problem or data set. If data are read from cards on the same unit as the control cards, card 1 prefaces the entire run; cards 2–5 preface each data set.

Card 2: Position 5: The number of independent variables (min 1, max 9).

Position 10 (units): The number of records to be read, where one record represents one individual for ungrouped data, or one cell for grouped or cross-tabulated data (min 8, max 2000).[6]

---

[6] Dimensions can be larger than given in the program. Dimensions should be as large as necessary for the problem at hand, and no larger than machine capacity.

Position 15: 1 if only linear model

2 if only exponential model

3 if first linear, followed by exponential

Position 20: 1 if only constrained model ($c_k = -b_k$)

2 if only unconstrained model (c_k independent of b_k)

3 if both

Position 25: Number of variables that are observed at both points in time. If only the dependent variable is observed twice, a 1 goes in this position. If all variables are observed twice, this is 1 plus the number in position 5 (min 1, max 10).

Position 28 (decimal point appears in position 28): The length of time between waves, in whatever time units desired.

Card 3: *Positions 3, 6, 9, . . .* (units position): There are as many numbers in this card as there are variables measured at both waves. Each number represents the variable number of one of these twice-measured variables. The first number is always 1, standing for the dependent variable. The number of numbers on this card is equal to the number in position 25 of card 2.

Card 4: *Position 5:* 1 if input data are to be printed out, 0 otherwise.

Position 10: 1 if predicted proportions in state 1 at time *t* are to be printed, 0 otherwise.

Position 15: 1 if a Pearson chi-square is to be calculated (only possible if data are from cross-tabulation and alternate records are cells that differ (1 or 0) on dependent variable at time 2); 0 otherwise.

Position 20: 1 if multiple R^2 is to be calculated; 0 otherwise.

Position 30 (decimal): The number of independent individuals represented by the data for the calculation of statistical tests. If this equals the sum of the weights, then this number can be deleted.

Card 5: This card contains the format specifications for the data. The conventions of Fortran format statements are used. For a *standard* format, reading from cards or card-image records, the decimal point for each of the variables described under *Input Data* below is in position 5, 10, . . . , 70. If there are more than fourteen total variables for each individual, two cards per individual are used. For this standard format, card 5 should read (14F5.0) in positions 3–10.

Input Data

To be read from unit 2, assumed to be read from cards or card-image records with blocksize 4560.

1. Data are read individual by individual (or for cross-tabulated data, cell by cell), in the following order:
    a. Value of the dependent attribute at the first wave, having the value 0 or 1
    b. Values of each of the independent attributes or variables at the first wave
    c. Value of the dependent attribute at the second wave (0 or 1)
    d. Values of any independent attributes or variables that are different the second time from the first; the number of such variables may range from zero to the total number of independent variables
    e. The weight of the individual. For a self-weighting sample, the weight is one. For nonself-weighting sample, the weight is the sampling weight associated with the individual. For the case in which the record represents all individuals in a cell of tabulation, the weight is the number of individuals in the cell if the sample is self-weighting, or the sun of the weights for individuals in the cell if it is not.
2. Data format is specified by the user on control card 5.

Alternate Options:

By modifying the Read statement in the program, variables can be read in a different order (for reading from records in which the data appear in a different order).

By modifying the JCL statements, data may be read from different units, different length records, differently blocked. JCL must in any case be specific to the machine and the operating system.

By replacing the statement with label 5010 ("5010 CONTINUE") with "5010 REWIND 2," the same records can be reread to extract a new set of variables for the next problem.

Example of Control Cards, Data, and Output

The control cards, data and output for the example in section 3.1 are presented with the appended program.

93

INPUT TO LONGIT.PANEL PROGRAM

(Example of Section 3.1)

```
   1
   1    8    3    3    1 1.
 1
    0    1    1    1
(20F4.0)
 1.  1.  1. 72.
 1.  1.  0.  5.
 0.  1.  1. 48.
 0.  1.  0. 80.
 1.  0.  1. 53.
 1.  0.  0. 12.
 0.  0.  1.  9.
 0.  0.  0.107.
```

OUTPUT FROM LONGIT.PANEL PROGRAM

LONGIT.PANEL PROGRAM FOR PANEL DATA   12/7/80

```
   1    8    3    3    1
```

ALL INDEPENDENT VARIABLES CONSTANT
ITERATION CONVERGED AFTER STEP :   6

RESTRICTED PARAMETERS: FIRST IS B0, LAST IS C0

LINEAR MODEL

COVARIANCE MATRIX
```
      0.00138   -0.00074   -0.00059
     -0.00074    0.00302    0.00291
     -0.00059    0.00291    0.00348
```

B COEFFICIENTS AND STANDARD ERRORS
```
   B( 0)=   0.1252    SE( 0)=   0.0372    B*( 0)=   0.2681
   B( 1)=   0.2820    SE( 1)=   0.0549    B*( 1)=   0.6039
   B( 2)=   0.3418    SE( 2)=   0.0590    B*( 2)=   0.7319
```

GOODNESS OF FIT TEST
CHI SQUARE=   5.15   WITH   1   D. F.

MULTIPLE R-SQUARE = 0.444

P-VECTOR :
 0.9520 0.9520 0.3252 0.3252 0.7267 0.7267 0.0999 0.0999
 ITERATION CONVERGED AFTER STEP :   6

RESTRICTED PARAMETERS: FIRST IS B0, LAST IS C0

EXPONENTIAL MODEL

COVARIANCE MATRIX
```
      0.09147   -0.08739    0.00959
     -0.08739    0.10388   -0.00630
      0.00959   -0.00630    0.07183
```

```
B COEFFICIENTS AND STANDARD ERRORS
    B( 0)=  -2.2241    SE( 0)=   0.3024    B*( 0)=   0.1082
    B( 1)=   1.4618    SE( 1)=   0.3223    B*( 1)=   4.3136
    B( 2)=  -1.3956    SE( 2)=   0.2680    B*( 2)=   0.2477


GOODNESS OF FIT TEST
CHI SQUARE=       1.29    WITH   1  D. F.

MULTIPLE R-SQUARE =  0.450

P-VECTOR :
 0.9553 0.9553 0.3632 0.3632 0.7916 0.7916 0.0910 0.0910
 ITERATION CONVERGED AFTER STEP :    5

UNRESTRICTED PARAMETERS: B0,B1,...,BN,C0,C1,...,CN

LINEAR MODEL


COVARIANCE MATRIX
     0.00092   -0.00092    0.00028   -0.00028
    -0.00092    0.00644   -0.00028    0.00093
     0.00028   -0.00028    0.00391   -0.00391
    -0.00028    0.00093   -0.00391    0.00544


B COEFFICIENTS AND STANDARD ERRORS
    B( 0)=   0.0900    SE( 0)=   0.0304    B*( 0)=   0.2959
    B( 1)=   0.4042    SE( 1)=   0.0803    B*( 1)=   1.3291
    B( 2)=   0.2141    SE( 2)=   0.0625    B*( 2)=   0.7041
    B( 3)=  -0.1285    SE( 3)=   0.0737    B*( 3)=  -0.4227


GOODNESS OF FIT TEST
CHI SQUARE=       0.00    WITH   0  D. F.

MULTIPLE R-SQUARE =  0.451

P-VECTOR :
 0.9351 0.9351 0.3750 0.3750 0.8154 0.8154 0.0776 0.0776
 ITERATION CONVERGED AFTER STEP :    6

UNRESTRICTED PARAMETERS: B0,B1,...,BN,C0,C1,...,CN

EXPONENTIAL MODEL


COVARIANCE MATRIX
     0.11394   -0.11394    0.01440   -0.01440
    -0.11394    0.13655   -0.01440    0.02985
     0.01440   -0.01440    0.08530   -0.08530
    -0.01440    0.02985   -0.08530    0.29362


B COEFFICIENTS AND STANDARD ERRORS
    B( 0)=  -2.4082    SE( 0)=   0.3375    B*( 0)=   0.0900
    B( 1)=   1.7032    SE( 1)=   0.3695    B*( 1)=   5.4917
    B( 2)=  -1.5413    SE( 2)=   0.2921    B*( 2)=   0.2141
    B( 3)=  -0.9172    SE( 3)=   0.5419    B*( 3)=   0.3996
```

95

GOODNESS OF FIT TEST
CHI SQUARE=   0.00   WITH   0 D. F.

MULTIPLE R-SQUARE = 0.451

P-VECTOR :
 0.9351 0.9351 0.3750 0.3750 0.8154 0.8154 0.0776 0.0776

                    LONGIT.PANEL PROGRAM

```
1
  1.      //LONGIT JOB (2ZB004,COL,Q,NORC),COLEMAN,RE=750K,
  2.      // TE=YES,ID='LONGIT.PANEL',RO=NORC,Q=0
  3.      // EXEC FORTXCLG
  4.      //FORT.SYSIN DD *
  5.
  6.
  7.      C
  8.      C
  9.      C
 10.            DIMENSION INDEX(20,2),IPIVOT(20),FMT(18),FMQ(18),
 11.           &Z(2000),W(2000),X(20,2000),SS(20,20),P(2000),XAT(20,2000),
 12.           &R(20),C(20),B(20),BL(20),D(2000),WEIGHT(2000),ZO(2000),
 13.           &XAT1(20,2000),A3(20),A5(20),XDEL(20),DXG(20,2),DXXG(20,20,2),
 14.           &CA6(20,20),CA7(20,20),CA9(20),CA11(20,20),XB(20),NCH(20)
 15.            COMMON R,INDEX,IPIVOT
 16.      C
 17.      C     NS=NUMBER OF INDEPENDENT VARIABLES, N=NUMBER OF CELLS OR
 18.      C     DISTINCT TYPES OF INDIVIDUALS AS READ IN ONE RECORD.
 19.      C     NLAG=1 IF ONLY LINEAR MODEL, 2 IF ONLY EXPONENTIAL, 3 IF BOTH
 20.      C     NRES=1 IF RESTRICTED PARAMETERS ONLY, 2 IF UNRESTRICTED ONLY,
 21.      C     3 IF BOTH
 22.      C     NVAR=NUMBER OF VARIABLES THAT CHANGE OVER TIME INCLUDING
 23.      C     THE DEPENDENT VARIABLE.  NVAR=1,...,NS+1
 24.      C     NCH(J)=VARIABLE NUMBER OF JTH VARIABLE THAT CHANGES, INCLUDING
 25.      C     DEPENDENT.  NCH(1) IS ALWAYS 1; NCH(NVAR) IS VARIABLE NUMBER
 26.      C     OF LAST CHANGING VARIABLE.
 27.      C
 28.      C
 29.            WRITE(6,8893)
 30.      8893 FORMAT(//1X'LONGIT.PANEL PROGRAM FOR PANEL DATA  12/7/80'/)
 31.            READ(2,8888)NJOBS
 32.            DO 5010 I22=1,NJOBS
 33.      C
 34.            SUM=0.
 35.            ISTEP=0.
 36.            ZSUM=0.
 37.            READ(2,8888)NS,N,NLAG,NRES,NVAR,T
 38.            READ(2,8886)(NCH(J),J=1,NVAR)
 39.      8886 FORMAT(20I3)
 40.      8888 FORMAT(5I5,F6.3)
 41.            WRITE(6,808)
 42.       808 FORMAT(//)
 43.            WRITE(6,8888)NS,N,NLAG,NRES,NVAR
 44.            READ(2,8788)JW,NWP,NC,NR,CNUM
 45.      8788 FORMAT(4I5,F10.0)
 46.      C
 47.      C     JW=1 IF DATA ARE TO BE WRITTEN, NWP=1 IF PREDICTED PROPORTION
 48.      C     NC=1 FOR PEARSON CHISQUARE, NR=1 FOR MULTIPLE R-SQUARE
 49.            DO 61 J=2,NVAR
 50.       61 NCH(J)=NCH(J) -1
```

```
51.           IF(NVAR.GE.2)WRITE(6,8891)(NCH(J),J=2,NVAR)
52.           IF(NVAR.LT.2)WRITE(6,8892)
53.      8891 FORMAT(/1X'NON-CONSTANT INDEPENDENT VARIABLES ARE: '20I4)
54.      8892 FORMAT(/1X'ALL INDEPENDENT VARIABLES CONSTANT')
55.           READ (2,8889)FMT
56.      8889 FORMAT(18A4)
57.           TN=.0001*NS
58.           NSN=NS+1
59.           NSF=NS+2
60.           NSK=2*NS+2
61.           DO 2 I1=1,N
62.           READ(2,FMT)ZO(I1),(XAT(J,I1),J=2,NSN),(R(J),J=1,NVAR),W(I1)
63.           IF(JW.EQ.1)WRITE(6,FMT)ZO(I1),(XAT(J,I1),J=2,NSN),(R(J),J=1,
64.          &NVAR),W(I1)
65.           XAT(1,I1)=1
66.           DO 423 J=1,NSN
67.       423 XAT1(J,I1)=XAT(J,I1)
68.           Z(I1)=R(1)
69.           IF(NVAR.EQ.1)GOTO 481
70.           DO 422 J=2,NVAR
71.           NT=NCH(J) +1
72.           XAT1(NT,I1)=R(J)
73.       422 CONTINUE
74.       481 CONTINUE
75.           ZSUM=ZSUM +Z(I1)
76.           SUM=SUM+W(I1)
77.         2 CONTINUE
78.           ZBAR=ZSUM/N
79.       653 LAG=NLAG
80.       654 ISTEP=0
81.           DO 6541 I=1,N
82.           DO 424 J=1,NSN
83.           X(J+NSN,I)=-XAT(J,I)
84.           X(J,I)=XAT(J,I)
85.       424 CONTINUE
86.           D(I)=Z(I)-ZBAR*1.05
87.      6541 WEIGHT(I)=W(I)/SUM
88.           DO 3 I=1,N
89.           DO 3 J=1,NSN
90.           BL(J)=0.
91.           BL(J+NSN)=0.
92.         3 CONTINUE
93.           NSV=NSK
94.           IF(NRES.NE.2)NSV=NSF
95.  C
96.      1000 IF(ISTEP.GE.100) GOTO 2000
97.  C
98.           DO 5 I=1,NSV
99.           DO 5 J=1,NSV
100.        5 SS(I,J)=0.0
101. C
102.          DO 15 I1=1,N
103.          DO 15 I=1,NSV
104.          DO 15 J=I,NSV
105.          SS(I,J)=SS(I,J)+X(I,I1)*X(J,I1)*WEIGHT(I1)
106.       15 SS(J,I)=SS(I,J)
107. C
108. C
109.          CALL INVER(SS,NSV)
110. C
111. C
112.          DO 35 I=1,NSV
```

97

```
113.          35 R(I)=0
114.      C
115.             DO 40 IC=1,N
116.             D(IC)=D(IC)*WEIGHT(IC)
117.             DO 45 J=1,NSV
118.             C(J)=0.0
119.             DO 45 I1=1,NSV
120.          45 C(J)=C(J)+SS(I1,J)*X(I1,IC)
121.             DO 40 I=1,NSV
122.             C(I)=C(I)*D(IC)
123.          40 R(I)=R(I)+C(I)
124.      C
125.             DO  81 I=1,NSV
126.          81 B(I)=BL(I)+R(I)
127.      C
128.      C
129.             ISTEP=ISTEP+1
130.      C
131.      C
132.             DO 83 I=1,NSV
133.             DIFR=ABS(B(I)-BL(I))
134.             IF(DIFR.GE.0.001) GOTO 89
135.          83 CONTINUE
136.             GOTO 106
137.      C
138.          89 DO 90 I=1,NSV
139.          90 BL(I)=B(I)
140.             DO 9003 I=1,N
141.             DO 9003 J=1,NSN
142.        9003 X(J,I)=XAT(J,I)
143.             CALL PANLU(NVAR,LAG,NRES,BL,X,NS,N,T,P,ZO,Z,WEIGHT,W,D,XAT1)
144.             GOTO 1000
145.      C
146.         106 WRITE(6,88)ISTEP
147.          88 FORMAT(1H0,' ITERATION CONVERGED AFTER STEP : ',I5)
148.      C
149.      C     THIS LARGE SECTION, TO LABEL 101, CALCULATES 2ND DERIVATIVES.
150.             DO 103 J=1,NSV
151.             DO 103 K=1,NSV
152.         103 SS(J,K)=0.
153.             DO 101 I=1,N
154.      C
155.      C     THIS PUTS IN PRODUCT OF FIRST DERIVATIVES
156.             D1=W(I)*(P(I) -Z(I))/(P(I)*(1-P(I)))
157.             RI=D1*D1/W(I)
158.             DO 102 J=1,NSV
159.             DO 102 K=1,NSV
160.         102 SS(J,K)=SS(J,K) +RI*X(J,I)*X(K,I)
161.             IF(NVAR.GT.1)GOTO 741
162.      C
163.      C     THIS SECTION FINDS 2ND DERIVATIVES FOR CONSTANT.
164.             G1=0.
165.             G2=0.
166.             DO 104 J=1,NSN
167.             G2=G2 +B(J+NSN)*XAT(J,I)
168.         104 G1=G1 +B(J)*XAT(J,I)
169.             IF(NRES.NE.2)G2=B(NSF) -G1 +B(1)
170.             IF(LAG.NE.2)GOTO 204
171.             G1=EXP(G1)
172.             G2=EXP(G2)
173.         204 CO=G1+G2
174.             C1=EXP(-CO*T)
```

98

```
175.              C2=(1-C1)/CO
176.              C3=(C2-C1*T)/(CO*T)
177.              D2=(ZO(I) -G1/CO)*C1*T
178.              IF(NRES.EQ.2)GOTO 143
179.      C
180.      C       THIS SECTION FINDS 2ND DERIVATIVES CONSTANT, RESTRICTED,
181.      C        BOTH LINEAR AND EXPONENTIAL
182.              D3=(G1-G2)*2*C3*T/CO
183.              DO 165 J=2,NSN
184.              IF(LAG.NE.2)GOTO 153
185.              DO 155 K=2,NSN
186.              SS(J,K)=SS(J,K) +D1*(D2*(T*(G1-G2)*(G1-G2) -CO) -2*G1*G2*D3)*
187.             &XAT(J,I)*XAT(K,I)
188.        155 CONTINUE
189.              SS(J,1)=SS(J,1) +D1*G1*(D2*(T*(G1-G2) -1) +G2*C1*T/CO -G2*D3)*
190.             &XAT(J,I)
191.              SS(1,J)=SS(J,1)
192.              SS(J,NSF)=SS(J,NSF) +D1*G2*(D2*(T*(G1-G2) +1) +G1*C1*T/CO +G1*
193.             &D3)*XAT(J,I)
194.              SS(NSF,J)=SS(J,NSF)
195.              GOTO 165
196.        153 D3=D1*(-C3*T)*XAT(J,I)
197.              SS(J,1)=SS(J,1) +D3
198.              SS(J,NSF)=SS(J,NSF) +D3
199.              SS(NSF,J)=SS(NSF,J) +D3
200.              SS(1,J)=SS(1,J) +D3
201.        165 CONTINUE
202.              IF(LAG.NE.2)GOTO 156
203.              SS(1,1)=SS(1,1) +D1*G1*(D2*(T*G1 -1) +(T*C1*2*G1*G2 -
204.             &G2*(G1-G2)*C2)/(CO*CO))
205.              SS(1,NSF)=SS(1,NSF) +D1*G2*G1*(D2*T +(G1-G2)*T*C3/CO)
206.              SS(NSF,1)=SS(1,NSF)
207.              SS(NSF,NSF)=SS(NSF,NSF) +D1*G2*(D2*(T*G2 -1) -(T*C1*2*G1*G2 +
208.             &G1*(G1-G2)*C2)/(CO*CO))
209.              GOTO 101
210.        156 SS(1,1)=SS(1,1) +D1*T*(D2 -2*C3*G2/CO)
211.              SS(NSF,1)=SS(NSF,1) +D1*T*(D2 +C3*(G1-G2)/CO)
212.              SS(1,NSF)=SS(NSF,1)
213.              SS(NSF,NSF)=SS(NSF,NSF) +D1*T*(D2 +2*C3*G1/CO)
214.              GOTO 101
215.      C
216.      C       THIS SECTION FINDS 2ND DERIVATIVES, CONSTANT, NONRESTRICTED,
217.      C       BOTH LINEAR AND EXPONENTIAL
218.        143 DO 107 J=1,NSN
219.              DO 105 K=J,NSN
220.              IF(LAG.EQ.2)GOTO 201
221.              SS(J,K)=SS(J,K) +D1*T*(D2 -C3*2*G2/CO)*XAT(J,I)*XAT(K,I)
222.              GOTO 105
223.        201 SS(J,K)=SS(J,K) +D1*G1*(D2*(T*G1-1) +(T*C1*2*G1*G2 -
224.             &G2*(G1-G2)*C2)/(CO*CO))*XAT(J,I)*XAT(K,I)
225.        105 SS(K,J)=SS(J,K)
226.              DO 107 K=NSF,NSK
227.              IF(LAG.EQ.2)GOTO 202
228.              SS(J,K)=SS(J,K) +D1*T*(D2 +C3*(G1-G2)/CO)*XAT(J,I)*XAT(K-NSN,I)
229.              GOTO 107
230.        202 SS(J,K)=SS(J,K) +D1*G2*G1*(D2*T +(G1-G2)*T*C3/CO)*
231.             &XAT(J,I)*XAT(K-NSN,I)
232.        107 SS(K,J)=SS(J,K)
233.              DO 109 J=NSF,NSK
234.              DO 109 K=J,NSK
235.              IF(LAG.EQ.2)GOTO 203
236.              SS(J,K)=SS(J,K) +D1*T*(D2+2*C3*G1/CO)*XAT(J-NSN,I)*XAT(K-NSN,I)
```

```
237.                GOTO 109
238.            203 SS(J,K)=SS(J,K) +D1*G2*(D2*(T*G2-1) -(T*C1*2*G1*G2 +
239.                &G1*(G1-G2)*C2)/(CO*CO))*XAT(J-NSN,I)*XAT(K-NSN,I)
240.            109 SS(K,J)=SS(J,K)
241.                GOTO 101
242.        C
243.        C       THIS SECTION FINDS 2ND DERIVATIVES, NONCONSTANT.
244.            741 GA1=0.
245.                GT1=0.
246.                GA2=0.
247.                GT2=0.
248.                DO 592 J=1,NSN
249.                XB(J)=XAT(J,I) +XAT1(J,I)
250.                GA1=GA1 +B(J)*X(J,I)
251.                GA2=GA2 +B(J+NSN)*X(J,I)
252.                GT1=GT1 +B(J)*XAT1(J,I)
253.                GT2=GT2 +B(J+NSN)*X(J,I)
254.            592 CONTINUE
255.                IF(NRES.NE.2)GA2=B(NSF) -GA1 +B(1)
256.                IF(NRES.NE.2)GT2=B(NSF) -GT1 +B(1)
257.                IF(LAG.NE.2)GOTO 443
258.        C
259.                GA1=EXP(GA1)
260.                GT1=EXP(GT1)
261.                GA2=EXP(GA2)
262.                GT2=EXP(GT2)
263.                CO4=GA1
264.                IF(ABS(C00-C01).GE..0001)CO4=(GT1-GA1)/(C01-C00)
265.                CO5=GA2
266.                IF(ABS(C02-C03).GE..0001)CO5=(GT2-GA2)/(C03-C02)
267.                CO=C04+C05
268.                C1=EXP(-CO*T)
269.                C4=CO+(C01-C00)/T
270.                C4S=C4*C4
271.                C8=GT1 -C1*GA1
272.                C10=GA1/C4 -ZO(I)
273.                DO 333 J=1,NSN
274.                XDEL(J)=XAT1(J,I)-X(J,I)
275.                A3(J)=X(J,I)*GA1
276.                IF(ABS(C00-C01).GE..0001)A3(J)=(-XDEL(J)*C04 +
277.                &XAT1(J,I)*GT1 -X(J,I)*GA1)/(C01-C00)
278.                A5(J)=X(J,I)*GA2
279.                IF(ABS(C02-C03).GE..0001)A5(J)=(-XDEL(J)*C05+
280.                &XAT1(J,I)*GT2-X(J,I)*GA2)/(C03-C02)
281.                CA9(J)=XAT1(J,I)*GT1 -XAT(J,I)*GA1*C1
282.                DXG(J,1)=XAT1(J,I)*GT1 -XAT(J,I)*GA1
283.                DXG(J,2)=XAT1(J,I)*GT2 -XAT(J,I)*GA1
284.                DO 333 K=1,NSN
285.                DXXG(J,K,1)=XAT1(J,I)*XAT1(K,I)*GT1 -XAT(J,I)*XAT(K,I)*GA1
286.                DXXG(J,K,2)=XAT1(J,I)*XAT1(K,I)*GT2 -XAT(J,I)*XAT(K,I)*GA2
287.                CA6(J,K)=DXXG(J,K,1) -A3(J)*XDEL(K) -A3(K)*XDEL(J)
288.                CA7(J,K)=DXXG(J,K,2) -A5(J)*XDEL(K) -A5(K)*XDEL(J)
289.                CA11(J,K)=XAT1(J,I)*XAT1(K,I)*GT1 -XAT(J,I)*XAT(J,I)*GA1*C1
290.        C       MUST GET EXPRESSION FOR CA6 AND CA7 WHEN GA1=GT1
291.            333 CONTINUE
292.        C
293.        C       THIS SUBSECTION FINDS 2ND DERIVATIVE EXPONENTIAL NONCONSTANT,
294.        C       BOTH RESTRICTED AND NONRESTRICTED.
295.                NSQ=NSK
296.                IF(NRES.NE.2)NSQ=NSF
297.                DO 307 J=1,NSN
298.                DO 305 K=J,NSN
```

```
299.              IF(NRES.NE.2)GOTO 308
300.              DUM6=CA6(J,K)
301.              DUM3J=A3(J)
302.              DUM3K=A3(K)
303.              GOTO 311
304.          308 DUM6=CA6(J,K) -CA7(J,K)
305.              DUM3J=A3(J) -A5(J)
306.              DUM3K=A3(K) -A5(K)
307.              IF(J.EQ.1)DUM3J=A3(J)
308.          311 SS(J,K)=SS(J,K) +D1*(DUM6*(T*C1*C10 -C8/C4S) +
309.             &DUM3J*DUM3K*(2*C8/(T*C4*C4S) -T*C1*(T*C10 +2*GA1/C4S)) +
310.             &DUM3J*(2*C8*XDEL(K)/(T*C4*C4S) -CA9(K)/C4S +GA1*C1*T*(XAT(K,I)
311.             & -XDEL(K)/(T*C4))/C4)  +DUM3K*(2*C8*XDEL(J)/(T*C4*C4S) -CA9(J)/
312.             &C4S +GA1*C1*T*(XAT(J,I) -XDEL(J)/(T*C4))/C4)  +CA11(J,K)/C4
313.             &-XDEL(J)*CA9(K)/(T*C4S) -XDEL(K)*CA9(J)/(T*C4S)  +2*XDEL(J)*
314.             &XDEL(K)*C8/(T*C4))
315.          305 SS(K,J)=SS(J,K)
316.              DO 307 K=NSF,NSQ
317.              SS(J,K)=SS(J,K) +D1*(A3(J)*A5(K-NSN)*(2*C8/(T*C4*C4S) -T*C1*
318.             &(T*C10 +2*GA1/C4S))  +A5(K-NSN)*(2*C8*XDEL(J)/(T*C4*C4S) -
319.             &CA9(J)/C4S +GA1*C1*T*(XAT(J,I) -XDEL(J)/(T*C4))/C4)  +2*XDEL(J)
320.             &*XDEL(K-NSN)*C8/(T*T*C4*C4S))
321.          307 SS(K,J)=SS(J,K)
322.              DO 309 J=NSF,NSQ
323.              DO 309 K=J,NSQ
324.              SS(J,K)=SS(J,K) +D1*(CA7(J,K)*(T*C1*C10 -C8/C4S)) +A5(J-NSN)*
325.             &A5(K-NSN)*(2*C8/(C4*C4S) -T*C1*(T*C10 +2*GA1/C4S))
326.          309 SS(K,J)=SS(J,K)
327.              GOTO 101
328.      C
329.      C     THIS SECTION FINDS 2ND DERIVATIVES FOR LINEAR NONCONSTANT.
330.          443 CO=(GA1 +GT1 +GA2 +GT2)/2
331.              C1=EXP(-CO*T)
332.              C2=(1-C1)/CO
333.              C3=(C2/T-C1)/CO
334.              C4=(1-C2/T)/CO
335.              D2T=(ZO(I) -GA1/CO)*C1*T*T
336.              AC5=(T*C1 -2*C3)/CO
337.              AC6=(C2 -2*C4)/CO
338.              AC8= -(T*C3 +3*AC6)/CO
339.              DUM=D2T -3*GA1*AC5/CO +GT1*AC8
340.              IF(NRES.NE.2)GOTO 493
341.      C
342.      C     THIS SUBSECTION FINDS 2ND DERIVATIVES FOR LINEAR NONCONSTANT,
343.      C     NONRESTRICTED.
344.              DO 207 J=1,NSN
345.              DO 205 K=J,NSN
346.              SS(J,K)=SS(J,K) +D1*(XB(J)*XB(K)*DUM +XB(J)*(AC5*XAT(K,I) +AC6*
347.             &XAT1(K,I))  +XB(K)*(AC5*XAT(J,I) +AC6*XAT1(J,I)))
348.          205 SS(K,J)=SS(J,K)
349.              DO 207 K=NSF,NSK
350.              SS(J,K)=SS(J,K) +D1*(XB(J)*XB(K-NSN)*DUM +XB(K-NSN)*(AC5*
351.             &XAT(J,I) +AC6*XAT1(J,I)))
352.          207 SS(K,J)=SS(J,K)
353.              DO 209 J=NSF,NSK
354.              DO 209 K=J,NSK
355.              SS(J,K)=SS(J,K) +D1*(XB(J-NSN)*XB(K-NSN)*DUM)
356.          209 SS(K,J)=SS(J,K)
357.              GOTO 101
358.      C
359.      C     THIS SUBSECTION FINDS 2ND DERIVATIVES FOR LINEAR NONCONSTANT,
360.      C     RESTRICTED.
```

101

```
361.        493 DO 265 J=2,NSN
362.            D3=D1*(AC5*XAT(J,I) +AC6*XAT1(J,I))
363.            SS(J,1)=SS(J,1) +D3
364.            SS(J,NSF)=SS(J,NSF) +D3
365.            SS(NSF,J)=SS(NSF,J) +D3
366.            SS(1,J)=SS(1,J) +D3
367.        265 CONTINUE
368.            SS(1,1)=SS(1,1) +D1*(DUM +2*(AC5+AC6))
369.            SS(NSF,1)=SS(NSF,1) +D1*(DUM +AC5 +AC6)
370.            SS(1,NSF)=SS(NSF,1)
371.            SS(NSF,NSF)=SS(NSF,NSF) +D1*DUM
372.    C
373.        101 CONTINUE
374.    C
375.            CALL INVER(SS,NSV)
376.    C
377.    C
378.            IF(NRES.NE.2)WRITE(6,1117)
379.            IF(NRES.EQ.2)WRITE(6,1118)
380.       1117 FORMAT(/1X'RESTRICTED PARAMETERS: FIRST IS B0, LAST IS C0')
381.       1118 FORMAT(/1X'UNRESTRICTED PARAMETERS: B0,B1,...,BN,C0,C1,...,CN')
382.            IF(LAG.EQ.2)GOTO 141
383.            WRITE(6,117)
384.        117 FORMAT(/1X,'LINEAR MODEL')
385.            GOTO 142
386.        141 WRITE(6,118)
387.        118 FORMAT(/1X,'EXPONENTIAL MODEL')
388.        142 WRITE(6,115)
389.            DO 113 K=1,NSV
390.        113 WRITE(6,110)(SS(K,J),J=1,NSV)
391.        115 FORMAT(//1X,'COVARIANCE MATRIX')
392.        110 FORMAT(5X,8F10.5)
393.            DO 723 K=1,NSV
394.            IF(LAG.EQ.2)BL(K)=EXP(B(K))
395.        723 IF(LAG.NE.2)BL(K)=B(K)/(B(1) +B(NSF))
396.            WRITE(6,112)
397.        128 DO 111 K=1,NSV
398.            SS(K,K)=SQRT(SS(K,K))
399.            K1=K-1
400.        111 WRITE(6,122)K1,B(K),K1,SS(K,K),K1,BL(K)
401.        112 FORMAT(//1X,'B COEFFICIENTS AND STANDARD ERRORS')
402.        122 FORMAT(5X,'B(',I2,')=',F9.4,5X,'SE(',I2,')=',F9.4,
403.           &5X,'B*(',I2,')=',F9.4)
404.            CALL TESTS(NC,NR,N,NSV,NS,CNUM,SUM,P,Z,XAT,W)
405.            IF(NWP.EQ.1)WRITE(6,888)
406.        888 FORMAT(1H0,'P-VECTOR :')
407.            IF(NWP.EQ.1)WRITE(6,878)(P(I),I=1,N)
408.        878 FORMAT(1X,10F7.4)
409.        108 IF(LAG.NE.3) GOTO 5000
410.            LAG=2
411.            GOTO 654
412.       5000 IF(NRES.NE.3)GOTO 5010
413.            NRES=2
414.            GOTO 653
415.       5010 CONTINUE
416.            STOP
417.       2000 WRITE(6,9991) ISTEP
418.       9991 FORMAT(1X,'ITERATION DID NOT CONVERGE IN ',I4,' STEPS ')
419.            GOTO 108
420.    C
421.            END
```

```
422.     C
423.           SUBROUTINE PANLU(NVAR,LAG,NRES,B,X,NS,N,T,PS,ZO,Z,WEIGHT,W,D,
424.          &XAT1)
425.           DIMENSION ZO(1000),X(20,1000),B(20),PS(1000),XAT1(20,1000),
426.          &Z(1000),WEIGHT(1000),W(1000),D(1000),A3(20),A5(20),XDEL(20)
427.     C
428.           NSN=NS+1
429.           NSF=NS+2
430.           NSK=2*NS+2
431.           D1=1.
432.           D2=1.
433.     C
434.           DO 90 I=1,N
435.     C
436.           IF(NVAR.EQ.1)GOTO 591
437.     C
438.     C     THIS SECTION FINDS 1ST DERIVATIVES FOR NONCONSTANT.
439.           GT1=0.
440.           GA1=0.
441.           IF(NRES.EQ.2)GOTO 691
442.           DO 692 J=2,NSN
443.           GA1=GA1 +B(J)*X(J,I)
444.           GT1=GT1 +B(J)*XAT1(J,I)
445.       692 CONTINUE
446.           GA2=B(NSF) -GA1
447.           GT2=B(NSF) -GT1
448.           GA1=B(1) +GA1
449.           GT1=B(1) +GT1
450.           GOTO 592
451.     C
452.       691 GA2=0.
453.           GT2=0.
454.           DO 592 J=1,NSN
455.           GA1=GA1 +B(J)*X(J,I)
456.           GA2=GA2 +B(J+NSN)*X(J,I)
457.           GT1=GT1 +B(J)*XAT1(J,I)
458.           GT2=GT2 +B(J+NSN)*XAT1(J,I)
459.       592 CONTINUE
460.           IF(LAG.NE.2)GOTO 443
461.     C
462.           C00=GA1
463.           C01=GT1
464.           C02=GA2
465.           C03=GT2
466.           GA1=EXP(GA1)
467.           GT1=EXP(GT1)
468.           GA2=EXP(GA2)
469.           GT2=EXP(GT2)
470.           C04=GA1
471.           IF(ABS(C00-C01).GE..0001)C04=(GT1-GA1)/(C01-C00)
472.           C05=GA2
473.           IF(ABS(C02-C03).GE..0001)C05=(GT2-GA2)/(C03-C02)
474.           C0=C04+C05
475.           C1=EXP(-C0*T)
476.           C4=C0+(C01-C00)/T
477.           C4S=C4*C4
478.           C8=GT1 -C1*GA1
479.           C10=GA1/C4 -ZO(I)
480.           PS(I)=ZO(I)*C1 +C8/C4
481.           DO 333 J=1,NSN
482.           XDEL(J)=XAT1(J,I)-X(J,I)
483.           A3(J)=X(J,I)*GA1
```

103

```
484.            IF( ABS(C00-C01).GE..0001)A3(J)=(-XDEL(J)*C04 +
485.         &XAT1(J,I)*GT1 -X(J,I)*GA1)/(C01-C00)
486.            A5(J)=X(J,I)*GA2
487.            IF(ABS(C02-C03).GE..0001)A5(J)=(-XDEL(J)*C05+
488.         &XAT1(J,I)*GT2-X(J,I)*GA2)/(C03-C02)
489.      333 CONTINUE
490.            IF(NRES.NE.2)GOTO 445
491.    C
492.    C      THIS SUBSECTION FINDS 1ST DERIVATIVES EXP. NONCONSTANT,NONRES.
493.            DO 92 J=1,NSN
494.            X(J+NSN,I)=A5(J)*(T*C1*C10 -C8/C4S)
495.       92 X(J,I)=A3(J)*T*C1*C10 -C8*(A3(J) +XDEL(J)/T)/C4S +
496.         &(XAT1(J,I)*GT1 -X(J,I)*GA1*C1)/C4
497.            GOTO 177
498.    C
499.    C      THIS SUBSECTION FINDS 1ST DERIV. EXP. NONCONSTANT RESTRICTED.
500.      445 DO 392 J=2,NSN
501.            X(J,I)=(A3(J)-A5(J))*T*C1*C10 -C8*(A3(J)-A5(J)+XDEL(J)/T)/C4S
502.         & +(XAT1(J,I)*GT1 -X(J,I)*GA1*C1)/C4
503.      392 CONTINUE
504.            X(1,I)=A3(1)*(T*C1*C10 -C8/C4S) +C8/C4
505.            X(NSF,I)=A5(1)*(T*C1*C10 -C8/C4S)
506.            GOTO 177
507.    C
508.    C      THIS SUBSECTION FINDS 1ST DERIVATIVES OF NONCONSTANT LINEAR.
509.      443 C0=(GA1 +GT1 +GA2 +GT2)/2
510.            C1=EXP(-C0*T)
511.            C2=(1-C1)/C0
512.            C3=(C2/T-C1)/C0
513.            C4=(1-C2/T)/C0
514.            PS(I)=Z0(I)*C1+GA1*C3+GT1*C4
515.            C6=(C2 -2*C4)/C0
516.            C10=GA1/C0 -Z0(I)
517.            D4=T*C1*C10 -2*GA1*C3/C0 +GT1*C6
518.    C
519.            IF(NRES.NE.2)GOTO 493
520.            DO 792 J=1,NSN
521.            X(J+NSN,I)=((X(J,I)+XAT1(J,I))/2)*D4
522.      792 X(J,I)=X(J+NSN,I)+X(J,I)*C3+XAT1(J,I)*C4
523.            GOTO 177
524.    C
525.      493 DO 492 J=2,NSN
526.      492 X(J,I)=C3*X(J,I) +C4*XAT1(J,I)
527.            X(NSF,I)= D4
528.            X(1,I)=C2 +X(NSF,I)
529.            GOTO 177
530.    C
531.    C      THIS SECTION FINDS FIRST DERVIATIVES FOR CONSTANT.
532.      591 G1=0.
533.            G2=0.
534.            DO 91 J=1,NSN
535.            G1=G1 +B(J)*X(J,I)
536.            G2=G2 +B(J+NSN)*X(J,I)
537.       91 CONTINUE
538.            IF(NRES.NE.2)G2=B(NSF) -G1 +B(1)
539.            IF(LAG.NE.2)GOTO 421
540.            G2=EXP(G2)
541.            G1=EXP(G1)
542.            D2=G2
543.            D1=G1
544.      421 IF(G1.LE.0)G1=0.001
545.            IF(G2.LE.0)G2=0.001
546.            C0=G1+G2
```

```
547.            C1=EXP(-CO*T)
548.            C2=(1-C1)/CO
549.            PS(I)=ZO(I)*C1+G1*C2
550.      C
551.            IF(NRES.EQ.2)GOTO 176
552.            IF(LAG.EQ.2)GOTO 178
553.            DO 192 J=2,NSN
554.        192 X(J,I)=X(J,I)*C2
555.            X(1,I)=((G1/CO-PS(I))*T+G2*C2/CO)
556.            X(NSF,I)=((G1/CO-PS(I))*T-G1*C2/CO)
557.            GOTO 177
558.        178 DO 292 J=2,NSN
559.        292 X(J,I)=X(J,I)*((G1/CO-PS(I))*(G1-G2)+
560.           &2*G1*G2*C2/CO)
561.            X(1,I)=G1*((G1/CO-PS(I))*T+G2*C2/CO)
562.            X(NSF,I)=G2*((G1/CO-PS(I))*T-G1*C2/CO)
563.            GOTO 177
564.        176 DO 892 J=1,NSN
565.            X(J+NSN,I)=X(J,I)*((G1/CO-PS(I))*T-G1*C2/CO)*D2
566.        892 X(J,I)=X(J,I)*((G1/CO-PS(I))*T+G2*C2/CO)*D1
567.        177 D(I)=Z(I)-PS(I)
568.            TEM=PS(I)*(1-PS(I))
569.            IF(TEM.LT.0.0291) TEM=0.0291
570.            WEIGHT(I)=W(I)/TEM
571.         90 CONTINUE
572.            RETURN
573.            END
574.      C
575.      C
576.            SUBROUTINE TESTS(NC,NR,N,NSV,NS,CNUM,SUMA,P,Z,X,W)
577.            DIMENSION P(2000),Z(2000),X(20,2000),W(2000)
578.            IF(CNUM.GT.0.)GOTO 19
579.            CNUM=SUMA
580.      C
581.      C     CALCULATION OF CHI SQUARE GOODNESS OF FIT TEST
582.         19 IF (NC.NE.1)GOTO 10
583.            NH=N/2
584.            NHH=NH-NSV
585.            CHI=0.
586.            DO 11 J=1,NH
587.            I=J*2-1
588.            I1=J*2
589.            IF(Z(I).EQ.1.)GOTO 13
590.            IT=I
591.            I=I1
592.            I1=IT
593.         13 CONTINUE
594.            DO 12 K=1,NS
595.            DIFR=X(K,I)-X(K,I1)
596.            IF(DIFR.NE.0.)GOTO 21
597.         12 CONTINUE
598.            WT=W(I)+W(I1)
599.         11 CHI=CHI +(CNUM/SUMA)*WT*((W(I)/WT -P(I))**2)/(P(I)*(1.-P(I)))
600.            WRITE(6,877)
601.            WRITE(6,879)CHI,NHH
602.        877 FORMAT(//1X,'GOODNESS OF FIT TEST')
603.        879 FORMAT(1X'CHI SQUARE=',F12.2,'    WITH',I4,' D. F.')
604.      C
605.      C     CALCULATION OF R SQUARE
606.         10 IF(NR.NE.1)GOTO 14
607.            D2=0.
608.            DNUM=0.
```

105

```
609.            DENOM=0.
610.            DEN2=0.
611.            ZB=0.
612.            PB=0.
613.            WT=0.
614.            DO 36 I=1,N
615.            DNUM=DNUM +Z(I)*P(I)*W(I)
616.            DENOM=DENOM +Z(I)*Z(I)*W(I)
617.            DEN2=DEN2 +P(I)*P(I)*W(I)
618.            ZB=ZB +Z(I)*W(I)
619.            PB=PB +P(I)*W(I)
620.         36 WT=WT +W(I)
621.            ZBS=ZB*ZB/WT
622.            PBS=PB*PB/WT
623.            RSQ=(DNUM -ZB*PB/WT)**2/((DENOM -ZBS)*(DEN2 -PBS))
624.            WRITE(6,196)RSQ
625.        196 FORMAT(/1X,'MULTIPLE R-SQUARE =',F7.3/)
626.    C
627.         14 RETURN
628.         21 WRITE(6,4)I,I1
629.          4 FORMAT(1X,'DATA OUT OF ORDER FOR CHI SQUARE TEST, I=',2I6)
630.            GOTO 10
631.            END
632.    C
633.            SUBROUTINE INVER(A,N)
634.    C
635.            DIMENSION A(20,20),INDEX(20,2),IPIVOT(20),PIVOT(20)
636.            COMMON PIVOT,INDEX,IPIVOT
637.            EQUIVALENCE (IROW,JROW),(ICOLUM,JCOLUM),(AMAX,T,SWAP)
638.    C
639.            DETERM=1.0
640.    C
641.            DO 20 J=1,N
642.         20 IPIVOT(J)=0
643.    C
644.            DO 550 I=1,N
645.            AMAX=0.0
646.    C
647.            DO 105 J=1,N
648.            IF(IPIVOT(J)-1) 60,105,60
649.    C
650.         60 DO 100 K=1,N
651.            IF(IPIVOT(K)-1) 80,100,740
652.    C
653.         80 IF(ABS(AMAX)-ABS(A(J,K))) 85,100,100
654.    C
655.         85 IROW=J
656.            ICOLUM=K
657.            AMAX=A(J,K)
658.    C
659.        100 CONTINUE
660.        105 CONTINUE
661.    C
662.            IPIVOT(ICOLUM)=IPIVOT(ICOLUM)+1
663.            IF(IROW-ICOLUM) 140,260,140
664.    C
665.        140 DETERM=-DETERM
666.    C
667.            DO 200 L=1,N
668.            SWAP=A(IROW,L)
669.            A(IROW,L)=A(ICOLUM,L)
670.        200 A(ICOLUM,L)=SWAP
```

```
671.    C
672.      260 INDEX(I,1)=IROW
673.          INDEX(I,2)=ICOLUM
674.          PIVOT(I)=A(ICOLUM,ICOLUM)
675.          DETERM=DETERM*PIVOT(I)
676.          A(ICOLUM,ICOLUM)=1.0
677.    C
678.          DO 350 L=1,N
679.          IF(PIVOT(I).NE.0) GOTO 349
680.          A(ICOLUM,L)=0.
681.          GOTO 350
682.      349 A(ICOLUM,L)=A(ICOLUM,L)/PIVOT(I)
683.      350 CONTINUE
684.    C
685.          DO 550 L1=1,N
686.          IF(L1-ICOLUM) 400,550,400
687.      400 T=A(L1,ICOLUM)
688.          A(L1,ICOLUM)=0.0
689.          DO 450 L=1,N
690.      450 A(L1,L)=A(L1,L)-A(ICOLUM,L)*T
691.    C
692.      550 CONTINUE
693.    C
694.          DO 710 I=1,N
695.          L=N+1-I
696.          IF(INDEX(L,1)-INDEX(L,2)) 630,710,630
697.      630 JROW=INDEX(L,1)
698.    C
699.          JCOLUM=INDEX(L,2)
700.    C
701.          DO 705 K=1,N
702.          SWAP=A(K,JROW)
703.          A(K,JROW)=A(K,JCOLUM)
704.          A(K,JCOLUM)=SWAP
705.      705 CONTINUE
706.    C
707.      710 CONTINUE
708.    C
709.      740 RETURN
710.          END
711.    //GO.FT02F001 DD UNIT=SYSDA,VOL=SER=NRES01,DISP=OLD,
712.    // DSN=$2ZB004.COL.INPUT.ANALTST3,DCB=(RECFM=FB,LRECL=80,BLKSIZE=4560)
713.    //GO.FT06F001 DD SYSOUT=A,DCB=(RECFM=FB,BLKSIZE=133)
714.    //
```

Chapter 4

Interdependent Systems and Structural Equations

In all the processes discussed up to this point, there has been a single dependent attribute. In chapter 3 the independent variables have been allowed to vary over time, but they remain exogenous, not affected by the attribute regarded as a dependent attribute.

Yet the existence of panel data has led many investigators to attempt to separate out the effects of two attributes on one another. Paul Lazarsfeld was one of the early formulators of the problem, which he termed the *16-fold table problem*. For a history of work on the subject, see Lazarsfeld (1972, 1978). See also Wiggins (1973), Goodman (1973), Coleman (1964a), Fienberg (1977), and Pelz and Andrews (1964).

The 16-fold table problem can be seen in a heuristic way by examining such a table obtained from a study of adolescents in high school. [The data were first analyzed by Coleman (1964a, p. 171), then by Goodman (1973) and Fienberg (1977) with loglinear methods.][1]

TABLE 4.1

Boys' Membership in Leading Crowd and Attitudes toward Membership, Fall 1957 and Spring 1958

	Membership Attitude		Spring 1958				
			11	10	01	00	Total
	1	1	458	140	110	49	751
Fall 1957	1	0	171	182	56	87	496
	0	1	184	75	531	281	1071
	0	0	85	97	338	554	1074

Heuristically, it seems that if membership in the leading crowd helps to maintain a positive attitude toward the leading crowd, then as one effect, those 751 boys who are 11 in the fall should be less likely to move to 10 in the spring than the 1071 who are 01 in the fall are likely to move to 00 in the spring. This has been called in the literature a *preserving effect*, in that occupancy of a given state on one attribute makes change less likely on the other attribute. In fact we find 140/751, or 19 percent moving from 11 to 10, and 281/1071, or 26 percent moving from 01 to 00. Thus there is a slight difference in the expected direction. There are several other comparisons that can be similarly made.

To move from heuristic considerations to an explicit model, it is possible to express a system of two interdependent attributes as a model with four states, consisting of the possible combinations of states 0 and 1 in each of the two attributes. The states may be labeled by the decimal equivalent of the binary number representing the combination of states on the two attributes:

	attribute	
state	2	1
3	1	1
2	1	0
1	0	1
0	0	0

In accordance with the general conception of two interdependent but distinct

[1] This example provides an interesting illustration of the point stated in chapter 1, that logit analysis applied to panel data does not allow interdependence of the attributes. Fienberg (1977) analyzes the same data with a logit model, testing the hypothesis of an effect of attitude on membership, and finds evidence of an effect, but the model does not allow simultaneously introducing the hypothesis of an effect of membership on attitude.

attributes, and a continuous process in which only one event can occur in an instant of time, the transitions are restricted to those that involve change in only one attribute, that is, $3 \overset{2}{\underset{1}{\lessgtr}} 0$. The model can be represented as in figure 4.1. Changes in attribute 1 are in the vertical direction, changes in attribute 2 are in the horizontal direction.

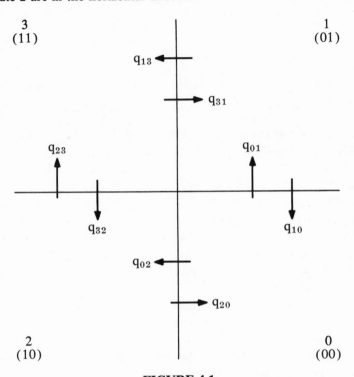

FIGURE 4.1

A System of Two Interdependent Attributes

The q_{hj}'s are decomposed as before, either linearly or exponentially-linearly. If we consider first changes in attribute 1, then with the linear decomposition, the vertical transition rates become

$$
\begin{aligned}
q_{23} &= b_0 + b_2 \\
q_{32} &= c_0 + c_2 \\
q_{01} &= b_0 \\
q_{10} &= c_0
\end{aligned}
\tag{4.1}
$$

where the subscript 2 refers to the independent attribute 2, which affects the transition rate on attribute 1, and where b_k is a component of the transition rate to state 1 of attribute 1, and c_k is a component of the transition rate to state 0. With the exponential decomposition, these are the same, except that the right-hand side of equations (4.1) are all exponents of e. If the assumption of identical and opposite effects in the two directions is made, that is, $c_k = -b_k$, the first two lines in the equations of (4.1) become

$$q_{23} = b_0 + b_2$$
$$q_{32} = c_0 - b_2$$

A minor notational change is necessary in systems with two or more dependent attributes. An additional subscript becomes necessary in order to designate the dependent variable. That is, b_k and c_k will be replaced by b_{jk} and c_{jk}, to designate effects of variable k on attribute j. For a model in which identical and opposite effects in the two directions are assumed, c_{jk} is equal to $-b_{jk}$ for $1 \leq k \leq n$, and will be denoted by $-b_{jk}$. Using this notation for the two-attribute system with equal and opposite effects in the two directions, or with differing effects in the two directions, the decomposition of the transition rates is:

for change in attribute 1 (vertical change):

	equal and opposite effects	effects in two directions independent	
$q_{23} =$	$b_{10} + b_{12}$	$= b_{10} + b_{12}$	
$q_{32} =$	$c_{10} - b_{12}$	$= c_{10} + c_{12}$	(4.2)
$q_{01} =$	b_{10}	$= b_{10}$	
$q_{10} =$	c_{10}	$= c_{10}$	

and for change in attribute 2 (horizontal change):

$q_{13} =$	$b_{20} + b_{21}$	$= b_{20} + b_{21}$	
$q_{31} =$	$c_{20} - b_{21}$	$= c_{20} + c_{21}$	
$q_{02} =$	b_{20}	$= b_{20}$	(4.3)
$q_{20} =$	c_{20}	$= c_{20}$	

The problem, then, in determining the effects in the interdependent system, is to estimate the parameters on the right-side of equations (4.2) and (4.3). Yet the system is fundamentally more complex than before: It is no longer a two-state system for which $p(t)$ can be explicitly written out as a function of the q's, as in equation (1.12). Instead, the full model must be written as a four-state system, for which the differential equations are given below:

$$\frac{dp_3}{dt} = -p_3(q_{32} + q_{31}) + p_2 q_{23} + p_1 q_{13},$$

$$\frac{dp_2}{dt} = -p_2(q_{20} + q_{23}) + p_0 q_{02} + p_3 q_{32},$$

$$\frac{dp_1}{dt} = -p_1(q_{10} + q_{13}) + p_0 q_{01} + p_3 q_{31}, \tag{4.4}$$

$$\frac{dp_0}{dt} = -p_0(q_{01} + q_{02}) + p_1 q_{10} + p_2 q_{20}.$$

These equations may be written with the b's replacing the q's, for the two different decompositions of the q's, and for the case in which c_{jk} is restricted to be equal to $-b_{jk}$ and for the case in which it is not.

Because the linear decomposition with the restriction that $c_{jk} = -b_{jk}$ allows certain simplifications in the analysis, I will treat it in this section. With these assumptions, the first two lines of equations (4.4) become

$$\frac{dp_3}{dt} = -p_3(c_{10} - b_{12} + c_{20} - b_{21}) + p_2(b_{10} + b_{12}) + p_1(b_{20} + b_{21}),$$

$$\frac{dp_2}{dt} = -p_2(c_{20} + b_{10} + b_{12}) + p_0 b_{20} + p_3(c_{10} - b_{12}). \tag{4.5}$$

Now since $p_3 + p_2$ is the probability of occupying state 1 on attribute 2, $dp_3/dt + dp_2/dt$ is the change in that probability. We can thus add the two lines of equations (4.5) to get the change in the probability of being in state 1 of attribute 2:

$$\frac{dp_3}{dt} + \frac{dp_2}{dt} = -(p_3 + p_2)c_{20} + (p_3 + p_1)c_{21} + (p_1 + p_0)c_{20}. \tag{4.6}$$

Inspection of equation (4.6) shows that it can be written wholly in terms of the probability of being in state 1 on attributes 1 and 2 independently. If we denote the probability of being in state 1 on attribute j as π_j, equation (4.6) becomes

$$\frac{d\pi_2}{dt} = -\pi_2 c_{20} + \pi_1 b_{21} + (1 - \pi_2)b_{20}$$

$$= -\pi_2(c_{20} + b_{20}) + \pi_1 b_{21} + b_{20}. \tag{4.7}$$

A geometric representation of the change in π_2 and of the equilibrium state can be given by showing movement in π_2 in the π_1, π_2 plane, and by showing the equilibrium line for attribute 2 by setting $d\pi_2/dt = 0$ in equation (4.7). This gives, for π_2 at equilibrium (π_{2e})

$$\pi_{2e} = \frac{b_{20} + \pi_1 b_{21}}{b_{20} + c_{20}}.$$ (4.8)

Figure 4.2 shows the direction of movement and the equilibrium line.

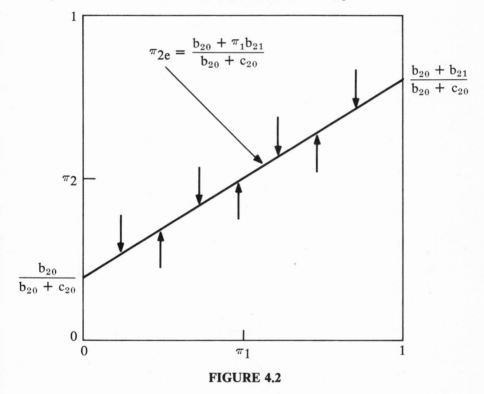

FIGURE 4.2

The equilibrium line in figure 4.2 is a straight line and it intersects the lines $\pi_1 = 0$ and $\pi_1 = 1$ somewhere between $\pi_2 = 0$ and $\pi_2 = 1$, as shown. This must be the case, since by assumption all transition rates are nonnegative, which means that b_{20}, $c_{20} \geq 0$, and $b_{20} + b_{21} > 0$, and $c_{20} - b_{21} \geq 0$ [see equation (4.3)]. If the effect of attribute 1, b_{21}, is positive, the equilibrium line is shown as in figure 4.2; if it is negative, the equilibrium line has a negative slope. That the arrows expressing movement are in fact toward the equilibrium line rather than away from it can be confirmed by examining the value of $d\pi_2/dt$ above and below the equilibrium line; this is the direction of change in π_2 when π_2 is greater than its equilibrium value $[(b_{20} + \pi_1 b_{21})/(b_{20} + c_{20})]$ and when it is less.

A similar analysis, beginning with the first and third line of equations (4.4), can be carried out for attribute 1 as a dependent variable. This gives equation (4.9) as the equation for change in π_1, analogous to equation (4.7), and equation (4.10) for the equilibrium value, analogous to equation (4.8):

$$\frac{d\pi_1}{dt} = -\pi_1(c_{10} + b_{10}) + \pi_2 b_{12} + b_{10}, \qquad (4.9)$$

$$\pi_{1e} = \frac{b_{10} + b_{12}\pi_2}{b_{10} + c_{10}}. \qquad (4.10)$$

The equilibrium line for attribute 1, together with changes as expressed by equation (4.9), is shown in figure 4.3, assuming a positive effect, b_{12}, of attribute 2 on attribute 1.

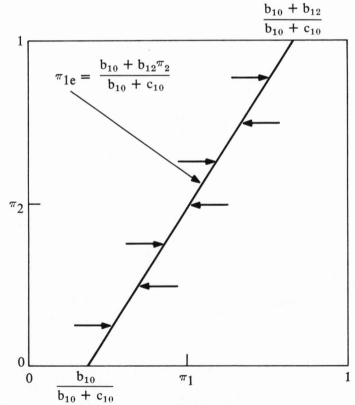

FIGURE 4.3

As in the case of attribute 2 as dependent, the intercepts at $\pi_2 = 0$ and $\pi_2 = 1$ are between 0 and 1, and the lines of movement are toward the equilibrium line, making it a stable equilibrium.

Change in each of the two attributes has been considered separately, but equations (4.7) and (4.9) are simultaneous. We may then consider what happens for the interdependent system, in which attribute 1 affects 2 and attribute 2 affects 1. One of the two possible configurations can be seen by superimposing the equilibrium line of figure 4.3 on that of figure 4.2 and noting the directions of change in the two variables in each of the four sectors thus formed. The result is shown in figure 4.4.

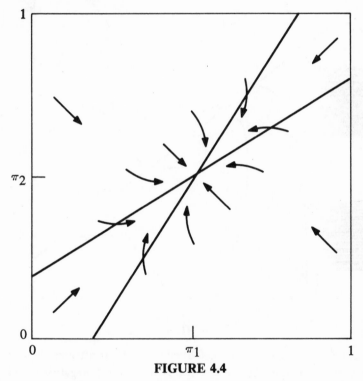

FIGURE 4.4

Figure 4.4 shows the two equilibrium lines for the attributes separately, and the equilibrium point toward which all the lines of movement are directed. This point represents the simultaneous solution of equations (4.8) and (4.10), which give, as the point of equilibrium of the system

$$\pi_1 = \frac{b_{10}(b_{20} + c_{20}) + b_{12}b_{20}}{(b_{20} + c_{20})(b_{10} + c_{10}) - b_{12}b_{21}} \tag{4.11}$$

$$\pi_2 = \frac{b_{20}(b_{10} + c_{10}) + b_{21}b_{10}}{(b_{20} + c_{20})(b_{10} + c_{10}) - b_{12}b_{21}} . \tag{4.12}$$

115

That π_1 and π_2 are both between 0 and 1 can be verified by examination of equations (4.11) and (4.12) together with reference to the fact that all q_{ij}'s are nonnegative, and to the decomposition given in equations (4.2) and (4.3).

There is, however, another possible configuration besides that of figure 4.4. If one of the attributes affects the other positively and the other effect is negative (so that b_{12} and b_{21} are of opposite signs), then in place of figure 4.4 we have figure 4.5.

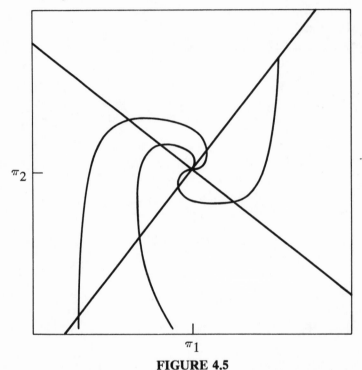

π_2

π_1

FIGURE 4.5

Figure 4.5 shows the case in which attribute 2 affects attribute 1 positively (that is, $b_{12} > 0$), but attribute 1 affects attribute 2 negatively (that is, $b_{21} < 0$). A configuration similar to figure 4.5, but with π_2 and π_1 exchanged, would result if $b_{12} < 0$ and $b_{21} > 0$. If both effects were negative, the system would be the mirror image of figure 4.4.

This qualitative analysis of a system with two interdependent attributes, linear decomposition of transition rates, and effects in the two directions equal and opposite gives a sense of the way these systems behave.

However, without the assumption that $c_{jk} = -b_{jk}$ ($k \geq 1$) for the two attributes, or with the exponential linear decomposition, the simplicity of this

116

structure would not have occurred. In both these cases $d\pi_2/dt$ and $d\pi_1/dt$ depend not only on π_1 and π_2, the proportions in state 1 on each of the attributes separately, but on an additional piece of information, for example, the proportion in state 1 in *both* attributes, denoted p_3 earlier. For the linear decomposition when $c_{jk} \neq -b_{jk}$, equation (4.7) changes to become

$$\frac{d\pi_2}{dt} = -\pi_2(b_{20} + c_{20}) + \pi_1 b_{21} + b_{21} - p_3(b_{21} + c_{21}). \qquad (4.13)$$

In this equation, there is an extra term, $-p_3(b_{21} + c_{21})$, which is zero only when $c_{21} = -b_{21}$. The equilibrium equation for π_2 alone becomes, in place of equation (4.8):

$$\pi_{2e} = \frac{b_{20} + c_{21}\pi_1 - p_3(b_{21} + c_{21})}{b_{20} + c_{20}}. \qquad (4.14)$$

If p_3 is a constant fraction k of π_1, then π_{2e} remains linearly related to π_1. Equation (4.14) becomes

$$\pi_{2e} = \frac{b_{20}}{b_{20} + c_{20}} + \frac{[b_{21} - k(b_{21} + c_{21})]\pi_1}{b_{20} + c_{20}} \qquad (4.15)$$

and a graph of π_{2e} as a function of π_1 would look like that of figure 4.2 for a particular value of k. The problem would arise in attempting to show simultaneously the effect of 1 on 2 and 2 on 1, for p_3 is not a constant fraction of π_2 (that is, of $p_3 + p_2$), as equations (4.4) indicate.

For the exponential decomposition, the analogue to equation (4.7) becomes

$$\frac{d\pi_2}{dt} = -\pi_2(e^{b_{20}} + e^{c_{20}}) + \pi_1[e^{b_{20}}(e^{b_{21}} - 1)]$$
$$+ e^{b_{20}} - p_3[e^{c_{20}}(e^{c_{21}} - 1) + e^{b_{20}}(e^{b_{21}} - 1)]. \qquad (4.16)$$

Again, this equation contains a term dependent on p_3, a term that does not vanish if $c_{20} = -b_{20}$. This term vanishes only if the effects b_{21} and c_{21} are zero. This case is even more intractible than the preceding one. It appears most sensible for the exponential decomposition to retain the full set of four equations (4.4).

In neither of these two cases, then, can the simple qualitative analysis of the system be carried as far as in the case where $c_{jk} = -b_{jk}$ (for $k \geq 1$).

To carry out quantitative analysis necessary to estimate parameters, as in the other processes discussed in these chapters, however, is not simple in any of these cases, because the system is no longer a two-state stochastic process.

What I will do in the succeeding sections of this chapter is to outline several analytical approaches. First, in what immediately follows, I apply the model of chapter 3, sections 5 and 6, with a single endogenous attribute and exogenous attributes which change linearly over time. This gives a first approximation to the system of interdependence. In section 1.0 is an approach which attempts to creep up on the interdependence by successive applications of the previous model, but after each, adjusting the value of the "independent" variable to eliminate the dependent variable's indirect effect on itself. The results of this approach are shown using the current example, and an improvement upon the approach which assumes no interdependence is shown. Yet the results remain only an approximation to the true values. In section 2.0 an extension of this approach is outlined, incorporating the simultaneity into the equations themselves. For a system of m endogenous attributes, this means beginning with m equations of the form of equation (3.23) from the preceding chapter, and modifying the equations to incorporate simultaneity, in somewhat the same way that is done in two-stage least squares. This too, however, requires some approximations, which produce unknown amounts of deviation from the true values, depending on the particular data.

Next, in sections 3.0 and 4.0 are two exact solutions for special cases. In section 3.0, the system is limited to two attributes, and the linear model. In section 4.0, the restriction to two attributes is removed, though the linear restriction remains. That solution, however, has an additional defect: it requires data that are grouped into transition matrices. Therefore, it does not have the flexibility of solutions which allow, in principle, each individual to have different values on independent variables.

Finally, in section 5, an exact solution for the general case is given. This eliminates all the approximations, restrictions, and defects of the preceding approaches, allowing solution of systems of m attributes with additional exogenous variables, with both the linear and exponential models. It is this solution for which a computer program (LONGIT·SIMUL) is appended, and results for two examples are given.

Although the sections of the chapter up to section 5 are partially blind alleys, they allow greater insight into the problem of systems of interdependence than would an immediate move to section 5. Thus the strategy of the chapter will be to chip away at the problem of interdependence before addressing it in its full complexity.

Now to turn to the problem itself. There is not a serious problem of estimation if the data are grouped into a transition matrix with sizeable numbers of individuals in each cell. In Coleman (1964a) I carried out an estimation of the q_{ij}'s using an iterative method based on equation (1.19), and then derived the measures of effect from the estimates of q_{ij}. This method, however, had the defect that it had unknown statistical properties. Cohen and Singer (1979) have developed a maximum likelihood method for estimation from grouped data like that of table 4.1.

For illustrative purposes, the results from Coleman (1964) are reproduced here, on a diagram like that of figure 4.1, where membership in the leading crowd is attribute 2, and attitude is attribute 1.[2]

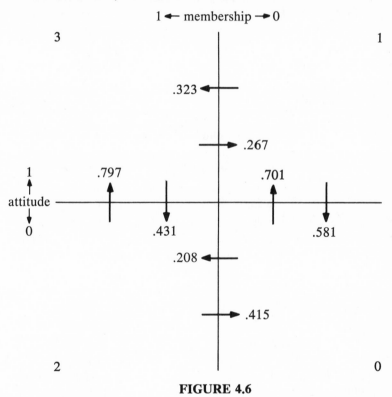

FIGURE 4.6

Referring to figure 4.1 and to the decomposition equations (4.2) and (4.3), the b's are shown in table 4.2, for the linear model with b_{jk} independent of c_{jk}.

[2] Cohen and Singer (1979) present an iterative maximum likelihood estimation method for the q_{ij}'s, which gives for these data approximately the same results as those of figure 4.6. This method is examined in more detail later in the chapter.

TABLE 4.2

Measures of Effect in an Interdependent System Calculated from Estimated Transition Rates Using Linear Decomposition

Changes in Attitude	Changes in Membership
$b_{10} = .701$	$b_{20} = .208$
$c_{10} = .581$	$c_{20} = .415$
$b_{12} = .096$	$b_{21} = .115$
$c_{12} = -.150$	$c_{21} = -.148$

The results indicate that each attribute has some effect on the other, though the effect of attitude on membership is greater than the effect of membership on attitude, both in absolute sizes of the b's and in their sizes relative to unexplained changes in the two attributes. The assumption that $c_{jk} = -b_{jk}$ is not exactly met for these data: The estimates of the preserving effects of membership and attitude (b_{12} and b_{21}) are slightly greater than the generating effects (c_{12} and c_{21}).

The approach illustrated by these results can be extended directly to three, four, or more interdependent attributes. Its principal defect, however, is that it requires grouped data, and as the number of attributes increases, the cell sizes ordinarily become too small for analysis. In addition, the approach does not allow controlling for other variables and attributes, as have all the other methods introduced thus far. The reason, of course, is that it does not make use of data at the individual level, so that each individual may be characterized by that individual's values on independent variables. The approach does have one virtue: It can be used equally well with either the exponential or linear decomposition and with or without the restriction that effects in the two directions be equal and opposite in sign.

An approximation of a model of interdependence between two or more attributes can be achieved by using the model of the preceding chapter for nonconstant independent variables. For example, using equation (3.22) or (3.26), with $p(0)$, $x_k(0)$, and $x_k(t)$ each being 0 or 1 allows estimation, for each of the two attributes, of b_{jo}, c_{jo}, and the effect of the other. However, the derivation of those models is dependent on the assumption that $x_k(\tau)$, the independent variable, changes linearly with time (or changes at the midpoint of time) and is thus independent of the value of the attribute currently treated as dependent. If the effect of the dependent attribute on the one(s) being taken in the equation as independent is small, the bias introduced will be small; but if the effect is large, the bias will be large. To illustrate use of this approach, despite the fact that it is only an approximation, the data of table 4.1 are analyzed by use of equation (3.26) with the

LONGIT·PANEL program. This of course does not exhibit the full power of the approach because grouped data are used. This estimation procedure allows the use of data in which each individual may have values for exogenous variables which differ from those of all others.

Using the LONGIT·PANEL program, with unconstrained effects and the assumption of a constant probability of change between the initial and final values of the independent attribute when the other is taken as dependent, gives the parameter estimates shown in table 4.3.

TABLE 4.3

Estimated Measures of Effect Assuming Exogenous Change in Independent Attributes, Using Model in Chapter 3, Section 6

Changes in Attitude	Changes in Membership
$b_{10} = .674$	$b_{20} = .203$
$c_{10} = .620$	$c_{20} = .432$
$b_{12} = .193$	$b_{21} = .140$
$c_{12} = -.199$	$c_{21} = -.176$

These estimates may be compared with those presented earlier, in which the full four-state model was used for analysis. The estimates are similar, but differ somewhat. The comparison, however, is not conclusive since the estimates presented earlier are not maximum likelihood estimates and in particular ignore numbers of cases in each of the initial-state patterns. A more conclusive comparison will be made below.

The estimates for each dependent attribute, with the other treated as a nonconstant independent variable, are based on the assumption that the attribute does not affect the other. Thus, if the true values of b_{12} and c_{12} were both 0, the model would be correctly specified, and the estimates of b_{21} and c_{21} (as well as b_{12} and c_{12} and b_{j0}, c_{j0}) would be the same as maximum likelihood estimates of a correctly specified model. It is the existence of nonzero values of b_{jk} and c_{jk} for variable j that violates the assumptions on which the estimates of b_{kj} and c_{kj} are based.

To see the impact of this violation in the present case, it is useful to carry out a better comparison than the one just suggested. What was done is this: The q_{ij}'s presented in figure 4.6 were used to generate a set of hypothetical data, similar, but not identical, to those of table 4.1. Then those hypothetical data were used as input to the LONGIT·PANEL program and estimates were obtained. The original transition rates as taken from figure 4.6, partitioned into c_{jk} and b_{jk}, are shown together with the estimates obtained by the program (using the linear model).

121

TABLE 4.4

*Comparison of True Values of Parameters in
Interdependent System with Those Estimated from
Model in Chapter 3*

	Changes in Attitude			Changes in Membership	
	true	estimated		true	estimated
b_{10}	.701	.651	b_{20}	.208	.198
c_{10}	.581	.585	c_{20}	.415	.421
b_{12}	.096	.212	b_{21}	.115	.136
c_{12}	−.150	−.159	c_{21}	−.148	−.163

These estimates are in some cases reasonably close, but in others they are quite distant from the true values. Of particular interest is the estimate of .212 for a value of .096. The true effects b_{21} and c_{21} are considerably larger relative to the random shocks (constant terms) b_{20} and c_{20} than are the true effects b_{12} and c_{12} relative to b_{10} and c_{10}. This means that b_{21} and c_{21} will be estimated better than will b_{12} and c_{12}, because the assumptions on which the estimates are made are less violently violated in estimating b_{21} and c_{21}.

Although the model with linear change in independent variables gives an approximation to the results for an interdependent system under certain circumstances, it is not entirely satisfactory. In fact, it is increasingly unsatisfactory as the system is more tightly interdependent. Consequently it is useful to attempt to model the full interdependence.

The preceding analysis gives a starting point and a basis for the full analysis of interdependence with individual-level data. In the preceding analysis the models with nonconstant independent variables were used to approximate an interdependent system, although in an interdependent system, the assumption on which these models is based is violated. In other words, in those models it is assumed when analyzing a dependent attribute that the independent attributes and variables have moved from $x_k(0)$ to $x_k(t)$ linearly with time (or with constant probability of change), independent of the value of the dependent attribute. If x_k is an attribute, taking on values of 0 or 1, this is equivalent to the assumption that x_k, given that it has changed between times 0 and t, had an equal probability of changing at each point in time.

In fact, what we have instead is x_k changing as a function of the dependent attribute itself. In the case of m dependent attributes we have m equations of the form of equation (3.23), for $j = 1, \ldots, m$ for the m attributes. (A leading subscript j is used with q_1 or q_0 to denote the dependent attribute j.)

$$p_j(t) = e^{-\int_0^t (_jq_0(\tau) + _jq_1(\tau))d\tau} \left[p_j(0) + \int_0^t e^{\int_0^\tau (_jq_0(\theta) + _jq_1(\theta))d\theta} \, _jq_1(\tau)d\tau \right] \quad (4.17)$$

(It is assumed for the present that the process is for a single individual; the subscript for that individual is suppressed.)

In the equations of the form of equation (4.17), $_jq_1(t)$ and $_jq_0(t)$ are, although constant for given values of the independent variables, $x_k(t)$, indirectly functions of time through their dependence on $x_k(t)$. In the preceding chapter they have already been freed from the assumption of constancy. As was evident in the preceding section, this can come close to the correct solution.

To consider the problem more fundamentally than before, we may return to the original system of differential equations, equation (1.2). With m endogenous attributes, each having two states, the full state space of the stochastic process consists of 2^m states. Equation (1.2) can be integrated when the exogenous attributes are constant, and the integral takes the form of equation (1.15). That is, a system of equations describing the full-state space of 2^m states of the form of equation (1.2) models correctly the interdependence among endogenous attributes. Even though the values of q_{ij} change for each dependent attribute, they change only as a function of the individual's state on other attributes, which is explicitly included in the model. On the other hand, if there are changes in exogenous variables, equation (1.15) cannot be used to mirror the process, since it assumes constant q_{ij} among the 2^m states.

A different approach is not to model the full-state space of 2^m states in order to estimate parameters with 2^m equations, but to try to consider the state of each attribute separately, to give m equations like that of equation (4.17). The problem with this, of course, is that the equation is only partially integrated, and the explicit integration of the remaining parts seems difficult indeed, since $q_0(\tau)$ and $q_1(\tau)$ depend upon the individual's state on other attributes that are themselves changing endogenously. The gains, if this obstacle can be overcome, are considerable. Since only m equations are to be estimated for m endogenous variables, the system is much smaller and more manageable for a given number of endogenous variables. The data requirements are far less for a system of m equations than for a system of 2^m. We are not interested in estimating the $2^m(2^m - 1)$ q_{ij}'s (for which examination of the full state-space is intrinsically necessary), but only in estimating the parameters c_{jk} and b_{jk}. If there are only the m endogenous variables, this means $2m^2$ parameters for the models with unrestricted parameters, and $m^2 + m$ parameters for the models with the restriction that $c_{jk} = -b_{jk}$ for $k \neq 0$. For each additional exogenous variable, another $2m$ or m parameters are introduced into the system.

The economy of the smaller system is very great, even when the number of endogenous variables is small. For example, in a system with three endogenous attributes, modeling the full state-space involves estimating 56 transition rates, while the number of c_{jk} and b_{jk} desired from such a system is only 6 for each endogenous attribute, or 18 altogether for the unrestricted model, and 12 for the restricted model. With additional exogenous attributes having two states each, the difference becomes even greater. With two such attributes, there are $2^2(56)$, or 224, transition rates to be estimated in the model of the full state-space (since a different set of transition rates must be estimated for each combination of values of the exogenous attributes), while the number of parameters in the unrestricted model is only 12 more, or 30 altogether. Thus it is clear that use of the model involving the full state-space would quickly exhaust even very large data sets.

The abundance of transition rates relative to the number of parameters in the linear or exponential model arises from two sources. As is evident from the earlier discussion, there are certain transitions assumed zero because they imply change on two or more attributes simultaneously. For example, in figure 4.1, the transition rates q_{12}, q_{21}, q_{03}, and q_{30} are all identically 0. The other source is the assumption of linearity (or linearity in exponents) in the composition of the transition rates. For example, with three endogenous attributes, there is a total of $2^3(2^3 - 1) = 56$ transition rates. But of these, only $3 \cdot 2^3 = 24$ (in general, $m2^m$) are nonzero through the assumption of nonsimultaneous change. But the number of parameters employed in the linear or exponential decomposition of these transition rates is only $2 \cdot 3^2 = 18$ (in general, $2 \cdot m^2$) for the unrestricted model or $3^2 + 3 = 12$ (in general, $m^2 + m$) for the restricted model. The use of interaction terms in the equations through which q is decomposed can bring the 18 or 12 up to 24, that is, in general up to $m \cdot 2^m$, but only to that point.

The excess of transition rates over c_{jk}'s and b_{jk}'s introduces another problem if the full state-space model is to be used as a way of estimating the c_{jk}'s and b_{jk}'s. After the transition rates are estimated, there remains a second problem of data reduction, that is, to go from the q's to the c's and b's.

These considerations make the use of equation (4.17) or some other approach that estimates directly the c's and b's in the interdependent system very desirable.

124

1. PURGING ENDOGENOUS EFFECTS

I will first outline an approach that improves upon the estimates obtained by use of equations (3.22) or (3.26) but does not fully capture interdependence. I will describe this first approach by giving a heuristic description of what is to be done. If we use the models for nonconstant independent variables in chapter 3, sections 3.4, 3.5, or 3.6, to calculate the predicted value $p_1^*(t)$ or $z_1(t)$ for an individual, this value includes within it the effect of $x_2(\tau)$. If we recalculate the predicted value *without* b_{12} and c_{12}, that is, without the effects of $x_2(\tau)$, we get a different calculated value, say $p_1^{**}(t)$. The difference between these, $p_1^*(t) - p_1^{**}(t)$, is an estimate of the contribution that $x_2(\tau)$ has made to $z_1(t)$. What we then do is *purge* $z_1(t)$ of the effect of $x_2(\tau)$ by subtracting out this estimated contribution (which of course may be positive or negative). We then have $z_1^*(t)$, which is $z_1(t) - [p_1^*(t) - p_1^{**}(t)]$, a purged value of $z_1(t)$ to use in the estimation of the effects of x_1 on x_2. A similar procedure is used for the estimation of the effects of x_2 on x_1. We now have for each individual $z_1(0)$, $z_2(0)$, and the two purged values, $z_1^*(t)$ and $z_2^*(t)$. The latter are then used, exactly as the original observations were used in the first estimation, to estimate new values of the coefficient vectors, $\mathbf{b}_1$, $\mathbf{c}_1$, $\mathbf{b}_2$, and $\mathbf{c}_2$.

But these new coefficients mean that the predicted values $p_j^*(t)$ and $p_j^{**}(t)$ (for $j = 1$, 2) will change, giving a different estimate of the contribution of $x_2(\tau)$ on $z_1(t)$ and $x_1(\tau)$ on $z_2(t)$. This different estimate means purging $z_1(t)$ and $z_2(t)$ again, to get new estimates of the coefficient vectors. This leads to an iterative process, which continues until values of the coefficient vectors change in succeeding iterations by less than a small predetermined value. At each iteration, the purge starts from $z_1(t)$.

What is done in this procedure is to take an interdependent system and, by purging the second-wave values of estimated effects of the other variable, create a system in which each attribute is primarily a function of exogenous variables.

It is useful to look at the purging more formally, to examine the assumptions it entails. What is done is to make use of equation (3.22) or equation (3.26) for nonconstant independent variables, and for all endogenous attributes k that affect attribute j, to remove from $x_k(t)$ an effect that results from attribute j. Using equation (3.26) for $p_k(t)$, in which we assume that all variables affecting it change linearly, we calculate two values of $p_k(t)$: $p_k(t)$ with and $p_k^*(t)$ without the effect of $x_j(0)$ and $x_j(t)$. Applying equation (3.26):

$$p_k(t) - p_k^*(t) = b_{kj}[x_j(0)a_3^{(k)} + x_j(t)a_4^{(k)}],$$

125

where $a_3^{(k)}$ and $a_4^{(k)}$ refer to the first and second quantities in braces in equation (3.26), and the superscript indicates that k is the dependent variable. See section 3.9 of chapter 6 for definitions. This is the quantity that is subtracted from $x_k(t)$ in the calculation of $p_j(t)$. The equation that is used in the estimation is that following this sentence, where b_{kj}, $a_3^{(k)}$, and $a_4^{(k)}$ are taken from the solution of the preceding iteration on attribute k, and $q_1^{(j)}(\tau)$ omits the effects of all endogenous attributes k on j.

$$p_j(t) = a_1^{(j)} x_j(0) + a_3^{(j)} q_1^{(j)}(0) + a_4^{(j)} \left[q_1^{(j)}(t) + \sum_k b_{jk}\{ x_k(t) \right.$$
$$\left. - b_{kj}[a_3^{(k)} x_j(0) + a_4^{(k)} x_j(t)]\} \right]$$

The form of the maximum likelihood estimating procedure remains the same as in the model in chapter 3, because this equation is just like that of equation (3.26). The quantity in brackets is merely a fixed value [which we would call $x_k(t)*$], a purged value of $x_k(t)$.

The approach described here seems a reasonable approach, but it is important to note that it is ad hoc and without theoretical justification. As a result, it is not surprising to find that this strategy does not fully extract the interdependence so that the equations in chapter 3 will, when used iteratively in the way described above, give the correct parameters for the interdependent system. In table 4.5, estimates are presented (from the linear model) that were obtained after this procedure converged, compared to the true values and those obtained by only a single use of the equations with nonconstant independent variables. The first two columns for each dependent attribute are taken from table 4.4.

TABLE 4.5

Comparison of True Values of Parameters in Interdependent System with Purging of Independent Variables

	estimated					estimated			
	(a) true	(b) linear change	(c) purge	(a − c)		(a) true	(b) linear change	(c) purge	(a − c)
b_{10}	.701	.651	.698	.003	b_{20}	.208	.198	.213	.005
c_{10}	.581	.585	.568	.013	c_{20}	.415	.421	.398	.017
b_{12}	.096	.212	.100	−.004	b_{21}	.115	.136	.104	.009
c_{12}	−.150	−.159	−.142	−.008	c_{21}	−.148	−.163	−.131	−.017
Average difference from true		.045	.007				.013	.013	

Overall, the purge does improve the estimates, although all of the improvement is in one of the dependent attributes. The principal improvement is in the two estimates with grossly incorrect values, b_{10} and b_{12}. For those, the deviations are reduced from .050 and .116 to .003 and .004, respectively. For the other parameters, the size of the deviations is not much different, although the estimates themselves are different.

The end result of this experiment is that the purging of one attribute's effect on a second when estimating the effect of the second on the first may come closer to the true values for an interdependent system than the simple assumption of linear change in each independent variable; but the values to which the estimates converge are not the correct values, and we do not know the direction or amount of the bias.

2. INTRODUCING SIMULTANEITY INTO THE EQUATIONS

In the preceding section, equations that assume exogenous change for the endogenous variables were used to obtain initial estimates; then, using these estimates, the observations at time t were purged of the indirect effects of the attribute on itself through other attributes. New estimates were obtained, and the whole procedure was repeated until convergence was reached.

A somewhat more fundamental approach is to introduce simultaneity into the basic equations (4.17) for $p_j(t)$ and to integrate those equations with the least damaging approximations. That is the approach of this section.

Returning to equation (4.17), let us consider the case of linear decomposition with $c_{jk} = -b_{jk}$ for all $k > 1$. In that case $q_1^{(j)}(\tau) + q_0^{(j)}(\tau) = q_1^{(j)} + q_0^{(j)} = a_0^{(j)}$, constant over time and individuals. To simplify exposition, let us consider only two endogenous attributes, denoted by j and k, and for each a (different) exogenous, nonconstant variable, denoted by 3 and 4. Then equation (4.17) becomes, for attribute j:

$$p_j(t) = e^{-a_0^{(j)}t} p_j(0) + e^{-a_0^{(j)}t} \int_0^t e^{a_0^{(j)}\tau} [q_1^{(j)}(\tau) + b_{jk}p_k(\tau)]d\tau \qquad (4.18)$$

where $q_1^{(j)}(\tau)$ is that part of $q_1^j(\tau)$ that omits the endogenous variables. In this case, $q_1^{(j)}(\tau) = b_{j0} + b_{j3}x_3(\tau)$.

Now $x_3(\tau)$ is assumed to vary linearly between times 0 and t, so that $x_3(\tau) = x_3(0) + [x_3(t) - x_3(0)]\tau/t$, and can be integrated out in equation (4.18). This gives us

$$p_j(t) = e^{-a_0^{(j)}t} p_j(0) + q_1^j\!\cdot(0)a_3^{(j)} + q_1^{(j)}(t)a_4^{(j)} + \int_0^t e^{a_0^{(j)}(\tau - t)} b_{jk}p_k(\tau)d\tau \quad (4.19)$$

where $a_3^{(j)}$ and $a_4^{(j)}$ are a_3 and a_4 as defined in section 3.9 of chapter 6.

Since a similar equation can be written for $p_k(\tau)$, that equation may be substituted into equation (4.19) to give

$$p_j(t) = e^{-a_0^{(j)}t} p_j(0) + q_1^{(j)}(0)a_3^{(j)} + q_1^{(j)}(t)a_4^{(j)} + \int_0^t e^{a_0^{(j)}(\tau - t)} b_{jk}[e^{-a_0^{(k)}} p_k(0)$$

$$+ q_{1*}^{(k)}(0)a_3^{(k)} + q_{1*}^{(k)}(\tau)a_4^{(k)} + \int_0^\tau e^{a_0^{(k)}(\theta - \tau)} b_{kj}p_j(\theta)d\theta]d\tau \quad (4.20)$$

where $q_{1*}^{(k)}(0)$ and $q_{1*}^{(k)}(\tau)$ are $q_1^{(k)}(0)$ and $q_1^{(k)}(t)$ with effects of $p_j(0)$ and $p_j(t)$ omitted. In this case, $q_{1*}^{(k)} = q_1^{(k)}$, but in general they are different: $q_1^{(k)}$ omits effects of all endogenous attributes, while $q_{1*}^{(k)}$ omits only the effect of the attribute on the left side of the equation, in this case j.

The quantities under only the first integral can be integrated out. Furthermore, if we use the approximation that $p_j(\theta)$ varies linearly with time between 0 and θ, then $p_j(\theta) = p_j(0) + [p_j(t) - p_j(0)]\theta/t$. This may be substituted in equation (4.20) and the whole thing integrated. Solving for $p_j(t)$ gives

$$p_j(t) = [q_1^{(j)}(0)a_3^{(j)} + q_1^{(j)}(t)a_4^{(j)} + p_j(0)\{a_1^{(j)} + b_{jk}b_{kj}(a_{22}^{(jk)} - a_{23}^{(jk)}/t)\}$$
$$+ b_{jk}\{x_k(0)a_{21}^{(jk)} + q_{1*}^{(k)}(0)a_{22}^{(jk)} + \Delta q_{1*}^{(k)}(t)a_{23}^{(jk)}/t\}]/(1$$
$$- b_{jk}b_{kj}a_{23}^{(jk)}/t) \qquad (4.21)$$

where $a_1^{(j)} = e^{-a_0^{(j)}t}$,

$$a_{21}^{(jk)} = \frac{e^{-a_0^{(k)}t} - e^{-a_0^{(j)}t}}{a_0^{(j)} - a_0^{(k)}},$$

$$a_{22}^{(jk)} = \frac{a_0^{(j)}(1 - e^{-a_0^{(k)}t}) - a_0^{(k)}(1 - e^{-a_0^{(k)}t})}{a_0^{(k)}a_0^{(j)}(a_0^{(j)} - a_0^{(k)})}$$

$$= \frac{a_2^{(k)} - a_2^{(j)}}{a_0^{(j)} - a_0^{(k)}},$$

$$a_{23}^{(jk)} = \frac{a_0^{(j)2}(e^{-a_k t} - 1) - a_0^{(k)2}(e^{-a_j t} - 1) + a_0^{(j)}a_0^{(k)}(a_0^{(j)} - a_0^{(k)})t}{a_0^{(j)2}a_0^{(k)2}(a_0^{(j)} - a_0^{(k)})}$$

$$= \frac{(-a_2^{(k)}a_0^{(j)} + a_2^{(j)}a_0^{(k)}) + (a_0^{(j)} - a_0^{(k)})t}{a_0^{(j)}a_0^{(k)}(a_0^{(j)} - a_0^{(k)})}.$$

$$\Delta q_{1*}^{(k)}(t) = q_{1*}^{(k)}(t) - q_{1*}^{(k)}(0)$$

Equation (4.21) gives a basis for estimation of effects in a system of endogenous attributes with exogenous variables as well. Equation (4.21) has been derived for the case of two endogenous attributes, but inspection of the derivation will show that it is applicable as well to systems with more than two endogenous variables merely by inserting a summation over the k endogenous varia-

bles, $\sum_{k=1}^{m} (k \neq j)$, to the left of the three points at which b_{jk} appears in

equation (4.21).

This equation does involve an approximation, that is, the assumption of linear change for $p_j(\theta)$. The approximation is so deeply embedded in the equation that it would seem likely not to have a large effect.

If this solution were to be applied to the case in which $c_k \neq -b_k$, then another approximation is involved. This is the approximation in setting $a_0^{(j)}$ and $a_0^{(k)}$ constant over time (though not over individuals). This assumption can, however, be weakened without affecting equation (4.21) but only the definition of $a_0^{(j)}$ and $a_0^{(k)}$. As was evident in the case of nonconstant independent variables in chapter 3, nothing is changed but the definition of $a_0^{(j)}$ if we no longer assume the variables affecting j to be constant, but rather to be changing linearly between the values at times 0 and t. This involves an approximation for the other endogenous variables, but an approximation that is again deeply embedded in the equation and may not greatly affect the estimates.

Application of this approach to the case of exponential decomposition, however, does not seem warranted. Equation (4.21) no longer holds, and the equation that would replace it requires more extensive approximations in order to solve for $p_j(t)$.

Modifications of the LONGIT·PANEL program can be made by those who wish to pursue this direction.

The next two sections, 3 and 4, are directed to solutions of the special cases of linear decomposition and restricted effects of $b_k = -c_k$, first for two attributes and then for any number of attributes. They are included here because the special case they deal with is of some interest as it is structurally identical to systems of linear relations among continuous variables. Thus, for mixed systems of attributes and continuous variables, these methods can be indiscriminately applied to their solution.

3. THE EXACT SOLUTION FOR TWO ATTRIBUTES WITH $c_k = -b_k$ FOR BOTH ENDOGENOUS ATTRIBUTES

The special virtues of the case in which effects of independent variables or attributes toward states 0 and 1 are linear and equal and opposite become evident here. If we now denote the probability of occupying state 1 on attribute j at time t as p_j [instead of the $\pi_j(t)$ used in equation (4.7) and (4.9)], the process can be described by two simultaneous linear differential equations, from equation (4.7) and (4.9) (and here we add exogenous attributes for a more general model):

$$\frac{dp_1}{dt} = -p_1 \sum_{\substack{j=0 \\ j \neq 1,2}}^{n} x_j(b_{1j} + c_{1j}) + \sum_{\substack{j=0 \\ j \neq 1,2}}^{n} b_{1j}x_j + b_{12}p_2, \qquad (4.22)$$

$$\frac{dp_2}{dt} = -p_2 \sum_{\substack{j=0 \\ j \neq 1,2}}^{n} x_j(b_{2j} + c_{2j}) + \sum_{\substack{j=0 \\ j \neq 1,2}}^{n} b_{2j}x_j + b_{21}p_1. \qquad (4.23)$$

These equations may be solved, but they require another equation if we are to end up with an equation in p_1 devoid of p_2 and any derivatives of p_2. Such an equation is provided by differentiating equation (4.22) again with respect to time:

$$\frac{d^2p_1}{dt^2} = \frac{-dp_1}{dt} \sum_{\substack{j=0 \\ j \neq 1,2}}^{n} x_j(b_{1j} + c_{1j}) + b_{12}\frac{dp_2}{dt}. \qquad (4.24)$$

Now dp_2/dt can be eliminated from equations (4.23) and (4.24):

$$\frac{d^2p_1}{dt^2} = \frac{-dp_1}{dt}\Sigma x_1(b_{1j} + c_{1j}) + b_{12}[-p_2\Sigma x_j(b_{2j} + c_{2j}) + \Sigma b_{2j}x_j + b_{21}p_1]. \quad (4.25)$$

Similarly, eliminate p_2 from equations (4.22) and (4.25) and collect terms:

$$\frac{d^2p_1}{dt^2} + \frac{dp_1}{dt}[\Sigma x_j(b_{1j} + c_{1j} + b_{2j} + c_{2j})] + p_1[\Sigma x_j(b_{1j} + c_{1j})\Sigma x_k(b_{2j} + c_{2k})$$
$$-b_{12}b_{21}] - \Sigma b_{1j}x_j\Sigma x_k(b_{2k} + c_{2k}) - b_{12}\Sigma b_{2k}x_k = 0. \quad (4.26)$$

Equation (4.26) is a second-order linear differential equation of the form

$$\frac{d^2x}{dy^2} + A\frac{dx}{dy} + Bx + C = 0,$$

and the general solution of this equation is

$$p_1(t) = k_1 e^{s_1 t} + k_2 e^{s_2 t} - \frac{C}{B} \quad (4.27)$$

where k_1 and k_2 are constants of integration, and

$$s_1, s_2 = \frac{-A \pm \sqrt{A^2 - 4B}}{2}.$$

First, to simplify notation, define $a_{hj} = b_{hj} + c_{hj}$. Then,

$$s_1, s_2 = \frac{x_j(a_{1j} + a_{2j}) \pm \sqrt{x_j(a_{1j} - a_{2j})^2}}{2}. \quad (4.28)$$

The constant k_1 may be evaluated by setting $t = 0$ in equation (4.27):

$$p_1(0) = k_1 + k_2 - \frac{C}{B}, \quad \text{or} \quad k_1 = p_1(0) - k_2 + \frac{C}{B}. \quad (4.29)$$

Substituting from equation (4.29) into equation (4.27):

$$p_1(t) = p_1(0)e^{s_1 t} + k_2(e^{s_2 t} - e^{s_1 t}) - \frac{C}{B}(1 - e^{s_1 t}). \quad (4.30)$$

131

To evaluate k_2, it is necessary to take the time derivative of equation (4.30) and set the result equal to the right-hand side of equation (4.22), with both evaluated at time (0):

$$\frac{dp_1}{dt}\bigg|_{t=0} = p_1(0)s_1 + k_2(s_2 - s_1) + \frac{C}{B}s_1$$

$$= -p_1(0)\Sigma a_{1j}x_{1j} + \Sigma b_{1j}x_j + b_{12}p_2(0). \quad (4.31)$$

Solving equation (4.31) for k_2 and substituting it back into equation (4.26) gives

$$p_1(t) = p_1(0)\frac{(s_1 e^{s_2 t} - s_2 e^{s_1 t})}{s_1 - s_2} + p_{1e}\frac{[s_1 - s_2 - (s_1 e^{s_2 t} - s_2 e^{s_1 t})]}{s_1 - s_2}$$

$$+ [p_1(0)\Sigma a_{1j}x_j - \Sigma b_{1j}x_j - b_{12}p_2(0)]\left[\frac{e^{s_1 t} - e^{s_2 t}}{s_1 - s_2}\right]. \quad (4.32)$$

The end result is equation (4.32) with s_1 and s_2 as given by equation (4.28). The quantity p_{1e} is from equation (4.26):

$$p_{1e} = \frac{\Sigma b_{1j}x_j\Sigma a_{2k}x_k + b_{12}\Sigma b_{2k}x_k}{\sum_j a_{1j}x_j \sum_k a_{2k}x_k - b_{12}b_{21}}. \quad (4.33)$$

This, as given earlier in equation (4.11), is the equilibrium value of $p_1(t)$, a result that can also be found by evaluating equation (4.32) at $t \to \infty$.

With the value of $p_1(t)$ as given in equation (4.30), and an analogous value for $p_2(t)$, then in principle it is possible to estimate b_{1j}, c_{1j}, b_{12}, and b_{2j}, c_{2j}, b_{21} so long as there is sufficient data. If there is a two-wave panel with no exogenous variables, with individuals identified according to state at time 0, then there are four initial values of $p_1(0)$, $p_2(0)$, (that is, 0,0; 0,1; 1,0; 1,1), and for each initial value there are two outcomes, $z_1(t)$ and $z_2(t)$. This means that there are eight degrees of freedom and six parameters to estimate, giving a sufficient number of degrees of freedom to estimate the parameters.

If there are exogenous variables as well, then there are two more parameters for each exogenous variable, and eight more degrees of freedom for each two-valued exogenous variable. This increases the excess degrees of freedom.

Obtaining first and second derivatives of $p_i(t)$ with respect to each parameter is extremely tedious. This is carried out in chapter 6.

If there are more than two endogenous attributes (or variables) creating a system of m simultaneous linear differential equations, then the solution is much more complicated than in the two-variable case. A three-attribute system requires solution of a third-order linear differential equation, and an m-attribute system requires solution of an m-order linear differential equation. Furthermore, in order to obtain these differential equations for solution, it is necessary first to eliminate $m(m-1)$ variables from the m-order differential equation ($p_h, \dfrac{dp_h}{dt}, \ldots, d^{m-1}p_h/d^{m-1} t = d^{m-1}t$ for all $m-1$ endogenous attributes h other than the one in question). It is simpler for $m > 2$ to turn to the general solution for a system of linear differential equations.

4. THE EXACT SOLUTION FOR AN m-ATTRIBUTE CASE WHERE $c_k = -b_k$ FOR ALL ENDOGENOUS ATTRIBUTES

With more than two equations of the form of equations (4.22) and (4.23), the method just described is infeasible, despite the restriction to linear decomposition and identical effects in opposite directions $(c_k = -b_k)$. In that case, one may turn to the general solution for a system of m linear differential equations, although, as will be evident, this method has shortcomings also.[3] The solution has a form similar to that of the general solution for the m-state Markov process, given in equation (1.15). If the system of differential equations expressed in matrix form is

$$\frac{dP}{dt} = \mathbf{G}P + \mathbf{s},$$

then the solution is, from any text on systems of linear differential equations,

$$\mathbf{P}(t) = e^{\mathbf{G}t}\mathbf{P}(0) + (e^{\mathbf{G}t} - \mathbf{I})\mathbf{G}^{-1}\mathbf{s}. \tag{4.34}$$

Here, unlike earlier examples, the vector $\mathbf{P}(t)$ is not a vector of state probabilities. $\mathbf{P}(t)$ instead is the vector of probabilities of occupancy of state 1 on each of the m attributes, like p_1 and p_2 in equations (4.22) and (4.23). Thus,

---

[3] Hummon, Doreian, and Teuter (1975) present a method based on taking logarithms of eigenvalues, such as that described in this section, not for a system of relationships among m attributes, but for a system of relationships among m continuous variables. Singer and Spilerman (1976a) use the same approach for estimating transition rates in the 2^m-state Markov process, beginning not with equation (4.34), but with equation (1.15).

for m attributes there are only m equations rather than 2^m. The vector $P(t)$ does not have the constraint that the sum of $p_j(t)$ over all endogenous attributes j must equal 1.0. Similarly, the matrix G does not have the form of a matrix of transition rates. Rather, the form is as follows.

G is an $m \times m$ matrix with elements g_{ij}, where [as a generalization of equations (4.22) and (4.23)]:

$$g_{ii} = -\Sigma (b_{ik} + c_{ik})x_k$$
$$g_{ij} = b_{ij}$$

(where k ranges over the set of exogenous variables, $k = 0, m + 1, \ldots, n$)
$i, j = 1, \ldots, m \quad (i \neq j)$

The vector s consists of terms

$$s_j = \Sigma b_{jk}x_k \qquad k = 0, m + 1, \ldots, n$$

where x_k is the value on exogenous variable k.

The notation e^{Gt} stands for the infinite series $I + Gt + (Gt)^2/2! + (Gt)^3/3! + \ldots$.

The parameters b_{ij} and c_{ij} may be estimated by use of either of two approaches. First, maximum likelihood methods may be applied directly to $P(t)$. The method proceeds as follows: First, equation (4.34) can be written

$$P(t) = RP(0) + s^* \tag{4.35}$$

where

$$R = e^{Gt}, \quad \text{and} \quad s^* = (R - I)G^{-1}s \tag{4.36}$$

With panel data, each individual is characterized by a vector $z(0)$ of length m, consisting of zeros and ones, with a one for each attribute in which he is in state 1 at time 0. He is also characterized by a vector $z(t)$, which has a one for each attribute in which he is in state 1 at time t. Then the element $p_j(t)$ from $p(t)$, the probability that the individual will be in state j at time t, is[4]

$$p_j(t) = \sum_k r_{jk}(t)z_k(0) + s_j^*$$

[4] Note that $r_{jk}(t)$ is not a transition probability in a markov process. It is the probability that the individual, positive on attribute j at time 0, will be positive on attribute k at time t. Thus $r_{jk}(t)$ has more nearly the character of an association between attribute j at time 0 and attribute k at time t.

The likelihood of observing the individual's response is

$$\mathcal{L} = \prod_{j=1}^{m} p_j(t)^{z_j(t)}, \text{ or} \tag{4.37}$$

$$\mathcal{L} = \prod_{j=1}^{m} \left(\sum_k r_{jk}(t) p_k(0) + s_j^* \right)^{z_j(t)} \tag{4.38}$$

The likelihood of observing the full set of responses at time t in the sample (given the initial responses at time 0) is given by the product of either of these individual likelihoods over all individuals.

The likelihoods may be maximized by methods such as those of section 5, as described in section 4.5 of chapter 6. The methods described in that section are directed to the general process rather than the restricted one of the present section and are therefore applied to the full transition matrix of size 2^m by 2^m, rather than the m by m matrix under consideration here. Thus, while the general approach of those methods may be used, the specific method must be modified. The modifications are discussed in chapter 6, section 4.4.

The second approach makes use of the fact that a function of a square matrix can be expressed as the eigenvectors of the matrix times that function of its eigenvalues. That is, if for the matrix $\mathbf{R}$, we have

$$\mathbf{R} = \mathbf{H}\Lambda\mathbf{H}^{-1}, \tag{4.39}$$

where Λ is a diagonal matrix of eigenvalues, and the columns of $\mathbf{H}$ are eigenvectors, then

$$f(\mathbf{R}) = \mathbf{H}f(\Lambda)\mathbf{H}^{-1}.$$

Starting with equation (4.35), estimation is carried out in two steps. First, from known values of $\mathbf{P}(0)$ and $\mathbf{P}(t)$, $\mathbf{R}$ and $\mathbf{s}^*$ are estimated. Then, finding the eigenvalues of $\mathbf{R}$ and using equation (4.36), it is possible to find $\mathbf{G}t$. Knowing t allows finding $\mathbf{G}$, and then equation (4.39) may be used, given knowledge of $\mathbf{s}^*$, $\mathbf{R}$, and $\mathbf{G}$, to find $\mathbf{s}$.

Empirical data are ordinarily of two forms. First, panel data at the individual level gives 2^m combinations of values on attributes $1, \ldots, m$. For example, when $m = 2$, we have four vectors of values of $\mathbf{P}(0)$: 0,0; 0,1; 1,0; 1,1. In this case we would have, for estimating the first row of $\mathbf{R}$, and s_1^*:

Value of P(0):

$$
\begin{array}{ll}
1 \quad 1 & p_1(t) = r_{11} + r_{12} + s_1^* \\
1 \quad 0 & p_1(t) = r_{11} + \phantom{r_{12} +} s_1^* \\
0 \quad 1 & p_1(t) = \phantom{r_{11} +} r_{12} + s_1^* \\
0 \quad 0 & p_1(t) = \phantom{r_{11} + r_{12} +} s_1^*
\end{array}
\qquad (4.40)
$$

Row i of **R**, together with **s***, is estimated by a weighted least-squares regression of $p_i(t)$ on **P**(0). Carrying out m such regressions gives **R** and **s***. For example, using data from table 4.1, the values of $p_1(t)$ and weights for the equations shown in equation (4.40), which would allow estimation of r_{11}, r_{12}, and s_1^*, are:

Values of **P**(0)	Values of $p_1(t)$	Weight
1 1	$(458 + 110)/751$	751
1 0	$(171 + 56)/496$	496
0 1	$(184 + 531)/1071$	1071
0 0	$(85 + 338)/1074$	1074

A similar set of values of $p_2(t)$ would allow estimation of r_{21}, r_{22}, and s_2^*. These become the starting points for the second step, which proceeds by estimating the eigenvalues of **R**.

If data are not at the individual level, so that $p_i(0)$ may lie anywhere between 0 and 1, then the procedure is unchanged. The only difference is that the least-squares regression is not based on the orthogonal structure given by equation (4.40).

Once **R** is estimated, then the eigenvalues and eigenvectors of **R** are found, logarithms of the eigenvalues are taken, and log **R** is found by

$$
\log \mathbf{R} = \mathbf{H} \log (\Lambda)\mathbf{H}^{-1} \qquad (4.41)
$$

We have $\log \mathbf{R} = e^{\mathbf{G}t}$ so that finding the eigenvalues and eigenvectors of **R**, taking the logarithm of the eigenvalues, and multiplying by eigenvectors as in equation (4.41) gives the matrix **G**t.

Having found the matrix **G**t, then dividing through by t gives **G**, which allows equation (4.39) to be used to obtain **s**. From equation (4.39):

$$
\mathbf{s} = \mathbf{G}(\mathbf{R} - \mathbf{I})^{-1}\mathbf{s}^*
$$

However, there are several problems outlined in Singer and Spilerman (1976a), that I will only refer to here. First, this assumes distinct eigenvalues. This does not always occur, but identical eigenvalues are unusual in empirical panel data. Second, it assumes that no eigenvalues are complex numbers.

The logarithm is a multivalued function. If λ is a real number, then log $\lambda = a + 2i\lambda k$, where $k = 0, \pm 1, \pm 2, \ldots$. It is necessary, then, to take the value of log λ when $k = 0$, which is the only value of log λ that is real. So long as all the eigenvalues λ_i are real and distinct, this ordinarily poses no problem. If they are not, the data are not compatible with a continuous-time Markov process, and these methods cannot be used. The practical problem is failure of compatibility of the data with a continuous-time Markov process due to sampling variations when data are sparse. Thus it may well be that data have been generated by a continuous-time Markov process but fail to give real and distinct eigenvalues.

This approach has some additional defects. First, it does not give maximum likelihood estimates of the **b** and **c** vectors directly. It gives estimates of another set of quantities, and the estimates of the **b** and **c** vectors are obtained from those quantities through a set of transformations. This does not, in general, give the same estimates of **b** and **c** as direct maximum likelihood estimates of those quantities.

Another defect of the method is that because it requires grouping of data, it requires extensive additional data if effects of exogenous attributes are to be examined. Separate calculation of eigenvalues is necessary for each empirical matrix representing distinct profiles of values on exogenous variables. For estimates to be stable, there must be a large enough sample of persons with a given profile of values on exogenous variables so that the observed matrix **R** is not greatly affected by sampling fluctuations. In practice, extensive grouping of data is necessary.

5. THE EXACT SOLUTION IN THE GENERAL CASE

As it turns out, some of the virtues of a method that would treat each endogenous attribute separately (achieving the necessary interdependence through iteration) are preserved by an exact method that is quite general. This method makes use of the general solution for a system of simultaneous equations. It also exploits the fact that in the 2^m by 2^m **Q** matrix arising from m interdependent attributes, there are not 2^m by $2^m - 1$ independent parameters, as would be the case in a general **Q** matrix, but instead is a number equal only to the total number of independent parameters in the model. If endogenous attribute j has n_j endogenous and exogenous variables affecting it, and the effects are free to differ in the two directions, there are $2n_1 + 2 + 2n_2 + 2 + \cdots + 2n_m + 2$ parameters. Thus, for example, if there are no exogenous attributes in a system of three endogenous attributes (all affecting each other), there are not $2^3 \cdot (2^2 - 1) = 56$ q_{ij}'s to estimate, but only eighteen parameters.

The general method of estimation uses the following strategy: From panel data with m endogenous attributes, we have an empirical vector for individual i whose origin was in state j, $\mathbf{z}_{ij}(t)$, with an element $z_{ijk}(t)$ (equal to 0 or 1) for each of the 2^m destination states k.[5] One element, say $z_{ijk}(t)$, is 1, the others are 0, representing the fact that individual i, whose origin was state j, ended in state k at time t. Since we have $\mathbf{P}(t) = \mathbf{P}(0)e^{\mathbf{Q}t}$, or $\mathbf{P}(t) = \mathbf{P}(0)\mathbf{R}(t)$, this $z_{ijk}(t)$ corresponds to an element $r_{ijk}(t)$ from the matrix $e^{\mathbf{Q}t}$. The likelihood of having obtained the sample as observed is the product of the N $r_{ijk}(t)$ over all i, where there is only the origin j and destination k for which $z_{ijk}(t) = 1$, appear in the product. Or, formally,

$$\mathcal{L} = \prod_{i=1}^{N} \prod_{j=1}^{2^m} \prod_{k=1}^{2^m} r_{ijk}(t)^{z_{ijk}(t)} \tag{4.42}$$

The estimation problem becomes one of finding the values of $\mathbf{b}$ and $\mathbf{c}$ that maximize $\mathcal{L}$. The procedures for such estimation involve finding first and second derivatives of $r_{ijk}(t)$ (which is an element from the infinite series matrix $e^{\mathbf{Q}t}$). That procedure is described in chapter 6.

The first and second derivatives for this method are presented in chapter 6; the appendix to this chapter contains the computer program LONGIT·SIMUL for estimating parameters, together with notes outlining the use of the program. In the examples below, the use of the method is illustrated.

6. INTERACTION TERMS IN INTERDEPENDENT SYSTEMS

Interaction terms were introduced in chapter 2 for cross-sectional data. Their introduction was particularly simple, for nothing more was required

---

[5] Note that in contrast to the preceding section, z for individual i is a 2^m by 2^m matrix with one 1 and the remaining cells 0, and $\mathbf{R}$ for individual i is the 2^m by 2^m transition matrix for i.

for the interaction between attributes i and j than to introduce a new independent attribute equal to $x_i x_j + (1 - x_i)(1 - x_j)$, and nothing more was required for the interaction between continuous variables i and j than to introduce a new independent variable equal to $x_i x_j$. That is, interaction terms are introduced exactly as in linear regression or other linear models.

For panel data with single dependent attributes, the same procedure may be used. In the case of independent variables which change over time, the interaction terms are defined at time 1 and time 2 via their constituent variables, and then these are treated as time 1 and time 2 observations just as for the original independent attributes.

But the matter is less simple for systems of endogenous attributes. A new attribute representing interaction between two endogenous attributes in their effect on a third, or between an endogenous and exogenous attribute in their effect on another endogenous attribute, cannot be introduced as an exogenous attribute, for it is not. And if it is introduced as an endogenous attribute, its change is logically derivative from the change in either of the attributes in terms of which it is defined.

What is necessary is to conceive of a new variable or attribute whose effect depends not on the presence or absence of one endogenous attribute, but upon the *joint* presence or absence of two (or more) endogenous attributes, or if the interaction is between an endogenous attribute and an exogenous variable, depends on the values of both.

Implementation of this is not carried out, as in the case of the models of chapters 2 and 3, by introducing a new independent attribute into the dataset, but rather by a modification of the computer program, together with information in the control cards which tells the attributes whose interaction is to be examined, and the attribute which is to be the dependent attribute for that effect.

In the appended LONGIT·SIMUL program, the appropriate modifications have been made, and with the dimension statements as given in the program, up to five such interaction terms can be included for all dependent attributes taken together. Instructions for preparation of control cards are given in the appendix to the chapter.

7. EXAMPLES

7.1. EXAMPLE

College Plans and Membership in the Leading Crowd: In the "purging" technique described in section 1 of this chapter, a strategy for testing how close the purge comes to capturing full interdependence was devised. This consisted of first estimating transition rates by an old (Coleman, 1964a, p. 171) method with the reverse-diagonal rates constrained to equal zero, then calculating transition proportions (i.e., hypothetical data) from these rates, and using the purge technique with these hypothetical data to determine how close the parameter estimates (and thus the transition rates) came to the correct rates which contain this interdependence. Because the number of parameters in the unrestricted model (8) equals the number of rates, full success of the purge would have given rates identical to those which generated the proportions. As table 4.5 shows, the purge moved the estimates closer to the true values, but did not give the true values.

With the exact method described in this section, the estimated parameters of course reproduce the true values of the parameters shown in table 4.5, the goal of the earlier approaches. Both algorithm 1, involving only the first derivative, and algorithm 2, involving both first and second derivatives (see chapter 6, section 5), give the exact result; algorithm 2, however, takes more processing time to reach convergence (though with the same number of iteration cycles).

The real data, of course, from table 4.1, having twelve degrees of freedom (taking the responses at the first wave as given), do not fit perfectly when they are used as input for estimating the eight parameters of the unrestricted model. In table 4.6 are shown the parameter estimates, with the linear decomposition and the exponential decomposition. The parameter estimates show nothing substantively new; but unlike earlier estimates, they are maximum likelihood estimates for the parameters of the interdependent system.

For many purposes a restricted model, with only one parameter for the effect of each attribute on each other attribute, is desirable. This of course eliminates the distinction between the effect of an attribute on movement to state 1 of another attribute, and its effect on movement to state 0. But in the present circumstance, table 4.6a shows that the estimates of effects in the two directions are sufficiently similar for both attributes relative to their standard errors, that it is reasonable to regard the effect as alike in the two directions, and to estimate the single parameter in the restricted

TABLE 4.6

Maximum Likelihood Estimates of Effects in the
Interdependent System of College Plans and
Membership in the Leading Crowd: Linear and
Exponential Decompositions

	a. Unrestricted Model			
	Linear		Exponential	
	estimate	s.e.	estimate	s.e.
b_{10}	.696	(.047)	−.362	(.067)
b_{12}	.109	(.095)	.145	(.124)
c_{10}	.596	(.045)	−.517	(.075)
c_{12}	−.153	(.068)	−.297	(.134)
b_{20}	.212	(.023)	−1.551	(.110)
b_{21}	.120	(.040)	.447	(.155)
c_{20}	.417	(.045)	−.874	(.108)
c_{21}	−.153	(.060)	−.457	(.173)
Steps to convergence	6		6	

	b. Restricted Model			
	Linear		Exponential	
	estimate	s.e.	estimate	s.e.
b_{10}	.687	(.037)	−.389	(.055)
b_{12}	.136	(.038)	.217	(.060)
c_{10}	.588	(.036)	.548	(.059)
b_{20}	.207	(.019)	−1.555	(.084)
b_{21}	.131	(.029)	.454	(.106)
c_{20}	.403	(.028)	−.876	(.083)
Steps to convergence	5		4	

model. Table 4.6b shows the estimates for this model, which has six parameters rather than eight. The estimates of effect are, as anticipated, between the two estimates which they replace, though not a simple average. The residual or unexplained effects in the two directions for the two attributes also differ slightly from those in the unrestricted model. It is useful to note that the standard errors for the measures of effect of the two attributes on each other are lower than the standard errors for the measures of effect in the unrestricted model. This is because the effective amount of data on which estimates of each of the restricted parameters are based is approximately double that on which estimates of each of the unrestricted parameters are based.

For both models and both attributes, the effects shown in the restricted model (b_{12} and b_{21}) are 3 to 4 times their standard errors, allowing the inference that membership in the leading crowd positively affects attitudes toward it, and attitudes toward the leading crowd positively affect membership in it. We can compare the sizes of the effects in column 1 of part a of the table with those shown in table 4.3 using the LONGIT·PANEL program (which treats each attribute as exogenous when taking the other as dependent). The comparison shows, as we would expect, that the estimates which ignore simultaneity are overestimates of the true effect of each attribute on the other, ranging from about a 14 percent overestimate to about an 80 percent overestimate.

The degree to which each of these models fits the observed data can be shown by comparing the original data used to estimate the parameters with the regenerated data, and calculating a χ^2 for each of the fits (see table 4.7). For the unrestricted model, there are four degrees of freedom (12–8),

TABLE 4.7

College Plans and Membership in the Leading Crowd: Original Data and Regenerated Data by Unrestricted and Restricted Models, Linear and Exponential Decomposition

	time t			
time 0	**state 11**	**state 10**	**state 01**	**state 00**
state 11				
original data	458	140	110	49
unrestricted	445.8	141.8	106.7	56.6
restricted linear	442.2	143.5	108.7	56.6
restricted exponential	441.7	145.4	106.9	57.1
state 10				
original data	171	182	56	87
unrestricted	171.3	187.1	50.3	87.2
restricted linear	173.6	187.3	50.1	84.9
restricted exponential	175.0	183.9	50.4	86.7
state 01				
original data	184	75	531	281
unrestricted	186.8	59.5	539.0	285.5
restricted linear	188.9	59.8	538.8	283.5
restricted exponential	187.0	60.0	542.9	281.1
state 00				
original data	85	97	338	554
unrestricted	96.0	98.8	332.4	546.8
restricted linear	96.1	97.1	330.3	550.4
restricted exponential	96.1	98.2	328.5	551.2

Tests of fit:	unrestricted	$8.02 = \chi^2_4$
	restricted linear	$8.23 = \chi^2_6$
	restricted exponential	$8.42 = \chi^2_6$

and for the restricted model, six degrees of freedom (12–6). For the unrestricted model, the models estimate eight transition rates (with the reverse-diagonal rates fixed at zero), and there are eight parameters, so that the linear and exponential models estimate identical transition rates and regenerate identical data. Thus there are three predictions, one from the unrestricted model and one each from the linear and exponential restricted models.

The values of χ^2 show that the deviations of the unrestricted model are somewhat worse than chance; deviations as large as those observed would occur by chance about 9 percent of the time. χ^2 for the two restricted models shows that deviations as large as those observed would occur by chance about 22 percent of the time. Thus the models fit reasonably well.

7.2. EXAMPLE

Cohen and Singer's Malaria Infection Data: Cohen and Singer (1979), in a study of interdependence of different types of malaria infection, wanted to examine whether these two types of infection inhibited each other, facilitated each other, or were independent. To study these questions, they used data from several measurements on the same population at different points in time. They analyzed the data with models like the restricted linear and exponential models discussed here, but with a different estimation procedure, based on taking the logarithm of e^{Qt}. That procedure has two principal difficulties, however, as discussed earlier in section 4: It does not begin with individual-level data, but with transition matrices, and thus cannot freely estimate the effects of exogenous variables which differ from individual to individual; and the logarithm of a matrix is a many-valued function, creating mathematical difficulties. The first of these two difficulties prevented extensive introduction of independent variables, because of the necessity for maintaining cell sizes at some reasonable level. Thus the only variable introduced was age, with seven age groups.[6] They calculated separate transition matrices for each of the seven groups for each pair of adjacent observations, and analyzed each of the transition matrices separately. In their published paper, data for only one population subgroup and one pair of observations are reported. These data are given in table 4.8, together with their maximum likelihood estimates of the logarithm of e^{Qt}, and estimates calculated with the LONGIT · SIMUL program, based on the infinite series which defines e^{Qt}.

[6] The necessity for having reasonable cell sizes also prevented simultaneous analysis of the three types of malarial infection that was measured. Cohen and Singer's analysis covers only two species of infection, which I will call p.m. and p.f., following their abbreviations.

TABLE 4.8

Data for Interdependence of Two Types of Malaria Infection, and Estimates of Parameters Obtained by Cohen and Singer, and Obtained by the LONGIT·SIMUL Program

	11	10	01	00
11				
observed	4	20	2	16
Cohen-Singer linear	2.7	21.2	1.6	16.4
LONGIT·SIMUL linear	2.8	20.6	2.2	16.5
Cohen-Singer exponential	2.1	20.8	1.0	18.1
LONGIT·SIMUL exponential	3.7	19.3	2.2	16.8
10				
observed	13	103	3	77
Cohen-Singer linear	9.9	105.8	4.3	76.0
LONGIT·SIMUL linear	8.9	107.7	4.5	75.0
Cohen-Singer exponential	10.0	109.1	3.9	73.0
LONGIT·SIMUL exponential	8.8	108.1	4.1	75.0
01				
observed	0	9	2	21
Cohen-Singer linear	1.0	9.1	1.6	20.4
LONGIT·SIMUL linear	0.9	8.5	2.2	20.4
Cohen-Singer exponential	0.7	9.1	0.8	21.4
LONGIT·SIMUL exponential	1.0	8.9	1.5	20.6
00				
observed	7	171	14	340
Cohen-Singer linear	12.7	164.6	13.0	341.7
LONGIT·SIMUL linear	11.0	166.0	12.8	342.2
Cohen-Singer exponential	12.3	160.4	12.2	347.0
LONGIT·SIMUL exponential	10.8	166.1	13.0	342.1

These data appear to show a reasonably good fit to the table. Calculation of χ^2 for the four estimations gives the results shown below. (The degrees of freedom are $12 - 6 = 6$):

$$\text{Cohen-Singer linear} \qquad 6.17 = \chi_6^2$$
$$\text{LONGIT·SIMUL linear} \qquad 4.47 = \chi_6^2$$
$$\text{Cohen-Singer exponential} \qquad 10.84 = \chi_6^2$$
$$\text{LONGIT·SIMUL exponential} \qquad 5.39 = \chi_6^2$$

Thus all models seem to fit reasonably well (though of course the sample size is small, making a large value of χ^2 less likely, and some of the cell sizes are rather small for use of χ^2). The linear model appears to fit slightly better than the exponential one by both estimation methods; and the estimation using the infinite series which defines e^{Qt} (that is, the LONGIT·SIMUL estimation) gives a closer fit than does the Cohen-Singer estimation.

The estimates of the parameters are shown in table 4.9, for the linear model and for the exponential model with the two estimation procedures. The standard errors of the LONGIT estimates, which are calculated along with the parameter estimates, are shown as well.

TABLE 4.9

Parameter Estimates for Linear Model and Exponential Model of Interdependence of Two Malaria Infections

	Linear			Exponential		
	Cohen/Singer	LONGIT·SIMUL		Cohen/Singer	LONGIT·SIMUL	
P.f. as dependent	estimate	estimate	s.e.	estimate	estimate	s.e.
b_{10}	.110	.090	(.038)	−1.570	−2.131	(.342)
b_{12}	.218	.179	(.091)	.704	.596	(.241)
c_{10}	3.304	2.839	(.656)	1.975	1.270	(.224)
P.m. as dependent						
b_{20}	.613	.610	(.061)	−.548	−.501	(.102)
b_{21}	−.179	−.301	(.346)	−.854	−.389	(.351)
c_{20}	.734	.713	(.104)	−.468	−.345	(.129)

The estimates of the model's parameters show greater differences than do the cell frequencies they generate shown earlier. The qualitative inferences that one would draw are similar: that infection by p.m. facilitates infection by p.f., and that the point estimate of p.f.'s effect on p.m. is that it inhibits infection by p.m. This reflects a system of interdependence like that shown in figure 4.5, rather than the more common system of figure 4.4. However, the standard errors generated by the LONGIT method show that the estimated facilitating effect of p.m. on p.f. is about two standard errors, a result that would have happened by chance only about five times out of a hundred if the true effect is zero, while the inhibiting effect of p.f. on p.m. is only one standard error in size, a result that would have occurred 30 times in a hundred if the true effect is zero. Thus it is reasonable to say that one can have some confidence that there is a facilitating effect of p.f. on p.m., but not much confidence about the other effect. (This of course is a result only from this one subgroup; Cohen and Singer present results for seven age groups and for various pairs of time points, with the general result that there appear to be facilitating effects of both infections on one another.)

Another difference between these estimation methods as applied to these data can be seen as well: the LONGIT parameters appear in general (with two exceptions) to be somewhat smaller than the Cohen-Singer parameters.

Whether this is a characteristic difference or is peculiar to these data is, of course, an open question.

Another comparison of the results of these approaches can be obtained by comparing the transition rates themselves. The Cohen-Singer method directly estimates these rates, while in the LONGIT method, it is the parameters of table 4.9 which are directly estimated, and from which the transition rates are constructed. The transition rates are shown in table 4.10.

TABLE 4.10

Estimated Transition Rates for Malaria Infection Data with Two Models and Two Estimation Methods

Estimates of transition rates from Cohen and Singer (upper is from linear model, lower is from exponential model)

	11	10	01	00
11		3.086	.914	
		3.561	1.469	
10	.328			.734
	.420			.626
01	.434			3.304
	.246			7.205
00		.613	.110	
		.578	.208	

Estimates of transition rates from LONGIT·SIMUL (upper is from linear model, lower is from exponential)

	11	10	01	00
11		2.660	1.014	
		1.962	1.045	
10	.269			.713
	.216			.709
01	.308			2.839
	.411			3.561
00		.610	.090	
		.606	.119	

One point is evident from the comparisons in table 4.10: The linear and exponential models give rates that are much closer together with the LONGIT estimation than with the Cohen-Singer estimation. The sum of the absolute differences between rates for the two models is 5.156 for the Cohen-Singer estimation, and only 1.920 for the LONGIT estimation.

146

This example has shown both the applicability of the LONGIT estimation method for simultaneous equations for the matrix infinite series, and some of its merits as compared to the Cohen-Singer method. The principal virtue, however, is that it does not require a transition matrix (and thus aggregated data) at all, but can be used when each individual has different values of independent variables. In this way it follows directly the approach of chapters 2 and 3.

It may, however, be that the LONGIT method has other defects unobserved here. It did show difficulties of convergence with these data; for the linear model, it converged only after approximate values of the parameters (for comparison with the estimated values in column 2 of table 4.9, those were: .085, .227, 3.088, .617, −.612, .679). Convergence was after seven steps when these approximate starting values were used, and for the exponential mode, after thirteen steps when arbitrary starting values were used. In practice, of course, approximate starting values can be obtained by use of the LON-GIT·PANEL program for each endogenous attribute with the others taken as exogenous.

It should be pointed out that the examples used here are much more restricted than those allowed by the model and calculable by the LONGIT·SI-MUL program, in three ways. First, they include only two endogenous attributes, while in principle any number may be included. The dimensions of the attached program allow five, but more can be introduced by modifying the dimension statements. Second, no exogenous attributes or variables have been included. The LONGIT·SIMUL program allows for a maximum of eighteen different exogenous attributes. Again, dimension statements may be changed to increase this, if the machine capacity allows it. Third, the examples have not shown interaction terms among the variables or attributes affecting endogenous attributes. The appended program allows five such terms for all the endogenous attributes together.

8. STATISTICAL TESTS FOR AN INTERDEPENDENT SYSTEM

In chapter 2, statistical tests for models with single dependent attributes were discussed, and they are incorporated in the LONGIT·CROSS and LONGIT·PANEL programs. The same tests with modifications can be used for systems of interdependent variables.

The value of R^2 as described in chapter 2, section 10, is a measure of the overall explanatory power of the independent variables. It would be possible to calculate a value of R^2 for the system of attributes as a whole, for there is a predicted proportion in each state of the system for each combination of values of exogenous variables and endogenous attributes. This predicted proportion could be compared to the observed proportion, as described for R^2 in chapter 2. But what is more useful in an interdependent system is something different: a set of values of R_i^2, one for each endogenous attribute i. The value of R_i^2 is the explanatory power of the independent variables in accounting for the values of the dependent attribute i.

The calculation of a χ^2 goodness of fit statistic is done in this case by calculating expected numbers of cases in each cell, given the time 1 distribution, and comparing them to the observed cell frequencies, using the Pearson goodness of fit statistic in chapter 2, equation (2.33). The number of degrees of freedom is the number of independent cell values minus the number of parameters.

The LONGIT·SIMUL computer program appended to the chapter calculates R_i^2 for each of the dependent attributes. It does not calculate the χ^2 goodness of fit test.

APPENDIX: USE OF LONGIT·SIMUL PROGRAM

This program is designed to use panel data, with observations or individuals at two points in time, to estimate parameters of effect among a set of two or more endogenous (dichotomous) attributes, and the effects of exogenous attributes or continuous variables upon each of the endogenous attributes.

It is assumed that for each individual, data exist at two points in time for each of the endogenous attributes, so that he can be classified in either state 0 or 1 on each attribute at each time. Dimension statements in the program allow up to five endogenous attributes. He is also characterized, either at one time point or at both, by values of up to eighteen exogenous attributes or variables. (While the maximum number of attributes and variables is five endogenous and eighteen exogenous, the maximum number of total parameters estimated in the model is eighty. This means that in the unrestricted model, there is a maximum of thirty-nine total independent variables considering all endogenous attributes together. With the restricted model, there is a maximum of seventy-nine. The maximum number of individuals with differing values of the variables is 1,000.

If there is more than one individual with the same values on all endogenous attributes at both times and on all independent variables (as is true, for example, for grouped data that are cross-classified into a tabulation), then all those with the same values can be read in a single record, with the number of individuals represented by that record being the "weight" for that record. This will reduce running time of the program. Also, running time will be reduced if records which have identical exogenous attributes or variables are adjacent in the input file. This means that the series convergence need be carried out only once for records with the same values of exogenous attributes.

Control Cards

To be read from Unit 2, assumed to be read from cards or card-image records with blocksize 4560.

Card 1: The number of different data sets or problems to be analyzed on this run. This number appears with the units position in column 5. There is no limit to the number of problems per run.

Cards 2–5: are repeated for each problem or data set. If data are read from cards on same unit as control cards (as assumed in the program as written), Card 1 prefaces entire run, Cards 2–5 preface each data-set.

Card 2: *Position 2:* The number of endogenous attributes (min = 2, max 5).

Position 5: The number of exogenous attributes and variables (min 0, max 18).

Position 10 (units): The number of records to be read, where one record represents one individual for ungrouped data, or one cell for grouped or cross-tabulated data (min 16, max 1,000).[7]

Position 15: 0 if only linear model
1 if only exponential model
2 if first linear, followed by exponential

Position 20: 1 if only constrained model $(c_k = -b_k)$
2 if only unconstrained model $(c_k$ independent of $b_k)$
3 if both

---

[7] Dimensions can be larger than given in the program. Dimensions should be as large as necessary for the problem at hand, and no larger than machine capacity.

Position 25: Number of variables that are observed at both points in time. If only the endogenous attributes are observed twice, the same number as in position 2 goes here. If all variables are observed twice, this is the number in position 2 plus the number in position 5 (min 2, max 23).

Position 28 (decimal point appears in position 28): The length of time between waves, in whatever time units desired.

Position 35: 0 if no interactions involving effects of endogenous attributes, 1 if one or more such interactions (max 5).

Position 40: 1 if algorithm involving first derivative only is desired, 2 if algorithm involving both first and second.

Card 3: *Positions 3, 6, 9, . . .* (units position): There are as many numbers in this card as there are variables measured at both waves. Each number represents the variable number of one of these twice-measured variables. The "variable number" means the location of the variable in the file of input data, beginning with endogenous attributes and continuing through exogenous. The number of numbers on this card is equal to the number in position 25 of Card 2.

Card 4: The number of independent variables for each endogenous attribute, including both other endogenous attributes and exogenous attributes or variables in positions 5, 10, 15, ... (min = 1, max 22). There is one number on this card for each endogenous attribute.

Card 5-1, 5-2, . . . : One card for each endogenous attribute. The card contains, in positions 5, 10, . . . , the variable numbers of the attributes or variables which affect that endogenous attribute. The number of numbers on each card is equal to the corresponding number on Card 4.

Card 6: (This card exists only if there are one or more interaction effects, i.e., if position 35 in Card 2 is not zero.) The number of interactions involving effects of at least one endogenous attribute as independent, for each endogenous attribute as dependent, in positions 5, 10, . . . (min 1, max 5; maximum of sum of these numbers is 5). Position 5 is for first endogenous attribute, as dependent, position 10 for second, and so on.

Card 7-1, 7-2, . . . : One card for each endogenous attribute which has at least one interaction effect as dependent, as shown in Card 6. In positions 5 and 10 are the two variable

150

numbers (in ascending order) of the two attributes or variables (at least one of which is endogenous) from which the first interaction term is composed. If there is a second, the numbers are in positions 15 and 20; and so on.

Card 8:   *Position 5:*   1 if input data are to be printed out; 0 otherwise.

         Position 10:   1 if predicted proportions in each state at time t are to be printed; 0 otherwise.

         Position 16:   1 if multiple R^2 is to be calculated, 0 otherwise.

Card 9:   This card contains the format specifications for the data. The conventions of Fortran format statements are used. For a "standard" format, reading from cards or card image records, the decimal point for each of the variables described under "Input Data" below is in position 5, 10, . . . , 70. If there are more than 14 total variables for each individual, two cards per individual are used. For this standard format, Card 5 should read (14F5.0) in positions 3–10.

Input Data

To be read from Unit 2, assumed to be read from cards or card-image records with blocksize 4560.

1. Data are read individual by individual, in the following order:

    a. Values of the endogenous attributes at the first wave, each having the value 0 or 1;

    b. Values of each of the exogenous attributes or variables at the first wave;

    c. Value of the endogenous attributes at the second wave (each 0 or 1);

    d. Values of any exogenous attributes or variables that are different at the second time than at the first; the number of such variables may range from zero to the total number of exogenous attributes or variables;

    e. The weight of the individual. For a self-weighting sample, the weight is one. For a non-self-weighting sample, the weight is the sampling weight associated with the individual. If the record represents all individuals in a cell of a tabulation, the weight is the number of individuals in the cell if the sample is self-weighting, or the sum of the weights for individuals in the cell if it is not.

2. Data format is specified by the user on control card 9.

Alternate Options

By modifying the Read statement in the program, variables can be read in a different order (for reading from records in which the data can appear in a different order).

By modifying the JCL statements, data may be read from different units, different length records, differently blocked. JCL must in any case be specific to the machine and operating system.

By replacing the statement with label 5010 ("5010 CONTINUE") with "5010 REWIND 2", the same records can be reread to extract a new set of variables for the next problem.

Example of Control Cards and Data

The control cards and data for the example in table 4.1 are presented with the program and accompanying output.

INPUT TO LONGIT.SIMUL PROGRAM

(Example of Section 7.1)

```
  1
  2    0   16    2    3    2    0    1.   1
1  2
  1    1
  2
  1
  1    1    1
(8F10.4)
```

1	1	1	1	458
1	1	1	0	110
1	1	0	1	140
1	1	0	0	49
1	0	1	1	184
1	0	1	0	531
1	0	0	1	75
1	0	0	0	281
0	1	1	1	171
0	1	1	0	56
0	1	0	1	182
0	1	0	0	87
0	0	1	1	85
0	0	1	0	338
0	0	0	1	97
0	0	0	0	554

OUTPUT FROM LONGIT.SIMUL PROGRAM

LONGIT.SIMULT PROGRAM FOR PANEL DATA WITH TWO OR MORE ENDOGENOUS VARIABLES   12/7/80
```
  2    0   16    0    2    2    0    1.00 1
```

ALL INDEPENDENT VARIABLES CONSTANT
```
  1    1
  1.0000    1.0000    1.0000    1.0000   458.0000
  1.0000    1.0000    1.0000    0.0      110.0000
  1.0000    1.0000    0.0       1.0000   140.0000
  1.0000    1.0000    0.0       0.0       49.0000
  1.0000    0.0       1.0000    1.0000   184.0000
  1.0000    0.0       1.0000    0.0      531.0000
  1.0000    0.0       0.0       1.0000    75.0000
  1.0000    0.0       0.0       0.0      281.0000
  0.0       1.0000    1.0000    1.0000   171.0000
  0.0       1.0000    1.0000    0.0       56.0000
  0.0       1.0000    0.0       1.0000   182.0000
  0.0       1.0000    0.0       0.0       87.0000
  0.0       0.0       1.0000    1.0000    85.0000
  0.0       0.0       1.0000    0.0      338.0000
  0.0       0.0       0.0       1.0000    97.0000
  0.0       0.0       0.0       0.0      554.0000
STEP  0  BM   0.200    0.0      0.100    0.300    0.0     -0.100
  0.200    0.100    0.0       0.300   -0.100    0.0
STEP  1  BM   0.360    0.0      0.161    0.438    0.0     -0.126
STEP  1  BM   0.212    0.113    0.0       0.379   -0.132    0.0
DIFR=    0.4431
STEP  2  BM   0.556    0.0      0.174    0.542    0.0     -0.137
STEP  2  BM   0.217    0.115    0.0       0.407   -0.142    0.0
DIFR=    0.3435
STEP  3  BM   0.676    0.0      0.125    0.589    0.0     -0.150
STEP  3  BM   0.213    0.121    0.0       0.414   -0.149    0.0
```

```
DIFR=      0.2312
STEP  4  BM   0.696   0.0      0.109   0.596   0.0     -0.153
STEP  4  BM   0.212   0.120    0.0     0.417  -0.153    0.0
DIFR=      0.0524
STEP  5  BM   0.696   0.0      0.109   0.596   0.0     -0.153
STEP  5  BM   0.212   0.120    0.0     0.417  -0.153    0.0
DIFR=      0.0028
STEP  6  BM   0.696   0.0      0.108   0.596   0.0     -0.153
STEP  6  BM   0.212   0.120    0.0     0.417  -0.153    0.0
DIFR=      0.0003
  ITERATION CONVERGED AFTER STEP :    6
     0.5091   0.3095   0.0920   0.0894   0.2666   0.5033   0.0556   0.1744
     0.1759   0.1015   0.3773   0.3453   0.0754   0.1421   0.1888   0.5936
     1    247.90     336.95     336.95     458.00
     2    280.38     358.35     358.35     458.00
     1    307.44     417.88     417.88     568.00
     2    433.43     553.96     467.89     598.00
     1    494.25     681.63     542.58     752.00
     2    473.17     634.63     510.23     782.00
     1    738.15    1041.51     902.46    1283.00
     2    505.25     774.07     527.48     857.00
     1    935.80    1359.18     978.86    1454.00
     2    609.41     962.29     651.05    1028.00
     1    946.98    1384.20    1003.88    1510.00
     2    733.69    1134.27     782.56    1210.00
     1   1014.20    1538.29    1037.79    1595.00
     2    781.91    1212.56     797.99    1295.00
     1   1067.99    1673.12    1172.61    1933.00
     2    796.24    1291.49     815.59    1392.00


MULTIPLE R-SQUARE FOR EACH ENDOGENOUS ATTRIBUTE
J= 1:     0.089
J= 2:     0.299


SIMULTANEOUS EQUATIONS MODEL WITH UNRESTRICTED PARAMETERS
   2 ENDOGENOUS ATTRIBUTES    0 EXOGENOUS VARIABLES
LINEAR MODEL


COVARIANCE MATRIX
      0.00220  -0.00279   0.00123  -0.00138  -0.00006   0.00011   0.00015  -0.00024
     -0.00279   0.00901  -0.00152   0.00347   0.00016  -0.00031  -0.00041   0.00067
      0.00123  -0.00152   0.00202  -0.00238   0.00010  -0.00019  -0.00008   0.00012
     -0.00138   0.00347  -0.00238   0.00460  -0.00023   0.00044   0.00018  -0.00031
     -0.00006   0.00016   0.00010  -0.00023   0.00054  -0.00076   0.00028  -0.00032
      0.00011  -0.00031  -0.00019   0.00044  -0.00076   0.00163  -0.00036   0.00055
      0.00015  -0.00041  -0.00008   0.00018   0.00028  -0.00036   0.00204  -0.00246
     -0.00024   0.00067   0.00012  -0.00031  -0.00032   0.00058  -0.00246   0.00366


    B( 1 0)=    0.6962    SE( 1 0)=    0.0469
    B( 1 2)=    0.1084    SE( 1 2)=    0.0949
    C( 1 0)=    0.5963    SE( 1 0)=    0.0450
    C( 1 2)=   -0.1531    SE( 1 2)=    0.0678


    B( 2 0)=    0.2121    SE( 2 0)=    0.0232
    B( 2 1)=    0.1196    SE( 2 1)=    0.0404
    C( 2 0)=    0.4171    SE( 2 0)=    0.0452
    C( 2 1)=   -0.1531    SE( 2 1)=    0.0600
```

154

LONGIT.SIMUL PROGRAM

```
1.      //LONGQUAL JOB (2ZB004,COL,Q,NORC),FORT,RE=1500K,
2.      // TE=YES,ID='LONGIT.SIMUL',RO=REG,Q=0,TI=1
3.      // EXEC FORTXCLG
4.      //FORT.SYSIN DD *
5.
6.
7.      C
8.      C
9.      C
10.            DIMENSION W(1000),SS(80,80),P(1000),XAT(18,1000),
11.           &R(80),B(80),BM(5,46),IORG(1000),IDES(1000),LJ(5),
12.           &L4(5,24),ITR(5,32),IDR(5,32),IRG(5,32),NIV(5),X(80),
13.           &ID(5,24,16),XAT2(24),NIP(22),FMT(18),IR(1000),XAT1(24)
14.           &,INTV(5,2,5),NINT(5),NCH(23)
15.            EQUIVALENCE (IORG(1000),IR(1000))
16.      C
17.      C      M=NUMBER OF ENDOGENOUS ATTRIBUTES (5 MAX), NIV(J)=NUMBER OF
18.      C      INDEPENDENT VARIABLES FOR ENDOGENOUS ATTRIBUTE J,
19.      C      L4(J,I) IS POSITION OF ITH INDEPENDENT VARIABLE OF J.
20.      C      NE=NUMBER OF EXOGENOUS ATTRIBUTES OR VARIABLES.
21.      C      IN ORDERED LIST OF VARIABLES, FIRST M VARIABLES IN LIST
22.      C      MUST BE ENDOGENOUS ATTRIBUTES.  N=NUMBER OF CELLS OR
23.      C      DISTINCT TYPES OF INDIVIDUALS AS READ IN ONE RECORD.
24.      C      T=TIME BETWEEN PANEL WAVES
25.      C      IE=0 FOR LINEAR, 1 FOR EXPONENTIAL, 2 FOR BOTH (LINEAR FIRST).
26.      C      NALG=1 FOR ALGORITHM USING FIRST DER. ONLY, 2 FOR ALGORITHM
27.      C      USING FIRST AND SECOND DERIVATIVES.
28.      C      NRES=1 IF RESTRICTED PARAMETERS ONLY, 2 IF UNRESTRICTED ONLY,
29.      C       3 IF RESTRICTED FIRST THEN UNRESTRICTED.
30.      C
31.      C      NSTEP=MAX STEPS IN SERIES CALCULATION OF TR. PROPORTIONS
32.      C      INT=0 OR BLANK IF NO INTERACTIONS, 1 IF ONE OR MORE.
33.      C      NINT(J)=NUMBER OF INTERACTIONS FOR DEPENDENT ATTRIBUTE J.
34.      C      FIRST VARIABLE IN INTERACTION MUST ALWAYS BE ENDOGENOUS. (IF
35.      C       INTERACTION BETWEEN TWO EXOGENOUS VARIABLES IS DESIRED,
36.      C       INSERT AS EXPLICIT VARIABLE IN INPUT DATA.)
37.      C      SECOND VARIABLE IN INTERACTION MAY BE ENDOGENOUS OR EXOGENOUS.
38.      C      INTV(J,1,K) IS ORIGINAL POSITION OF FIRST OF TWO VARIABLES
39.      C       IN KTH INTERACTION FOR DEPENDENT ATTRIBUTE J.
40.      C      INTV(J,2,K) IS ORIGINAL POSITION OF SECOND.
41.      C      L4(J,K+NVJ)=POSITION OF NEW VARIABLE.
42.      C      NVAR=NUMBER OF VARIABLES THAT CHANGE OVER TIME INCLUDING
43.      C      THE ENDOGENOUS VARIABLES.  NVAR=1,...,M+NE (MAX)
44.      C      NCH(J)=VARIABLE NUMBER OF JTH VARIABLE THAT CHANGES, INCLUDING
45.      C      ENDOGENOUS ONES.  NCH(1),...,NCH(M) ARE ALWAYS 1,...,M;
46.      C      NCH(NVAR) IS VARIABLES NUMBER OF LAST CHANGING VARIABLE.
47.            NSTEP=30
48.
49.            WRITE(6,8893)
50.      8893 FORMAT(//1X'LONGIT.SIMULT PROGRAM FOR PANEL DATA WITH TWO OR MORE
51.           &ENDOGENOUS VARIABLES   12/7/80')
52.            READ(2,8888)NJOBS
53.            DO 5010 I22=1,NJOBS
54.      C
55.      C
56.
57.
58.
59.            NALG=1
60.            WRITE(6,8888)M,NE,N,IE,NRES,NVAR,INT,T,NALG
61.            READ(2,8886)(NCH(J),J=1,NVAR)
```

```
62.        8886 FORMAT(20I3)
63.             MP=M+1
64.             DO 61 J=1,NVAR
65.          61 NCH(J)=NCH(J) -1
66.             IF(NVAR.GT.M)WRITE(6,8891)(NCH(J),J=MP,NVAR)
67.             IF(NVAR.LE.M)WRITE(6,8892)
68.        8891 FORMAT(/1X'NON-CONSTANT INDEPENDENT VARIABLES ARE: '20I4)
69.        8892 FORMAT(/1X'ALL INDEPENDENT VARIABLES CONSTANT')
70.             DO 32 J=1,5
71.             DO 31 I=1,2
72.             DO 31 K=1,5
73.          31 INTV(J,I,K)=0
74.          32 NINT(J)=0
75.             READ (2,8882)(NIV(J),J=1,M)
76.             WRITE(6,8882)(NIV(J),J=1,M)
77.        8888 FORMAT(7I5,F8.2,I2)
78.             NS=NE+M
79.             KA=0
80.             DO 33 J=1,M
81.             NIV(J)=NIV(J) +1
82.             NVJ=NIV(J)
83.             READ (2,8882)(L4(J,I),I=2,NVJ)
84.             L4(J,1)=1
85.        8882 FORMAT(10I5)
86.             IF(INT.GT.0)READ(2,8882)(NINT(J1),J1=1,M)
87.             IF(INT.GT.0)WRITE(6,8882)(NINT(J1),J1=1,M)
88.             INTJ=NINT(J)
89.             IF(INTJ.GT.0)READ (2,8882)((INTV(J,I,K),I=1,2),K=1,INTJ)
90.             IF(INTJ.GT.0)WRITE(6,8882)((INTV(J,I,K),I=1,2),K=1,INTJ)
91.             NVP=NVJ +NINT(J)
92.             IF(NINT(J).EQ.0)GOTO 35
93.             DO 34 K=1,INTJ
94.             IF(J.EQ.1)GOTO 37
95.             JM=J-1
96.             DO 36 J1=1,JM
97.             INTJ1=NINT(J1)
98.             IF(INTJ1.EQ.0)GOTO 36
99.             DO 36 K1=1,INTJ1
100.            IF(INTV(J,1,K).EQ.INTV(J1,1,K1).AND.INTV(J,2,K).EQ.
101.           &INTV(J1,2,K1))GOTO 38
102.         36 CONTINUE
103.         37 KA=KA+1
104.            L4(J,K+NVJ)=NS+1+KA
105.            GOTO 34
106.         38 L4(J,K+NVJ)=L4(J1,K1+NIV(J1))
107.         34 CONTINUE
108.         35 CONTINUE
109.            DO 33 I=2,NVP
110.            L4(J,I)=L4(J,I) +1
111.         33 CONTINUE
112.            READ(2,8788)JW,NWP,NR
113.        8788 FORMAT(3I5)
114.      C
115.      C    JW=1 IF DATA ARE TO BE WRITTEN, NWP=1 IF PREDICTED PROPORTION
116.      C     IN EACH STATE IS TO BE WRITTEN, NR=1 IF R-SQUARE IS TO BE
117.      C     CALCULATED FOR EACH DEPENDENT ATTRIBUTE.
118.            READ(2,8889)FMT
119.        8889 FORMAT(18A4)
120.            TN=.0001*NS
121.            NSN=NS+1+KA
122.            NSM=NS-M+KA
123.            NSN2=2*NSN
124.            IEH=IE
```

```
125.            NRESH=NRES
126.            NSM=NS-M
127.     C      CREATING SOME INITIAL PARAMETERS
128.            NC=2**M
129.            LH1=2**(M-1)
130.            SUM=0.
131.     C
132.            DO 79 J=1,M
133.            LJ(J)=2**(J-1)
134.            DO 75 JD=1,NC
135.       75 ITR(J,JD)=0
136.            DO 77 K=1,NSN2
137.       77 BM(J,K)=0.
138.       79 CONTINUE
139.     C      LJ(J) IS DIFFERENCE IN INDICES FOR STATE CHANGES IN J.
140.     C
141.     C      CALCULATE ORIGIN AND DESTINATION STATES FOR EACH ENDOG. VARIABLE
142.            DO 51 J=1,M
143.            J2=M+1-J
144.            LJ2=LJ(J2)
145.            I5=0
146.            JM=J-1
147.            DO 51 IJ=1,NC
148.            IR(IJ)=IJ -1
149.            IF(JM.EQ.0)GOTO 52
150.            DO 52 J3=1,JM
151.            J4=M+1-J3
152.            JQ=2**(J4-1)
153.            IF(IR(IJ)/J4.GE.1)IR(IJ)=IR(IJ)-JQ
154.       52 CONTINUE
155.            IF(IR(IJ)/J2.GE.1)GOTO 51
156.            I5=I5+1
157.            ITR(J2,IJ)=IJ +LJ2
158.            IDR(J2,IJ)=0
159.            ITR(J2,IJ+LJ2)=IJ
160.            IDR(J2,IJ+LJ2)=1
161.            IRG(J2,I5)=IJ
162.       51 CONTINUE
163.     C      ITR(J2,JD) IS THE ORIGIN STATE IN VARIABLE J2 FOR EACH
164.     C      DESTINATION STATE JD.
165.     C      IDR(J2,JD)=1 IF DESTINATION JD IS STATE 1; 0 IF IT IS STATE 0.
166.     C      DIMENSIONS ARE ITR(M,NC),IDR(M,NC)
167.     C      IRG(J,I) IS ORIGIN STATE FOR EACH OF THE NC/2 TRANSITIONS TO
168.     C      STATE 1 ON ATTRIBUTE J.
169.     C
170.     C      FORMAT : FMT SHOULD BE SPECIFIED FOR X1,X2,W
171.     C              X1 - VECTOR AT TIME 1
172.     C              X2 - VECTOR AT TIME 2
173.     C              W  - WEIGHTS
174.            DO 2 I1=1,N
175.            IORG(I1)=1
176.            IDES(I1)=1
177.            READ(2,FMT)(XAT1(J),J=2,NSN),(R(J),J=1,NVAR),W(I1)
178.            IF(JW.EQ.1)WRITE(6,FMT)(XAT1(J),J=2,NSN),(R(J),J=1,NVAR),W(I1)
179.            XAT1(1)=1.
180.            DO 423 J=1,NSN
181.      423 XAT2(J)=XAT1(J)
182.            DO 422 J=1,NVAR
183.            NT=NCH(J) +2
184.            XAT2(NT)=R(J)
185.      422 CONTINUE
186.     C      CALCULATE ORIGIN AND DESTINATION FOR EACH INDIVIDUAL IS.
187.            DO 2 J2=1,NS
```

157

```
188.           J3=J2+1
189.           IF(J3.GT.MP)GOTO 92
190.           IORG(I1)=IORG(I1) +XAT1(J3)*LJ(J2)
191.           IDES(I1)=IDES(I1) +XAT2(J3)*LJ(J2)
192.           IF(J3.LE.MP)GOTO 2
193.        92 XAT(J3-MP,I1)=(XAT1(J3) +XAT2(J3))/2.
194.         2 CONTINUE
195.     C
196.     C THIS IS PLACE TO COME BACK TO FOR RECYCLING WITH NEW MODEL.
197.      2001 CONTINUE
198.           NA=2
199.           IF(NRES.NE.2)NA=1
200.           NEXIT=0
201.           ISTEP=0
202.           NBT=0
203.           DO 321 J=1,M
204.           NJP=NIV(J) +NINT(J)
205.           NIP(J)=2*NJP
206.           IF(NRES.NE.2)NIP(J)=NJP +1
207.       321 NBT=NBT+NIP(J)
208.     C     NIP(J) IS TOTAL NUMBER OF PARAMETERS WITH J AS DEPENDENT.
209.     C     NBT IS TOTAL NUMBER OF PARAMETERS.
210.           DO 322 J2=1,M
211.           LJ2=LJ(J2)
212.           NJ2=NIV(J2)
213.           NJP=NJ2 +NINT(J2)
214.           BM(J2,1)=.2
215.           IF(IE.EQ.1)BM(J2,1)=-1.61
216.           BM(J2,NSN+1)=BM(J2,1)
217.           DO 322 K1=1,NJP
218.           K2=L4(J2,K1)
219.           IF(K2.EQ.1)GOTO 503
220.           BM(J2,K2)=.1
221.           IF(IE.EQ.1)BM(J2,K2)=.3
222.           BM(J2,K2+NSN)=-BM(J2,K2)
223.           BM(J2,NSN+1)=BM(J2,NSN+1) -BM(J2,K2+NSN)
224.           IF(NRES.NE.2)BM(J2,K2+NSN)=0.
225.       503 KN=0
226.           DO 501 IN=1,LH1
227.           IS2=IRG(J2,IN)
228.           KN=KN+1
229.           ID(J2,K2,KN)=0
230.           IF(K2.EQ.1)GOTO 504
231.           IF(K2.GT.MP.AND.K2.LE.NSN)GOTO 504
232.           IF(K2.GT.NSN)GOTO 513
233.           IF(IDR(K2-1,IS2).EQ.0)GOTO 501
234.       504 ID(J2,K2,KN)=IS2
235.           GOTO 501
236.       513 IVAR1=INTV(J2,1,K1-NJ2)
237.           IVAR2=INTV(J2,2,K1-NJ2)
238.           IF(IVAR2.GT.MP)GOTO 512
239.           IF(IDR(IVAR1,IS2).EQ.0.OR.IDR(IVAR2,IS2).EQ.0)GOTO 501
240.           ID(J2,K2,KN)=IS2
241.           GOTO 501
242.       512 IF(IDR(IVAR1,IS2).EQ.0)GOTO 501
243.           ID(J2,K2,KN)=IS2
244.       501 CONTINUE
245.       322 CONTINUE
246.     C     STATE IS2 IS THE KNTH ORIGIN STATE FOR WHICH THE INDEPENDENT
247.     C     VARIABLE K2 IS NONZERO FOR DEPENDENT VARIABLE J2, IN A
248.     C     POSITIVE DIRECTION. (ALSO THIS +LJ2 IS NONZERO; AND
249.     C     IS2,IS2 IS NEGATIVE, AS IS IS2+LJ2,IS2+LJ2.)  THIS IS STORED
```

```
250.      C       IN ID(J2,K2,KN).
251.              WRITE(6,69)ISTEP,((BM(J,K),K=1,NSN2),J=1,M)
252.      C
253.       1000 IF(ISTEP.GE.25)GOTO 2000
254.      C
255.      C
256.              CALL       SIMEQ(N,M,NC,NSN,NSTEP,NIV,LJ,IORG,IDES,IDR,NIP,
257.             &IRG,LH1,BM,T,X,NBT,XAT,W,R,SS,NEXIT,P,L4,ID,IE,NALG,NA
258.             &,NINT,INTV,NWP,NR)
259.      C
260.      C
261.      C
262.              ISTEP=ISTEP+1
263.      C
264.      C
265.              DIFR=0.
266.              NX=0
267.              DO 67 J2=1,M
268.              NJ2=NIV(J2) +NINT(J2)
269.              DO 68 K=1,NJ2
270.              K2=L4(J2,K)
271.              K3=NX+K
272.              K5=K3+NJ2
273.              BM(J2,K2)=BM(J2,K2) +R(K3)
274.              IF(NRES.EQ.2)BM(J2,K2+NSN)=BM(J2,K2+NSN) +R(K5)
275.              IF(NRES.NE.2.AND.K.EQ.1)BM(J2,NSN+1)=BM(J2,NSN+1) +R(K5)
276.              DIFR=DIFR +ABS(R(K3) +R(K5))
277.           68 CONTINUE
278.              NX=NX +NIP(J2)
279.           67 CONTINUE
280.              DO 138 J=1,M
281.              WRITE(6,69)ISTEP,(BM(J,K),K=1,NSN2)
282.          138 CONTINUE
283.           69 FORMAT(1X,'STEP',I3,'  BM',(6F8.3))
284.              WRITE(6,78)DIFR
285.           78 FORMAT(1X,'DIFR=',F10.4)
286.              IF (DIFR.GE..001)GOTO 1000
287.              WRITE(6,88)ISTEP
288.           88 FORMAT(1H0,' ITERATION CONVERGED AFTER STEP : ',I5)
289.              NEXIT=1
290.              CALL       SIMEQ(N,M,NC,NSN,NSTEP,NIV,LJ,IORG,IDES,IDR,NIP,
291.             &IRG,LH1,BM,T,X,NBT,XAT,W,R,SS,NEXIT,P,L4,ID,IE,NALG,NA
292.             &,NINT,INTV,NWP,NR)
293.              IF(NRES.NE.2)WRITE(6,126)M,NSM
294.              IF(NRES.EQ.2)WRITE(6,127)M,NSN
295.              IF(IE.NE.1)WRITE(6,128)
296.              IF(IE.EQ.1)WRITE(6,129)
297.          126 FORMAT(//1X'SIMULTANEOUS EQUATIONS MODEL WITH RESTRICTED PARAMETER
298.             &S',/1X,I4,' ENDOGENOUS ATTRIBUTES',I4,' EXOGENOUS VARIABLES')
299.          127 FORMAT(//1X'SIMULTANEOUS EQUATIONS MODEL WITH UNRESTRICTED PARAMET
300.             &ERS',/1X,I4,' ENDOGENOUS ATTRIBUTES',I4,' EXOGENOUS VARIABLES')
301.          128 FORMAT(1X'LINEAR MODEL')
302.          129 FORMAT(1X'EXPONENTIAL MODEL')
303.              WRITE(6,115)
304.              DO 113 K=1,NBT
305.          113 WRITE(6,110)(SS(K,J),J=1,NBT)
306.          115 FORMAT(//1X,'COVARIANCE MATRIX')
307.          110 FORMAT(5X,8F10.5)
308.              K=0
309.              DO 121 J=1,M
310.              NTJ=NIV(J) +NINT(J)
311.              WRITE (6,44)
```

```
312.          44 FORMAT(/)
313.             K1=-1
314.             DO 111 L=1,NTJ
315.             K2=L4(J,L)
316.             IB=NSN*(IA-1)
317.             BA=BM(J,K2+IB)
318.             K=K +1
319.             K1=K2 -1
320.             SS(K,K)=SQRT(SS(K,K))
321.         111 WRITE(6,122)J,K1,BM(J,K2),J,K1,SS(K,K)
322.             IF(NRES.NE.2)NTJ=1
323.             DO 119 L=1,NTJ
324.             K2=L4(J,L)
325.             K=K+1
326.             K1=K2 -1
327.             SS(K,K)=SQRT(SS(K,K))
328.             WRITE(6,123)J,K1,BM(J,K2+NSN),J,K1,SS(K,K)
329.         123 FORMAT(5X,'C(',2I2,')=',F10.4,5X,'SE(',2I2,')=',F10.4)
330.         119 CONTINUE
331.         121 CONTINUE
332.         112 FORMAT(//5X,'B COEFFICIENTS AND STANDARD ERRORS')
333.         122 FORMAT(5X,'B(',2I2,')=',F10.4,5X,'SE(',2I2,')=',F10.4)
334.       C     THIS IS DUMMY INSTRUCTION FOR CALLING TESTS
335.             IF(IE.NE.2)GOTO 436
336.             IE=1
337.             GOTO 2001
338.         436 IF(NRES.NE.3)GOTO 5010
339.             NRES=2
340.             IF(IEH.EQ.2)IE=2
341.             GOTO 2001
342.        5010 CONTINUE
343.             STOP
344.       C
345.       C
346.        2000 WRITE(6,9991) ISTEP
347.             WRITE (6,44)
348.        9991 FORMAT(1X,'ITERATION DID NOT CONVERGE IN ',I4,' STEPS ')
349.             STOP
350.             END
351.
352.
353.
354.       C
355.       C     THIS SUBROUTINE PREPARES SIMULTANEOUS EQN. DATA FOR INVERSION
356.             SUBROUTINE SIMEQ(N,M,NC,NSN,NSTEP,NIV,LJ,IORG,IDES,IDR,NIP,
357.      &IRG,LH1,BM,T,X,NBT,XAT,W,CA,SS,NEXIT,PJ,L4,ID,IE,NALG,NA
358.      &,NINT,INTV,NWP,NR)
359.       C
360.             DIMENSION NIV(5),LJ(5),IORG(1000),IDES(1000),
361.      &L4(5,24),IDR(5,32),IRG(5,32),BM(5,46),XAT(18,1000),TT2(32,32),
362.      &W(1000),D(80),X(80),PJ(1000),QT(32,32),CA(80),SS(80,80),
363.      &RT(32,32,80),RAT(32,32),RBT(32,32),ZP(5),ZSUM(5),PB(5),PST(5)
364.      &,RA2(32,32,80),TT(32,32),TS(32,32),NIP(22),P(32,32)
365.      &,T3(24),U(32,32),TEMP(32,32),V(32,32,80)
366.      &,ID(5,24,16),RS(32,32),VA(32,32),RX(32,32),INTV(5,2,5),NINT(5)
367.       C
368.             EQUIVALENCE (RS(16,16),RX(16,16)),(TEMP(16,16),U(16,16))
369.             NE=NSN-M-1
370.             MP=M+1
371.             NRES=2
372.             IF(NA.EQ.1)NRES=1
373.       C
```

```
374.            NSET=0
375.            NFLAG=0
376.            IF(NALG.EQ.1.AND.NEXIT.NE.1)NFLAG=1
377.
378.            DO 189 J=1,M
379.            PB(J)=0.
380.            ZSUM(J)=0.
381.            PST(J)=0.
382.            ZP(J)=0.
383.        189 CONTINUE
384.            WT=0.
385.    C
386.            DO 5 J=1,NBT
387.            CA(J)=0.
388.            D(J)=0.
389.            DO 5 K=1,NBT
390.          5 SS(J,K)=0.
391.    C
392.            AD1=T
393.    C       THIS IS MULTIPLIER FOR 1ST DERIVATIVE, LINEAR DECOMPOSITION.
394.    C
395.            DO 211 IS=1,N
396.            JO=IORG(IS)
397.            JD=IDES(IS)
398.    C       CALCULATE QT, PJ, AND RT ONLY FOR IS WHO DIFFER ON EXOGENOUS
399.    C        VARIABLES.
400.            IF(IS.EQ.1)GOTO 225
401.            IM=IS-1
402.            DO 226 J=1,M
403.            NJ =NIV(J) +NINT(J)
404.            DO 226 K=2,NJ
405.            K2=L4(J,K)
406.            IF(K2.LE.MP.OR.K2.GT.NSN) GOTO 226
407.            IF(XAT(K2-MP,IS).NE.XAT(K2-MP,IM))GOTO 225
408.        226 CONTINUE
409.            IF(NFLAG.NE.1)GOTO 600
410.            GOTO 51
411.    C       CALCULATE QS FOR STATE CHANGES IN ALL ENDOGENOUS VARIABLES
412.        225 DO 82 J2=1,M
413.            LJ2=LJ(J2)
414.            NJ2=NIV(J2)
415.            NJP=NJ2 +NINT(J2)
416.            DO 91 I1=1,LH1
417.            I2=IRG(J2,I1)
418.            J1=I2+LJ2
419.            QT(I2,J1)=0.
420.            QT(J1,I2)=0.
421.            DO 83 K=1,NJP
422.            K2=L4(J2,K)
423.            IF(K2.GT.1.AND.K2.LE.M+1.AND.IDR(K2-1,J1).EQ.0)GOTO 83
424.            IF(K2.LE.M+1)GOTO 7
425.            IF(NJP.EQ.NJ2)GOTO 8
426.            IF(K2.GT.NSN.AND.INTV(J2,2,K-NJ2).LE.M)GOTO 7
427.          8 CONTINUE
428.    C       CALCULATE Q TO STATE 1 ON VARIABLE J2
429.            QT(I2,J1)=QT(I2,J1) +BM(J2,K2)*XAT(K2-MP,IS)
430.    C       CALCULATE Q TO STATE 0 ON VARIABLE J2
431.            IF(NRES.EQ.2)QT(J1,I2)=QT(J1,I2) +BM(J2,K2+NSN)*XAT(K2-MP,IS)
432.            IF(NRES.NE.2)QT(J1,I2)=QT(J1,I2) -BM(J2,K2)*XAT(K2-MP,IS)
433.            GOTO 83
434.          7 QT(I2,J1)=QT(I2,J1) +BM(J2,K2)
435.            IF(NRES.EQ.2.OR.K2.EQ.1)QT(J1,I2)=QT(J1,I2) +BM(J2,K2+NSN)
```

161

```
436.            IF(NRES.NE.2.AND.K2.NE.1)QT(J1,I2)=QT(J1,I2) -BM(J2,K2)
437.         83 CONTINUE
438.            QT(I2,J1)=QT(I2,J1)*T
439.            QT(J1,I2)=QT(J1,I2)*T
440.            IF(IE.EQ.1)GOTO 90
441.            IF(QT(I2,J1).LT.0.)QT(I2,J1)=0.
442.            IF(QT(J1,I2).LT.0.)QT(J1,I2)=0.
443.            GOTO 91
444.         90 QT(I2,J1)=EXP(QT(I2,J1))
445.            QT(J1,I2)=EXP(QT(J1,I2))
446.         91 CONTINUE
447.         82 CONTINUE
448.      C
449.            DO 27 I=1,NC
450.            QT(I,I)=0.
451.            DO 27 J=1,NC
452.            IF(J.EQ.I)GOTO 27
453.            QT(I,I)=QT(I,I) -QT(I,J)
454.         27 CONTINUE
455.            IF(JSC.EQ.1)WRITE(6,19)((QT(I,J),J=1,NC),I=1,NC)
456.            JSC=0
457.         19 FORMAT(1X,'QS',8F9.4)
458.      C    CALCULATE DESTINATION PROBABILITIES FOR INDIVIDUAL IS
459.            DO 49 I=1,NC
460.            DO 49 J=1,NC
461.         49 P(I,J)=0.
462.            DO 10 I=1,NC
463.            P(I,I)=1
464.            DO 10 J=1,NC
465.            RS(I,J)=QT(I,J)
466.         10 P(I,J)=QT(I,J) + P(I,J)
467.            DO 100 ISTEP=2,NSTEP
468.            TEST=0
469.            DO 20 I=1,NC
470.            DO 20 J=1,NC
471.            TEMP(I,J)=0
472.            DO 30 K=1,NC
473.         30 TEMP(I,J)=QT(I,K)*RS(K,J)/ISTEP +TEMP(I,J)
474.            P(I,J)=P(I,J) + TEMP(I,J)
475.            TEST=TEST + ABS(TEMP(I,J))
476.         20 CONTINUE
477.            DO 39 I=1,NC
478.            DO 39 J=1,NC
479.         39 RS(I,J)=TEMP(I,J)
480.            IF(TEST.LT..001)GOTO 50
481.        100 CONTINUE
482.            WRITE(6,1)ISTEP,TEST
483.          1 FORMAT(1X,'NONCONVERGENCE OF P VECTOR AFTER',I5,'  STEPS.  LAST
484.          & STEP ADDS',F10.4)
485.            STOP
486.         50 CONTINUE
487.            IF(NEXIT.NE.1.OR.NWP.NE.1)GOTO 184
488.        888 FORMAT(/1X,'P-VECTOR FOR VALUES OF IND. VAR. = ',18F6.2)
489.            WRITE(6,878)((P(I,J),J=1,NC),I=1,NC)
490.        878 FORMAT(3X,8F8.4)
491.        184 CONTINUE
492.        600 PJ(IS)=P(JO,JD)
493.            IF(NEXIT.NE.1.OR.NR.NE.1)GOTO 601
494.            WT=WT+W(IS)
495.            DO 187 J=1,M
496.            PT=0.
497.            DO 188 JS=1,NC
498.            IF(IDR(J,JS).NE.1)GOTO 188
```

```
499.          PT=PT +P(JO,JS)*W(IS)
500.      188 CONTINUE
501.          PB(J)=PB(J) +PT
502.          PST(J)=PST(J) +PT*PT/W(IS)
503.          IF(IDR(J,JD).NE.1)GOTO 187
504.          ZP(J)=ZP(J) +PT
505.          ZSUM(J)=ZSUM(J) +W(IS)
506.          WRITE(6,879)J,PST(J),PB(J),ZP(J),ZSUM(J)
507.      879 FORMAT(1XI3,4F10.2)
508.      187 CONTINUE
509.
510.      601 NX=1
511.          K3=0.
512.          DO 501 J1=1,M
513.          LJ1=LJ(J1)
514.          NJ1=NIV(J1)
515.          NJP=NJ1 +NINT(J1)
516.          DO 502 I1=1,2
517.          KX=0
518.          DO 503 K1=1,NJP
519.          NJT=NIP(J1) +NX
520.          AT4=AD1
521.          DO 493 I=1,NC
522.          DO 493 J=1,NC
523.      493 TS(I,J)=0.
524.          K4=L4(J1,K1)
525.          K3=K3+1
526.          IF(K4.GT.MP.AND.K4.LE.NSN)AT4=AD1*XAT(K4-MP,IS)
527.          IF(K4.LE.NSN)GOTO 391
528.          KX=KX+1
529.          IF(INTV(J1,2,KX).GT.M)AT4=AD1*XAT(K4-MP,IS)
530.      391 AT1=AT4
531.          DO 498 KN=1,LH1
532.          IS2=ID(J1,K4,KN)
533.          IF(IS2)498,498,497
534.      497 IS1=IS2+LJ1
535.          IF(I1.NE.1)GOTO 490
536.          IF(IE.NE.1)GOTO 550
537.          TS(IS2,IS1)=AT1*QT(IS2,IS1)
538.          TS(IS2,IS2)=-TS(IS2,IS1)
539.          IF(NRES.EQ.2.OR.K4.EQ.1)GOTO 498
540.          AT1=-AT1
541.          GOTO 461
542.      550 TS(IS2,IS1)=AT1
543.          TS(IS2,IS2)=-AT1
544.          IF(NRES.EQ.2.OR.K4.EQ.1)GOTO 498
545.          AT1=-AT1
546.          GOTO 551
547.      490 IF(IE.NE.1)GOTO 551
548.      461 TS(IS1,IS2)=AT1*QT(IS1,IS2)
549.          TS(IS1,IS1)=-TS(IS1,IS2)
550.          GOTO 498
551.      551 TS(IS1,IS2)=AT1
552.          TS(IS1,IS1)=-AT1
553.      498 CONTINUE
554.          IF(NFLAG.EQ.1)GOTO 792
555.          KW=0
556.          K7=K3-1
557.          DO 799 J2=J1,M
558.          LJ2=LJ(J2)
559.          NJ2=NIV(J2)
560.          N2P=NJ2+NINT(J2)
```

```
561.          NZ=1
562.          IF(J2.EQ.J1)NZ=I1
563.          DO 799 I2=NZ,2
564.          NY=1
565.          IF(NRES.NE.2.AND.I2.EQ.2)N2P=1
566.          IF(J2.EQ.J1.AND.I2.EQ.I1)NY=K1
567.          DO 719 K2=NY,N2P
568.          K7=K7+1
569.          K9=L4(J2,K2)
570.          AT3=AD1
571.          DO 71 I=1,NC
572.          DO 71 J=1,NC
573.          TT(I,J)=0.
574.       71 V(I,J,K7)=0.
575.          IF(K9.GT.MP.AND.K9.LE.NSN)AT3=AD1*XAT(K9-MP,IS)
576.          IF(K9.LE.NSN)GOTO 72
577.          KW=KW+1
578.          KY=KW
579.          IF(KY.GT.NINT(J1))KY=KW-NINT(J1)
580.          IF(INTV(J1,2,KY).GT.M)AT3=AD1*XAT(K9-MP,IS)
581.       72 AT2=AT3*AT4
582.          AT1=AT3
583.          DO 798 KN=1,LH1
584.          IS2=ID(J2,K9,KN)
585.          IF(IS2)798,798,797
586.      797 IS1=IS2+LJ2
587.
588.          IF(I2.NE.1)GOTO 790
589.          IF(IE.NE.1)GOTO 750
590.          TT(IS2,IS1)=AT1*QT(IS2,IS1)
591.          TT(IS2,IS2)=-TT(IS2,IS1)
592.          IF(NRES.EQ.2.OR.K9.EQ.1)GOTO 798
593.          AT1=-AT1
594.          GOTO 761
595.      750 TT(IS2,IS1)=AT1
596.          TT(IS2,IS2)=-AT1
597.          IF(NRES.EQ.2.OR.K9.EQ.1)GOTO 798
598.          AT1=-AT1
599.          GOTO 751
600.      790 IF(IE.NE.1)GOTO 751
601.      761 TT(IS1,IS2)=AT1*QT(IS1,IS2)
602.          TT(IS1,IS1)=-TT(IS1,IS2)
603.          GOTO 798
604.      751 TT(IS1,IS2)=AT1
605.          TT(IS1,IS1)=-AT1
606.      798 CONTINUE
607.
608.          DO 770 I=1,NC
609.          DO 770 J=1,NC
610.          RA2(I,J,K7)=TT(I,J)
611.          IF(I.EQ.J.OR.IE.NE.1)GOTO 770
612.          IF(TS(I,J).EQ.0.OR.TT(I,J).EQ.0)GOTO 770
613.          D2=AT2*QT(I,J)
614.          V(I,J,K7)=D2
615.          V(I,I,K7)=-D2
616.      770 CONTINUE
617.      719 CONTINUE
618.          IF(NRES.NE.2)N2P=1
619.      799 CONTINUE
620.      792 CONTINUE
621.    C
622.          DO 556 I=1,NC
623.          DO 555 J=1,NC
```

164

```
624.              RT(I,J,K3)=0.
625.              RAT(I,J)=0.
626.          555 RBT(I,J)=0.
627.          556 RBT(I,I)=1.
628.          561 DO 504 ISTEP=2,NSTEP
629.              T2=0.
630.              FSTEP=ISTEP
631.              DO 505 I=1,NC
632.              DO 505 J=1,NC
633.              AUK=0.
634.              AKAN=0.
635.              U(I,J)=0.
636.              DO 554 K=1,NC
637.              AUK=QT(I,K)*RAT(K,J) +AUK
638.              AKAN=TS(I,K)*RBT(K,J) +AKAN
639.          554 U(I,J)=QT(I,K)*RBT(K,J) +U(I,J)
640.              RX(I,J)=(AUK +AKAN)/(FSTEP-1.)
641.          505 CONTINUE
642.              DO 557 I=1,NC
643.              DO 557 J=1,NC
644.              RBT(I,J)=U(I,J)/(FSTEP-1.)
645.              RAT(I,J)=RX(I,J)
646.              T2=T2 +ABS(RAT(I,J))
647.          557 RT(I,J,K3)=RT(I,J,K3) +RAT(I,J)
648.              IF(NFLAG.EQ.1)GOTO 514
649.              IF(NSET.EQ.1)GOTO 514
650.
651.              KW=0
652.              K7=K3-1
653.              DO 509 J2=J1,M
654.              LJ2=LJ(J2)
655.              NJ2=NIV(J2)
656.              N2P=NJ2+NINT(J2)
657.              NZ=1
658.              IF(J2.EQ.J1)NZ=I1
659.              DO 509 I2=NZ,2
660.              NY=1
661.              IF(NRES.NE.2.AND.I2.EQ.2)N2P=1
662.              IF(J2.EQ.J1.AND.I2.EQ.I1)NY=K1
663.              DO 519 K2=NY,N2P
664.              K7=K7+1
665.              K9=L4(J2,K2)
666.              AT3=AD1
667.              DO 494 I=1,NC
668.              DO 494 J=1,NC
669.              TT(I,J)=0.
670.          494 TT2(I,J)=0.
671.              IF(K9.GT.MP.AND.K9.LE.NSN)AT3=AD1*XAT(K9-MP,IS)
672.              IF(K9.LE.NSN)GOTO 392
673.              KW=KW+1
674.              KY=KW
675.              IF(KY.GT.NINT(J1))KY=KW-NINT(J1)
676.              IF(INTV(J1,2,KY).GT.M)AT3=AD1*XAT(K9-MP,IS)
677.          392 AT1=AT3
678.              DO 698 KN=1,LH1
679.              IS2=ID(J2,K9,KN)
680.              IF(IS2)698,698,697
681.          697 IS1=IS2+LJ2
682.              IF(I2.NE.1)GOTO 690
683.              IF(IE.NE.1)GOTO 650
684.              TT(IS2,IS1)=AT1*QT(IS2,IS1)
685.              TT(IS2,IS2)=-TT(IS2,IS1)
```

165

```
686.          IF(NRES.EQ.2.OR.K9.EQ.1)GOTO 698
687.          AT1=-AT1
688.          GOTO 661
689.     650 TT(IS2,IS1)=AT1
690.          TT(IS2,IS2)=-AT1
691.          IF(NRES.EQ.2.OR.K9.EQ.1)GOTO 698
692.          AT1=-AT1
693.          GOTO 651
694.     690 IF(IE.NE.1)GOTO 651
695.     661 TT(IS1,IS2)=AT1*QT(IS1,IS2)
696.          TT(IS1,IS1)=-TT(IS1,IS2)
697.          GOTO 698
698.     651 TT(IS1,IS2)=AT1
699.          TT(IS1,IS1)=-AT1
700.     698 CONTINUE
701.          IF(IE.NE.1)GOTO 492
702.          AT2=AT3*AT4
703.          DO 474 KN=1,LH1
704.          IS2=IRG(J1,KN)
705.          IS1=IS2 +LJ1
706.          IF(TS(IS2,IS1).EQ.0..OR.TT(IS2,IS1).EQ.0.)GOTO 487
707.          D2=AT2*QT(IS2,IS1)
708.          TT2(IS2,IS1)=D2
709.          TT2(IS2,IS2)=-D2
710.     487 IF(TS(IS1,IS2).EQ.0..OR.TT(IS1,IS2).EQ.0.)GOTO 474
711.          D2=AT2*QT(IS1,IS2)
712.          IF(NRES.EQ.2)GOTO 489
713.          IF(K4.EQ.1.AND.K9.EQ.1)GOTO 489
714.          IF(K4.NE.1.AND.K9.NE.1)GOTO 489
715.          D2=-D2
716.     489 TT2(IS1,IS2)=D2
717.          TT2(IS1,IS1)=-D2
718.     474 CONTINUE
719.     492 CONTINUE
720.          T3(K7)=0.
721.          DO 524 I=1,NC
722.          DO 524 J=1,NC
723.          AUJ=0.
724.          AJAN=0.
725.          AV=0.
726.          AJUK=0.
727.          AKUJ=0.
728.          AJKAN=0.
729.          DO 508 K=1,NC
730.          AUJ=QT(I,K)*RA2(K,J,K7) +AUJ
731.          AJAN=TT(I,K)*RBT(K,J) +AJAN
732.          AJKAN=TT2(I,K)*RBT(K,J) +AJKAN
733.          AV=QT(I,K)*V(K,J,K7) +AV
734.          AJUK=TT(I,K)*RAT(K,J) +AJUK
735.     508 AKUJ=TS(I,K)*RA2(K,J,K7) +AKUJ
736.          VA(I,J)=(AV +AJUK +AKUJ +AJKAN)/FSTEP
737.          RX(I,J)=(AUJ +AJAN)/FSTEP
738.          T3(K7)=T3(K7) +ABS(VA(I,J))
739.     524 CONTINUE
740.          SS(K3,K7)=SS(K3,K7) -V(JO,JD,K7)*W(IS)/PJ(IS)
741.          DO 536 I=1,NC
742.          DO 536 J=1,NC
743.          RA2(I,J,K7)=RX(I,J)
744.     536 V(I,J,K7)=VA(I,J)
745.     519 CONTINUE
746.          IF(NRES.NE.2)N2P=1
747.     509 CONTINUE
748.          DO 526 K7= K3,NBT
```

```
749.            IF(T3(K7).GT..001)GOTO 504
750.        526 CONTINUE
751.            NSET=1
752.        514 IF(T2.LT..001)GOTO 507
753.        504 CONTINUE
754.            GOTO 202
755.        507 NSET=0
756.            X(K3)=RT(JO,JD,K3)/PJ(IS)
757.        503 CONTINUE
758.            IF(NRES.NE.2)NJP=1
759.        502 CONTINUE
760.            NX=NX+NIP(J1)
761.        501 CONTINUE
762.            GOTO 200
763.        202 CONTINUE
764.          4 FORMAT(1X,I5,2X'TERMS NOT ENOUGH IN INF. SERIES 1ST DERIV FOR'I3)
765.            STOP
766.         51 PJ(IS)=P(JO,JD)
767.            DO 602 K3=1,NBT
768.            X(K3)=RT(JO,JD,K3)/PJ(IS)
769.        602 CONTINUE
770.        200 CONTINUE
771.            DO 220 J=1,NBT
772.            D(J)=D(J) +X(J)*W(IS)
773.            DO 220 K=J,NBT
774.            SS(J,K)=SS(J,K) +X(J)*X(K)*W(IS)
775.            SS(K,J)=SS(J,K)
776.        220 CONTINUE
777.        211 CONTINUE
778.      C
779.          9 CALL INVER(SS,NBT)
780.      C
781.            DO 6 K=1,NBT
782.            DO 6 J=1,NBT
783.            CA(J)=CA(J) +D(K)*SS(K,J)
784.          6 CONTINUE
785.      C
786.            IF(NEXIT.NE.1.OR.NR.NE.1)GOTO 186
787.            DO 185 J=1,M
788.            NUM=ZP(J) -PB(J)*ZSUM(J)/WT
789.            DEN1=ZSUM(J)*(1. -ZSUM(J)/WT)
790.            DEN2=PST(J) -PB(J)*PB(J)/WT
791.            PB(J)=NUM*NUM/(DEN1*DEN2)
792.        185 CONTINUE
793.            WRITE(6,196)(J,PB(J),J=1,M)
794.        196 FORMAT(/1X,'MULTIPLE R-SQUARE FOR EACH ENDOGENOUS ATTRIBUTE',
795.           &/(1X,'J=',I2,': ',F8.3))
796.      C
797.        186 RETURN
798.            END
799.
800.            SUBROUTINE INVER(A,N)
801.      C
802.            DIMENSION A(80,80),INDEX(80,2),IPIVOT(80),PIVOT(80)
803.            COMMON PIVOT,INDEX,IPIVOT
804.            EQUIVALENCE (IROW,JROW),(ICOLUM,JCOLUM),(AMAX,T,SWAP)
805.      C
806.            DETERM=1.0
807.      C
808.            DO 20 J=1,N
809.         20 IPIVOT(J)=0
810.      C
811.            DO 550 I=1,N
```

167

```
812.          AMAX=0.0
813.   C
814.          DO 105 J=1,N
815.          IF(IPIVOT(J)-1) 60,105,60
816.   C
817.       60 DO 100 K=1,N
818.          IF(IPIVOT(K)-1) 80,100,740
819.   C
820.       80 IF(ABS(AMAX)-ABS(A(J,K))) 85,100,100
821.   C
822.       85 IROW=J
823.          ICOLUM=K
824.          AMAX=A(J,K)
825.   C
826.      100 CONTINUE
827.      105 CONTINUE
828.   C
829.          IPIVOT(ICOLUM)=IPIVOT(ICOLUM)+1
830.          IF(IROW-ICOLUM) 140,260,140
831.   C
832.      140 DETERM=-DETERM
833.   C
834.          DO 200 L=1,N
835.          SWAP=A(IROW,L)
836.          A(IROW,L)=A(ICOLUM,L)
837.      200 A(ICOLUM,L)=SWAP
838.   C
839.      260 INDEX(I,1)=IROW
840.          INDEX(I,2)=ICOLUM
841.          PIVOT(I)=A(ICOLUM,ICOLUM)
842.          DETERM=DETERM*PIVOT(I)
843.          A(ICOLUM,ICOLUM)=1.0
844.   C
845.          DO 350 L=1,N
846.          IF(PIVOT(I).NE.0) GOTO 349
847.          A(ICOLUM,L)=0.
848.          GOTO 350
849.      349 A(ICOLUM,L)=A(ICOLUM,L)/PIVOT(I)
850.      350 CONTINUE
851.   C
852.          DO 550 L1=1,N
853.          IF(L1-ICOLUM) 400,550,400
854.      400 T=A(L1,ICOLUM)
855.          A(L1,ICOLUM)=0.0
856.          DO 450 L=1,N
857.      450 A(L1,L)=A(L1,L)-A(ICOLUM,L)*T
858.   C
859.      550 CONTINUE
860.   C
861.          DO 710 I=1,N
862.          L=N+1-I
863.          IF(INDEX(L,1)-INDEX(L,2)) 630,710,630
864.      630 JROW=INDEX(L,1)
865.   C
866.          JCOLUM=INDEX(L,2)
867.   C
868.          DO 705 K=1,N
869.          SWAP=A(K,JROW)
870.          A(K,JROW)=A(K,JCOLUM)
871.          A(K,JCOLUM)=SWAP
872.      705 CONTINUE
873.   C
874.      710 CONTINUE
```

168

```
875.     C
876.        740 RETURN
877.           END
878.     //GO.FT02F001 DD UNIT=SYSDA,VOL=SER=NRES01,DISP=OLD,
879.     // DSN=$2ZB004.COL.SIMUL.INPUT5,DCB=(RECFM=FB,LRECL=80,BLKSIZE=4560)
880.     //GO.FT06F001 DD SYSOUT=A,DCB=(RECFM=FB,BLKSIZE=133)
881.     //
?
```

Chapter 5

Events

In all the preceding chapters, observations on states were assumed. Either an individual would be observed in a given state, or the individual would be asked in an interview what state he was in. For processes of the sort under consideration, however, there is another possible kind of observation: observation of the event by which the individual changes from one state to another.

The structure of continuous-time stochastic processes is one in which the individual resides in one state or another, with these times punctuated by events that move him into a new state. In the formal model the event is instantaneous and serves only to mark the time point at which a change of state occurs. In applying such models to reality, "events" may occupy some period of time, but the period is sufficiently short that, for the purposes at hand, events may be considered instantaneous. For example, in research on geographic mobility, the "states" of the model may be residences, and the "events" may be moves from one residence location to another. But a move takes one or more days, and for some purposes, one might want to define a new state, *moving,* bounded by two events, leaving the old residence and arriving at the new residence. Such decisions depend wholly upon the purpose for which the model is applied.

In some applications of these processes, it is not possible to identify the time at which an event occurred, but only to identify the current state of an individual. For example, in the study of attitudes or moods, it is often possible for the individual to report his current attitude or mood, but not when his attitude or mood changed. Nor is it possible for an external observer to note the occurrence of such a change. There may be some question about the appropriateness of discrete-state models for describing this situation. That is, there may be changes in an unobservable continuous-state space together with a response mechanism in which the observed response (such as good mood or bad mood) is a function of the position in the unobservable continuous-state space. But whether or not such a more complex model might be applicable, it is nevertheless true that discrete-state conceptions of what is taking place are widely used in analysis of such attitude and mood phenomena.

So long as this is the case, it must be recognized that for this class of phenomena, observations must be limited to states; events can only be inferred by successive reports of residence in different states. For these phenomena observations or records of events are not in principle possible, and methods described in chapters 3 and 4 are necessary.

However, for the class of phenomena in which events can be observed and recorded, the observation of events provides an attractive alternative to the observation of states. Their attraction lies in the fact that they often provide richer information about the process than does mere observation of the state. This can be seen by the information contained in observation of an event and that contained in observation of a state. In observation of occupancy of state i (say the job currently held by a person), the information consists only of occupancy of that state (rather than the other defined states) at that time. If the expected occupancy time of that state is t_i [which equals $1/q_i$ by equation (1.24)], then we can expect that for any time point during a period t_i units long, we would have made the same observation with no new information. But observation of the time at which an event occurs gives us information about a precise time point; on either side of that point, the person is in a different state. To look at it more simply, observation on state occupancy in a two-state process gives data of only zero or one, one bit of information, while the time of an event stated to an accuracy of 1 in a range of 0–1,000 gives about ten bits of information ($2^{10} = 1,024$).

It is also often feasible to obtain information on events in surveys, administrative records, or other systematic modes of observation. Administrative records ordinarily contain the dates of changes in status (job changes, salary changes, leaves of absence, enrollment changes), and surveys can often provide information about events in the recent past. If there is a multiwave panel, waves succeeding the first can often provide data about events that have intervened since the preceding panel wave. In cross-sectional surveys, it is possible to obtain information on the number of events of a certain type since a given date (for example, number of times admitted to a hospital, number of absences from school or job) and information on the time since (or date of) the last event of a given type. In other cases, it is possible to obtain information about the sequence of events of different types although the exact time of each event is not known.

This combination of rich information about the process and observational feasibility means that data on events provide attractive alternatives to data of states for estimating parameters in a social or psychological process. Before discussing the equations that allow this, it is useful to make a conceptual clarification concerning events and two-state processes.

Until now, I have discussed primarily two-state processes with states 0 and 1 and nonzero transition rates q_0 to state 0 and q_1 to state 1. The question is, are the processes involving events compatible with this?

For some empirical applications, the answer is clearly yes. If the event of interest is admission to a hospital, then we have two transition rates, q_1, the rate of admission to hospital, given that one is not in, and q_0, the rate of discharge from the hospital, given that one is in. If we know the proportion of time that the average person is in the hospital, and the average length of time between admissions, we can use equations (2.17) and (1.24) to give estimates of the rates of admission and exit. The estimate of the rate of admission, q_1, is simply the inverse of the average time between admissions [by equation (1.24)]. The rate of discharge is found by use of $p_1 = q_1/(q_1 + q_0)$, together with the direct estimate of p_1 (the proportion of total time spent in the hospital). Solving for q_0, we have $q_0 = q_1 \dfrac{(1 - p_1)}{p_1}$. The estimate of the average length of stay can also be found as $1/q_0$.

However, in some cases, it is somewhat artificial to assume as two-state processes. Consider the act of buying a book. It is possible to consider two states, the state of not buying and the state of buying, with transition rates toward buying given that one is not buying, and toward not buying given that one is buying. This, however, is somewhat artificial for a single reason: The two transition rates are of very different orders of magnitude. Suppose a person buys a book, on the average, once every two weeks. And suppose he spends ten minutes, on the average, in doing so. In two weeks there are 20,160 minutes, so he spends 1/2016 of his time in buying books; or to put it differently, the transition rate to buying books, expressed in minutes^{-1}, is 1/20160, while the transition rate to not buying is 1/10.

When such different orders of magnitude exist, the principal interest is ordinarily in the smaller transition rate (in this case, the rate toward buying), and the factors that affect it. It is often possible to ignore the second state and the second transition rate and consider this as a *point process,* in which the event does not move the person into a different state but simply occurs. Seen in this way, the event is buying a book, and the person is seen as having a transition rate toward that event at all times. In effect, what is done in such applications is to ignore the minuscule period of time that he spends in the other state. The analogue to the continuous-time Markov process for point processes is the Poisson process, as derived in equation (1.29).

In some cases, such as hospital admissions, our interest may be limited to the slower process, that is, admissions, even though the more rapid one is not quite negligible. It is possible for analytical purposes to convert a two-state process into a point process by subtracting out the small amount of time spent in the second state.

In all of the cases treated in this chapter, events of a given type will be analyzed separately—either through treating them as point processes, as just described, or through considering separately the periods of time spent in different states, as will be described with event histories in a subsequent section.

1. NUMBER OF EVENTS

One common form of data in questionnaries and interviews is the number of events that have occurred since a particular time. For example, a questionnaire administered to students in school may ask the student how many days he has been late to school during the last month.[1] Or a person may be asked how many times he has changed jobs in the last five years. Or a worker may be asked how many accidents requiring at least a trip to the infirmary he has had in the last year.

All of these examples generate data of the same form: the number of events in a fixed period of time. For such data, the Poisson probability, from equation (1.29), shows the relationship between the transition rate q_1, the period of time t, and the probability of a given number of events, $p_n(t)$, when the transition rate is constant:

$$p_n(t) = \frac{e^{-q_1 t}(q_1 t)^n}{n!}.$$ (5.1)

[1] In applying the model to such data, it should be recognized that because there is not a continuous time line with a constant transition rate, but instead twenty-two Bernoulli trials, one on each school day, there is an approximation involved in the application. The approximation is, however, innocuous so long as the probability of being tardy is small.

If we now allow the possibility that transition rates may be a function of various characteristics of individuals, according to a linear decomposition of q_1, equation (5.1) becomes

$$p_n(t) = \frac{e^{-t \sum_k b_k x_k} \left(t \sum_k b_k x_k \right)^n}{n!}. \tag{5.2}$$

Note that since we have only a single transition rate, q_1, there are not two models, for $c_k = -b_k$ and $c_k \neq -b_k$, as in the preceding chapters. There is simply the one parameter, b_k, for the particular kind of event under consideration. It is also important to note that with the kind of data considered in this section, there is no perfectly natural way in which to allow for independent variables that vary with time. Since we do not observe x_k at the times when events occur, but have only summary information about the number of events since a given time, then ordinarily the values of x_k will be known only at the time the observation is made.

There is one exception to this: If a question about the number of events is asked concerning a period between waves of a panel study, then values of x_k may be known at both the start and the end of the period for which the question is asked. If $x_k(0)$ is the value at the start, $x_k(t)$ is the value at the end, and it is reasonable to use a linear interpolation, equation (5.2) can be modified to make use of this information. The equation for the process is $\dfrac{dp_0}{dt} = q_1 p_0$. When x_k is a linear function of τ between $x_k(0)$ and $x_k(t)$, this equation, integrated to find the probability of no event, gives, for the case of linear decomposition of q_1:

$$p_0(t) = e^{-t \sum_k b_k \bar{x}_k} \tag{5.3}$$

where $\bar{x}_k = [x_k(t) + x_k(0)]/2$.

To find $p_1(t)$, we use a modification of equation (1.28),

$$p_1(t) = \int_0^t e^{-\tau \sum b_k [x_k(\tau) + x_k(0)]/2} \, q_1(\tau) e^{-(t-\tau) \sum b_k [x_k(\tau) + x_k(t)]/2} \, d\tau \tag{5.4}$$

This equation may be solved to give

$$p_1(t) = e^{-t \sum b_k \bar{x}_k} \, t \sum b_k \bar{x}_k. \tag{5.5}$$

This has the same form as the equation for constant x_k and the solution for $p_2(t), \ldots, p_n(t)$ gives the same form, so that by induction the equation for $p_n(t)$ becomes simply

$$p_n(t) = \frac{e^{-t \sum_k b_k \bar{x}_k} \left(t \sum_k b_k \bar{x}_k \right)^n}{n!} \tag{5.6}$$

This equation or equation (5.2) may be used to estimate the values of b_k if we have for each individual the values of x_k (or $\bar{x}_k$ in the case of linear change in x_k) and the number of events in time period t. The values of b_k are found as those values that maximize the likelihood of $\prod_i p_{n_i}(t)$, where $p_{n_i}(t)$ is the probability that individual i was involved in n_i events in time period t. The maximum likelihood estimates are given in chapter 6.

If the form of decomposition of q_1 is exponentially linear, then equation (5.1) becomes

$$p_n(t) = \frac{e^{-te \sum_k b_k x_k} \left(te^{\sum_k b_k x_k} \right)^n}{n!}. \tag{5.7}$$

As in the linear case, estimates of b_k may be found by maximum likelihood methods described in chapter 6.

Also as in the linear case, it is possible to introduce nonconstant independent variables where $x_k(t)$ and $x_k(0)$ are both measured, and linear interpolation is assumed between 0 and t. However, this is not a simple form for $p_n(t)$ in this case, so that the b_k's cannot be easily estimated.

Maximum likelihood methods of estimation for this form of data are described in chapter 6, but no computer programs are appended.

2. TIME SINCE LAST EVENT

A second common form of data in questionnaires and interviews is the time since the last event. The probability of an event occurring for the first time at time t is the probability of no event until t multiplied by probability of an event at t. Since a Markov process is identical backward and forward, this product is not only the probability that an event will occur at a future time t measured from the present ($t = 0$), but also the probability that it will have occurred t time units backward from the present. If $\pi(t)$ is the probability that the first event is t units in the past, then if we use subscript i for individual i, $\pi_i(t_i)$ is the probability that no event had occurred until time t_i, times the probability that an event occurs at t_i:

$$\pi_i(t_i) = e^{-q_i t_i} q_i. \tag{5.8}$$

Using the linear decomposition of q, this becomes

$$\pi_i(t_i) = e^{-t_i \sum b_k x_{ki}} \sum b_k x_{ki}. \tag{5.9}$$

Equation (5.8) assumes constant x_k. If x_k is a function of time, varying linearly between t_i and 0, then as before it is possible to take account of this variation by using the mean value of x_{ki} between $x_k(t_i)$ and $x_k(0)$, that is, $\bar{x}_k$ [$=(x_k(0) + x_k(t_i)]/2$) in place of x_k in the exponent in equation (5.9). The equation becomes

$$\pi_i(t_i) = e^{-t_i \sum_k b_k \bar{x}_{ki}} \sum_k b_k x_{ki}(t_i). \tag{5.10}$$

This sort of data will often not be available because the time t_i will vary over individuals, and $x_k(t_i)$ will be unknown. However, it is possible that such information can be obtained in an interview or questionnaire by questions following the one about the time of the last event (for example, "What was your income at that time?"). In that case, equation (5.10) gives the probability of the event as a function of average income between the initial reference point and the event, and of income at the time of the event.

The estimation of the values of b_k is obtained through maximizing the likelihood of $\prod_{i=1}^{N} \pi_i(t_i)$ with respect to the b_k.

For exponential linear decomposition, equation (5.9) becomes

$$\pi_i(t_i) = e^{-t_i e^{\sum_k b_k x_{ki}}} e^{\sum_k b_k x_{ki}} \tag{5.11}$$

This equation can be used in maximum likelihood estimation, as described

176

in chapter 6, to obtain values of b_k that maximize the likelihood of having obtained responses $t_1, \ldots, t_n$ from the sample of n individuals.

If x_k is a function of t, and is assumed to vary linearly between t_i and 0, then the probability of no event during this period is found by integrating $dp/p = -q_1(t)dt$ between t_i and 0. Integration of this equation when q_1 is a function of t gives $p_i(t_i) = \exp\left(-\int_0^{t_i} q(\tau)d\tau\right)$, and this integral when x varies linearly between times 0 and t_i gives

$$\int_0^{t_i} q(\tau)d\tau = \frac{t_i[q_i(t_i) - q_i(0)]}{\sum b_k[x_{ki}(t_i) - x_{ki}(0)]} . \tag{5.12}$$

If the right-hand side of equation (5.12) is denoted by $\alpha_i t_i$, the probability that the most recent event for person i was at time t_i is

$$\pi_i(t_i) = e^{-\alpha_i t_i} q_i(t_i), \text{ where } q_i(t_i) = e^{\sum b_k x_{ki}(t_i)} . \tag{5.13}$$

As in the earlier cases, the techniques for finding the values of b_k, which maximize the likelihood of having obtained the observed responses, are given in chapter 6. As in the preceding form of data, no computer program is appended.

3. SEQUENCES OF EVENTS

Another form of data from processes such as these consists of the order of events in a sequence. D. R. Cox (1972a, 1975) has developed a *partial likelihood* method for analysis of such sequences that is not full-maximum likelihood but gives estimates that have most of the properties of maximum likelihood estimates. This method is described in chapter 6. However, I will discuss here the general ideas behind the method in order to give a sense of the range of their application.

In application of the method we think of a sequence of events, which for present will be a simple case in which there can be at most one event for each person, and there is only one type of event, say death. In such a sequence there is at the outset a total transition rate consisting of the sum of each person's transition rate. The total transition rate is reduced after the first person has died and continues to be reduced after others have died. At any point in time, the probability of person i dying next (assuming that the transition rates are constant over time or are all amplified or reduced over time to the same degree) is $q_1(t)/\Sigma q_j(t)$, where the summation in the denominator extends over the set of remaining persons, the *risk set* at this point in time.

Consider a set of persons, each of whom can carry out some action. For example, the set of persons may be ninth-grade boys in a given school, and the action may be some form of delinquency. We know something about each of the boys, such as his grades in school, his family's income, and his parents' educational levels. If we observe which of the boys commits a delinquent act first, second, third, and so on over all the acts that occur, then we should be able to infer something about the effects of grades, family income, and parents' education on the probability of committing a delinquent act in a period of time.

Cox's method of partial likelihood provides an efficient method of estimating these effects and, furthermore, does so by using only the order in which the boys committed these acts, without the necessity of knowing the times at which they were committed. It is the order in which events occur to persons with different characteristics rather than the actual times of the events that contains most of the information about the effect those characteristics have on the transition rate toward that event, so long as the effect is multiplicative rather than additive. Efron (1977) proves that Cox's partial likelihood method, which uses only order information, asymptotically contains all the information about effects of independent variables. Knowing the actual times of the events gives information about the absolute sizes of the transition rates, but gives little information beyond that contained by the order of events about amplification or suppression of transition rates by various independent variables that differ across individuals.

Cox's method of partial likelihood was initially developed as a way of estimating the effects of various factors on survival, with initial application to life tables. In the applications that Cox considered, only one event at most can occur to each individual, for example, death, or in industrial applications, failure of the item. However, there are other applications in which the actions are not taken by different persons, though the actions may be independent. One application occurs if a person is asked to rank a set of items, and create a sequence by this ranking. In such a rank-order, the risk set is reduced by one at each step. If the items are characterized by values on one or more variables or attributes, which may affect their transition rate to being ranked, the analysis will show the effects of these variables and attributes. If a group of cities is observed to pass fluoridation laws in a particular sequence, then the sequence of actions can be analyzed by this method, and the effects of characteristics on the rate of passage can be estimated. If an organization makes a sequence of appointments to similar jobs in the organization, and if the appointments are independent, knowledge of the sequence and characteristics of the persons appointed at each point in the sequence (as well as those not appointed) can be used to discover the effects of these characteristics on appointment rates.

Neither is it necessary that in a sequence of actions by different persons, the action be taken no more than once by a given person. These methods have been used to examine effects of various factors on the rate of becoming unemployed, where the number of periods of unemployment may range fron none to several (see DiPrete, 1979). They have also been used to study factors affecting marriage and divorce rates, with some persons getting married or divorced more than once during the period of observation (Hannan, Tuma, and Groeneveld, 1978).

In these cases of multiple events for the same person, there are transition rates back into the state from which the first event occurred: back into employment from unemployment, back into marriage from divorce. Thus, after this second kind of event occurs, the person is once again in the risk set for the first kind of event. After becoming once again employed, the person is again in the risk set for unemployment. In order to analyze such data, all that is necessary is to ascertain the risk set for a given kind of event at the point when such an event occurs.

It is useful to consider further the case in which the event can recur for the individual, as in the case of delinquent acts. In such a case, dependence between acts may be explicitly modeled by including among the independent variables information about the occurrence of earlier events for that individual (for example, including as an independent variable the number of previous acts of delinquency). Even further extensions can be made, for individuals need not be assumed to be independent. Dependence among acts of different individuals can be modeled by incorporating among the independent variables information about prior acts of other individuals with whom the individual has some connection. For example, in a study of doctors' introduction of a new drug, Coleman, Katz, and Menzel (1966) obtained from pharmacies information on the dates each doctor first prescribed the drug. Information about the doctors included the city in which each practiced (the sample was limited to four small cities), which doctor or doctors each shared an office with, what hospital each had an appointment in, what doctor each turned to most often for advice, and what doctors were their closest friends. Since nearly all doctors in these cities were in the sample, a partial likelihood analysis of doctors' introduction of drugs could be carried out with independent variables (changing over time), such as the fraction of doctors in the particular doctor's city who had introduced the drug, the fraction of those with whom he shared an office who had done so, the fraction of those at his hospital who had done so, the fraction of his friends, and a 0–1 variable for introduction by the doctor he reported he turned to most for advice. This would give measures of the effect of each of these relationships on the transition rate toward introducing the drug.

The method may be extended as well to the study of different types of events or acts where there are multiple types of acts possible. For example, in the study of delinquency, there are different types of delinquency, and the method can be used to examine effects of different variables on each type of delinquent act, as well as to examine effects of the prior occurrence of one type of act on the subsequent occurrence of another. Or with consumer diary panels, in which consumers record the date and brand of purchase of various types of goods, it is possible to use such data to examine effects of various consumer characteristics, as well as the brand of the preceding purchase on the probability per unit time of purchase of a given brand.

The formal method of analysis of such sequences is carried out in chapter 6. Here I will present examples to illustrate use of the method.

3.1. EXAMPLE

Six Cases, One Independent Attribute: The first example will be hypothetical, to show just how the calculation is carried out. There are six bottles of white wine, three randomly drawn from a given year's production at vineyard A, three randomly drawn from the same year's production at vineyard B. The wine is tasted and rated according to taste. The order of the wines is A_1, A_2, B_1, A_3, B_2, B_3. The question is, how much better do we estimate the wine from vineyard A to be on the basis of these data? And how confident can we be that vineyard A's wines are better than vineyard B's?

In obtaining the estimate, it is necessary to calculate the following quantities on each iteration (see chapter 6 for derivation of these quantities). Although there is only one independent attribute in this case, I will write the quantities in more general form, to indicate the nature of the calculations when there are more independent variables. The following equations are written for s independent variables, n events, and m individuals. The quantities are:

$$q_i^*(t_j) = e^{-\lambda_j} q_i(t_j) = e^{\sum b_k x_{ki}}. \tag{5.14}$$

The quantity $q_i(t_j)$ is the transition rate for individual i at event j (here assumed constant by having $x_{ki}(t_j) = x_{ki}$), composed of the effects of independent variables k and the effect of the particular period j (expressed as λ_j). Only the effects of the independent variables, $q_i^*(t_j)$, are calculated:

$$y_{ij} = \frac{q_i(t_j)}{\sum q_h(t_j)\delta_{hj}} \left(= \frac{q_i^*(t_j)}{\sum_h q_h^*(t_j)\delta_{hj}} \right). \qquad (5.15)$$

The quantity y_{ij} is the transition rate for individual i (in this example the "individual" is a wine bottle) when event j occurs (in this example, when bottle j is chosen), divided by the sum of the rates over all individuals (bottles) still remaining at this point. (δ_{hj} is one if the bottle is among those remaining for consideration at time j, it is zero otherwise.) The quantity y_{ij} is a conditional probability that i was chosen at time j, given that a choice was made, and given that the risk set consisted of the individuals for whom $\delta_{hj} = 1$.

$$g_{kj} = \sum_{i=1}^{m} x_{ki}y_{ij}\delta_{ij}. \qquad (5.16)$$

The quantity g_{kj} is the sum, over all individuals in the risk set at the time of event j, of the conditional probability y_{ij} times the value of independent variable k for the individual (in this case, there is only one independent variable, with a value of 1 for vineyard A, 0 for vineyard B). g_{kj} can be thought of as the effective strength of the independent variable k toward being chosen at time j.

$$d_k = \sum_{j=1}^{m} (x_{kj} - g_{kj}). \qquad (5.17)$$

The quantity d_k is the sum of the difference between the value of the independent variable k for individual j and the quantity g_{kj}, the strength of k at the time j was chosen. And finally,

$$a_{hk} = \sum_{j=1}^{n} \sum_{i=1}^{m} x_{hi}x_{ki}y_{ij\ ij} - \sum_{j=1}^{n} g_{hj}g_{kj}. \qquad (5.18)$$

The quantity a_{hk} has a form like that of a cross-product, heuristically the sum over all events j of the difference between the joint strength of variables h and k at event j and the product of the separate strengths of h and k.

For iteration at the v stage, we have

$$\mathbf{b}^v = \mathbf{b}^{v-1} + \mathbf{d}^{v-1}(\mathbf{a}^{v-1})^{-1}$$

where this is written in matrix form, with $\mathbf{b}^v$ a $1 \times s$ vector of parameters at stage v, $\mathbf{d}$ a $1 \times s$ vector of elements d_k, and $\mathbf{a}$ an $s \times s$ matrix of elements a_{hk}.

Two points should be made about these equations. First, and perhaps the most important virtue of this method, the period-specific component of the transition rate drops out of the calculations, since $q_i(t_j)$ appears only relative to other qs at the same time as t_j in the equation for y_{ij}. That is, a multiplier e^{λ_j} appears in both numerator and denominator. Second, in this example, since there is only one independent variable, there is only one quantity d, only one quantity a, and only five quantities g_j for the five points at which a decision was made. We have only one quantity b to estimate.

To carry out the calculation, we can begin with a starting value of $b = 0$. The calculations are:

For iteration $v = 1$:

$q_i(t_j) = e^{\lambda_j}$ for all i, $q_i^*(t_j) = 1.0$ for all i.

	$j =$	1	2	3	4	5
1	(A_1)	1/6				
2	(A_2)	1/6	1/5			
3	(B_1)	1/6	1/5	1/4		
y_{ij} $i = 4$	(A_3)	1/6	1/5	1/4	1/3	
5	(B_2)	1/6	1/5	1/4	1/3	1/2
6	(B_3)	1/6	1/5	1/4	1/3	1/2

$j =$	1	2	3	4	5
$g_j =$	1/2	2/5	1/4	1/3	0

$d = 1/2 + 3/5 - 1/4 + 2/3 + 0 = 1.517$

$a = 1.483 - 1/2^2 - 2/5^2 - 1/4^2 - 1/3^2 = .900$

$b = b^{(0)} + d/a = 1.687$

For iteration $v = 2$:

$j =$	1	2	3	4	5
1	.281				
2	.281	.391			
y_{ij} $i = 3$	.052	.072	.119		
4	.281	.391	.643	.730	
5	.052	.072	.119	.135	.500
6	.052	.072	.119	.135	.500
$g_j =$	.843	.782	.643	.730	0

$d = .157 + .218 - .643 + .270 = .002$

$a = 3.000 - .843^2 - .782^2 - .643^2 - .730^2 = 0.732$

$b = 1.687 + .002/1.416 = 1.688$

Effective convergence occurred after only two iterations, giving an estimated value of 1.688 for b. This means, in the present example, that a wine drawn at random from the cellars of vineyard A is $e^{1.688}$ or 5.41 times as likely to be chosen in a taste comparison with one from vineyard B.

The second derivative of the likelihood function is merely the negative of the matrix of elements a_{jk}, or in this case the negative of a. A lower bound for the variance of b, which asymptotically equals the variance for b, is given by the negative of the inverse of this (see chapter 6), or in this case, $-(-.732)^{-1} = 1.366$. Of course, the small number of cases means that this may underestimate the true variance. The estimate of the standard deviation is the square root of this, or 1.169. The estimate of b is about 1.44 times the estimated standard deviation, which means that according to this estimate of the variance, the chance is about 3 in 40 that the wines from vineyard A do not taste better than those from vineyard B (that is, about 3 in 40 chances that b is actually not greater than zero). In this case we can check the variance estimate, since by random drawings there are 2 chances out of 20 (or 4 in 40) of a drawing as extreme as this in favor of vineyard A. This means that the variance estimate from the inverse of a is close to the true variance, although somewhat smaller.

3.2. EXAMPLE

Effect of a Drug on Remission of Leukemia: Cox, in his 1972 paper, presented an example of a drug used on twenty-one patients with leukemia, compared to a control group of twenty-one patients with leukemia to whom the drug was not administered. The example, which contains censored data, will be useful for comparison with the maximum likelihood method discussed in the next section. The example also contains *ties,* that is, two or more events occurring at the same point in time, as measured. Such ties are ordinarily due to a recording of time in intervals rather than with precision. In this case, a week was the recording interval. The data are listed in table 5.1.

TABLE 5.1

Length of Remission of Leukemia in Weeks After Initiation of Drug Treatment (or, for Control Patients, Start of Observation)

Experimental group:	6*, 6, 6, 6, 7, 9*, 10*, 10, 11*, 13, 16, 17*, 19*, 20, 22, 23, 25*, 32*, 32*, 34*, 35*.
Control group:	1, 1, 2, 2, 3, 4, 4, 5, 5, 8, 8, 8, 8, 11, 11, 12, 12, 15, 17, 22, 23

* An asterisk indicates that the observation was censored after this point.

183

The table suggests that the drug has a strong effect. For those who were observed until the disease recurred, the average length of remission was 12.9 weeks for the treated patients and 8.7 weeks for the control group, or about 1.5 times as long for the treated patients as for the control group. Since in a continuous-time Markov process the expected time to the event is the inverse of the transition rate, then if these events are occurring through such a process, this comparison indicates that the transition rate to recurrence for the control-group patients is about 1.5 times that of the experimental patients.

Yet this crude comparison undoubtedly gives an estimate of the effect that is biased downward, since it ignores all those patient records that were censored, and most of those censored records occurred late in the observation period. Even if the worst were assumed, and all the experimental patients who were censored were assumed to have had a recurrence at the time of censoring, the average length of remission would be nearly twice that of the control group. The method of partial likelihood makes use of this censored data (or most of it, as I will indicate later) and thus should show an even greater effect.

Hand calculations could be used for this example as for the last, because there remains only one independent variable and thus no matrix to invert. However, the LONGIT·EVENTP program contained in the appendix was used in this case, giving a value of $b = -1.51$ with a standard error of .412. This means that the drug reduces the recurrence rate to $e^{-1.51} = 0.216$ of its size in the absence of the drug. Cox obtained for this example a $b = -1.65$ (1972, p. 198). He did not calculate the standard deviation from the second derivative of the log likelihood but obtained confidence intervals from the log likelihood function. These give approximately .478 for the standard deviation.

The difference in estimates of b between -1.51 and -1.65 is most likely due to the treatment of ties. For ties the method must be modified, since it is based on the use of conditional probabilities that i acted at time t_j, given that someone acted at time t. Cox recognizes that whenever time is measured in discrete units, there is some chance that a period as measured will be terminated by more than one event. In the example Cox presents, time is measured in weeks, and a number of periods are terminated by two events, with one terminated by three and one terminated by four. Cox treats this situation by a discrete-time analysis, and the conditional probability of the single event occurring at time t_j, given that an event occurred, is replaced by the conditional probability that a particular set M_j of m_j events occurred at time t_j, given that some set of m_j occurred at t_j. This is $\prod_{i \in M_j} q_i(t_j) / \Sigma \prod_{k \in N_j}$

$q_k(t_j)$, where the sum in the denominator is taken over all distinct sets N_j of size m_j of individuals in the risk set at time t_j.

In a comment on Cox's paper, Richard Peto (Cox, 1972a, p. 207) points out that for continuous time Cox's conditional probability for tied events is an approximation to the true probability (which, for example, in the case of two events is $(q_1/\Sigma q_i)[q_2/(\Sigma q_i - q_1)] + (q_2/\Sigma q_i)[q_1/(\Sigma q_i - q_2)]$. He suggests an alternative approximation that is easier to compute, which is, in the case

of m_j events, $\prod_{i \in M_j} q_i(t_j)/\binom{r_j}{m_j}\left(\sum_{i \in R_j} q_i(t_j)/N\right)^{m_j}$, where r_j is the number in the

risk set at time t_j and m_j is the number who acted, and R_j is the risk set at time t_j. In the LONGIT·EVENTP program, I have used Peto's suggestion, which, as it turns out, is the marginal likelihood proposed for this case by Kalbfleisch (Cox, 1972, p. 215).

4. EVENT HISTORIES

Full records of the continuous history of events provide the most complete data possible for analysis of processes of the sort discussed in this book. These records contain not only the order information required for use of the method of partial likelihood, but also, as in the second example above, information about the times at which events occurred. If events are for convenience labeled according to order of occurrence so that $t_1 < t_2 < \ldots < t_m$, then it is possible to write the probability of the sequence $t_1, \ldots, t_m$ as

$$e^{-\int_0^t q \cdot (\tau)d\tau} q_{i_1}(t_1) e^{\int_{t_1}^{t_2} q \cdot (\tau)d\tau} q_{i_2}(t_2) \ldots e^{-\int_{t_{m-1}}^{t_m} q \cdot (\tau)d\tau} q_{i_m}(t_m), \quad (5.19)$$

where $q \cdot (\tau)$ is the sum of the transition rates at time τ for all those in the risk set at that time, and $q_{i_j}(t_j)$ is the transition rate for the person i_j who acted at time t_j. However, while the probability of such a set of times for the designated actions can be written down in this fashion, maximum likelihood methods for event histories using equation (5.19) are difficult to arrive at (see Hannan, Tuma, and Groeneveld, 1979). What is more feasible in some circumstances is to use either of two strategies that simplify the situation. One strategy is to use Cox's partial likelihood for estimating the effects of independent variables—either varying over time or constant over time—as in example 3.2, and then, take those estimates as given, and maximize the likelihood of the observed times, given these estimates. An idea of the way this may be done can be given here, although the full method is outlined in chapter 6.

Nancy Tuma and Michael Hannan, in a series of papers and a forthcoming book, have done most to introduce the analysis of event histories into social research. A look at their papers listed in the reference section will give an idea of the broad fruitfulness of this mode of analysis.

4.1. ESTIMATING THE ABSOLUTE RATE AT EACH TIME PERIOD, GIVEN THE PARTIAL LIKELIHOOD ESTIMATES

The probability of event i occurring at a given time t, given that some event out of those at risk [in set $R(t)$] occurred at time t, is simply the ratio $q_i(t)/\sum_{j \in R(t)} q_j(t)$. If the denominator, $\sum_{j \in R(t)} q_j(t)$, which is the total transition rate at time t, is denoted by $q \cdot (t)$, then the probability that no event occurs between times t_{i-1} and t_i, and that the event occurred for person i at time t_i, is given by [see equation (5.8)]:

$$p_i(t_i) = e^{-\int_{t_{i-1}}^{t_i} q \cdot (\tau) d\tau} q_i(t_i) \tag{5.20}$$

and this can also be written

$$p_i(t_i) = e^{-\int_{t_{i-1}}^{t_i} q \cdot (\tau) d\tau} q \cdot (t_i) \frac{q_i(t_i)}{q \cdot (t_i)}. \tag{5.21}$$

We know the fraction on the right-hand side from use of Cox's partial likelihood as described in the earlier section. The remainder of the right-hand side is independent of the characteristics of person i, and it becomes possible, as described in chapter 6, to solve for $q \cdot (t_i)$, the total transition rate at the time period t_{i-1}, t_i. Or, since all components of $q \cdot (t_i)$ except the period-specific component have been estimated, the period-specific component

186

can be estimated. (Since there is no event in this time interval, $q \cdot (t)$ can be regarded as constant over this period.)[2]

4.2. EXAMPLE

Period-Specific Rates in Leukemia Recurrence: For certain applications, it is useful to calculate the period-specific components of transition rates. The method by which these are calculated is described in chapter 6. Here we need note only that these components are calculated given the effects of independent variables determined according to Cox's method of partial likelihood. With those values, it is possible to estimate the period-specific rates when the value of each independent variable is zero. Obviously, the estimates of period-specific rates will depend very much on the length of the period and the number of individuals who acted in this period relative to the number of individuals still at risk. Table 5.2 presents the estimates of the period-specific rates. These rates show, apart from their fluctuation, that the probability per unit time of recurrence increases with time.

TABLE 5.2

Period-specific Transition Rates to Recurrence of Leukemia

Period	λ	Rate Without Drug
1	−2.55	.078
2	−2.47	.085
3	−3.70	.025
4	−2.33	.097
5	−2.23	.108
6	−1.71	.183
7	−2.75	.064
8	−1.35	.259
9	−1.73	.177
10	−1.69	.185
11	−1.45	.232
12	−1.89	.151
13	−1.16	.313
14	−1.68	.186
15	−1.64	.194
16	−1.05	.350
17	−0.14	.869

[2] If independent variables are changing regularly over time, then $q \cdot (t)$ can be assumed to change within this interval. In that case, since for time period i,

$$q \cdot (t) = \sum_{k \in R(t_i)} e^{\lambda_i} e^{\mathbf{bx}_{k(t)}} = e^{\lambda_i} \sum_{k \in R(t_i)} e^{\mathbf{bx}_{k(t)}},$$

λ_i can be estimated since the summation can be calculated after having estimated the **b** vector by partial likelihood methods.

5. MAXIMUM LIKELIHOOD BY USE OF MULTIPLE SMALL INTERVALS

A second strategy can be used for analysis of event histories. A continuous record for an individual consists of a set of events (perhaps from different states, perhaps into different states) spaced in time. If there is more than one individual, then, as indicated earlier, the combined records can be divided into time segments punctuated by events. If time is not measured precisely, more than one event may be recorded at the same time. For example, in the data analyzed by Cox on the experiment involving use of a drug for treating leukemia, the time was measured in weeks, and as shown earlier, most weeks contained more than one event. If time were measured precisely, of course, there would be no such ties. But time is never measured with complete precision, and the units are often sufficiently large that some ties exist.

What can be done in a case like this is to divide up the total time period into segments. In the experiment of table 5.1 the natural unit is the unit of measurement, one week. Then for each week, it is possible to divide persons into three groups: (a) those for whom the event occurred during the period; (b) those who were present at the beginning and the end of the period, but for whom no event occurred; and (c) those who were not present during all or a portion of the period. The last class includes both those who were no longer at risk at the beginning of the period and those for whom observation was censored during the period.

Classes (a) and (b) constitute all those at risk during the period in question. If we call p_i the probability of remaining in the state, then this is given for individual i by

$$p_i = e^{-\int_{t_1}^{t_2} q_i(\tau) d\tau} \qquad (5.22)$$

The probability that the event occurs to all those in class (a) and that all those in class (b) remain in the state is the product of $(1 - p_i)$, for all persons i in class (a) and p_k for all persons k in class (b), that is,

$$\mathcal{L} = \prod_{i \epsilon A}(1 - p_i) \prod_{k \epsilon B} p_k \cdot \qquad (5.23)$$

This product is the likelihood of the observed outcomes in this period, and will form the basis, in chapter 6, for the maximum likelihood estimation of

188

the effects of independent variables on q. But, following the pattern of the earlier section, we are interested in two different assumptions about the form of effect of independent variables on q: linear effects and exponential effects. And in each of these cases, the independent variables x_{ki} may be constant or may change linearly over the time period, with observation at both the beginning and the end of the period. Thus it is useful, for purposes of estimation in chapter 6, to restate the value of $\int_{t_1}^{t_2} q(\tau)d\tau$ in each of these cases, as derived in chapter 3:

Linear, constant $\mathbf{x}$: $\displaystyle\int_{t_1}^{t_2} q_i(\tau)d\tau = \mathbf{bx}_i(t_2 - t_1)$

Linear, nonconstant $\mathbf{x}$: $\displaystyle\int_{t_1}^{t_2} q_i(\tau)d\tau = \mathbf{b\bar{x}}_i(t_2 - t_1)$

where $\bar{\mathbf{x}}_i = [\mathbf{x}_i(t_2) + \mathbf{x}_i(t_1)]/2$

Exponential, constant $\mathbf{x}$: $\displaystyle\int_{t_1}^{t_2} q_i(\tau)d\tau = e^{\mathbf{bx}_i}(t_2 - t_1)$

Exponential, nonconstant $\mathbf{x}$: $\displaystyle\int_{t_1}^{t_2} q_i(\tau)d\tau = \frac{e^{\mathbf{bx}_i(t_2)} - e^{\mathbf{bx}_i(t_1)}}{\mathbf{b}(\mathbf{x}(t_2) - \mathbf{x}(t_1))}(t_2 - t_1)$

In the estimation, observations over all time periods are treated together, that is, the likelihood of the observed times of events is

$$\mathcal{L} = \prod_{j=1}^{J} \prod_{i \in A_j} (1 - p_{ij}) \prod_{k \in B_j} p_{kj},$$ (5.24)

where $j = 1, \ldots, J$ indexes the number of time segments. It might at first appear that this is a conditional likelihood rather than a full likelihood since the likelihood for each period given in equation (5.23) is conditional upon the composition of the risk set at that period. But the composition of the risk set at period j is determined by the observed outcomes at periods $j - 1, j - 2, \ldots, 1$. Thus this is a full likelihood.

Another way of seeing this is to consider one individual i who is present up through period j. As presented in equation (5.24), the likelihood of this occurrence is given by the product $p_{i1}, p_{i2}, \ldots, p_{ij}$, or

$$\prod_{h=1}^{j} e^{-\int_{t_{h-1}}^{t_h} q_i(\tau)d\tau}$$

189

These are independent probabilities, and this is simply another way of writing the probability

$$p_i(t_0,\ t_j) \quad (= e^{-\int_{t_0}^{t_j} q_i(\tau) d\tau})$$

that i is present from time 0 to time t.

The transition rate for period j when all independent variables are zero can either be taken as a constant, b_0, as in the case of panels, left unconstrained to differ for all time periods, or assumed to be some explicit function of time. If it is unconstrained, then each time period is treated as a dummy variable. The example in section 5.2 will show the possible options. In the method of partial likelihood, these parameters are "nuisance parameters," which drop out and do not appear in the calculation (though they may subsequently be estimated conditionally upon the partial likelihood estimates, as indicated in the preceding section).

In addition to continuous-record data, a different form of data may be analyzed by this model as well. These are data from panels of two or more waves when there is only an event in one direction between waves. For example, if the first grade of a school is observed at two points in time, and children are observed for whether or not they are able to read at the two times, only one kind of event can reasonably have occurred between the two observations: learning to read.[3] Or if doctors are observed at two points in time and asked if they have ever prescribed a given drug, then apart from response error, there is only one kind of event that will have changed their response: having introduced the drug into their practice.

With such data, there are numerous ties in the sense discussed earlier, because those for whom the event occurred early in the interobservation period are not distinguished from those for whom it occurred later.

The model takes a particularly simple form when there are only two time periods. Consider the case of a single independent attribute, x_1, constant over time, and assume for simplicity the linear decomposition model. Then at the first observation, there are two types of persons for whom the event has not yet occurred (that is, two types of persons in the risk set): those with $x_1 = 0$ and those with $x_1 = 1$. For the first, the probability of remaining in the state is $p_1 = e^{-(b_0 + b_1)t}$; and for the second, the probability of remaining in the state is $p_0 = e^{-b_0 t}$. We observe for each of these groups a proportion that actually did remain in the state, say p_1^* and p_0^*. Then a simple estimate

---

[3] Logically, it is the case that a reverse movement is possible in this example; in some cases, however, no reverse movement is logically possible. Both kinds of cases can reasonably be studied with this model.

of b_0 is $b_0 = -\dfrac{1}{t} \log p_0^*$, and a simple estimate of b_1 is $b_1 = -\dfrac{1}{t} \log p_1^* +$

$\dfrac{1}{t}\log p_0^*$. When the number of variables is greater, when the number of individuals of each type differs, and when there are more than two points of observation, the need for more general methods of estimation arises. The approach just outlined, in which the likelihood of observed outcomes over all time periods and all individuals is maximized, satisfies that need.

5.1. EVENT-DEFINED INTERVALS

The method of this section can be carried one step further, by recognizing that there is always a minimum observation unit of time. In the leukemia example analyzed by partial likelihood, this unit is a week. It is because such minimum observation units exist, and because they are of some duration, that the problem of ties in the method of partial likelihood arises.

Consider first that we use this minimum observation unit for the small intervals discussed in the preceding section. In the leukemia example, there are thirty-five weeks altogether, with the week as the minimum observation unit, that means thirty-five such intervals. If the time unit is denoted as θ, then there are intervals θ_j, $j = 1, \ldots, J$, where J is the total observation period. In general, however, there will be fewer than J intervals terminated by an event or a censor. In the leukemia example, there are only seventeen intervals terminated by an event, and only seven more terminated by a censor. For eleven intervals (for example, the fourteenth week, see table 5.1) there are no events and no censors. If we consider the total interval between two events (say between the event in week 13 and the event in week 15), then for all weeks except the last all individuals remain in the state. The probability of individual i's having done so for interval θ_j is $p_i(\theta_j)$. Now the total time period between the two events is some multiple of θ_j, say n_j units. Then if the event initiating the period is at θ_j, the event terminating it is at θ_{j+n_j}. In the leukemia example, the interval between the event at the thirteenth week and the fifteenth week is two weeks, so that for $j = 13$, $n_j = 2$. The period is terminated at θ_{13+2}, or θ_{15}. For the first $n_j - 1$ small intervals within the event-defined period, all individuals in the risk set will be in class (b) referred to earlier, that is, all remain in the state. This occurs for individual i with probability $p_i(\Delta\theta_j)$ where $\Delta\theta_j$ is the time period θ_j to θ_{j+n_j-1}. The subset of individuals who act at time $j + n_j$ are in class (a) during this last $j + n_j$ interval [which we may denote as interval $k (= j + n_j)$], while those who remain are in class (b), and those for whom we have no further information because of censoring are in class (c). The probability of remaining at

191

this interval k is $p_i(\theta_k)$, the probability of acting is $1 - p_i(\theta_k)$. We do not know if those censored acted or remained, so for each of them a probability of 1 enters into the likelihood function. Defining $z_{ij} = 1$ if individual i does not act at time $j + n_j - 1$, 0 otherwise, and $u_{ij} = 1$ if individual i acts at time $j + n_j - 1$, 0 otherwise, then $z_{ij} + u_{ij} = 1$ for all who were not censored, and $z_{ij} + u_{ij} = 0$ for all those who were censored.[4] The likelihood of having observed this occurrence is

$$\mathcal{L}_j = \prod_{i \in R_j} p_i(\Delta\theta_j) p_i(\theta_k)^{z_{ij}} [1 - p_i(\theta_k)]^{u_{ij}} \qquad (5.25)$$

where R_j is all those at risk during interval j.

The likelihood function over the whole time period consists of the product of terms like that in equation (5.25); but rather than a product of J terms, the number of terms in the product is only the number of intervals terminated by an event or a censor. In the leukemia example, that means rather than a product of 35 terms, a product of $17 + 7 = 24$ terms. In cases where the unit of observation is small relative to the spacing of events, the difference between these two calculations can become very large; and what would be prohibitive to calculate by use of equation (5.24), with intervals defined by the unit of observation, becomes quite feasible by use of a product of terms like that in equation (5.25), with intervals defined by events and censors. Equation (5.25) shows the general form; for interval j terminated solely by censors, $z_{ij} = u_{ij} = 0$ for all individuals i; and the right-hand side of equation (5.25) becomes simply $\prod p_i(\Delta\theta_j)$.

5.2. EXAMPLE

The Leukemia Case Reanalyzed: Use of the method just described with Cox's leukemia example will show some of the similarities and differences

---

[4] The above assumes that censoring is a random event, independent of any external influences. Alternately, censoring can be treated as a second kind of event, and the transition rate to censoring can, like the event of interest, be explained by independent variables. In this case, if $q_{1i}(\theta_k)$ is the transition rate for the event of interest at time θ_k, and $q_{2i}(\theta_k)$ is the rate for censoring at θ_k, the likelihood given in equation (5.25) would become

$$\mathcal{L}_j = \prod_{i \in R_j} p_i(\Delta\theta_j) p_i(\theta_k)^{z_{ij}} \left[\frac{q_{1i}(\theta_k)}{q_{1i}(\theta_k) + q_{2i}(\theta_k)} \{1 - p_i(\theta_k)\} \right]^{u_{ij}} \left[\frac{q_{2i}(\theta_k)}{q_{1i}(\theta_k) + q_{2i}(\theta_k)} \{1 - p_i(\theta_k)\} \right]^{1 - z_{ij} - u_{ij}}$$

This is a special case of the likelihood for multiple types of events treated simultaneously. I will not treat multiple types of events in this section. The principal virtue of doing so is the greater capability it offers for estimating period-specific components of transition rates, not any increased efficiency in estimating effects of independent variables. That is, the effects on each type of event can be estimated by treating the likelihood for each event separately. In partial likelihood methods, there is a gain in precision of the estimate if multiple types of events are treated simultaneously.

of the two methods. First it should be pointed out that the partial likelihood method, by using only intervals terminated by events, fails to use all the information available and may bias the estimate. In this example table 5.1 shows that there are the following intervals at which there is information loss with partial likelihood: week 9, weeks 18–19, week 20, weeks 24–25, weeks 26–32, weeks 33–34, and week 35. For the individual censored after week 9, for example, the information that he had no event through week 8 is used by partial likelihood since week 8 was terminated by events on the part of others; but the information that he had no event during week 9 is lost.

Because all of this lost information is for the experimental subjects in this case, and because most of it is beyond the average time of the event for these subjects, the failure to use this information should bias the estimate. This is shown in the following comparison, in which the maximum likelihood method is used, first ignoring censored periods and then including them. The effect of the drug was estimated while simultaneously estimating a period-specific effect for each period: results are shown in table 5.3.

TABLE 5.3

*Estimated Effect of Drug on Remission of Leukemia: Compari-
son of Partial Likelihood with Maximum Likelihood, Using
Periods Terminated by Events and Periods Terminated by Events
or Censors*

	b	s.e.	$|b/s.e.|$
Cox (1972) partial likelihood	−1.65	≃(.43)	3.86
Maximum likelihood: events only	−1.64	(.42)	3.89
Maximum likelihood: events & censors	−1.76	(.44)	4.00

The table shows first that the partial likelihood estimate agrees very closely with the maximum likelihood estimate using only periods terminated by events, but second that this is an understatement compared to the maximum likelihood estimate which also uses information about periods terminated by censors.[5] The amount of information lost is small in this case, but it is one-sided information, thus producing a downwardly biased estimate. It should be evident that this bias is specific to the present example; other data may show a different degree or direction of bias or none at all, depending on the way in which the censoring occurred. In a subsequent section, I will indicate how this bias can be corrected.

---

[5] I have taken for comparison Cox's partial likelihood estimate. My own, using a different method for dealing with ties, gave −1.51, as indicated earlier in the chapter.

193

Comparing the maximum likelihood and partial likelihood estimates based only on event-periods shows that the partial likelihood estimate is very nearly the same number of times its standard deviation as the maximum likelihood estimate. The maximum likelihood using full information is a slightly greater multiple of its standard deviation, 4.00 compared to 3.86 or 3.89. This reflects the value of the additional information in the present case.

The LONGIT·EVENTM program calculates a general constant, effects due to the independent variables, (optionally) a time trend, and (optionally) period-specific effects. The model for exponential decomposition in this example is

$$q(t) = e^{b_0 + b_1 x_1 + \lambda_t}$$

where $x_1 = 1$ if the drug is present, 0 otherwise; λ_t is the period-specific component. For comparability with the period-specific components of partial likelihood, in which no general constant comparable to b_0 is calculated, the sum of b_0 and λ_t must be used. The general constant and period-specific effects for the exponential decomposition, along with standard deviations, are given in the following list. The column headed rate without drug can be directly compared to that of table 5.2, for it is calculated as $e^{b_0 + \lambda_t}$.

period	λ_t	s.e.	rate without drug
constant	−1.49	(0.82)	
1	−0.98	(1.06)	.085
2	−0.89	(1.06)	.093
3	−1.52	(1.27)	.050
4	−0.74	(1.05)	.108
5	−0.63	(1.05)	.120
6	−0.15	(0.97)	.195
7	−1.21	(1.27)	.067
8	−0.28	(0.92)	.170
9	−0.86	(1.60)	.095
10	−0.04	(1.05)	.217
11	0.23	(1.04)	.285
12	−0.30	(1.25)	.167
13	−0.89	(1.25)	.093
14	−0.08	(1.25)	.208
15	−1.20	(1.25)	.068
16	0.55	(1.03)	.391
17	—	—	.226

Comparing the rates with those from table 5.2 shows that they are about 10 percent higher, except for a few periods (8, 9, 13, 15, 17) in which the rates are quite discrepant. The effect of the drug gives a multiplier which is about 20 percent less than that calculated with partial likelihood, which means that the maximum likelihood method estimates the rates at each period for those without the drug about 10 percent higher than does partial likelihood, and the rates for those with the drug about 10 percent lower.

5.3. RELATIVE VIRTUES OF THE TWO METHODS

The preceding example shows a defect in partial likelihood estimates, a defect which depends on the amount and kind of censoring. But there are other considerations as well. There appear to be two major virtues to partial likelihood: its simplicity of calculation, and its use of only order relations among the events. As for the second, it can be shown that with the exponential decomposition of the transition rate (that used in partial likelihood), the maximum likelihood method could use only order data as well, absorbing into the period-specific component the effects of different time intervals. In that case, the first term in equation (5.25) vanishes.

The greater ease of calculation is a definite virtue of partial likelihood. For the case of a single independent variable (as in the leukemia example) partial likelihood requires no inversion of matrices, while the maximum likelihood method with full freedom for period-specific rates requires inverting in each iteration a matrix of order equal to the number of event- or censor-terminated periods. The size of the matrix to be inverted with the maximum likelihood method is the number of independent variables plus the number of event- or censor-terminated periods, while for partial likelihood it is only the number of independent variables. This advantage, however, is not as great as it once was given the increased computing power available. And it is partially if not wholly offset in cases where there are many ties. A major advantage of the maximum likelihood method is that it is no more complicated with any number of ties than it is without ties.

The maximum likelihood method does offer another advantage: a wider range of parameterizations of the transition rate. Partial likelihood depends upon a multiplicative parameterization, such as an exponential linear decomposition, while the maximum likelihood method can also use additive decomposition.

The LONGIT·EVENTP program in the appendix carries out partial likelihood calculations, and the LONGIT·EVENTM program carries out maximum likelihood calculations.

5.4. EXAMPLE

Innovations in Hospitals: Some organizations adopt innovations more rapidly than do others, and sociologists have been interested in the factors responsible for adopting innovations slowly or quickly. One study has examined a particular managerial innovation in hospitals, attempting to answer this question by studying characteristics of approximately 1,000 hospitals (some adopted the innovation, others did not) and their administrators.[6] I have taken a portion of this data and a small number of the hospitals to illustrate the use of the maximum likelihood analysis of continuous records. The data are listed in table 5.4.

TABLE 5.4

Management Innovations and Other Characteristics of Sixteen Hospitals in Maine, New Hampshire, and Massachusetts

	Date of Innovation	State	Admissions, 1951	Admissions Growth, 1951–78	Admissions: Employees 1951	Employee Growth, 1951–78	Teaching Status, 1961
1	NO	12	4583	2.09	16.6	2.30	NO
2	1973	11	3392	3.65	24.4	7.01	NO
3	NO	11	3536	2.27	24.4	3.77	NO
4	NO	11	4472	1.70	17.8	2.68	NO
5	NO	13	5776	1.49	23.0	2.83	NO
6	NO	13	6463	1.07	19.5	2.53	NO
7	NO	13	6161	1.42	19.6	4.68	YES
8	1974	13	12996	0.88	26.2	2.91	YES
9	1963	13	11439	1.40	11.6	2.45	YES
10	NO	13	10176	0.97	22.3	3.15	YES
11	NO	11	7166	1.26	23.5	2.34	YES
12	1971	13	33686	0.48	8.8	0.53	YES
13	1970	11	9122	2.30	16.6	4.32	YES
14	1965	13	22663	1.31	8.3	2.03	YES
15	1964	12	7164	1.60	14.0	3.08	YES
16	1969	13	10124	1.29	13.5	3.99	YES

Four independent variables and three independent attributes were created from these data. The four variables are simply those listed in the table, and the attributes are teaching status (Yes = 1, No = 0), state of Maine (Maine = 1, other = 0), state of New Hampshire (New Hampshire = 1, other = 0). There is some arbitrariness about coding the time at which the event (innovation) occurred, because in the absence of period-specific effects, the starting point of the process affects the estimates. (If period-specific effects are included, the effect for the period terminated by the first adoptions auto-

[6] Lawton R. Burns (1981). I am indebted to Mr. Burns for making these data available to me.

196

matically adjusts so that the estimates for all but the first period are unaffected, and those for the first period are simply inversely proportional to its length. With partial likelihood times are not taken into account, only order is, so the starting date is irrelevant.) The starting point here was taken as 1960, so that the second hospital listed in the table adopted innovations thirteen years after the starting point.

With these data, an analysis was carried out using the maximum likelihood method. Three different models were tested: one with only a constant term plus the seven independent variables; one with a constant term, a time trend, and the seven variables; and one with a constant term, the seven independent variables, and nine period-specific effects. As might be imagined, the third did not converge: there were seventeen parameters to be estimated, and only sixteen observations. The model including the time trend (nine parameters) also did not converge. These were obviously severe tests in estimating models with many parameters and minimal data. With a greater number of hospitals, these models should converge.

The model with the constant and the seven independent variables did converge, and the results are presented in table 5.5.

TABLE 5.5

Effects of Seven Hospital Characteristics
on Management Innovation

	Linear Model	
	b	s.e.
State of Maine	−3.49	(2.46)
State of New Hampshire	0.26	(1.75)
Admissions, 1951	0.0001	(0.0001)
Admissions Growth, 1951–78	4.70	(2.83)
Admission: Employee Ratio, 1951	0.08	(0.16)
Employee Growth, 1951–78	−0.50	(0.95)
Teaching Status, 1951	5.52	(2.99)
Constant	−15.3	(8.19)

The large positive and negative values of the components of transition rates indicate the marginal stability of this model with these data. With a larger number of cases the absolute values of these estimates, along with the sizes of their standard errors, would most likely decline. Nevertheless, some initial indications of effects are available even with these marginal data. The only variables that approach being twice their standard errors are admissions growth and teaching status: The hospitals that grew most and the teaching hospitals had higher rates of adopting the innovation. The signs of the other variables suggest that with larger amounts of data, there might be a positive effect of the hospital size (as measured by number of admissions in 1951); with even less certainty, there might be a negative effect of employee growth (controlling, as in the model, for admissions growth) and a positive effect of the 1951 admissions-to-employee ratio. Thus, the suggestion of these data is that larger, growing, teaching hospitals with fewer employees relative to admissions are more quick to adopt the innovation. The small amount of data, of course, make any such inference quite tentative.

6. EXTENSIONS OF PARTIAL LIKELIHOOD AND MAXIMUM LIKELIHOOD METHODS

In this section several extensions of the approaches examined in the previous sections are described. First to be discussed is a method for eliminating the bias in partial likelihood due to censoring that is recorded at times intervening between events. This leads to an extension of the partial likelihood method to the simultaneous examination of more than one kind of event. Finally I will examine the extension of both partial likelihood and maximum likelihood to sequences of events of differing types between which there are dependencies.

6.1. THE PROBLEM OF INTERVENING CENSORS IN PARTIAL LIKELIHOOD

In the use of partial likelihood, information of two kinds is not used. Information about the timing of events beyond that necessary to establish event order is lost; in addition, information about the persistence of certain censored cases is lost as well. The latter is illustrated in the leukemia example by the experimental patients who were censored at weeks 9, 19, 20, 25, 32, 34, and 35. The information that is *not* lost about the patient censored at week 20, for example, is his presence up through week 17, which is the last week at which an event occurred before week 20. The information that *is* lost is his presence in weeks 18, 19, and 20.

Since all the lost information occurs for the experimental patients, and since there are altogether forty-seven patient-weeks of risk that are unrecorded, the failure to use information about censors creates a distinct bias. The size of the bias is reflected by the difference between the maximum likelihood estimates of −1.64 when censors are ignored, and −1.76 when the full information is used.

198

This raises the question of whether information about censors might not be used in partial likelihood. (Cox's rationale for ignoring censors in his 1972 paper is that "No information can be contributed about β by time intervals in which no failures occur because the component $\lambda_0(t)$ [the period-specific component of the transition rate] might conceivably be identically zero in such intervals." But under most reasonable prior assumptions about the transition rates, the probability that $\lambda_0(t)$ would be identically zero when it is not zero in adjoining periods is vanishingly small. Thus there seems no reason not to use this information if it is possible to do so.)

To use the information it is necessary to return to the initial formulation of partial likelihood. In that formulation the probability of observing a period beginning at time t and terminated at time $t + \Delta t$ by a jump from individual i is

$$p_i = e^{-\int_t^{t+\Delta t} q(\tau)d\tau} q_i(t + \Delta t),$$

where $q(\tau)$ is the sum of all transition rates from all individuals at time τ. The quantity $q_i(t + \Delta t)$ is restated as a product of two terms. The first constitutes the probability that an event occurs at time $t + \Delta t$, while the second is the conditional probability that it is i who acts, given that an action takes place. Thus what we have is $p_i = \alpha \beta_i$, where α is the probability that an event took place at time t, and β_i is the conditional probability that the event was an act of individual i, given that some event took place.[7]

If we consider censors as events that can occur at any point in time, then we may generalize the above formulation to one in which there are two types of events. Now $q(\tau)$ consists of the sum of transition rates at time τ over both types of events, and if $p_{ij} = \alpha \beta_{ij}$ is the probability that the period was terminated by an event of type j from individual i, then β_{ij} is the conditional probability that an event of type j from individual i occurred, given that some event occurred. In parameterizing the transition rates for events of each type, it is necessary to be careful because their overall levels may vary. Thus the event in which we are interested (in Cox's example, death of the patient), which I will denote as $q_{i1}(\tau)$ for individual i at time τ, is

$$q_{i1}(\tau) = e^{\lambda_\tau + \sum_k b_{k1}x_{ki}(\tau)},$$

[7] Note that p_i is itself a conditional probability, for it is conditional upon the composition of the risk set at time t. If there were no censoring, the probability that the risk set came to be as observed through one particular path would be given by the product of the prior terms; but because of censoring, the product of the prior terms does not give the desired unconditional probability.

where λ_τ is the period-specific component of the rate. In Cox's original formulation, λ_τ vanishes because it appears in both the numerator and denominator of the conditional probability $q_i(\tau)/\Sigma q_j(\tau)$. To include censoring as a second type of event, we must assume that the process of censoring is subject to the same period-specific component, but that in addition it contains another component, positive or negative (denoted below by ϕ_2), giving its overall level relative to event 1. Also, it may be subject to the effects of various factors characterizing the individual, just as is event 1. Then the transition rate for event 2 is

$$q_{i2}(\tau) = e^{\lambda_\tau + \phi_2 + \sum_k b_{k2}x_{ki}},$$

where the independent variables may, but need not, be the same as those for the event of interest, but the coefficients b_{k2} are of course different in general from b_{k1}. The quantity ϕ_2 is necessary to adjust the rate of the censor to that of the event of interest.

In some cases, we may assume that the probability of censoring is the same for everyone so that $\Sigma b_{k2}x_{ki} = 0$ for all i.

If we formulate the matter in this way, then each censoring of an observation, whether it occurs at the end of a period terminated by an event or terminates a period itself, is taken into account in estimation. If there are no effects of independent variables hypothesized for the censor, then the estimation is just as in Cox's formulation, except that an additional parameter ϕ_2 is estimated, giving the rate of censoring relative to the rate of the event in question. If effects of independent variables are introduced, then a second **b**-vector is estimated as well.

To show the effects of not ignoring the periods terminated by censoring, Cox's leukemia example will be used, first neglecting any effects of independent variables and estimating only ϕ_2, and then allowing the censoring to be a function of the experimental treatment.[8]

6.2. EXAMPLE

The Leukemia Case Again: If censoring is considered simply as another event, each individual has two transition rates at each time period. For time period t, if we neglect any effect of the experiment on censoring, the transition rates for individuals who have had the drug and for those who have not are as follows:

---

[8] In this example, where censoring is clearly related to experimental treatment, it appears that observation was stopped because the disease was declared in complete remission.

To recurrence:

$$\text{with drug } q_1(t) = e^{\lambda_\tau + b}$$
$$\text{without drug } q_1(t) = e^{\lambda_\tau}$$

To censoring:

$$\text{with drug } q_2(t) = e^{\lambda_\tau + \phi_2}$$
$$\text{without drug } q_2(t) = e^{\lambda_\tau + \phi_2}$$

The task, then, is to estimate b, ϕ_2, and λ_τ.

Inspection of the data (table 5.1) shows that when censoring is considered as a different kind of event, there are now twenty-four periods rather than seventeen. Thirteen are terminated by one or more recurrences, four are terminated by both recurrence and censors, and seven are terminated by censors. Using all of these periods, and maximizing the conditional likelihood with respect to b and ϕ_2, gives values as shown in table 5.6.

TABLE 5.6

Partial Likelihood Estimates of Effect of Drug on Leukemia and Adjustment Parameter for Censoring as a Second Event

	Estimate	s.e.
ϕ_2	−1.90	(.382)
b	−1.88	(.431)

Values for λ_τ are:

Period	λ				
1	−2.72	9	−2.64	17	−0.91
2	−2.65	10	−1.93	18	−1.55
3	−3.25	11	−1.48	19	−0.10
4	−2.51	12	−1.66	20	−0.39
5	−2.42	13	−2.11	21	0.28
6	−1.62	14	−1.38	22	2.45
7	−2.94	15	−1.91	23	1.20
8	−1.54	16	−1.17	24	1.20

This estimate of −1.88 for b is considerably larger than the partial likelihood estimate when censored intervals are not taken into account. This difference seems primarily related to the additional periods of observation brought about by those individuals who were censored after all recurrences had taken place (weeks 25–35).

When an effect of the drug on censoring is introduced, this changes the transition rate $q_2(t)$ with the drug to

$$q_2(t) = e^{\lambda_T + \phi_2 + b_2}$$

I was not able to achieve complete convergence for this model because there are no censors for the individuals who did not take the drug. This means that the estimate of ϕ_2 that maximizes the likelihood of this absence of censors is $\phi_2 \rightarrow -\infty$, and the corresponding estimate of b_2 is $b_2 \rightarrow +\infty$. Nevertheless, complete stability of b_1 and λ_T are achieved through the iterations by which ϕ_2 and b_2 slowly diverge. The value of b_1 and its standard error are

$$b_1 = -1.81; \quad \text{s.e.} = .424$$

This analysis, incorporating the effect of the drug on censoring, slightly reduces the estimated effect.

There is, however, one variable to which censoring appears strongly related, and that is time. Censoring is much more likely to occur later than earlier. Thus an additional model, in which the transition rate for censors is $q_2 = e^{\lambda_T + \phi_2 + b_2 t}$, was examined. Time is not introduced into the transition rate to recurrence, which remains $e^{\lambda_T + b_1}$ for those who received the drug and e^{λ_T} for those who did not. Estimates of b_1, b_2, and ϕ_2 are shown in table 5.7.

TABLE 5.7

Partial Likelihood Estimates of Effect of Drug on Leukemia, with Parameter for Censoring, and with Censoring Assumed to be a Function of Time

	Estimate	s.e.
ϕ_2	−3.46	(.858)
b_1	−1.57	(.419)
b_2	0.11	(.051)

This shows the adjustment for censoring to be much more negative, but with a strong, positive time trend. With these parameters for the censors the estimate of the effect of the drug is substantially reduced, though it is not as low as before censored periods were taken into account.

It is clear from this example that taking into account periods terminated by a censor can affect the estimates of the effects of independent variables on the event of interest. What is perhaps somewhat surprising is that the specific way the censoring is modeled also can have a substantial effect on the estimates.

6.3. MULTIPLE EVENTS OR INDIVIDUAL HETEROGENEITY

If there is more than one kind of event, then the additional events can be subject to analysis in exactly the same way as censoring is, which in principle is nothing other than a second kind of event. The analysis just described is not limited to two types of events, and in principle any number of types of events can be analyzed simultaneously. From such an analysis would come an event-specific component, ϕ_k, for each event k except the first (comparable to a constant term in a regression equation), and a vector of effect parameters $\mathbf{b}_k$, for each event, including the first. In addition, the period-specific components can be estimated through a constrained maximum likelihood method that takes the parameters estimated by partial likelihood as given.

If there are several events per individual, then the logic of the analysis can be extended to the calculation of parameters for individual heterogeneity. That is, a parameter ψ_i can be included in the transition rate for individual i and estimated. This provides a measure of individual heterogeneity that is constant across time periods.

6.4. DOUBLE CONDITIONALITY FOR TREATING CENSORED PERIODS

A second method of treating periods terminated by a censor is simpler than the first and allows relaxation of the assumption that the period-specific component of the censoring transition rate is the same as that of the event of interest. It is applicable, however, only when we know that a period was terminated by an event or a censor. Thus, if there are ties between events and censors, as there are likely to be when time is measured in discrete units that are not small relative to the rates in question, this method is not strictly applicable. If there are no ties, or if ties can be handled by an approximation, it constitutes a generalization of Cox's method.

We go back to the observation of a period, say period ℓ, terminated by an event of type j on the part of individual i, and the decomposition of its probability $p_{\ell ij}$ into two components: $p_{\ell ij} = \alpha_\ell \beta_{ij}$, where α_ℓ is the probability that period ℓ is terminated by a jump or a censor, and β_{ij} is the conditional probability that it was terminated by an event of type j (jump or censor) from individual i. Now, however, we decompose somewhat differently, into $\alpha_i \beta_j \gamma_{ij}$, where α_i is as before, the probability that no event occurred during the period, and then some event occurred at the end of the period; β_j is the conditional probability that it was an event of type j, given that an event occurred; and γ_{ij} is the conditional probability that it was an event (of type j) from individual i, given that an event of type j occurred.

6.5. MULTIPLE EVENT TYPES IN THE MAXIMUM LIKELIHOOD METHOD

In the use of partial likelihood methods, the simultaneous estimation of parameters for more than one type of event aids the estimation of each one. This occurs because partial likelihood methods are able to use only information about periods terminated by events, and when intervening events remove individuals from the risk set (as in the case of the individual censored at week 9, for example, in Cox's leukemia example), information about their presence in the period since the last event of the type under examination is lost. Consequently, simultaneous analysis of all types of events that affect the risk sets for any one type of event benefits the estimation for each type. This arises, of course, because of one of the principal virtues of the partial likelihood method: the method does not require knowledge of the timing of events, but only their order, and thus it does not use such information when it exists. Intervening events can sometimes aid in recovering that information.

This is not true, however, for the maximum likelihood method. The time a member of the risk set is lost is used in the analysis because periods of both types are included in the analysis: those that are terminated by an event of the type under analysis, and those that are not. Thus, the information that is only retrieved by simultaneous analysis of other events in partial likelihood is never lost in the present maximum likelihood method. Consequently, nothing is gained in maximum likelihood by simultaneously estimating multiple event types unless there is dependence among events (as will be treated shortly). The analysis for different event types can be carried out independently without a loss of information.

6.6. HETEROGENEITY AMONG INDIVIDUALS IN THE MAXIMUM LIKELIHOOD METHOD

Heterogeneity among individuals in cases where individuals experience several events was introduced above for partial likelihood methods. With the

204

maximum likelihood method discussed earlier, heterogeneity requires only that a 0–1 variable x_{ki} be introduced for each individual i, taking on the value 1 for $k = i$ and 0 otherwise. The parameter expressing that individual's quicker or slower rate of action, controlling for the effect of variables that are included in the decomposition of the transition rate, is the coefficient for that 0–1 variable.

6.7. DEPENDENCE AMONG EVENTS AND ANALYSIS OF SYSTEM FUNCTIONING

The methods for analyzing event sequences outlined in this chapter, both partial likelihood and maximum likelihood, offer possibilities of analyzing systems—either social systems or the individual as a system—in quite powerful ways. I will explain this by reference to what is called the *natural history* approach in sociology. In this approach, some phenomenon in a social system is studied, and the sequence of events that occurs in the system is noted. Such a sequence, which may occur in the study of social conflict, community decision making, friendship formation, organizational decline, collective behavior, or in many other areas, is then presumed to express something like the natural history of the events in the phenomenon under study. Ordinarily several such sequences are studied in order to reduce the chance that the sequence observed was not a natural history at all, but was merely fortuitous. From such regularities, qualitative generalizations are often expressed about the development of a social phenomenon. The general idea is often one of a cumulative process, in which each event in a sequence helps determine the outcome of subsequent events.

Max Weber expressed something of the same thing when he wrote that one event in a historical sequence *loads the dice* in shaping the outcome of subsequent events. The common saying that an event *set in motion* certain succeeding events expresses the same idea.

The methods introduced up to this point have not been appropriate to such data and inferences, because they have dealt with single events or, in the case of multiple events, events that were independent of one another. The methods, however, lend themselves to the study of such event dependencies within a system and thus to the study of systemic phenomena of the sort that have been described by the natural history approach.

To fix ideas, it is useful to think of a substantive illustration. The unit under consideration is an authority structure, with a superordinate (which may be an individual or a larger body) and a set of subordinates. Events are as follows (and I use events that have been proposed, in the literature on revolts and revolutions, as important determinants of subsequent events):

A: Economic growth and social development
B: An economic downturn
C: Demands for policy change by opponents among subordinates
D: Punishment of opposition by superordinate
E: Acquiescence of superordinate to opponents' demands
F: Active support for opposition among some subordinates
G: Active support for superordinate among some subordinates

There are two major strands of theory among revolution theorists. Their theories have something like the following matrices of dependence among events. In these matrices, a plus sign means that the event type in the row is hypothesized to affect the column event type positively. A minus sign means a negative effect.

Type I Theories		Dependent Event						
		A	B	C	D	E	F	G
Frustration-Aggression Theories A			+	⊖				
B				⊕			⊕	
Causal C					+	+	+	
Event D				⊕		−	⊕	⊖
E				⊖	−		⊖	⊕
F				+	−	+	+	+
G				+	−		+	+

Type II Theories		Dependent Event						
		A	B	C	D	E	F	G
Power Theories A			+	⊕			⊕	
B								
Causal C					+	+	+	
Event D				⊖		−	⊖	⊕
E				⊕	−		⊕	⊖
F				+	−	+	+	+
G				+	−		+	+

The circled cells in the two tables indicate just where the theories' principal differences lie. With data on the sequences of these events from a number of administrative authority systems (starting with the initiation of economic growth), it would be possible to estimate parameters that would test the theories. (I have grossly simplified the task for the purpose of exposition. For serious work it would be necessary to restrict observations to a class of systems that was relatively homogeneous and then to incorporate more detail among the events.)

What is necessary is a simple addition to the partial likelihood or maximum likelihood methods discussed in preceding sections: The transition rate toward a particular type of event (say event C in the current example) would have independent variables representing events A, B, D, E, and F. Until each of those events occurred in a particular unit under observation, the variable $x_{ki}(t)$ representing that event would have the value 0 for that unit. After the event occurred (if it did occur), the variable would have the value 1.[9]

With such an addition to the methods described earlier, events need not only depend on exogenous variables or attributes but also on one another, and the sequences of events can be used to estimate the parameters for these dependencies.

APPENDIX: USE OF LONGIT·EVENTP AND LONGIT·EVENTM PROGRAMS

These programs are designed to use records characterizing an individual (or other unit) and the events he experiences, either by their time of occurrence or by their order. Rank-order data, in which each individual (or other unit) is ranked relative to the others, is included in the latter type of data. The program estimates parameters of effect of the qualitative attributes or continuous variables on the transition rate to the event in question.

An individual may experience zero or one event, may be intermittently in or out of the risk set, and may have his presence in the risk set terminated either by an event or by a censor. He may be characterized by values of up to nine independent attributes or variables, and each of these may be constant or differing from period to period. It is assumed that there is a common time frame for all the units (for example, individuals) so that the time of event for one may be aligned with the time of event for each of the others. This alignment creates "periods" during which nothing happens until the end of the period, when one or more events or censors occur. The programs use either a partial likelihood (EVENT·P) or maximum likeli-

---

[9] It would also be possible, of course, to have a time dependency with two parameters, $(\beta_k + \eta_k\tau)x_{ki}(t)$, where τ is time measured from the occurrence of the event. If the effect weakens over time, η_k is less than 0.

hood (EVENT·M) estimation method. Different individuals may have differing weights. The EVENT·P program will analyze up to five types of events simultaneously.

Control Cards and Input Data

All data are read after control cards for that data set.

PROGRAM[10]

P M

x x *Card 1:* *Position 5:* Number of jobs

Remaining control cards and data to be read for each job:

x x *Card 2:* *Position 5:* 0 if no independent variable changes over time, 1 if one or more varies at different event times.

Position 10: Number of time periods, terminated either by event or censor. (max 50)

Position 15: Number of individuals. (max 50)

Position 20: Number of independent variables. (min 1, max 9)

Position 25: (EVENT·M only; leave blank for EVENT·P) 0 if only one constant term is estimated, 1 if an additional term for each event-terminated period but the last is estimated.

Position 30: 0 if no time trend is estimated, 1 if it is.

Position 35: 1 if each record has a weight of 1, 0 if weights are to be read in explicitly.

Position 40: 1 if times of events are always 1 unit apart, 0 if times are to be read in explicitly.

Position 45: (EVENT·M only) 1 for exponential model, 0 for linear.

Position 50: (EVENT·P only) number of event types for which calculation is to be done. (max 5)

x x *Card 3* (present only if Position 5 on control card 2 is 1): *Positions 6–16:* 0 if independent variable is constant over time, 1 if it is nonconstant (in which case a value is read for each time at which a period terminates. Position 6 is first independent variable, 7 is second, and so on).

---

[10] In the columns at left, x = present for that program, 0 = absent.

x 0   *Card 4P* (EVENT·P only): *Positions 5, 10, . . . :* Position 5 = 1 if first variable is included for first type of event, 0 otherwise; position 10 = 1 if first variable is included for second type of event, and so on, then continue (to position 50, using a second card if necessary beyond that) with second variable for each type of event, and so on.

0 *x*   *Card 4M* (EVENT·M only): *Position 5:* Number of periods terminated not by an event, but by censor only.

0 *x*   *Card 4½M* (EVENT·M only, read only if position 5 on 4M above is 1 or greater): *Positions 5, 10, . . . , 50 (max):* Use additional cards if more than 10 positions are needed. Period numbers (in order) terminated not by event, but by censor.

x *x*   *Data 5:* In positions 1, . . . , 80 (use more cards if there are more than eighty persons in sample) 1 in position *i* if person *i* was present at beginning of first period, 0 otherwise.

x *x*   *Data 5½:* In positions 1, . . . , 80 do same for second period, and so on for each period.

x *x*   *Data 6:* Card gives variable format for reading values of dependent variable and independent variables, in positions 1 to 18.

x *x*   *Data 7:* If card 3 has 0 in position 6: Value of first independent variable for first individual.

If card 3 has 1 in position 6: Value of first independent variable for first individual at beginning of first time period.

Continue on, each record having only one value of one variable. Period changes first (for nonconstant variables), then variable, and last individual.

x *x*   *Data 8* (exists only when position 40 on card 2 is 0):

Positions 5, 10, . . . , for Periods 1, 2, . . . , : Times at which events or censors (which terminate periods) occur.

x *x*   *Data 9:*

Positions 3, 6, . . . , 78: (Using as many cards as necessary, with twenty-six individuals to a card) In each position corresponding to an individual, the period number at which event (or censor) occurred for that individual. If no event occurred, the number of last period plus one is used.

x 0   *Data 10* (EVENT·P only):

Positions 3, 6, . . . , 78: At each position corresponding to an individual, place the number representing the event type that occurred for that individual. If none occurred until the end, use event type corresponding to censor.

INPUT TO LONGIT.EVENTM PROGRAM

(Example of Section 5.2, Table 5.3)

```
1
0   24   42    1    1    0    1    0    1    7   1.
7
9   17   18   21   22   23   24
11111111111111111111111111111111111111111111
00111111111111111111111111111111111111111111
00000111111111111111111111111111111111111111
00000011111111111111111111111111111111111111
00000000111111111111111111111111111111111111
00000000011111111111111111111111111111111111
00000000000001111111111111111111111111111111
00000000000000011111111111111111111111111111
00000000000000000011111111111111111111111111
00000000000000000000111111111111111111111111
00000000000000000000011111111111111111111111
00000000000000000000000011111111111111111111
00000000000000000000000000111111111111111111
00000000000000000000000000001111111111111111
00000000000000000000000000000011111111111111
00000000000000000000000000000000111111111111
00000000000000000000000000000000001111111111
00000000000000000000000000000000000011111111
00000000000000000000000000000000000000111111
00000000000000000000000000000000000000001111
00000000000000000000000000000000000000000011
00000000000000000000000000000000000000000001
   (40F2.0)
0.
0.
0.
0.
0.
0.
0.
0.
0.
1.
1.
1.
1.
1.
0.
0.
0.
0.
1.
1.
1.
1.
0.
0.
0.
0.
1.
0.
```

```
1.
1.
0.
1.
1.
1.
0.
0.
1.
1.
1.
1.
1.
1.
 1.   2.   3.   4.   5.   6.   7.   8.   9.  10.  11.  12.  13.  15.  16.  17.
19.  20.  22.  23.  25.  32.  34.  35.
 1  1  2  2  3  4  4  5  5 40  6  6  6  7  8  8  8  8 40 40 10 40 11 11 12 12
13 14 15 40 16 40 40 19 19 20 20 40 40 40 40 40
```

OUTPUT FROM LONGIT.EVENTM PROGRAM

LONGIT.EVENTM MLE FOR CONTINUOUS RECORDS 9/10/80

```
 0   24   42   1   1   0   1   0   1
ITERATION CONVERGED AFTER STEP :   9  / DIFFERENCE =      0.0000331997871 /
```

EXPONENTIAL MODEL

COVARIANCE MATRIX
```
      0.67443  -0.18240  -0.64644  -0.64384  -0.64159  -0.63890  -0.63460  -0.63454
     -0.63948  -0.63143  -0.63101  -0.62984  -0.62032  -0.61400  -0.60996  -0.60581
     -0.59739  -0.59258
     -0.18240   0.19235   0.15288   0.15014   0.14777   0.14493   0.14040   0.14033
      0.14554   0.13705   0.13661   0.13538   0.12534   0.11867   0.11441   0.11003
      0.10116   0.09609
     -0.64644   0.15288   1.12328   0.62080   0.61892   0.61666   0.61306   0.61300
      0.61715   0.61040   0.61004   0.60907   0.60109   0.59579   0.59240   0.58892
      0.58187   0.57784
     -0.64384   0.15014   0.62080   1.11903   0.61681   0.61459   0.61106   0.61100
      0.61507   0.60845   0.60810   0.60714   0.59930   0.59410   0.59077   0.58736
      0.58043   0.57647
     -0.64159   0.14777   0.61892   0.61681   1.61519   0.61281   0.60933   0.60928
      0.61328   0.60676   0.60642   0.60547   0.59776   0.59263   0.58936   0.58600
      0.57918   0.57529
     -0.63890   0.14493   0.61666   0.61459   0.61281   1.11115   0.60725   0.60720
      0.61113   0.60473   0.60439   0.60347   0.59590   0.59088   0.58767   0.58437
      0.57768   0.57387
     -0.63460   0.14040   0.61306   0.61106   0.60933   0.60725   1.10455   0.60389
      0.60770   0.60150   0.60118   0.60028   0.59295   0.58808   0.58497   0.58178
      0.57530   0.57160
     -0.63454   0.14033   0.61300   0.61100   0.60928   0.60720   0.60389   0.93721
      0.60765   0.60146   0.60113   0.60023   0.59291   0.58804   0.58494   0.58174
      0.57527   0.57157
     -0.63948   0.14554   0.61715   0.61507   0.61328   0.61113   0.60770   0.60765
      1.61160   0.60517   0.60483   0.60390   0.59630   0.59126   0.58804   0.58473
      0.57801   0.57417
     -0.63143   0.13705   0.61040   0.60845   0.60676   0.60473   0.60150   0.60146
      0.60517   0.84973   0.59880   0.59793   0.59077   0.58602   0.58299   0.57987
      0.57354   0.56993
```

211

-0.63101	0.13661	0.61005	0.60810	0.60642	0.60439	0.60118	0.60113
0.60483	0.59880	1.59851	0.59762	0.59048	0.58575	0.58272	0.57961
0.57331	0.56971						
-0.62984	0.13538	0.60907	0.60714	0.60547	0.60347	0.60028	0.60023
0.60390	0.59793	0.59761	1.09872	0.58968	0.58499	0.58199	0.57891
0.57266	0.56910						
-0.62032	0.12534	0.60109	0.59930	0.59776	0.59590	0.59295	0.59291
0.59630	0.59077	0.59048	0.58968	1.08653	0.57879	0.57602	0.57317
0.56738	0.56408						
-0.61400	0.11867	0.59579	0.59410	0.59263	0.59088	0.58808	0.58804
0.59126	0.58602	0.58575	0.58499	0.57879	1.57475	0.57205	0.56935
0.56388	0.56075						
-0.60996	0.11441	0.59240	0.59077	0.58936	0.58767	0.58498	0.58494
0.58804	0.58299	0.58272	0.58199	0.57602	0.57205	1.57240	0.56692
0.56164	0.55862						
-0.60581	0.11003	0.58892	0.58736	0.58600	0.58437	0.58178	0.58174
0.58473	0.57987	0.57961	0.57891	0.57317	0.56935	0.56692	1.56452
0.55933	0.55644						
-0.59739	0.10116	0.58187	0.58043	0.57918	0.57768	0.57530	0.57527
0.57801	0.57354	0.57331	0.57266	0.56738	0.56388	0.56164	0.55933
1.55505	0.55200						
-0.59259	0.09609	0.57784	0.57647	0.57529	0.57387	0.57160	0.57157
0.57417	0.56993	0.56971	0.56910	0.56408	0.56075	0.55862	0.55644
0.55200	1.06258						

B COEFFICIENTS AND STANDARD ERRORS

B(0)=	-1.4865	SE(0)=	0.8212
B(1)=	-1.7578	SE(1)=	0.4386
B(1)=	-0.9819	SE(1)=	1.0598
B(2)=	-0.8933	SE(2)=	1.0578
B(3)=	-1.5151	SE(3)=	1.2709
B(4)=	-0.7437	SE(4)=	1.0541
B(5)=	-0.6298	SE(5)=	1.0510
B(6)=	-0.1467	SE(6)=	0.9681
B(7)=	-1.2112	SE(7)=	1.2695
B(8)=	-0.2826	SE(8)=	0.9218
B(9)=	-0.8649	SE(9)=	1.5985
B(10)=	-0.0402	SE(10)=	1.0482
B(11)=	0.2306	SE(11)=	1.0424
B(12)=	-0.3024	SE(12)=	1.2549
B(13)=	-0.8896	SE(13)=	1.2540
B(14)=	-0.0842	SE(14)=	1.2508
B(15)=	-1.2015	SE(15)=	1.2470
B(16)=	0.5487	SE(16)=	1.0308
B(17)=	0.0	SE(17)=	0.0

LONGIT.EVENTM PROGRAM

```
1.    //LONGIT JOB (2ZB004,COL,Q,NORC),COLEMAN,RE=500K,
2.    // TE=YES,ID='LONGIT.EVENTM',RO=REG,Q=0
3.    // EXEC FORTXCLG
4.    //FORT.SYSIN DD *
5.          DIMENSION NELTA(50,50),XV(50,5,50),T(50),NPER(50),X(5,50),
6.         &Q(50,50),B(55),BL(55),A(50,50),DWX(55),Z(50,50),S(55,55),
7.         &R(55),G(50),DT(50),INJ(5),FMT(18),W(50),NC(50)
8.    C
9.          WRITE(6,8880)
10.   8880 FORMAT(//1X'LONGIT.EVENTM MLE FOR CONTINUOUS RECORDS 9/10/80'/)
11.   C
12.          READ(2,1)NJOBS
```

212

```
13.            DO 5010 I22=1,NJOBS
14.    C       READ IN INC=1 FOR NON-CONSTANT INDEPENDENT VARIABLES, O FOR CONSTANT
15.    C       IE=1 FOR EXPONENTAIL, O FOR LINEAR
16.    C       MS= NUMBER OF TIME PERIODS, TERMINATED EITHER BY EVENT OR CENSOR
17.    C       N= NUMBER OF INDIVIDUALS
18.    C       NS= NUMBER OF INDEPENDENT VARIABLES
19.    C       IC=0 IF ONLY ONE CONSTANT TERM IS ESTIMATED, I IF AN ADDITIONAL
20.    C       TERM FOR EACH EVENT-TERMINATED PERIOD BUT THE LAST IS ESTIMATED.
21.    C       IT=0 IF NO TIME TREND IS ESTIMATED, 1 IF IT IS.
22.    C       TIME IS NOT ENTERED EXPLICITLY AS AN INDEPENDENT VARIABLE.
23.    C       INC=0 IF NO INDEPENDENT VARIABLE CHANGES OVER TIME, 1 IF ONE
24.    C       OR MORE VARIES AT DIFFERENT EVENT TIMES.
25.    C       INJ(J)=0 IF INDEPENDENT VARIABLE J IS CONSTANT OVER TIME, 1 IF
26.    C       IT IS MEASURED AT EACH TIME POINT.
27.    C       ORDER OF INDEPENDENT VARIABLES IS: CONSTANT, NS EXPLICIT
28.    C       VARIABLES, TIME (IF IT=1), CONSTANT TERMS FOR TIME PERIODS
29.    C       1,...,MS-1 (IF IC=1).
30.    C       NWT=1 IF EACH RECORD HAS A WEIGHT OF 1, O OTHERWISE.  IF NWT
31.    C       EQUALS O, WEIGHTS MUST BE READ IN EXPLICITLY.
32.    C       NTIM=1 IF TIMES OF EVENTS ARE 1 UNIT APART, O OTHERWISE.
33.    C       IF NTIM EQUALS O, TIMES MUST BE READ IN EXPLICITLY.
34.            READ (2,1)INC,MS,N,NS,IC,IT,NWT,NTIM,IE
35.            NSN=NS+1
36.            WRITE(6,1)INC,MS,N,NS,IC,IT,NWT,NTIM,IE
37.            IF(INC.EQ.1)READ (2,6)(INJ(J),J=2,NSN)
38.       6 FORMAT(5X10I1)
39.       1 FORMAT(10I5)
40.    C       NCEN= NUMBER OF PERIODS TERMINATED BY CENSOR.
41.            READ(2,1)NCEN
42.    C       NC(I)= PERIOD NUMBER TERMINATED BY CENSOR.
43.            IF(NCEN.GE.1)READ(2,1)(NC(I),I=1,NCEN)
44.            INJ(1)=0
45.            MSP=MS +1
46.            MSM=MS
47.            MSL=MS -NCEN
48.            ISTEP=0
49.            IE=1
50.            DO 10 L=1,MS
51.            G(L)=0.
52.    C       READ NELTA(L,I)=1 IF I IS PRESENT AT BEGINNING OF PERIOD L, O OTHERWISE
53.            READ(2,2)(NELTA(L,I),I=1,N)
54.      10 CONTINUE
55.            READ (2,8889)FMT
56.    8889 FORMAT(18A4)
57.       2 FORMAT(80I1)
58.    C       READ INDEPENDENT VARIABLES, INTERMIXED CONSTANT AND NON-CONST.
59.            DO 172 I=1,N
60.            DO 173 L=1,MSP
61.            XV(L,1,I)=1.
62.     173 CONTINUE
63.            X(1,I)=1.
64.            DO 172 J=2,NSN
65.            IF(INJ(J).NE.1)READ(2,FMT)XV(1,J,I),W(I)
66.            IF(INJ(J).EQ.1)READ(2,FMT)(XV(L,J,I),L=1,MSP),W(I)
67.            IF(NWT.EQ.1)W(I)=1
68.            DO 174 L=1,MSP
69.            IF(INJ(J).NE.1)XV(L,J,I)=XV(1,J,I)
70.     174 CONTINUE
71.            X(J,I)=XV(1,J,I)
72.     172 CONTINUE
73.            NS=NS+1
74.    C       READ TIMES OF EVENTS
```

```
75.          IF(NTIM.EQ.0)READ(2,4)(T(L),L=1,MS)
76.        4 FORMAT(16F5.1)
77.          IF(NTIM.EQ.0)GOTO 152
78.          DO 152 L=1,MS
79.          T(L)=L
80.      152 CONTINUE
81.          DUM=0.
82.          DO 95 L=1,MS
83.          DT(L)=T(L)-DUM
84.       95 DUM=T(L)
85.          IF(IT.EQ.0)GOTO 17
86.          NS=NS+1
87.          INJ(NS)=1
88.          DO 17 I=1,N
89.          DO 17 L=1,MS
90.          XV(L,NS,I)=T(L)
91.       17 CONTINUE
92.          NSPP=NS+MSM-1
93.          NSP=NS+MSL-1
94.          IF(IC.EQ.0)NSP=NS
95.          IF(IC.EQ.0)NSPP=NS
96.          NSR=NS+1
97.          TN=.00001*NSP
98.          DO 11 K=1,NSP
99.       11 B(K)=0.
100.    C    READ NUMBER OF PERIOD AT WHICH I JUMPED
101.         READ (2,5)(NPER(I),I=1,N)
102.        5 FORMAT(26I3)
103.         DO 93 I=1,N
104.         DO 97 L=1,MS
105.       97 Z(I,L)=1.
106.         L=NPER(I)
107.       93 Z(I,L)=0.
108.         IF(NSPP.LE.NSR)GOTO 171
109.         DO 171 K=NSR,NSPP
110.         X(K,I)=1.
111.      171 CONTINUE
112.         DUM=1.
113.         DUM2=0.
114.         IF(IE.EQ.1)DUM2=1.
115.    C
116.    C    CALCULATE Q FOR FIRST ITERATION
117.         DO 13 I=1,N
118.         L=NPER(I)
119.       13 G(L)=G(L)+W(I)
120.         SUMB=0.
121.         I1=1
122.         DO 14 L=1,MS
123.         IF(L.NE.NC(I1))GOTO 33
124.         I1=I1 +1
125.         GOTO 14
126.       33 SUMA=0.
127.         DO 12 I=1,N
128.       12 SUMA=SUMA+NELTA(L,I)*DT(L)*W(I)
129.         SUMB=SUMB +G(L)/SUMA
130.         DO 14 I=1,N
131.         Q(I,L)=G(L)/SUMA
132.       14 CONTINUE
133.         SUMB=SUMB/MSL
134.         I1=1
135.         DO 19 L=1,MS
136.         IF(L.NE.NC(I1))GOTO 19
137.         I1=I1 +1
```

214

```
138.          DO 18 I=1,N
139.       18 Q(I,L)=SUMB
140.       19 CONTINUE
141.          GOTO 53
142.    C
143.    C     BEGIN LOOP
144.       89 DO 90 I=1,NSP
145.       90 BL(I)=B(I)
146.          IF(ISTEP.GT.30 )GOTO 56
147.          DO 53 I=1,N
148.          I1=1
149.          DO 54 L=1,MS
150.          Q(I,L)=0.
151.          DO 55 K=1,NS
152.          IF(INJ(K).EQ.1)X(K,I)=(XV(L,K,I) +XV(L+1,K,I))/2
153.          Q(I,L)=Q(I,L) +B(K)*X(K,I)
154.       55 CONTINUE
155.          IF(IC.EQ.0)GOTO 59
156.          IF(L.NE.NC(I1))GOTO 30
157.          I1=I1 +1
158.       30 LA=L -I1 +1
159.          IF(LA.GE.MSL)GOTO 59
160.          Q(I,L)=Q(I,L) +B(NS+LA)
161.       59 IF(IE.EQ.1.AND.INC.NE.1) Q(I,L)=EXP(Q(I,L))
162.       54 CONTINUE
163.       53 CONTINUE
164.    C     BRANCH TO PROCESS D(K) AND S(K) FOR EXPONENTIAL  NON-CONSTANT
165.          IF(IE.EQ.1.AND.INC.EQ.1)GOTO 99
166.    C
167.    C     PROCESSING D(K) AND S(K,J) FOR LINEAR AND CONSTANT EXPONENTIAL
168.          DO 15 J=1,NSP
169.          DWX(J)=0.
170.          DO 15 K=1,NSP
171.       15 S(J,K)=0.
172.          I1=1
173.          DO 94 L=1,MS
174.          LA=L -I1 +1
175.          IF(L.NE.NC(I1))GOTO 76
176.          I1=I1 +1
177.          LA=L -I1 +1
178.       76 DO 16 I=1,N
179.          IF(NELTA(L,I).EQ.0)GOTO 16
180.          IF(IE.EQ.1)DUM=Q(I,L)
181.          P=EXP(-Q(I,L)*DT(L))
182.          PHI=DT(L)*DUM*(Z(I,L) -P)/(1.-P)
183.          TM2=DT(L)*DUM -DUM2
184.          TEM2= -PHI*(TM2 -PHI)*W(I)
185.          TEM= -PHI*W(I)
186.          DO 36 J=1,NS
187.          IF(INC.EQ.1)X(J,I)=(XV(L,J,I) +XV(L+1,J,I))/2.
188.          DWX(J)=DWX(J) +X(J,I)*TEM
189.          DO 36 K=1,NS
190.          IF(INJ(K).EQ.1)X(K,I)=(XV(L,K,I) +XV(L+1,K,I))/2.
191.          S(J,K)=S(J,K) +X(J,I)*X(K,I)*TEM2
192.       36 CONTINUE
193.          IF(IC.EQ.0)GOTO 16
194.          IF(LA.GE.MSL)GOTO 16
195.          DO 68 J=1,NS
196.          S(J,NS+LA)=S(J,NS+LA) +X(J,I)*TEM2
197.       68 S(NS+LA,J)=S(NS+LA,J) +X(J,I)*TEM2
198.          S(NS+LA,NS+LA)=S(NS+LA,NS+LA) +TEM2
199.          DWX(NS+LA)=DWX(NS+LA)+TEM
200.       16 CONTINUE
```

215

```
201.        94 CONTINUE
202.       812 FORMAT(8F8.3)
203.        21 CONTINUE
204.
205.           CALL INVER(S,NSP)
206.
207.           DO 40 K=1,NSP
208.           R(K)=0.
209.           DO 40 J=1,NSP
210.        40 R(K)=R(K) +DWX(J)*S(J,K)
211.           DO 81 K=1,NSP
212.        81 B(K)=BL(K) +R(K)
213.           ISTEP=ISTEP+1
214.           IST=IST+2
215.           IST=IST-10
216.       139 DIFR=0.
217.           DO 83 K=1,NSP
218.           DIF=ABS(B(K)-BL(K))
219.        83 DIFR=DIFR +DIF
220.           IF(DIFR.GT.TN)GOTO 89
221.           WRITE(6,88)ISTEP,DIFR
222.        88 FORMAT(1H0,'ITERATION CONVERGED AFTER STEP : ',I3,
223.          &'  / DIFFERENCE = ',F20.13,' '///)
224.           IF(IE.EQ.1)GOTO 141
225.           WRITE(6,117)
226.       117 FORMAT(/1X,'LINEAR MODEL')
227.           GOTO 142
228.       141 WRITE(6,118)
229.       118 FORMAT(/1X,'EXPONENTIAL MODEL')
230.       142 WRITE(6,115)
231.           DO 113 K=1,NSP
232.       113 WRITE(6,110)(S(K,J),J=1,NSP)
233.       115 FORMAT(//1X,'COVARIANCE MATRIX')
234.       110 FORMAT(5X,8F10.5)
235.           WRITE(6,112)
236.           I2=1
237.       128 DO 111 K=1,NSPP
238.           K2=K
239.           KC=K -NSN
240.           IF(KC.NE.NC(I2))GOTO 32
241.           I2=I2 +1
242.           GOTO 111
243.        32 IF(K.EQ.NSPP)GOTO 111
244.           S(K2,K2)=SQRT(S(K2,K2))
245.           K1=K-1
246.           IF(K.GT.NSN)K1=K-I2+1-NSN
247.           IF(K.GT.NSN)K2=K1+NS
248.           WRITE(6,122)K1,B(K2),K1,S(K2,K2)
249.       111 CONTINUE
250.       112 FORMAT(//1X,'B COEFFICIENTS AND STANDARD ERRORS')
251.       122 FORMAT(5X,'B(',I2,')=',F9.4,5X,'SE(',I2,')=',F9.4)
252.      5010 CONTINUE
253.           STOP
254.        56 WRITE(6,102)ISTEP,DIFR
255.       102 FORMAT(1X,'NO CONVERGENCE AFTER STEP',I4,';  DIFFERENC=',F10.4)
256.           GOTO 5010
257.     C
258.        99 CONTINUE
259.           WRITE(6,811)
260.       811 FORMAT(/1X'EXPONENTIAL NON-CONSTANT NOT IMPLEMENTED.')
261.           GOTO 5010
262.           END
263.           SUBROUTINE INVER(A,N)
```

```
264.    C
265.            DIMENSION A(55,55),INDEX(55,2),IPIVOT(55),PIVOT(55)
266.            COMMON PIVOT,INDEX,IPIVOT
267.            EQUIVALENCE (IROW,JROW),(ICOLUM,JCOLUM),(AMAX,T,SWAP)
268.    C
269.            DETERM=1.0
270.    C
271.            DO 20 J=1,N
272.        20 IPIVOT(J)=0
273.    C
274.            DO 550 I=1,N
275.            AMAX=0.0
276.    C
277.            DO 105 J=1,N
278.            IF(IPIVOT(J)-1) 60,105,60
279.    C
280.        60 DO 100 K=1,N
281.            IF(IPIVOT(K)-1) 80,100,740
282.    C
283.        80 IF(ABS(AMAX)-ABS(A(J,K))) 85,100,100
284.    C
285.        85 IROW=J
286.            ICOLUM=K
287.            AMAX=A(J,K)
288.    C
289.       100 CONTINUE
290.       105 CONTINUE
291.    C
292.            IPIVOT(ICOLUM)=IPIVOT(ICOLUM)+1
293.            IF(IROW-ICOLUM) 140,260,140
294.    C
295.       140 DETERM=-DETERM
296.    C
297.            DO 200 L=1,N
298.            SWAP=A(IROW,L)
299.            A(IROW,L)=A(ICOLUM,L)
300.       200 A(ICOLUM,L)=SWAP
301.    C
302.       260 INDEX(I,1)=IROW
303.            INDEX(I,2)=ICOLUM
304.            PIVOT(I)=A(ICOLUM,ICOLUM)
305.            DETERM=DETERM*PIVOT(I)
306.            A(ICOLUM,ICOLUM)=1.0
307.    C
308.            DO 350 L=1,N
309.            IF(PIVOT(I).NE.0) GOTO 349
310.            A(ICOLUM,L)=0.
311.            GOTO 350
312.       349 A(ICOLUM,L)=A(ICOLUM,L)/PIVOT(I)
313.       350 CONTINUE
314.    C
315.            DO 550 L1=1,N
316.            IF(L1-ICOLUM) 400,550,400
317.       400 T=A(L1,ICOLUM)
318.            A(L1,ICOLUM)=0.0
319.            DO 450 L=1,N
320.       450 A(L1,L)=A(L1,L)-A(ICOLUM,L)*T
321.    C
322.       550 CONTINUE
323.    C
324.            DO 710 I=1,N
325.            L=N+1-I
326.            IF(INDEX(L,1)-INDEX(L,2)) 630,710,630
327.       630 JROW=INDEX(L,1)
```

```
328.      C
329.           JCOLUM=INDEX(L,2)
330.      C
331.           DO 705 K=1,N
332.           SWAP=A(K,JROW)
333.           A(K,JROW)=A(K,JCOLUM)
334.           A(K,JCOLUM)=SWAP
335.      705 CONTINUE
336.      C
337.      710 CONTINUE
338.      C
339.      740 RETURN
340.           END
341.  //GO.FT02F001 DD UNIT=SYSDA,VOL=SER=NRES01,DISP=OLD,
342.  // DSN=$2ZB004.COL.INPUT.SECY,DCB=(RECFM=FB,LRECL=80,BLKSIZE=4560)
343.  //GO.FT06F001 DD SYSOUT=A,DCB=(RECFM=FB,BLKSIZE=133)
344.  //
```

INPUT TO LONGIT.EVENTP PROGRAM

(Example of Section 6.2, Table 5.7)

```
 1
 0  24  42   1   1   1   1   0   1   2
 1   0   0   1
11111111111111111111111111111111111111111
00111111111111111111111111111111111111111
00001111111111111111111111111111111111111
00000111111111111111111111111111111111111
00000001111111111111111111111111111111111
00000000011111111111111111111111111111111
00000000000001111111111111111111111111111
00000000000001111111111111111111111111111
00000000000000001111111111111111111111111
00000000000000000011111111111111111111111
00000000000000000000111111111111111111111
00000000000000000000001111111111111111111
00000000000000000000001111111111111111111
00000000000000000000000011111111111111111
00000000000000000000000000111111111111111
00000000000000000000000000001111111111111
00000000000000000000000000000011111111111
00000000000000000000000000000000111111111
00000000000000000000000000000000001111111
00000000000000000000000000000000000011111
00000000000000000000000000000000000000111
00000000000000000000000000000000000000011
00000000000000000000000000000000000000001
  (40F2.0)
0.
0.
0.
0.
0.
0.
0.
0.
0.
1.
1.
1.
1.
```

```
1.
0.
0.
0.
0.
1.
1.
1.
1.
0.
0.
0.
0.
1.
0.
1.
1.
0.
1.
1.
1.
0.
0.
1.
1.
1.
1.
1.
1.
```

```
1.   2.   3.   4.   5.   6.   7.   8.   9.  10.  11.  12.  13.  15.  16.  17.
19.  20.  22.  23.  25.  32.  34.  35.
 1   1   2   2   3   4   4   5   5   6   6   6   6   7   8   8   8   8   9  10  10  11  11  11  12  12
13  14  15  16  16  17  18  19  19  20  20  21  22  22  23  24
 1   1   1   1   1   1   1   1   1   2   1   1   1   1   1   1   1   1   2   2   1   2   1   1   1   1
 1   1   1   2   1   2   2   1   1   1   1   2   2   2   2   2
```

OUTPUT FROM LONGIT.EVENTP PROGRAM

```
0    24    42    1    1    1    1    0    1    2
```
ITERATION CONVERGED AFTER STEP :   5 / DIFFERENCE =   0.0000594854355 /

EXPONENTIAL MODEL

COVARIANCE MATRIX
```
      0.73650    0.00650   -0.03724
      0.00650    0.17522    0.00439
     -0.03724    0.00439    0.00257
```


B COEFFICIENTS AND STANDARD ERRORS
```
    B( 0)=  -3.4625    SE( 0)=   0.8582
    B( 1)=  -1.5661    SE( 1)=   0.4186
    B( 2)=   0.1141    SE( 2)=   0.0507
```

B COEFFICIENTS FOR TIME PERIODS IN PARTIAL LIKELIHOOD
```
    B( 1)=  -2.5976    SE( 1)=   0.7071
    B( 2)=  -2.5242    SE( 2)=   0.7071
    B( 3)=  -3.1382    SE( 3)=   1.0000
```

219

```
B( 4)=  -2.4077      SE( 4)=   0.7071
B( 5)=  -2.3188      SE( 5)=   0.7071
B( 6)=  -1.5281      SE( 6)=   0.5000
B( 7)=  -2.8662      SE( 7)=   1.0000
B( 8)=  -1.4775      SE( 8)=   0.5000
B( 9)=  -2.5984      SE( 9)=   1.0000
B(10)=  -1.9013      SE(10)=   0.7071
B(11)=  -1.4682      SE(11)=   0.5774
B(12)=  -1.6794      SE(12)=   0.7071
B(13)=  -2.1652      SE(13)=   1.0000
B(14)=  -1.4930      SE(14)=   1.0000
B(15)=  -2.0820      SE(15)=   1.0000
B(16)=  -1.3766      SE(16)=   0.7071
B(17)=  -1.2373      SE(17)=   1.0000
B(18)=  -1.9081      SE(18)=   1.0000
B(19)=  -0.5500      SE(19)=   0.7071
B(20)=  -0.9705      SE(20)=   0.7071
B(21)=  -0.6311      SE(21)=   1.0000
B(22)=   0.9052      SE(22)=   0.7071
B(23)=  -0.5451      SE(23)=   1.0000
B(24)=  -0.6460      SE(24)=   1.0000
```

LONGIT.EVENTP PROGRAM

```
1.      //LONGIT JOB (2ZB004,COL,Q,REG),COLEMAN,RE=500K,
2.      // TE=YES,ID='LONGIT.EVENTP',RO=REG,Q=0
3.      // EXEC FORTXCLG
4.      //FORT.SYSIN DD *
5.              DIMENSION XV(50,5,50),Q(50,10),NELTA(50,50),IE(50,50),NET(50),
6.           &S(5,5),PSI(5,5),DWX(5),BL(5),B(5),YBAR(50,10),TM(5,5),KV(5,10),
7.           &NPER(50),R(5),FMT(18),G(50),T(51),X(50,50),SUMQ(50),NV(5,10),
8.           &DT(50),INJ(5),W(50),NJL(50),INDEX(50,15),NE(50)
9.      C
10.             EQUIVALENCE (YBAR(50,10),Q(50,10))
11.     C   READ IN INC=1 FOR NON-CONSTANT INDEPENDENT VARIABLES, 0 FOR CONSTANT
12.     C   MS= NUMBER OF TIME PERIODS
13.     C   N= NUMBER OF INDIVIDUALS
14.     C   NS= NUMBER OF INDEPENDENT VARIABLES
15.     C   IC IS NOT USED IN  THIS PROGRAM.
16.     C   IT=0 IF NO TIME TREND IS ESTIMATED, 1 IF IT IS.
17.     C    TIME IS NOT ENTERED EXPLICITLY AS AN INDEPENDENT VARIABLE.
18.     C   INC=0 IF NO INDEPENDENT VARIABLE CHANGES OVER TIME, 1 IF ONE
19.     C    OR MORE VARIES AT DIFFERENT EVENT TIMES.
20.     C   INJ(J)=0 IF INDEPENDENT VARIABLE J IS CONSTANT OVER TIME, 1 IF
21.     C    IT IS MEASURED AT EACH TIME POINT.
22.     C   ORDER OF INDEPENDENT VARIABLES IS: CONSTANT, NS EXPLICIT
23.     C    VARIABLES, TIME (IF IT=1), CONSTANT TERMS FOR TIME PERIODS
24.     C   NWT=1 IF EACH RECORD HAS A WEIGHT OF 1, 0 OTHERWISE.  IF NWT
25.     C    EQUALS 0, WEIGHTS MUST BE READ IN EXPLICITLY.
26.     C   NTIM=1 IF TIMES OF EVENTS ARE 1 UNIT APART, 0 OTHERWISE.
27.     C    IF NTIM EQUALS 0, TIMES MUST BE READ IN EXPLICITLY.
28.     C   IPL=1 IF PERIOD-SPECIFIC COMPONENTS ARE TO BE CALCULATED, 0
29.     C    OTHERWISE.
30.             READ(2,1)NJOBS
31.             NJOBS=1
32.             DO 5010 I22=1,NJOBS
33.             READ (2,1)INC,MS,N,NS,IC,IT,NWT,NTIM,IPL,MT
34.             NSN=NS +1
35.             NSA=NSN
36.             IF(IT.EQ.1)NSA=NSN+1
37.             WRITE(6,1)INC,MS,N,NS,IC,IT,NWT,NTIM,IPL,MT
```

```
38.              IF(INC.EQ.1)READ (2,6)(INJ(J),J=2,NSN)
39.         6 FORMAT(5X10I1)
40.         1 FORMAT(10I5)
41.              MSP=MS +1
42.              KV(1,1)=0
43.              IF(MT.GT.1)GOTO 24
44.              DO 25 K=2,NSA
45.        25 KV(K,1)=1
46.              GOTO 23
47.        24 CONTINUE
48.    C      KV(K,J)=1 IF VARIABLE K IS INCLUDED FOR EVENT TYPE J, 0 OTHERWISE.
49.              READ(2,1)((KV(K,J),J=1,MT),K=2,NSA)
50.              DO 21 J=2,MT
51.              KV(1,J)=1
52.        21 CONTINUE
53.        23 CONTINUE
54.              ISTEP=0
55.              NSP=0
56.              DO 22 K=1,NSA
57.              DO 22 J=1,MT
58.              NV(K,J)=0
59.              IF(KV(K,J).EQ.1)NV(K,J)=NSP+1
60.        22 NSP=NSP +KV(K,J)
61.              DO 10 L=1,MS
62.    C      READ NELTA(I,L)=1 IF I IS OBSERVED AT START & END OF PERIOD L, 0 OTHERWISE
63.              READ(2,2)(NELTA(I,L),I=1,N)
64.        10 CONTINUE
65.              READ (2,8889)FMT
66.      8889 FORMAT(18A4)
67.         2 FORMAT(80I1)
68.    C      READ INDEPENDENT VARIABLES, INTERMIXED CONSTANT AND NON-CONST.
69.              DO 172 I=1,N
70.              DO 172 J=2,NSN
71.              IF(INJ(J).NE.1)READ(2,FMT)XV(1,J,I),W(I)
72.              IF(INJ(J).EQ.1)READ(2,FMT)(XV(L,J,I),L=1,MSP),W(I)
73.              IF(NWT.EQ.1)W(I)=1
74.              DO 174 L=1,MSP
75.              IF(INJ(J).NE.1)XV(L,J,I)=XV(1,J,I)
76.       174 CONTINUE
77.       172 CONTINUE
78.              DO 173 I=1,N
79.              DO 173 L=1,MSP
80.       173 XV(L,1,I)=1.
81.    C      READ TIMES OF EVENTS
82.              IF(NTIM.EQ.0)READ(2,4)(T(L),L=1,MS)
83.         4 FORMAT(16F5.1)
84.              IF(NTIM.EQ.0)GOTO 153
85.              DO 152 L=1,MS
86.              T(L)=L
87.       152 CONTINUE
88.       153 CONTINUE
89.              DUM=0.
90.              DO 95 L=1,MS
91.              DT(L)=T(L)-DUM
92.        95 DUM=T(L)
93.              IF(IT.NE.1)GOTO 39
94.              DO 38 I=1,N
95.              DO 38 L=1,MSP
96.        38 XV(L,NSA,I)=T(L)
97.              NSN=NSA
98.        39 CONTINUE
```

221

```
  99.              TN=.0005*NSP
 100.              DO 11 K=1,NSP
 101.         11 B(K)=0.
 102.      C       READ NUMBER OF PERIOD AT WHICH I JUMPED
 103.              READ (2,5)(NPER(I),I=1,N)
 104.          5 FORMAT(26I3)
 105.      C       READ NET(I)=EVENT TYPE FOR PERSON I.
 106.              IF(MT.LT.2)GOTO 28
 107.              READ (2,5)(NET(I),I=1,N)
 108.              GOTO 126
 109.         28 CONTINUE
 110.              DO 26 I=1,N
 111.              NET(I)=1
 112.         26 CONTINUE
 113.        126 CONTINUE
 114.      C
 115.      C       NJL(L)=NUMBER WHO JUMP AT PERIOD L.
 116.      C       INDEX(L,J)=INDEX OF JTH PERSON WHO JUMPED AT PERIOD L.
 117.              DO 161 L=1,MS
 118.      C       CA CULATING NE(L)=NUMBER IN RISK SET AT PERIOD L.
 119.              NE(L)=0
 120.              DO 164 I=1,N
 121.              NE(L)=NE(L) +NELTA(I,L)
 122.        164 CONTINUE
 123.        161 NJL(L)=0
 124.              DO 160 I=1,N
 125.              L=NPER(I)
 126.              NJL(L)=NJL(L)+1
 127.              J=NJL(L)
 128.              INDEX(L,J)=I
 129.        160 CONTINUE
 130.      C
 131.      C       IE(L,J)=INDEX OF J(TH PERSON IN RISK SET AT PERIOD L.
 132.              DO 130 L=1,MS
 133.              J=1
 134.              DO 130 I=1,N
 135.              IF(NELTA(I,L).EQ.0)GOTO 130
 136.              IE(L,J)=I
 137.              J=J+1
 138.        130 CONTINUE
 139.      C
 140.      C       CALCULATING COMBINED VALUES OF INDEPENDENT VARIABLES FOR ALL
 141.      C       WHO JUMPED AT TIME L AND STORING IT IN X(L,K).
 142.              DO 167 L=1,MS
 143.              NL=NJL(L)
 144.              DO 165 K=1,NSP
 145.        165 X(L,K)=0.
 146.              IF(NL.EQ.0)GOTO 167
 147.              DO 166 J=1,NL
 148.              I=INDEX(L,J)
 149.              IT=NET(I)
 150.              DO 166 K=1,NSN
 151.              IF(KV(K,IT).EQ.0)GOTO 166
 152.              KA=NV(K,IT)
 153.              X(L,KA)=X(L,KA) +XV(L,K,I)
 154.        166 CONTINUE
 155.        167 CONTINUE
 156.      C
 157.      C       BEGIN LOOP
 158.         89 DO 90 K=1,NSP
 159.              DWX(K)=0.
 160.              DO 90 J=1,NSP
```

222

```
161.              S(K,J)=0.
162.          90 BL(K)=B(K)
163.             IF(ISTEP.GT.30 )GOTO 56
164.             DO 31 L=1,MS
165.             NEL=NE(L)
166.             SUMQ(L)=0.
167.             DO 18 I=1,NEL
168.             IX=IE(L,I)
169.             DO 18 J=1,MT
170.             Q(I,J)=0.
171.             DO 20 K=1,NSN
172.             IF(KV(K,J).EQ.0)GOTO 20
173.             KA=NV(K,J)
174.             Q(I,J)=Q(I,J) +BL(KA)*XV(L,K,IX)
175.          20 CONTINUE
176.             Q(I,J)=EXP(Q(I,J))
177.          18 SUMQ(L)=SUMQ(L) +Q(I,J)
178.             DO 29 J=1,MT
179.             DO 29 I=1,NEL
180.          29 YBAR(I,J)=Q(I,J)/SUMQ(L)
181.             DO 33 K=1,NSP
182.             G(K)=0.
183.             DO 33 J=1,NSP
184.          33 TM(K,J)=0.
185.             DO 32 K=1,NSN
186.             DO 32 JE=1,MT
187.             IF(KV(K,JE).EQ.0)GOTO 32
188.             KA=NV(K,JE)
189.             DO 35 I=1,NEL
190.             IX=IE(L,I)
191.             G(KA)=G(KA) +YBAR(I,JE)*XV(L,K,IX)
192.             DO 311 J=1,NSN
193.             IF(KV(J,JE).EQ.0)GOTO 311
194.             KB=NV(J,JE)
195.             TM(KA,KB)=TM(KA,KB) +XV(L,K,IX)*XV(L,J,IX)*YBAR(I,JE)
196.         311 CONTINUE
197.          35 CONTINUE
198.          32 CONTINUE
199.             DO 34 K=1,NSP
200.             DWX(K)=DWX(K) +X(L,K) -NJL(L)*G(K)
201.             DO 34 J=1,NSP
202.             S(K,J)=S(K,J) +NJL(L)*(TM(J,K) -G(K)*G(J))
203.          34 CONTINUE
204.          31 CONTINUE
205. C
206.             CALL INVER(S,NSP)
207.
208.             DO 40 K=1,NSP
209.             R(K)=0.
210.             DO 40 J=1,NSP
211.          40 R(K)=R(K) +DWX(J)*S(J,K)
212.             DO 81 K=1,NSP
213.          81 B(K)=BL(K) +R(K)
214.             ISTEP=ISTEP+1
215.         139 DIFR=0.
216.             DO 83 K=1,NSP
217.             DIF=ABS(B(K)-BL(K))
218.          83 DIFR=DIFR +DIF
219.             IF(DIFR.GT.TN)GOTO 89
220.             WRITE(6,88)ISTEP,DIFR
221.          88 FORMAT(1H0,'ITERATION CONVERGED AFTER STEP : ',I3,
222.            &' / DIFFERENCE = ',F20.13,' '//)
```

223

```
223.          141 WRITE(6,118)
224.          118 FORMAT(/1X,'EXPONENTIAL MODEL')
225.          142 WRITE(6,115)
226.              DO 113 K=1,NSP
227.          113 WRITE(6,110)(S(K,J),J=1,NSP)
228.          115 FORMAT(//1X,'COVARIANCE MATRIX')
229.          110 FORMAT(5X,8F10.5)
230.              WRITE(6,112)
231.          128 DO 111 K=1,NSP
232.              S(K,K)=SQRT(S(K,K))
233.              K1=K-1
234.          111 WRITE(6,122)K1,B(K),K1,S(K,K)
235.          112 FORMAT(//1X,'B COEFFICIENTS AND STANDARD ERRORS')
236.          122 FORMAT(5X,'B(',I2,')=',F9.4,5X,'SE(',I2,')=',F9.4)
237.              IF(IPL.EQ.1)GOTO 27
238.         5010 CONTINUE
239.              STOP
240.           56 WRITE(6,102)ISTEP,DIFR
241.          102 FORMAT(1X,'NO CONVERGENCE AFTER STEP',I4,';  DIFFERENC=',F10.4)
242.              GOTO 5010
243.   C
244.   C          CALCULATING TIME-SPECIFIC RATES FOR PARTIAL LIKELIHOOD.
245.           27 DO 156 L=1,MS
246.              NEL=NE(L)
247.              SUMA1=0.
248.              SUMA2=0.0
249.              DO 155 I=1,NEL
250.              IX=IE(L,I)
251.              IF(NPER(IX).EQ.L)SUMA1=SUMA1 +1
252.          155 CONTINUE
253.              S(L,L)=1./SUMA1
254.          156 B(L)=  LOG(SUMA1) -LOG(SUMQ(L)) +LOG(DT(L))
255.              WRITE(6,132)
256.              DO 101 K=1,MS
257.              S(K,K)=SQRT(S(K,K))
258.          101 WRITE(6,122)K,B(K),K,S(K,K)
259.          132 FORMAT(/1X'B COEFFICIENTS FOR TIME PERIODS IN PARTIAL LIKELIHOOD')
260.          162 FORMAT(5X,'B(',I2,')=',F9.4,5X,'SE(',I2,')=',F9.4)
261.              GOTO 5010
262.              END
263.   C
264.              SUBROUTINE INVER(A,N)
265.   C
266.              DIMENSION A(5,5),INDEX(5,2),IPIVOT(5),PIVOT(5)
267.              COMMON PIVOT,INDEX,IPIVOT
268.              EQUIVALENCE (IROW,JROW),(ICOLUM,JCOLUM),(AMAX,T,SWAP)
269.   C
270.              DETERM=1.0
271.   C
272.              DO 20 J=1,N
273.           20 IPIVOT(J)=0
274.   C
275.              DO 550 I=1,N
276.              AMAX=0.0
277.   C
278.              DO 105 J=1,N
279.              IF(IPIVOT(J)-1) 60,105,60
280.   C
281.           60 DO 100 K=1,N
282.              IF(IPIVOT(K)-1) 80,100,740
283.   C
284.           80 IF(ABS(AMAX)-ABS(A(J,K))) 85,100,100
```

224

```
285.   C
286.      85 IROW=J
287.         ICOLUM=K
288.         AMAX=A(J,K)
289.   C
290.     100 CONTINUE
291.     105 CONTINUE
292.   C
293.         IPIVOT(ICOLUM)=IPIVOT(ICOLUM)+1
294.         IF(IROW-ICOLUM) 140,260,140
295.   C
296.     140 DETERM=-DETERM
297.   C
298.         DO 200 L=1,N
299.         SWAP=A(IROW,L)
300.         A(IROW,L)=A(ICOLUM,L)
301.     200 A(ICOLUM,L)=SWAP
302.   C
303.     260 INDEX(I,1)=IROW
304.         INDEX(I,2)=ICOLUM
305.         PIVOT(I)=A(ICOLUM,ICOLUM)
306.         DETERM=DETERM*PIVOT(I)
307.         A(ICOLUM,ICOLUM)=1.0
308.   C
309.         DO 350 L=1,N
310.         IF(PIVOT(I).NE.0) GOTO 349
311.         A(ICOLUM,L)=0.
312.         GOTO 350
313.     349 A(ICOLUM,L)=A(ICOLUM,L)/PIVOT(I)
314.     350 CONTINUE
315.   C
316.         DO 550 L1=1,N
317.         IF(L1-ICOLUM) 400,550,400
318.     400 T=A(L1,ICOLUM)
319.         A(L1,ICOLUM)=0.0
320.         DO 450 L=1,N
321.     450 A(L1,L)=A(L1,L)-A(ICOLUM,L)*T
322.   C
323.     550 CONTINUE
324.   C
325.         DO 710 I=1,N
326.         L=N+1-I
327.         IF(INDEX(L,1)-INDEX(L,2)) 630,710,630
328.     630 JROW=INDEX(L,1)
329.   C
330.         JCOLUM=INDEX(L,2)
331.   C
332.         DO 705 K=1,N
333.         SWAP=A(K,JROW)
334.         A(K,JROW)=A(K,JCOLUM)
335.         A(K,JCOLUM)=SWAP
336.     705 CONTINUE
337.   C
338.     710 CONTINUE
339.   C
340.     740 RETURN
341.         END
342.   //GO.FT02F001 DD UNIT=SYSDA,VOL=SER=NRES01,DISP=OLD,
343.   // DSN=$2ZB004.COL.INPUT.SEC5,DCB=(RECFM=FB,LRECL=80,BLKSIZE=4560)
344.   //GO.FT06F001 DD SYSOUT=A,DCB=(RECFM=FB,BLKSIZE=133)
345.   //
```
?

Chapter 6

Maximum Likelihood Estimates

1. MAXIMUM LIKELIHOOD ESTIMATION

There are various estimation strategies that may be used in special cases of these models. However, the one estimation method that may be used for nearly all the combinations of model and data discussed here is that of maximum likelihood. The likelihood function differs depending on the kind of data available (cross-sectional, panel, continuous records, and dichotomous response versus multiple responses), and the maximum likelihood equations differ depending on the kind of decomposition of the transition rates.

The use of a single estimation procedure across all data types and model types has several virtues. It increases comparability of the estimates from different forms of data by eliminating differences due to the estimation method; it makes comparability between the two forms of causal structure (q as a linear function of the x_k, and q as an exponential linear function of the x_k) more feasible; and it can form a single approach around which a general estimation computer program can be written. I will describe the estimation procedures for cross-sectional data, panel data, event-record data of various sorts, and finally for continuous records.

The general idea underlying maximum likelihood estimation is: Under a given model that is hypothesized to have generated the data, it is possible to write the likelihood that a particular observation will have occurred. For example, if a set of observations z_i $(i = 1, \ldots, n)$ that take on values of 0 or 1 are hypothesized to have been generated by a set of Bernoulli processes with parameters p_i, $i = 1, \ldots, n$, then the likelihood of having observed $z_i = 1$ is p_i, and the likelihood of having observed $z_i = 0$ is $1 - p_i$. The likelihood of having observed the whole set of values z_i is the product, over the whole set, of p_i corresponding to the observations $z_i = 1$ and $1 - p_i$ corresponding to the observation $z_i = 0$. This product can be conveniently

written as $\displaystyle\prod_{i=1}^{n} p_i{}^{z_i} (1 - p_i)^{1 - z_i}$.

Maximum likelihood methods obtain estimates of the parameter values that maximize the likelihood that the particular data will have been generated, given the hypothesized generating model. In general, so long as the number of parameters is less than or equal to the number of observations, a set of parameter values that maximize the likelihood can be found. For example, in the illustration just described, if each individual i is assumed to have a different parameter p_i, then the values of p_i that maximize the likelihood of the observed sample are simply $p_i = z_i$, that is, $p_i = 1$ whenever $z_i = 1$, and $p_i = 0$ whenever $z_i = 0$. This, of course, is a trivial case, because such an assumption of n parameters to generate n observations contains no parsimony. The case of interest is where the number of parameters is less than the number of observations. In that instance the maximization of the likelihood with respect to the parameters is ordinarily carried out by setting equal to zero the first partial derivatives of the likelihood with respect to each of the parameters and solving the resulting set of simultaneous equations for the parameters. Because the maximum of the logarithm of a function occurs at the same point as the maximum of the function itself, it is possible to use first derivatives of the log likelihood rather than first derivatives of the likelihood itself. And because the likelihood is in the form of a product, while its logarithm is in the form of a sum, it is easier to find the partial derivatives of the logarithm rather than the likelihood itself.

Besides obtaining estimates of the parameters of a model, it is also useful to obtain estimates of the standard deviations of these parameter estimates to gain an idea of the sampling variability of the estimated values. This allows the construction of confidence intervals for the true value of the parameter or the determination of how likely it is that the true value differs from zero in the observed direction. The use of maximum likelihood estimation methods is especially conducive to finding standard deviations. The Fisher information matrix is the inverse of the covariance matrix of the parameters. And the Fisher information matrix is equal to the negative of the expected values of the second derivatives of the log likelihood with respect to all pairs of parameters. Thus, having estimated the parameter values that maximize the likelihood, the values of the second derivatives of the log likelihood at this point can be used to find the covariance matrix and estimates of the standard deviations of the estimates. This is the general strategy followed in estimation procedures to be outlined in this chapter and contained in the LONGIT computer programs listed in the appendices to chapters 2, 3, 4, and 5.

1.1. THE GENERAL ESTIMATION METHOD TO BE USED HERE

The subsequent sections of this chapter will specify the likelihood functions for a particular form of data, and for a particular model, finding first and second partial derivatives of the log likelihood with respect to the parameters of that model. In the present section, I will outline the general form of the maximum likelihood solutions, and I will lay out the structure of the algorithms used in the LONGIT computer programs to estimate parameters in the models.

First, suppose we can write the likelihood function for the observed sample under the assumed model. This is not a trivial task but one with a wide range of difficulty, depending on the form of the observations and the model assumed to generate them. If the sample consists of a set of independent observations assumed to be generated by a bernoulli process, then the likelihood function is very simply written, as in the preceding illustration. On the other hand, the relationship between the fundamental parameters of the model (that is, the parameters whose values are to be estimated) and the probability of observing a particular outcome may be very complex, as, for example, in the general m-state markov process with constant transition rates, where the matrix of transition probabilities between times 0 and t is related to the transition rates through an infinite series of $m \times m$ matrices (see equation 1.16).

It is not always possible to write the likelihood function for the observed sample under a given assumed model. However, this task is reserved for the sections dealing with different data forms and different models. Here we assume the existence of the likelihood function, denoted by $\mathscr{L}$, and its logarithm, denoted by L.

Then the maximum of the function exists at those parameter values at which each of the first partial derivatives with respect to the parameters equals zero, and the second partial derivatives are negative. In the present section, I will use b_j as the generic term for the jth parameter, although the parameters are variously designated β_j, b_j, c_j, and λ_j in the different models. The use of b_j here is to be understood as covering all these cases. Similarly, the range of j is here generically taken as $1, \ldots, m$, where the total number of parameters equals m. In the models described in subsequent sections, this range will sometimes be designated differently, to facilitate notation for that model. The vector of first partial derivatives with respect to all the parameters will be denoted L', and the vector of second partial derivatives with respect to all pairs of parameters will be denoted L''.

The maximum of the likelihood exists at

$$\frac{\partial L}{\partial b_j} = 0, \frac{\partial^2 L}{\partial b_j \partial b_k} < 0, \qquad j = 1, \ldots, m \qquad (6.1)$$

or, in vector notation, $L' = 0$, $L'' < 0$.

If these m first derivatives were linear in $\mathbf{b}$, it would be possible to solve them directly. However, this is not true in general, so it is necessary to use an iterative method for estimating $\mathbf{b}$, picking a starting point $\mathbf{b}^{(0)}$ and then climbing toward $\mathbf{b}^{(e)}$, the value of $\mathbf{b}$ that maximizes L, in successive iterations. If v denotes the iteration number, then what is desired is to have a method that will calculate $\mathbf{b}^{(v+1)}$ from $\mathbf{b}^{(v)}$ such that for each j, $b_j^{(v+1)}$ is closer to $b_j^{(e)}$ than is $b_j^{(v)}$.

One algorithm for doing this takes advantage of the fact that the second derivative of a function must be negative in the neighborhood of a maximum of the function, while it is positive in the neighborhood of a minimum of the function. If in the one-parameter case $b^{(v)}$ represents the value of b on the v iteration, and $b^{(v+1)}$ the value on the $(v + 1)$ iteration, this implies that if $b^{(v+1)} - b^{(v)} = -L'/L''$, $b^{(v+1)}$ will be at a higher value of L than will be $b^{(v)}$.[1] Thus the iteration will be moving in the direction of the maximum. This fact can be used through equation (6.2) to calculate a value of $b^{(v+1)}$ given a value of $b^{(v)}$, thus providing an iterative algorithm in the one-parameter case:

---

[1] This statement can be verified geometrically by examination of the slope and its change on the two sides of a maximum and the two sides of a minimum. To the left of a maximum the slope is positive and the change in slope is negative so that L'/L'' is negative, and by equation (6.2), $b^{(v+1)}$ is to the right of $b^{(v)}$, toward the maximum. To the right of a maximum the slope is negative and the change in slope is negative so that L'/L'' is positive, and by equation (6.2), $b^{(v+1)}$ is to the left of $b^{(v)}$, again toward the maximum. The opposite results hold to the left and right of a minimum, making $b^{(v+1)}$ farther from the minimum than $b^{(v)}$.

$$b^{(v+1)} = b^{(v)} - \frac{L'}{L''}, \tag{6.2}$$

where L' and L'' are derivatives evaluated at $b^{(v)}$.

The multiparameter generalization of equation (6.2) for the vector of parameters $\mathbf{b}$ is given by equation (6.3):

$$\mathbf{b}^{(v+1)} = \mathbf{b}^{(v)} - \mathbf{L}'(\mathbf{L}'')^{-1} \tag{6.3}$$

Equation (6.3) provides an algorithm for iteratively finding $\mathbf{b}^{(e)}$, given a starting point $\mathbf{b}^{(0)}$. It was compared for cross-sectional data and for the model of chapter 4, section 5 with the Newton-Raphson algorithm to be subsequently described, and it was found to require more time and often more iterations to convergence. This, together with the fact that each iteration requires more calculations, led it to be discarded in favor of the Newton-Raphson method. However, I should emphasize that I have compared these algorithms only for a few data sets and models, on one criterion, and more extensive comparisons might show its superiority for some purposes.

The Newton-Raphson algorithm (see Haberman, 1974, for a more extensive discussion) is based on the use of only the first derivative, L', together with a Taylor series expansion of some function ρ of $\mathbf{b}$, which can be compared to the observations. In the models where the data observed are occupancy of states (chapter 2 with cross-sectional data and chapters 3 and 4 with panel data), the function $\rho(\mathbf{b})$ is p_i or $p_i(t)$, the probability that individual i occupies state 1, or in the multiresponse case, p_{ij} or $p_{ij}(t)$, the probability that individual i occupies state j. In the models where the data observed refer to events (chapter 5), $\rho(\mathbf{b})$ is q_i, the transition rate for the event in question.

It is ordinarily possible to write $\partial L / \partial b_j$ as the sum over individuals i of the products of three quantities: the derivative with respect to b_j of the function ρ, the difference between the observations z_i and ρ, and a third quantity, which I shall call w_i. This third quantity, which may be thought of heuristically as a weight for individual i, is also a function of $\mathbf{b}$. Thus the derivative of L at the v iteration may be written

$$\frac{\partial L^{(v)}}{\partial b_j} = \sum_{i=1}^{N} w_i^{(v)} [z_i - \rho^{(v+1)}] \frac{\partial \rho^{(v)}}{\partial b_j} \tag{6.4}$$

where $\rho^{(v+1)}$ is written, because in setting equation (6.4) equal to zero the equality will not hold with $\rho^{(v)}$ unless the likelihood is already at its maximum.

Thus $\rho_i^{(v+1)}$ is that value of ρ_i that makes the equations hold when used in the system of equations resulting from setting the right-hand side of equation (6.4) equal to zero. Under conditions of regularity and for small enough steps that value of ρ_i will be a value that is closer to the one at which L is maximum than is $\rho_i^{(v)}$.

But the task is not to solve for the N values of $\rho_i^{(v+1)}$, for there are only m equations, one for each parameter b_j. It is, rather, to solve for the m values of $b_j^{(v+1)}$, which taken together with the values of the independent variables, x_{ji}, give the N values of $\rho_i^{(v+1)}$. It is for this that the Taylor series expansion is used.

The Taylor series expansion of ρ around $\mathbf{b}^{(v)}$ may be written (using only the linear terms):

$$\rho_i^{(v+1)} = \rho_i^{(v)} + \sum_{k=1}^{n} [b_k^{(v+1)} - b_k^{(v)}] \frac{\partial \rho_i^{(v)}}{\partial b_k}. \tag{6.5}$$

Substituting for $\rho_i^{(v+1)}$ from equation (6.5) into the right-hand side of equation (6.4) and setting it equal to zero gives

$$0 = \sum_{i=1}^{N} \left[w_i^{(v)} \{z_i - \rho_i^{(v)}\} \frac{\partial \rho_i^{(v)}}{\partial b_j} - w_i^{(v)} \sum_{k=1}^{m} \{b_k^{(v+1)} - b_k^{(v)}\} \frac{\partial \rho_i^{(v)}}{\partial b_k} \frac{\partial \rho_i^{(v)}}{\partial b_j} \right]. \tag{6.6}$$

For simplicity of notation let us denote the first partial derivative of $\rho_i^{(v)}$ with respect to b_k, that is, $\partial \rho_i^{(v)}/\partial b_k$, as $x_{ki}^{*(v)}$. (The usefulness of using a modification of the symbol x_{ki} for the value of the independent variable k for individual i lies in the fact that for some models in chapters 2 through 5, this first derivative equals x_{ki}, and in most cases it is a linear function of x_{ki}.) Then, in order to write equation (6.6) in simpler matrix form, let us define the following vectors and matrices:

$\mathbf{d}^{(v)} \equiv \{d_i^{(v)}\}$ a $1 \times N$ row vector with an element $d_i^{(v)}$ for each individual, where $d_i^{(v)} = z_i - \rho_i^{(v)}$;

$\mathbf{w}^{(v)} \equiv \{w_{ij}^{(v)}\}$ an $N \times N$ diagonal matrix with $w_{ii}^{(v)} = w_i^{(v)}$, and $w_{ij}^{(v)} = 0$ for all $j \neq i$;

$\mathbf{b}^{(v)} \equiv \{b_k^{(v)}\}$ a $1 \times m$ row vector of the parameters $b_k^{(v)}$ at the v iteration;

$\mathbf{x}^{*(v)} \equiv \{x_{ki}^{*(v)}\}$ an $m \times N$ matrix with elements $x_{ki}^{*(v)}$, which is the first partial derivative of $\rho_i^{(v)}$ with respect to b_k^v, $\partial \rho_i/\partial b_{kj}$,

and the transpose of a matrix $\mathbf{s}$ is identified as $\mathbf{s}^{tr}$.

With these definitions, equation (6.6) can be written in matrix notation,

231

$$\mathbf{d}^{(v)}\mathbf{w}^{(v)}\mathbf{x}^{*(v)tr} + \mathbf{b}^{(v)}\mathbf{x}^{*(v)}\mathbf{w}^{(v)}\mathbf{x}^{*(v)tr} = \mathbf{b}^{(v+1)}\mathbf{x}^{*(v)}\mathbf{w}^{(v)}\mathbf{x}^{*(v)tr} \qquad (6.7)$$

Solving for $\mathbf{b}^{(v+1)}$ gives

$$\mathbf{b}^{(v+1)} = \mathbf{b}^{(v)} + \mathbf{d}^{(v)}\mathbf{w}^{(v)}\mathbf{x}^{*(v)tr}[\mathbf{x}^{*(v)}\mathbf{w}^{(v)}\mathbf{x}^{*(v)tr}]^{-1} \qquad (6.8)$$

Equation (6.8) constitutes the algorithm I have used in calculating the maximum likelihood estimates in nearly all the cases. Exceptions are indicated in later sections of the chapter. This algorithm requires obtaining first derivatives of ρ; and on each iteration it requires calculating the vector $\mathbf{d}^{(v)}$, the diagonal matrix $\mathbf{w}^v$ (which in the LONGIT programs is stored as a vector) and the matrix $\mathbf{x}^{*(v)}$, using the response observations z_i, the observations on independent variables, x_{ji}, and the v estimates of the $b_j, \mathbf{b}^{(v)}$. Its use also requires employing starting values $\mathbf{b}^{(0)}$, $\mathbf{w}^{(0)}$, and $\mathbf{x}^{*(0)}$.

The use of starting values that are close to final values obviously reduces the number of iterations necessary for convergence. For certain purposes it may be desirable to find approximate starting values by using some noniterative approximation, possibly a least-squares method of some sort. However, in most applications it is sufficient to use starting values of the sort that follow. In the LONGIT programs used for calculating examples in chapters 2 and 3, the following starting values are used:

$$b_j^{(0)} = 0 \text{ for all } j$$

$$d_i^{(0)} = z_i - 1.01\,\bar{z} \quad \text{where } \bar{z} = \frac{1}{N}\sum_{i=1}^{N} z_i$$

$$w_{ii}^{(0)} = 1.0 \text{ for all } i$$

$$x_{ji}^{*(0)} = x_{ji} \text{ for all independent variables } j \text{ and individuals } i$$

Convergence Criterion: The test for convergence can either be used on the $1 \times m$ vector $\mathbf{b}$, the parameters of the process, or on the $1 \times N$ vector $\boldsymbol{\rho}$, which is calculated from $\mathbf{b}$. In either case, convergence occurs when the values on the $(v + 1)$ iteration equal those on the v iteration within the desired degree of accuracy of $\mathbf{b}$ or $\boldsymbol{\rho}$.

An appropriate convergence criterion is given below:

$$\sum_{j=1}^{m} |b_j^{(v+1)} - b_j^{(v)}| < \epsilon$$

where ϵ is some small value, its size depending on the desired degree of

232

accuracy for a single b_j, and on the number of parameters m. The value of ϵ used in the LONGIT program, and for the examples in this book, is either $\epsilon = .0001m$ or $\epsilon = .001m$.

Second Derivatives of L and the Covariance Matrix: Equation (6.8) can be used for finding maximum likelihood estimates of **b**. For finding standard deviations of **b**, it is necessary to estimate the matrix of second derivatives of **L** with respect to all pairs of parameters. Thus if we define **L''** as

$$\mathbf{L''} \equiv \{L_{jk}''\}, \text{ where } L_{jk}'' \text{ is defined as } \frac{\partial^2 L}{\partial b_j \partial b_k},$$

and

$\boldsymbol{\sigma} \equiv \{\sigma_{jk}\}$, where σ_{jk} is defined as the estimate obtained from the matrix of second derivatives,

then

$$\boldsymbol{\sigma} = (-\mathbf{L''})^{-1}. \tag{6.9}$$

Thus, to find the covariance matrix it is necessary to calculate the second derivatives of L based on the maximum likelihood estimates of **b**.

The subsequent sections treating different data forms and different models are directed at finding first and second derivatives of the log likelihood with respect to b_j (and via the first derivative of L, finding the first derivative of p_i), and at indicating appropriate starting values for the iterative estimation algorithm.

2. CROSS-SECTIONAL DATA ON OCCUPANCY OF STATES

If person i is in state 1 with probability p_i, then the likelihood of the observed sample z_i $(i = 1, \ldots, N)$ $(z_i = 0, 1)$, is

$$\mathcal{L} = \prod_{i=1}^{N} p_i{}^{z_i}(1 - p_i)^{1-z_i} \tag{6.10}$$

The probability p_i is a function of $\boldsymbol{\beta}$ and x_i, as indicated in equation (2.19),

233

and the maximum likelihood estimate of β is that estimate which produces the values of p_i and q_i that maximize $\mathscr{L}$.

The maximum of $\mathscr{L}$ with respect to β_j may be found by differentiating the right-hand size of equation (6.10) with respect to β_j and setting the derivative equal to zero. For n independent variables, there are $n + 1$ parameters, and this gives us $n + 1$ equations, which when solved simultaneously give the vector β.

It is simpler to differentiate the logarithm of $\mathscr{L}$ rather than $\mathscr{L}$, and since $\log \mathscr{L}$ (conventionally denoted by L) has its maximum at the same point as $\mathscr{L}$, its derivative will suffice. First, taking logarithms,

$$L = \log \mathscr{L} = \sum_{i=1}^{N} [z_i \log p_i + (1 - z_i) \log (1 - p_i)] \cdot \qquad (6.11)$$

Differentiating by β_j $(j = 0, \ldots, n)$ gives

$$\frac{\partial L}{\partial \beta_j} = \sum_{i=1}^{N} \left(\frac{z_i}{p_i} \frac{\partial p_i}{\partial \beta_j} - \frac{(1 - z_i)}{1 - p_i} \frac{\partial p_i}{\partial \beta_j} \right) \qquad (6.12)$$

$$= \sum_{i=1}^{N} \frac{z_i - p_i}{p_i(1 - p_i)} \frac{\partial p_i}{\partial \beta_j} = 0.$$

Thus, for cross-sectional data on states, whatever the model, we have for use of the algorithm of section 1:

Section 1   *Section 2*

b_j	$= \beta_j$
p_i	$= p_i$
w_i	$= \{p_i(1 - p_i)\}^{-1}$
z_i	$= 1$ if i is observed to be in state 1, 0 otherwise
m	$= n + 1$ (where n is the number of independent variables)

What differs for different models is $\partial p_i/\partial b_j$. These will be derived for the linear and exponential decompositions shortly.

It is also necessary to find the second derivative of L to obtain an estimate of the covariance matrix. Taking the derivative of equation (6.12) with respect to β_k gives the second derivative of L.[2]

---

[2] If $z_i \neq 0$ or 1, then equation (6.13) and equation (6.14) are not correct. In place of $(z_i - p_i)^2$ is $z_i(1 - p_i) + p_i(p_i - z_i)$. This change is necessary if analysis uses aggregate data such that z_i is a proportion between zero and one.

234

$$\frac{\partial^2 L}{\partial \beta_j \partial \beta_k} = \left[\sum_{i=1}^{N} \frac{z_i - p_i}{z_i(1 - p_i)} \frac{\partial^2 p_i}{\partial \beta_j \partial \beta_k} - \frac{(z_i - p_i)^2}{p_i^2(1 - p_i)^2} \frac{\partial p_i}{\partial \beta_j} \frac{\partial p_i}{\partial \beta_k} \right]. \qquad (6.13)$$

If we define

$$\phi_i \equiv \frac{z_i - p_i}{p_i(1 - p_i)},$$

Then equation (6.13) may be written

$$L_{jk}'' = \sum_{i=1}^{N} \left[\phi_i \frac{\partial^2 p_i}{\partial \beta_j \partial \beta_k} - \phi_i^2 \frac{\partial p_i}{\partial \beta_j} \frac{\partial p_i}{\partial \beta_k} \right]. \qquad (6.14)$$

Thus, for each of the two models, linear and exponential, the task of estimating the vector β and the covariance matrix is reduced to the use of the indicated correspondences between the quantities of this section and the quantities defined in section 1, together with finding the first and second partial derivatives of p_i with respect to the β_j's. Then equation (6.8) is used to find the vector β, and equation (6.9) together with equation (6.14) is used to find the covariance matrix σ.

2.1. LINEAR DECOMPOSITION: THE LINEAR PROBABILITY MODEL

From equation (2.19) the linear decomposition gives

$$p_i = \sum_{j=0}^{n} \beta_j x_{ji}.$$

The first derivative with respect to β_j is

$$\frac{\partial p_i}{\partial \beta_j} = x_{ji}. \qquad (6.15)$$

Therefore, $x_{ji}^{*(v)} = x_{ji}$. The second derivative with respect to β_j and β_k is

$$\frac{\partial^2 p_i}{\partial \beta_j \partial \beta_k} = 0. \qquad (6.16)$$

Thus, for use of equation (6.8) $x_{ji}^{*(v)} = x_{ji}$ for all iterations. And for use of

235

equation (6.9) $L''_{jk} = \sum\limits_{i=1}^{N} \phi_i^2 \, x_{ji}x_{ki}$. For this simplest case I will write out equation (6.8) in terms of p_i and b_j, to give a sense of how the calculation is carried out at each iteration. For the other cases I will simply give the first and second partial derivatives, which together with the quantities defined in section 2, are used in equation (6.8) to solve iteratively for **b** and in equation (6.9) to solve for σ once convergence has been attained. There are $n + 1$ equations, $j = 0, \ldots, n$, of the following form [from equation (6.7)]:

$$\sum_{i=1}^{N} \frac{[z_i - p_i^{(v)}]}{p_i^{(v)}[1 - p_i^{(v)}]} \, x_{ji} + \sum_{i=1}^{N} \sum_{k=0}^{n} b_k^{(v)} \frac{x_{ki}x_{ji}}{p_i^{(v)}[1 - p_i^{(v)}]}$$

$$= \sum_{i=1}^{N} \sum_{k=0}^{n} b_k^{(v+1)} \frac{x_{ki}x_{ji}}{p_i^{(v)}[1 - p_i^{(v)}]} . \qquad (6.17)$$

Inversion of the matrix with elements $\dfrac{x_{ki}x_{ji}}{p_i^{(v)}[1 - p_i^{(v)}]}$ and right-multiplication of the vector consisting of elements

$$\frac{[z_i - p_i^{(v)}]x_{ji}}{p_i^{(v)}[1 - p_i^{(v)}]}$$

by the inverted matrix gives a vector with elements that are $b_k^{(v+1)} - b_k^{(v)}$. Adding the vector $\mathbf{b}^{(v)}$ to this gives the new vector, $\mathbf{b}^{(v+1)}$.

2.2. EXPONENTIAL LINEAR DECOMPOSITION: THE MULTIVARIATE LOGIT MODEL

From equation (2.23) exponential decomposition of the transition rates gives

$$p_i = \frac{1}{1 + e^{-\sum\limits_{k=0}^{n} \beta_k x_{ki}}}$$

The first derivative with respect to β_j is

$$\frac{\partial p_i}{\partial \beta_j} = x_{ji}p_i(1 - p_i).$$

Therefore,

$$x_{ji}^{*(v)} = x_{ji}p_i^{(v)}[1 - p_i^{(v)}], \tag{6.18}$$

and the second derivative with respect to β_j and β_k is

$$\frac{\partial^2 p_i}{\partial \beta_j \partial \beta_k} = x_{ji}x_{ki}p_i(1 - p_i)(1 - 2p_i). \tag{6.19}$$

Substitution of the right-hand side of equation (6.18) into equation (6.8), together with the other quantities defined immediately after equation (6.12) gives the equation for estimation of β for the exponential linear decomposition. However, in this case a simplification in the calculations is possible.

$$w_{ii}^{(v)} x_{ji}^{*(v)} = \frac{x_{ji}p_i^{(v)}[1 - p_i^{(v)}]}{p_i^{(v)}[1 - p_i^{(v)}]} = x_{ji}$$

so that

$$x_{ki}^{*(v)} w_{ii}^{(v)} x_{ji}^{*(v)} = x_{ji}x_{ki}p_i^{(v)}[1 - p_i^{(v)}]. \tag{6.20}$$

This simplification reduces the computations necessary on each iteration, which can reduce computation time. Similarly, there is a simplification in L_{jk}'': From equation (6.19) and equation (6.14)

$$L_{jk}'' = \sum_{i=1}^{N} \frac{(z_i - p_i)\, x_{ji}x_{ki}p_i\,(1 - p_i)(1 - 2p_i)}{p_i\,(1 - p_i)} - \frac{(z_i - p_i)^2\, x_{ji}x_{ki}p_i^2\,(1 - p_i)^2}{p_i^2\,(1 - p_i)^2}$$

$$= \sum_{i=1}^{N} - x_{ji}x_{ki}p_i\,(1 - p_i). \tag{6.21}$$

Use of equation (6.8), as in section 2.1, gives the iterative alogrithm for finding β and use of equation (6.9) gives the covariance matrix σ.

The parameters estimated from cross-sectional data do not give absolute values of transition rates. For the exponential model, they are in effect multipliers of the absolute rate (that is, e^{β_k} is a multiplier). Here, unlike the linear case, the estimated parameters β_k (for $k \geq 1$) are the same as the b_k in the model, except that they are multiplied by a factor of 2. What are *not* estimated, and cannot be with cross-sectional data, are b_0 and c_0, which give the absolute sizes of the transition rates in the two directions. With cross-sectional data all that is estimated is the difference, $b_0 - c_0$, which when exponentiated gives the ratio of the absolute sizes of the transition rates in the two directions when all independent variables x_k ($k \geq 1$) are 0.

3. PANEL DATA ON OCCUPANCY OF STATES

With cross-sectional data it is possible to estimate only the relative effects of independent variables, that is, the ratio of b_k to the effects of unmeasured variables on z: $\beta_k = b_k/(b_0 + c_0)$. However, since panel data show evidence of the amount of change that has taken place, it should be possible to estimate the absolute sizes of the effects on q_{hj}. This is also apparent from equation (3.2), in which $p_i(t)$ is a linear function of b_k, while in equation (2.19), p_i for cross-sectional data is a linear function of β_k.

With panel data there are two observations of the state of the dependent attribute for each individual, $z_i(0)$ and $z_i(t)$, where the times of the panel are taken as 0 and t. To make use of the information about change of state that exists in the sample to estimate b, we take the first observation as given and calculate the probability of occupying state 1 at time t given $z_i(0)$.[3] From equation (3.23), this is, for the general Markov case with time-varying transition rates,

$$p(t) = e^{-\int_0^t [q_1(\tau) + q_0(\tau)]d\tau} \left\{ z(0) + \int_0^t e^{\int_0^t [q_1(\theta) + q_0(\theta)]d\theta} q_1(\tau)d\tau \right\}.$$

As in cross-sectional data with state occupancy, if individual i is in state 1 at time t with probability $p_i(t)$, then the likelihood of the observations $z_i(t)$ ($i = 1, \ldots, N$) is

$$\mathcal{L} = \prod_{i=1}^{N} p_i(t)^{z_i(t)} [1 - p_i(t)]^{1 - z_i(t)}. \tag{6.22}$$

---

[3] By taking $z_i(0)$ as given, the likelihood thus constructed can be regarded as a conditional likelihood—conditional upon state occupancy at time 0. This is related to what some investigators call *left censoring*. If the initial state, $z_i(0)$, is unrelated to the independent variables of interest, then left censoring, or conditioning upon $z_i(0)$, does not affect parameter estimates. If the initial state is related to the independent variable, then estimates may be affected. This is a problem that has not been well studied. See section 9 of chapter 3 for a discussion of left censoring.

Here $p_i(t)$ is a conditional probability, and we are examining the likelihood of the observations $z_i(t)$ conditional upon observations $z_i(0)$. The probability $p_i(t)$ is a function of $z_i(0)$, **b**, **c**, and x_{ki} ($k = 0, \ldots, n$), and the maximum likelihood estimates of **b** and **c** are those estimates that generate the values of $p_i(t)$ which maximize $\mathcal{L}$ for the given $z_i(0)$ and x_{ki}.

The log likelihood obtained by taking the logarithm of equation (6.22) is like that in equation (6.11) for cross-sectional data, and the first derivative of L is like that in equation (6.12):

$$\frac{\partial L}{\partial b_k} = \sum_{i=1}^{N} \frac{z_i(t) - p_i(t)}{p_i(t)(1 - p_i(t))} \frac{\partial p_i(t)}{\partial b_k} \qquad 0 \le k \le n \qquad (6.23)$$

with $\partial L / \partial c_k$ like equation (6.23), except that c_k replaces b_k in the equation.

For use of the algorithm of section 1, comparison of equation (6.4) and equation (6.23) gives the following correspondences:

Section 1		*Section 3*
p_i	$=$	$p_i(t)$
w_i	$=$	$\{p_i(t)[1 - p_i(t)]\}^{-1}$
z_i	$=$	$z_i(t)$: $= 1$ if i is observed to be in state 1 at time t; $= 0$ otherwise
m	$=$	$n + 2$ (unrestricted model), $2n + 2$ (unrestricted model), where n is the number of independent variables
b_j	$=$	b_k, $k = 0, \ldots, n$ ($j = 1, \ldots, n + 1$) and either c_0 ($j = n + 2$) restricted model, or c_k $k = 0, \ldots, n$ ($j = n + 2, \ldots, 2n + 2$) unrestricted model

As in the case of cross-sectional data, the second derivative of L can be expressed in terms of first and second derivatives of $p_i(t)$. The equation is identical to equation (6.13) except that $p_i(t)$ replaces p_i, $z_i(t)$ replaces z_i, and b_j and b_k replace β_j and β_k.[4]

$$\frac{\partial^2 L}{\partial b_j \partial b_k} = \sum_{i=1}^{N} \left[\phi_i(t) \frac{d^2 p_i(t)}{db_j db_k} - \phi_i(t)^2 \frac{\partial p_i(t)}{\partial b_j} \frac{\partial p_i(t)}{\partial b_k} \right] \qquad (6.24)$$

---

[4] As in the cross-sectional case, if $z_i(t) \ne 0$ or 1, as would be the case if aggregate data are used, then in place of $\phi_i(t)^2$ in the right-hand term is

$$\frac{z_i(t)[1 - p_i(t)] + p_i(t)[p_i(t) - z_i(t)]}{\{p_i(t)[1 - p_i(t)]\}^2}$$

where we define

$$\phi_i(t) \equiv \frac{z_i(t) - p_i(t)}{p_i(t)(1 - p_i(t))}$$

and b_k is used generically to include both b_k and c_k.

In the different models that are treated in chapter 3, the only differences relevant to maximum likelihood estimation are in $\partial p_i(t)/\partial b_j$, $\partial^2 p_i(t)/\partial b_j \partial b_k$, and the number of parameters. The models, differing according to decomposition of the transition rates, restricted ($c_k = -b_k$ for $k \geq 1$) or unrestricted, and constant or nonconstant independent variables, are shown in the following table. The numbers in the cells indicate the section in which that model is treated.

| independent variables: | constant | | nonconstant | |
restriction on effects:	unrestricted	restricted	unrestricted	restricted
decomposition: linear:	3.1	3.2	3.3	3.4
exponential:	3.5	3.6	3.7	3.8

For models treated in each of these sections, the task of estimating b and c is reduced to the use of correspondences given in this section together with the first derivatives of p_i given in sections 3.1 to 3.8, in equation (6.8). The covariance matrix σ is obtained by use of the same correspondences, equation (6.9) together with equation (6.24), and the first and second derivatives from sections 3.1 to 3.8.

3.1. LINEAR DECOMPOSITION, UNRESTRICTED EFFECTS, AND CONSTANT INDEPENDENT VARIABLES

From equation (3.1), $p_i(t)$ is

$$p_i(t) = z_i(0)a_1 + q_{1i}a_2$$

where a_1 and a_2 are defined in section 3.9.

(Subscripts for individual i will be deleted from a_0, a_1, and a_2 for notational convenience. One should keep in mind that these quantities differ for different individuals i.) First, it is useful to find the first derivatives of a_0, a_1, and a_2 with respect to b_k and c_k.

$$\frac{\partial a_0}{\partial b_k} = \frac{\partial a_0}{\partial c_k} = x_{ki}$$

$$\frac{\partial a_1}{\partial b_k} = \frac{\partial a_1}{\partial c_k} = -x_{ki} t a_1$$

$$\frac{\partial a_2}{\partial b_k} = \frac{\partial a_2}{\partial c_k} = x_{ki} \frac{(t a_1 - a_2)}{a_0}$$

Then the first derivatives of $p_i(t)$ with respect to b_k and c_k are:

$$\frac{\partial p_i(t)}{\partial b_k} = x_{ki} \left[\left\{ \frac{q_{1i}}{a_0} - z_i(0) \right\} a_1 t + \frac{q_{0i} a_2}{a_0} \right] \tag{6.25}$$

$$\frac{\partial p_i(t)}{\partial c_k} = x_{ki} \left[\left\{ \frac{q_{1i}}{a_0} - z_i(0) \right\} a_1 t - \frac{q_{1i} a_2}{a_0} \right] \tag{6.26}$$

The second derivatives take three different forms in this model because of the two different forms taken by the first derivatives. With a_3 defined as in section 3.9, these are:

$$\frac{\partial^2 p_i(t)}{\partial b_j \partial b_k} = x_{ji} x_{ki} \left[\left\{ z_i(0) - \frac{q_{1i}}{a_0} \right\} a_1 t^2 - 2 q_{0i} \frac{a_3 t}{a_0} \right] \tag{6.27}$$

$$\frac{\partial^2 p_i(t)}{\partial b_j \partial c_k} = x_{ji} x_{ki} \left[\left\{ z_i(0) - \frac{q_{1i}}{a_0} \right\} a_1 t^2 + \left\{ q_{1i} - q_{0i} \right\} \frac{a_3 t}{a_0} \right] \tag{6.28}$$

$$\frac{\partial^2 p_i(t)}{\partial c_j \partial c_k} = x_{ji} x_{ki} \left[\left\{ z_i(0) - \frac{q_{1i}}{a_0} \right\} a_1 t^2 + 2 q_{1i} \frac{a_3 t}{a_0} \right] \tag{6.29}$$

Use of equations (6.25) and (6.26) in equation (6.8), and use of equations (6.25)–(6.29) in equation (6.24) and then in equation (6.9) gives the equations for estimating **b**, **c**, and the covariance matrix.

3.2. LINEAR DECOMPOSITION, RESTRICTED EFFECTS ($c_k = -b_k$ FOR $k \geq 1$), AND CONSTANT INDEPENDENT VARIABLES

The equation for $p_i(t)$ is given, as in the preceding section, by

$$p_i(t) = z_i(0) a_1 + q_{1i} a_2 .$$

The difference is that in this case, a_1, a_2, and a_0 are constant across individuals.

This changes the first and second derivatives for $k \neq 0$ since for $1 \leq k \leq n$, $\partial a_0/\partial b_k = \partial a_1/\partial b_k = \partial a_2/\partial b_k = 0$. The first derivatives for b_0 and c_0 remain as in equations (6.25) and (6.26), with of course $x_{0i} = 1$ for all i. The first derivatives are these:

$$\frac{\partial p_i(t)}{\partial b_k} = x_{ki}a_2 \qquad 1 \leq k \leq n \qquad\qquad (6.30)$$

$$\frac{\partial p_i(t)}{\partial b_0} \text{ as in equation (6.25)},$$

$$\frac{\partial p_i(t)}{\partial c_0} \text{ as in equation (6.26)}.$$

These three cases of first derivatives generate six cases of second derivatives, which may be found by differentiating equations (6.25), (6.26), and (6.30) by b_k, b_0, and c_0. These are

$$\frac{\partial^2 p_i(t)}{\partial b_j \partial b_k} = 0 \qquad 1 \leq k, j \leq n \qquad\qquad (6.31)$$

$$\frac{\partial^2 p_i(t)}{\partial b_k \partial b_0} = -x_{ki}a_3 t \qquad 1 \leq k \leq n \qquad\qquad (6.32)$$

$$\frac{\partial^2 p_i(t)}{\partial b_k \partial c_0} = -x_{ki}a_3 t \qquad 1 \leq k \leq n \qquad\qquad (6.33)$$

$$\frac{\partial^2 p_i(t)}{\partial b_0 \partial b_0} \text{ as in equation (6.27) with } j = k = 0$$

$$\frac{\partial^2 p_i(t)}{\partial b_0 \partial c_0} \text{ as in equation (6.28) with } j = k = 0$$

$$\frac{\partial^2 p_i(t)}{\partial c_0 \partial c_0} \text{ as in equation (6.29) with } j = k = 0.$$

Use of equations (6.25), (6.26), and (6.30) in equation (6.8), and use of equations (6.25)–(6.33) in equation (6.24) and then in equation (6.9) gives us the equations for iteratively estimating $\mathbf{b}$ and c_0 and for subsequently estimating the covariance matrix.

3.3. LINEAR DECOMPOSITION, UNRESTRICTED EFFECTS, AND NONCONSTANT INDEPENDENT VARIABLES

To treat this case the assumption is made in chapter 3 that the independent variables $x_{ki}(\tau)$ change linearly between times 0 and t, or if they are 0–1 attributes, that the expected value of $x_{ki}(\tau)$ is linear between 0 and t. That is, $x_{ki}(\tau) = x_{ki}(0) + [x_{ki}(t) - x_{ki}(0)]\tau/t$.

With this assumption, the definitions of the quantities a_1, a_2, a_3 defined earlier remain the same, but the definition of a_0 changes:

$$a_0 = \tfrac{1}{2}[q_1(0) + q_1(t) + q_0(0) + q_0(t)]$$

From equation (3.26), $p_i(t)$ is given by

$$p_i(t) = z_i(0)a_1 + q_1(0)a_3 + q_1(t)a_4,$$

where a_4 is defined as shown in section 3.9. To find the first derivative of $p_i(t)$ with respect to b_k and c_k, we first find the derivatives of a_3 and a_4:

$$\frac{\partial a_3}{\partial b_k} = \frac{\partial a_4}{\partial c_k} = \bar{x}_k a_5$$

where a_5 is defined as in section 3.9:

$$\frac{\partial a_4}{\partial b_k} = \frac{\partial a_4}{\partial c_k} = \bar{x}_k a_6$$

where a_6 is defined as in section 3.9. Using this together with the derivative of a_2 given in section 3.1, for the first derivatives of $p_i(t)$ with respect to b_k and c_k we obtain:

$$\frac{\partial p_i(t)}{\partial b_k} = \bar{x}_{ki} \left\{ \left[\frac{q_{1i}(0)}{a_0} - z_i(0) \right] a_1 t - 2q_{1i}(0)\frac{a_3}{a_0} + q_{1i}(t)a_6 \right\} + x_{ki}(0)a_3$$
$$+ x_{ki}(t)a_4 \quad (6.34)$$

$$\frac{\partial p_i(t)}{\partial c_k} = \bar{x}_{ki} \left\{ \left[\frac{q_{1i}(0)}{a_0} - z_i(0) \right] a_1 t - 2q_{1i}(0)\frac{a_3}{a_0} + q_{1i}(t)a_6 \right\}. \quad (6.35)$$

To obtain second derivatives of $p_i(t)$, it is useful to find the first derivatives of a_5 and a_6 with respect to b_k and c_k:

243

$$\frac{\partial a_5}{\partial b_k} = \frac{\partial a_5}{\partial c_k} = \bar{x}_{ki} a_7$$

where a_7 is defined as in section 3.9:

$$\frac{\partial a_6}{\partial b_k} = \frac{\partial a_6}{\partial c_k} = \bar{x}_{ki} a_8$$

where a_8 is defined as in section 3.9: The three second derivatives are

$$\frac{\partial^2 p_i(t)}{\partial b_j \partial b_k} = \bar{x}_{ji} \bar{x}_{ki} \left\{ t^2 a_1 \left[z_i(0) - \frac{q_{1i}(0)}{a_0} \right] - 3 q_{1i}(0) \frac{a_5}{a_0} + q_{1i}(t) a_8 \right\}$$
$$+ \bar{x}_j [a_5 x_{ki}(0) + a_6 x_{ki}(t)] + \bar{x}_k [a_5 x_{ji}(0) + a_6 x_{ji}(t)] \quad (6.36)$$

$$\frac{\partial^2 p_i(t)}{\partial b_j \partial c_k} = \bar{x}_{ji} \bar{x}_{ki} \left\{ t^2 a_1 \left[z_1(0) - \frac{q_{1i}(0)}{a_0} \right] - 3 q_{1i}(0) \frac{a_5}{a_0} + q_{1i}(t) a_8 \right\}$$
$$+ \bar{x}_k [a_5 x_j(0) + a_6 x_{ji}(t)] \quad (6.37)$$

$$\frac{\partial^2 p_i(t)}{\partial c_j \partial c_k} = \bar{x}_{ji} \bar{x}_{ki} \left\{ t^2 a_1 \left[z_i(0) - \frac{q_{1i}(0)}{a_0} \right] - 3 q_{1i}(0) \frac{a_5}{a_0} + q_{1i}(t) a_8 \right\}. \quad (6.38)$$

Note that in equation (6.37) there is an asymmetry that does not exist for the other second derivatives. If the matrix of second derivatives is divided into four quadrants with $\partial^2 p_i(t)/(\partial b_j \partial c_k)$ in the upper-right and lower-left quadrants, then these submatrices are not symmetric, although the matrix as a whole is symmetric. That is, $\partial^2 p_i(t)/\partial b_j \partial c_k \neq \partial^2 p_i(t)/\partial b_k \partial c_j$ when $k \neq j$.

Equations (6.34) and (6.35) in conjunction with equation (6.8) give the equation for iteratively estimating **b** and **c**, and equations (6.34)–(6.38) together with equation (6.9) and equation (6.24) give the proper equation for estimating the covariance matrix.

3.4. LINEAR DECOMPOSITION, RESTRICTED EFFECTS ($c_k = -b_k$ FOR $k \geq 1$), AND NONCONSTANT INDEPENDENT VARIABLES

The equation for $p_i(t)$ is that given in the preceding section.

Using the definitions of a_1, a_2, a_3, a_4, a_5, and a_6 given in earlier sections, the three first derivatives are

$$\frac{\partial p_i(t)}{\partial b_k} = a_3 x_{ki}(0) + a_4 x_{ki}(t), \qquad 1 \leq k \leq n \tag{6.39}$$

$$\frac{\partial p_i(t)}{\partial b_0} \text{ as in equation (6.34) with } k = 0$$

$$\frac{\partial p_i(t)}{\partial c_0} \text{ as in equation (6.35) with } k = 0$$

The second derivatives of $p_i(t)$ for each of the six cases generated by these three forms of the first derivative are

$$\frac{\partial^2 p_i(t)}{\partial b_j \partial b_k} = 0 \tag{6.40}$$

$$\frac{\partial^2 p_i(t)}{\partial b_k \partial b_0} = a_5 x_{ki}(0) + a_6 x_{ki}(t) \tag{6.41}$$

$$\frac{\partial^2 p_i(t)}{\partial b_k \partial c_0} = a_5 x_{ki}(0) + a_6 x_{ki}(t) \tag{6.42}$$

$$\frac{\partial^2 p_i(t)}{\partial b_0 \partial b_0} = t^2 z_i(0) a_1 + q_{1i}(0) a_7 + q_{1i}(t) a_8 - 2 a_3 t \tag{6.43}$$

$$\frac{\partial^2 p_i(t)}{\partial b_0 \partial c_0} = t^2 z_i(0) a_1 + q_{1i}(0) a_7 + q_{1i}(t) a_8 - a_3 t \tag{6.44}$$

$$\frac{\partial^2 p_i(t)}{\partial c_0 \partial c_0} = t^2 z_i(0) a_1 + q_{1i}(0) a_7 + q_{1i}(t) a_8 . \tag{6.45}$$

Equations (6.43)–(6.45) are identical to equations (6.36)–(6.38), respectively, with $j = k = 0$. Equations (6.40)–(6.42) are simplified by the fact that the assumption of $c_k = -b_k$ for $k \geq 1$ means that derivatives of a_1, a_2, a_3, a_4, a_5, and a_6 with respect to b_k are zero. Also, equations (6.40)–(6.42) can be seen to reduce, when all $x_{ki}(0) = x_{ki}(t)$, to equations (6.31)–(6.33), and equations (6.43)–(6.45) can similarly be seen to reduce to equations (6.27)–(6.29) (for $j = k = 0$), when $q_i(t) = q_i(0)$.

245

Use of these first and second derivatives with equations (6.8) and (6.9) allows estimation of $\mathbf{b}$ and c_0 with the iterative algorithm described in section 1 and subsequent estimation of the covariance matrix.

3.5. EXPONENTIAL DECOMPOSITION, UNRESTRICTED EFFECTS, AND CONSTANT INDEPENDENT VARIABLES

The equation for $p_i(t)$ is, as in the previous cases with constant independent variables,

$$p_i(t) = z_i(0)a_1 + q_{1i}a_2$$

where a_1 and a_2 are as defined in section 3.9.

The derivatives of a_0, a_1, *and* a_2 with respect to b_k and c_k are

$$\frac{\partial a_0}{\partial b_k} = \frac{\partial(e^{\Sigma b_k x_{ki}} + e^{\Sigma c_k x_{ki}})}{\partial b_k} = x_{ki}q_{1i},$$

$$\frac{\partial a_0}{\partial c_k} = x_{ki}q_{0i},$$

$$\frac{\partial a_1}{\partial b_k} = \frac{\partial(e^{-a_0 t})}{\partial b_k} = x_{ki}q_{1i}ta_1,$$

$$\frac{\partial a_1}{\partial c_k} = x_{ki}q_{0i}ta_1,$$

$$\frac{\partial a_2}{\partial b_k} = \frac{\partial\left(\dfrac{1 - a_1}{a_0}\right)}{\partial b_0} = \frac{x_{ki}q_{1i}(ta_1 - a_2)}{a_0} = -x_{ki}q_{1i}ta_3,$$

$$\frac{\partial a_2}{\partial c_k} = \frac{x_{ki}q_{0i}(ta_1 - a_2)}{a_0} = -x_{ki}q_{0i}ta_3.$$

With these derivatives, the derivatives of $p_i(t)$ with respect to b_k and c_k are

$$\frac{\partial p_i(t)}{\partial b_k} = x_{ki}q_{1i}\left\{\left[\frac{q_{1i}}{a_0} - z_i(0)\right]a_1 t + \frac{q_{0i}}{a_0}a_2\right\} \tag{6.46}$$

$$\frac{\partial p_i(t)}{\partial c_k} = x_{ki}q_{0i}\left\{\left[\frac{q_{1i}}{a_0} - z_i(0)\right]a_1 t - \frac{q_{1i}}{a_0}a_2\right\}. \tag{6.47}$$

Note that equations (6.46) and (6.47) are like the corresponding equations (6.25) and (6.26) for the linear decomposition, except for multiplication by q_{1i} and q_{0i}, respectively.

The three different forms of the second derivatives are

$$\frac{\partial^2 p_i(t)}{\partial b_k \partial b_j} = x_{ki}x_{ji}q_{1i}\left\{ ta_1\left[\frac{2q_{1i}q_{0i}}{a_0^2} + \left(\frac{q_{1i}}{a_0} - z_i(0)\right)\left(1 - tq_{1i}\right)\right]\right.$$
$$\left. - q_{0i}(q_{1i} - q_{0i})\frac{a_2}{a_0^2}\right\} \tag{6.48}$$

$$\frac{\partial^2 p_i(t)}{\partial b_k \partial c_j} = x_{ki}x_{ji}q_{1i}q_{0i}\left\{ ta_1\left[\frac{q_{0i} - q_{1i}}{a_0} - \left(\frac{q_{1i}}{a_0} - z_i(0)\right)t\right] + (q_{1i} - q_{0i})\frac{a_2}{a_0^2}\right\} \tag{6.49}$$

$$\frac{\partial^2 p_i(t)}{\partial c_k \partial c_j} = x_{ki}x_{ji}q_0\left\{ ta_1\left[-\frac{2q_{1i}q_{0i}}{a_0^2} + \left(\frac{q_{1i}}{a_0} - z_i(0)\right)\left(1 - tq_{0i}\right)\right]\right.$$
$$\left. - q_{1i}(q_{1i} - q_{0i})\frac{a_2}{a_0^2}\right\}. \tag{6.50}$$

Equations (6.46)–(6.50) may be used as before with equations (6.8), (6.9), and (6.24) to find **b, c,** and the covariance matrix.

3.6. EXPONENTIAL DECOMPOSITION, RESTRICTED EFFECTS ($c_k = -b_k$ FOR $k \geq 1$), AND CONSTANT INDEPENDENT VARIABLES

Equation (3.1) for $p_i(t)$ is as before. Making use of the derivatives of a_1 and a_2 in the preceding section, the first derivatives are

$$\frac{\partial p_i(t)}{\partial b_k} = x_{ki}\left\{\left[\frac{q_{1i}}{a_0} - z_i(0)\right]\left[q_{1i} - q_{0i}\right]a_1 t + 2\frac{q_{1i}}{a_0} a_2\right\}, \quad 1 \leq k \leq n \qquad (6.51)$$

$\dfrac{\partial p_i(t)}{\partial b_0}$ as in equation (6.46) with $k = 0$

$\dfrac{\partial p_i(t)}{\partial c_0}$ as in equation (6.47) with $k = 0$

The second derivatives are found to be:

$$\frac{\partial^2 p_i(t)}{\partial b_k \partial b_j} = x_{ki}x_{ji}\left\{ta_1\left[\frac{q_{1i}}{a_0} - z_i(0)\right]\left[a_0 - t(q_{1i} - q_{0i})^2\right]\right.$$
$$\left. - \frac{4q_{1i}q_{0i}}{a_0}(q_{1i} - q_{0i})a_3 t\right\}, \quad 1 \leq k, j \leq n \quad (6.52)$$

$$\frac{\partial^2 p_i(t)}{\partial b_k \partial b_0} = x_{ki}q_{1i}\left\{ta_1\left[\frac{q_{1i}}{a_0} - z_i(0)\right]\left[1 - t(q_{1i} - q_{0i})\right] + \frac{q_{0i}}{a_0}\right.$$
$$\left. - 2a_3 t\frac{q_{0i}}{a_0}(q_{1i} - q_{0i})\right\}, \quad 1 \leq k \leq n \quad (6.53)$$

$$\frac{\partial^2 p_i(t)}{\partial b_k \partial c_0} = x_{ki}q_{0i}\left\{ta_1\left[\frac{q_{1i}}{a_0} - z_i(0)\right]\left[-1 - t(q_{1i} - q_{0i})\right] + \frac{q_{1i}}{a_0}\right.$$
$$\left. + 2a_3 t\frac{q_{1i}}{a_0}(q_{1i} - q_{0i})\right\} \quad 1 \leq k \leq n \quad (6.54)$$

$\dfrac{\partial^2 p_i(t)}{\partial b_0 \partial b_0}$ as in equation (6.48) with $k = j = 0$

$\dfrac{\partial^2 p_i(t)}{\partial b_0 \partial c_0}$ as in equation (6.49) with $k = j = 0$

$\dfrac{\partial^2 p_i(t)}{\partial c_0 \partial c_0}$ as in equation (6.50) with $k = j = 0$

Equations (6.51), (6.46), (6.47), (6.52), (6.53), (6.54), (6.48), (6.49), and (6.50) can be used to define the appropriate quantities in equations (6.8) and (6.9) [with the use of equation (6.24)], to obtain **b**, c_0, and the covariance matrix.

3.7. EXPONENTIAL DECOMPOSITION, UNRESTRICTED EFFECTS, AND NONCONSTANT INDEPENDENT VARIABLES

The probability of occupying state 1 at time t is, from equation (3.22):

$$p_i(t) = z_i(0)\alpha_1 + \frac{q_{1i}(t) - q_{1i}(0)\alpha_1}{\alpha_4}$$

where the definitions of α_1 and α_4 are as shown in section 3.9. Taking the partial derivative of $p(t)$ with respect to b_k gives

$$\frac{\partial p(t)}{\partial b_k} = \alpha_{3k}\alpha_1 t \{q_{1i}(0)/\alpha_4 - z_i(0)\} - \frac{\{\alpha_3 k + \Delta x_{kt}/t\}\,\alpha_8}{\alpha_4^2} + \frac{\alpha_{9k}}{\alpha_4} \qquad (6.55)$$

where definitions of α_{3k}, α_8, α_{9k}, Δx_{kt} are given in section 3.9. Similarly, the partial derivative of $p(t)$ with respect to c_k is

$$\frac{\partial p(t)}{\partial c_k} = \alpha_{5k}\left\{\alpha_1 t\left[\frac{q_{1i}(0)}{\alpha_4} - z_i(0)\right] - \frac{\alpha_8}{\alpha_4^2}\right\} \qquad (6.56)$$

where α_{5k} is defined in section 3.9. In the second derivatives, new quantities α_{6jk}, α_{7jk}, α_{10}, and α_{11jk} appear. These are defined in section 3.9. Note that

$$\frac{\partial \alpha_{5k}}{\partial b_j} = \frac{\partial \alpha_{3k}}{\partial c_j} = 0$$

and that

$$\frac{\partial \alpha_4}{\partial b_j} = \alpha_{3j} + \frac{\Delta x_j}{t},$$

$$\frac{\partial \alpha_4}{\partial c_j} = \alpha_{5j}.$$

The three second derivatives are found to be, after some work:

$$\frac{\partial^2 p_i(t)}{\partial b_k \partial c_j} = \alpha_{6jk}\left(t\alpha_1\alpha_{10} - \frac{\alpha_8}{\alpha_4^2}\right) + \alpha_{3k}\alpha_{3j}\left\{\frac{2\alpha_8}{t\alpha_4^3} - t\alpha_1\left[t\alpha_{10} + \frac{2q_{1i}(0)}{\alpha_4^2}\right]\right\}$$

$$+ \alpha_{3k}\left\{\frac{2\alpha_8 x_j}{t\alpha_4^3} - \frac{\alpha_{9j}}{\alpha_4^2} + \frac{q_{1i}(0)\alpha_1 t}{\alpha_4}\left[x_{ji}(0) - \frac{\Delta x_j}{t\alpha_4}\right]\right\}$$

$$+ \alpha_{3j}\left\{\frac{2\alpha_8 x_k}{t\alpha_4^3} - \frac{\alpha_{9k}}{\alpha_4^2} + \frac{q_{1i}(0)\alpha_1 t}{\alpha_4}\left[x_{ki}(0) - \frac{\Delta x_j}{t\alpha_4}\right]\right\}$$

$$+ \frac{\alpha_{11jk}}{4} - \frac{\Delta x_k \alpha_{9j}}{t\alpha_4^2} - \frac{\Delta x_j \alpha_{9k}}{t\alpha_4^2} + \frac{2\Delta x_j \Delta x_k \alpha_8}{t^2\alpha_4^3} \tag{6.57}$$

$$\frac{\partial^2 p_i(t)}{\partial b_k \partial c_j} = \alpha_{3k}\alpha_{5j}\left\{\frac{2\alpha_8}{t\alpha_4^3} - t\alpha_1\left[t\alpha_{10} + \frac{2q_{1i}(0)}{\alpha_4^2}\right]\right\}$$

$$+ \alpha_{5j}\left\{\frac{2\alpha_8 \Delta x}{t\alpha_4^3} - \frac{\alpha_{9k}}{\alpha_4^2} + \frac{q_{1i}(0)\alpha_1 t}{\alpha_4}\left[x_{ki}(0) - \frac{\Delta x_k}{t\alpha_4}\right]\right\}$$

$$+ \frac{2\Delta x_j \Delta x_k \alpha_8}{t^2\alpha_4^3} \tag{6.58}$$

$$\frac{\partial^2 p_i(t)}{\partial c_k \partial c_j} = \alpha_{7jk}\left(t\alpha_1\alpha_{10} - \frac{\alpha_8}{\alpha_4^2}\right) + \alpha_{5k}\alpha_{5j}\left\{\frac{2\alpha_8}{\alpha_4^3} - t\alpha_1\left[t\alpha_{10} + \frac{2q_{1i}(0)}{\alpha_4^2}\right]\right\}. \tag{6.59}$$

These first and second derivatives given in equations (6.55)–(6.59) are used in equations (6.8) and (6.24) to find **b**, **c**, and the covariance matrix.

3.8. EXPONENTIAL DECOMPOSITION, RESTRICTED EFFECTS ($c_k = -b_k$ FOR $k \geq 1$), AND NONCONSTANT INDEPENDENT VARIABLES

This case is like the preceding one except there are three different cases of derivatives: for b_0, c_0, and b_k, $k = 1, \ldots, n$.

First, derivatives of some quantities that appear in the equation for $p_i(t)$ are

$$\frac{\partial \alpha_0}{\partial b_k} = \alpha_{3k} - \alpha_{5k} \qquad 1 \leq k \leq n,$$

$$\frac{\partial \alpha_0}{\partial b_0} = \alpha_{30} = \frac{\Delta q_1}{\Delta \log q_1},$$

$$\frac{\partial \alpha_0}{\partial c_0} = \alpha_{50} = \frac{\Delta q_0}{\Delta \log q_0},$$

$$\frac{\partial \alpha_4}{\partial b_k} = \alpha_{3k} - \alpha_{5k} + \frac{\Delta x_k}{t} \qquad 1 \leq k \leq n,$$

$$\frac{\partial \alpha_4}{\partial b_0} = \alpha_{30},$$

$$\frac{\partial \alpha_4}{\partial c_0} = \alpha_{50}.$$

Using these, the derivatives of $p(t)$ in the three cases are

$$\frac{\partial p(t)}{\partial b_k} = (\alpha_{3k} - \alpha_{5k})\alpha_1 t[q_{1i}(0)/\alpha_4 - z_i(0)] - \frac{\alpha_8\left(\alpha_{3k} - \alpha_{5k} + \frac{\Delta x_k}{t}\right)}{\alpha_4^2} + \frac{\alpha_{9k}}{\alpha_4} \qquad (6.60)$$

$$\frac{\partial p(t)}{\partial b_0} = \alpha_1 t\alpha_{30}[q_{1i}(0)/\alpha_4 - z_i(0)] - \frac{\alpha_8\alpha_{30}}{\alpha_4^2} \qquad 1 \leq k \leq n \qquad (6.61)$$

$$\frac{\partial p(t)}{\partial c_0} = \alpha_1 t\alpha_{50}[q_{1i}(0)/\alpha_4 - z_i(0)] - \frac{\alpha_8\alpha_{50}}{\alpha_4^2}. \qquad (6.62)$$

There are six forms of second derivative from these three forms of first derivative. Three of these follow directly from the unconstrained model:

$$\frac{\partial^2 p_i(t)}{\partial b_0 \partial b_0} \text{ as in equation (6.57) with } k=j=0$$

$$\frac{\partial^2 p_i(t)}{\partial b_0 \partial c_0} \text{ as in equation (6.58) with } k=j=0$$

$$\frac{\partial^2 p_i(t)}{\partial c_0 \partial c_0} \text{ as in equation (6.59) with } k=j=0$$

Note that all quantities in equations (6.57)–(6.59) where Δx_j or Δx_k is present as a multiplier vanish in these cases, since $\Delta x_0 = 0$.

The other three second derivatives have no direct correspondence in section 3.7, but are slightly modified forms of equations (6.57)–(6.59). They are found to be, after some work:

$$\frac{\partial^2 p_i(t)}{\partial b_k \partial b_j} \text{ as in equation (6.57) with: } \qquad (1 \leq k,\, j \leq n)$$

$\alpha_{6jk} - \alpha_{7jk}$ in place of α_{6jk}

$\alpha_{3k} - \alpha_{5k}$ in place of α_{3k}

$\alpha_{3j} - \alpha_{5j}$ in place of α_{3j}

$$\frac{\partial^2 p_i(t)}{\partial b_k \partial b_0} \text{ as in equation (6.57) with: }$$

$\alpha_{6k0} - \alpha_{7k0}$ in place of α_{6jk},
$\alpha_{3k} - \alpha_{5k}$ in place of α_{3k}.

However, the form is sufficiently modified that it is useful to write out this derivative.

$$\frac{\partial^2 p_i(t)}{\partial b_k \partial b_0} = (\alpha_{6k0} - \alpha_{7k0})\left(t\alpha_1 \alpha_{10} - \frac{\alpha_8}{\alpha_4^2} \right)$$

$$+ (\alpha_{3k} - \alpha_{5k})\alpha_{30} \left\{ \frac{2\alpha_8}{t\alpha_4^3} - t\alpha_1 \left[t\alpha_{10} + \frac{2q_{1i}(0)}{\alpha_4^2} \right] \right\}$$

$$+ \alpha_{30} \left\{ \frac{2\alpha_8 \Delta x_k}{t\alpha_4^3} - \frac{\alpha_{9k}}{t\alpha_4^2} + \frac{q_{1i}(0)\alpha_1 t}{\alpha_4} \left[x_{ki}(0) - \frac{\Delta x_k}{t\alpha_4} \right] \right\}$$

$$+ (\alpha_{3k} - \alpha_{5k})\left(-\frac{\alpha_8}{\alpha_4^2} + \frac{q_{1i}(0)\alpha_1 t}{\alpha_4} \right)$$

$$+ \frac{\alpha_{9k}}{\alpha_4} - \frac{\Delta x_k \alpha_8}{t\alpha_4^2} \qquad (1 \leq k \leq n) \qquad (6.63)$$

$\dfrac{\partial^2 p_i(t)}{\partial b_k \partial c_0}$ as in equation (6.58) with $\alpha_{3k} - \alpha_{5k}$ in place of α_{3k}. $(1 \leq k \leq n)$

These first and second derivatives may be used with equations (6.8) and (6.24) to obtain **b**, c_0, and the covariance matrix.

3.9. SUMMARY OF PANEL MODELS

The first and second partial derivatives set out in sections 3.1–3.8 constitute the missing elements necessary to obtain estimates from panel data. These are in some cases exceedingly complicated, and especially for the cases with nonconstant independent variables, they result in considerable complexity in the computer programs designed to estimate **b**, **c**, and covariances.

The LONGIT computer program appended to chapter 3 contains all these models. The program has not, however, been optimized, either for time of calculation or for program size. It is likely that considerable improvements on running time can be made in the program by further work.

For easy reference to terms used throughout sections 3.1–3.8, the definitions of these terms are given, all together, in the list below.

$a_0 \equiv q_{1i} + q_{0i}$ (constant independent variables)

$\quad\ \equiv \frac{1}{2}[q_{1i}(0) + q_{1i}(t) + q_{0i}(0) + q_{0i}(t)]$ (nonconstant independent variables)

$a_1 \equiv e^{-a_0 t}$

$a_2 \equiv \dfrac{1 - a_1}{a_0}$

$a_3 \equiv \dfrac{a_2 - t a_1}{t a_0}$

$a_4 \equiv \dfrac{t - a_2}{t a_0}$

$a_5 \equiv \dfrac{t a_1 - 2 a_3}{a_0}$

$a_6 \equiv \dfrac{a_2 - 2 a_4}{a_0}$

$a_7 \equiv \dfrac{-t^2 a_1 - 3 a_5}{a_0}$

$a_8 \equiv \dfrac{-t a_3 - 3 a_6}{a_0}$

(In the linear decomposition, $\bar{x}_k a_5$, $\bar{x}_k a_6$, $\bar{x}_k a_7$, and $\bar{x}_k a_8$ are the first derivatives of a_3, a_4, a_5, and a_6, respectively.)

The following quantities are used only in the exponential decomposition with nonconstant independent variables:

$$\Delta q_h = q_{hi}(t) - q_{hi}(0) \qquad h = 0, 1$$

$$\Delta \log q_h = \log q_{hi}(t) - \log q_{hi}(0) \qquad h = 0, 1$$

$$a_0 \equiv \frac{\Delta q_1}{\Delta \log q_1} + \frac{\Delta q_0}{\Delta \log q_0}$$

$$a_1 \equiv e^{-a_0 t}$$

$$a_4 \equiv a_0 + \frac{\Delta \log q_1}{t}$$

$$a_{3k} \equiv \frac{\partial a_0}{\partial b_k} = \frac{\Delta(x_k q_1) - \Delta x_k \Delta q_1 / \Delta \log q_1}{\Delta \log q_1}$$

$$a_{5k} \equiv \frac{\partial a_0}{\partial c_k} = \frac{\Delta(x_k q_0) - \Delta x_k \Delta q_0 / \Delta \log q_0}{\Delta \log q_0}$$

$$a_{6jk} \equiv \frac{\partial a_{3k}}{\partial b_j} = \frac{\Delta(x_j x_k q_1) - a_{3k}\Delta x_j - a_{3j}\Delta x_k}{\Delta \log q_1}$$

$$a_{7jk} \equiv \frac{\partial a_{5k}}{\partial c_j} = \frac{\Delta(x_j x_k q_0) - a_{5k}\Delta x_j - a_{5j}\Delta x_k}{\Delta \log q_0}$$

$$a_8 \equiv q_{1i}(t) - a_1 q_{1i}(0)$$

$$a_{9k} \equiv \frac{\partial a_8}{\partial b_k} = x_{ki}(t)q_{1i}(t) - x_{ki}(0)a_1 q_{1i}(0)$$

$$a_{10} \equiv \frac{q_{1i}(0)}{a_4} - z_i(0)$$

$$a_{11jk} \equiv \frac{\partial a_{9k}}{\partial b_j} = x_{ji}(t)x_{ki}(t)q_{1i}(t) - x_{ji}(0)x_{ki}(0)a_1 q_{1i}(0)$$

$$\Delta x_k \equiv x_{ki}(t) - x_{ki}(0)$$

$$\Delta(x_k q_h) \equiv x_{ki}(t)q_{hi}(t) - x_{ki}(0)q_{hi}(0) \qquad h = 0, 1$$

$$\Delta(x_j x_k q_h) \equiv x_{ji}(t)x_{ki}(t)q_{hi}(t) - x_{ji}(0)x_{ki}(0)q_{hi}(0) \qquad h = 0, 1$$

4. INTERDEPENDENCE WITH PANEL DATA

A number of methods for treating systems of interdependent attributes were introduced in chapter 4. Some of these involved new maximum likelihood estimation while others did not. In this section and succeeding subsections through 4.5, I will review these, introducing the relevant maximum likelihood estimation procedures where new ones are involved.

First the estimation procedure used in Coleman (1964a) was mentioned. This treats a system of m endogenous dichotomous attributes as a Markov process with 2^m states, and estimates the $2^m \times (2^m - 1)$ transition rates (or a subset of these, if certain rates are constrained to be zero) through an iterative process. The estimation method, however, suffers from a number of disadvantages: It has unknown statistical properties, it requires grouped data (which means its data demands become excessive as m increases or as exogenous variables are introduced), and it estimates the large number of transition rates rather than directly estimating the smaller number of parameters specified in the model.

A second procedure mentioned was that of Cohen and Singer (1979), which also treats the system of m endogenous attributes as a markov process with 2^m states. This procedure does provide maximum likelihood estimates but suffers from the second and third disadvantages of the method just described.

Because of the disadvantages, three approaches were introduced using approximations of some sort but overcoming the second and third disadvantages by using individual-level data and directly estimating the parameters specified in the model. One of those will be mentioned in this section; the others will be treated in subsections 4.1 and 4.2, corresponding to sections 1 and 2 of chapter 4.

The first and crudest approximation to a system of relationships among m endogenous attributes is to treat each attribute independently and to assume that each of the other endogenous attributes (as well as the exogenous variables) changes linearly between the two waves of the panel. This approach uses chapter 3, sections 4, 5 and 6 for restricted and unrestricted models and linear and exponential decomposition of transition rates. The approximation lies in the fact that change in other endogenous attributes is not linear between the two waves of the panel but depends on the state of the other endogenous attributes, including the one under consideration. Table 4.4 shows the errors introduced by this approximation in the example presented in table 4.1. Thus the result of this approach is to eliminate the disadvantages associated with the two methods just discussed, which require grouping, but it does so at the cost of providing estimates with some unknown error.

4.1. PURGING ENDOGENOUS EFFECTS

The first improvement upon this approximation was introduced in section 1 of chapter 4. This involved *purging* of the effects of attribute j on the value of other endogenous attributes at the second wave of the panel, to give a value $x_k^*(t)$ for those endogenous attributes k, which constituted a modification of the observed values of $x_k(t)$; $x_k^*(t)$ is intended to be the value of $x_k(t)$ that would be expected in the absence of the effects of the attribute under consideration. In this approach the estimates obtained in the preceding method are used for the first purge, leading to new estimates of the effects of each endogenous attribute on each other. These new estimates are used in the second purge, and so on, until convergence is achieved. The models of chapter 3, section 6 (linear) and 5 (exponential) are used in estimation of the parameters for each endogenous attribute, and the only modification involved is the construction of modified values $x_k^*(t)$ for each other endogenous attribute when estimating the effects on the attribute under consideration. As indicated, the process is continued until convergence is realized.

No new maximum likelihood estimates are involved in this modification, although a different computer program is necessary, incorporating the algorithms of subsections 3.3, 3.4, 3.7 and 3.8 of this chapter into a second level of iteration, in which provisional estimates of $p_j(t)$ for all endogenous attributes from one iteration are used to modify the estimates in the next iteration. The procedure is described in some detail in chapter 4.

4.2. INTRODUCING SIMULTANEITY INTO THE EQUATIONS FOR THE LINEAR MODEL WITH $c_k = -b_k$

In the case of m endogenous attributes and $n - m$ exogenous attributes, the probability of being in state 1 on attribute j at time t, given one's state at time 0 on all endogenous and exogenous attributes, can be approximated by equation (6.64), which is a generalization of equation (4.21) from two to m endogenous attributes.

$$p_j(t) = \left[q_{1\cdot}^{(j)}(0)a_3^{(j)} + q_{1\cdot}^{(j)}(t)a_4^{(j)} + x_j(0)\left\{ a_1^{(j)} + \sum_{\substack{k=1 \\ k\neq j}}^{m} b_{jk}b_{kj}(a_{22}^{(jk)} - a_{23}^{(jk)}/t) \right\} \right.$$

$$\left. + \sum_{\substack{k=1 \\ k\neq j}}^{m} b_{jk}\{x_k(0)a_{21}^{(jk)} + q_{1*}^{(k)}(0)a_{22}^{(jk)} + \Delta q_{1*}^{(k)}(t)a_{23}^{(jk)}/t\} \right] /$$

$$(1 - \Sigma b_{jk}b_{kj}a_{23}^{(jk)}/t). \qquad (6.64)$$

Definitions are given in chapter 4, section 2.

256

The approximation involved in writing the set of equations for p_j ($j = 1$, . . . , m) consisted of assuming $p_j(\theta)$ under the last integral in equation (4.20) to vary linearly between fixed values of $z_j(0)$ and $p_j(t)$, thus allowing the integration to be carried out and the equation to be solved for $p_j(t)$. Heuristically the numerator in equation (6.64) can be thought of as follows: The product involving a quantity in braces multiplying $x_j(0)$ is the contribution to $p_j(t)$ from the initial value; the products involving $q_{1.}^{(j)}(0)$ and $q_{1.}^{(j)}(t)$ are the contributions to $p_j(t)$ from exogenous attributes or variables, which may be constant or changing; and the product involving a quantity in braces multiplying b_{jk} is the contribution to $p_j(t)$ from endogenous attributes k.

The likelihood that a particular set of observations $z_{ji}(t)$ at time t for endogenous attributes $1, \ldots, j, \ldots, m$ over individuals $1, \ldots, i, \ldots, N$ is the product of the likelihood functions for each of the j attributes [as given in equation (6.22)], as follows:

$$\mathcal{L} = \prod_{j=1}^{m} \prod_{i=1}^{N} p_{ji}(t)^{z_{ji}} [1 - p_{ji}(t)]^{1 - z_{ji}(t)}. \tag{6.65}$$

The first derivative of the log likelihood with respect to any of the parameters of the model (for which I use b_{jk} as the generic symbol, expressing the effect of attribute or variable k on attribute j in either a positive or negative direction) is

$$\frac{\partial L}{\partial b_{jk}} = \sum_{i=1}^{N} \frac{z_{ji}(t) - p_{ji}(t)}{p_{ji}(t)[1 - p_{ji}(t)]} \frac{\partial p_{ji}(t)}{\partial b_{jk}}, \quad (j = 1, \ldots, m) \tag{6.66}$$

For estimating the variance of the estimates, second derivatives are necessary. The second derivative of L with respect to b_{jk} and b_{jh} is a direct extension of that for panel data with a single dependent attribute, as shown in equation (6.24):

$$\frac{\partial^2 L}{\partial b_{jk} \partial b_{jh}} = \sum_{i=1}^{N} \left[\phi_{ji}(t) \frac{\partial^2 p_{ji}(t)}{\partial b_{jk} \partial b_{jh}} - \phi_{ji}(t)^2 \frac{\partial p_{ji}(t)}{\partial b_{jk}} \frac{\partial p_{ji}(t)}{\partial b_{jh}} \right] \tag{6.67}$$

where $\phi_{ji}(t)$ is defined as

$$\phi_{ji}(t) = \frac{z_{ji}(t) - p_{ji}(t)}{p_{ji}(t)(1 - p_{ji}(t))}.$$

Thus the task of finding the values of b_{jk} that maximize the likelihood of

257

the observations under the model is no different than that of the previous section, except that the algorithm must use the partial derivatives of $p_{ji}(t)$ as given in equation (6.64), and the algorithm must be carried out not only for N individuals, but for m attributes for each of those individuals. The principal task of this section therefore is to find the first and second derivatives of $p_{ji}(t)$ [given as $p_j(t)$ in equation (6.64)].

Inspection of equation (6.64) shows that there are three cases of first derivatives:

(1) All b_{jk} and c_{jk} appear in $a_0^{(j)}$, upon which $a_1^{(j)}$, $a_3^{(j)}$, $a_4^{(j)}$, $a_{21}^{(jk)}$, $a_{22}^{(jk)}$, and $a_{23}^{(jk)}$ depend.

(2) Only b_{jk} for exogenous attributes $(k > m)$ appear in $q_1^{(j)}(0)$ and $q_1^{(j)}(t)$.

(3) Only b_{jk} for endogenous attributes $(k \leq m,\ k \neq j)$ appear explicitly as b_{jk} in equation (6.64).

Thus there are three different cases of derivatives of $p_{ji}(t)$, a core from (1), which exists for all parameters and which is the complete derivative for all c_{jk}; an added portion from (2) for b_{jk} for exogenous attributes; and a different added portion from (3) for b_{jk} for endogenous attributes. There are nine second derivatives, formed from the pair-wise combinations of the three classes of parameters, and of these, six distinct cases since the derivatives are symmetric in the independent variables.

First it is useful to express the derivatives of the various quantities involved in (1) as functions of the derivatives of $a_0^{(j)}$. The superscript j is used to identify the dependent variable. With that addition these quantities follow the definitions of subsection 3.9 of this chapter, or in the case of $a_{21}^{(jk)}$, $a_{22}^{(jk)}$, and $a_{23}^{(jk)}$, they are explicitly defined in section 2 of chapter 4 [at equation (4.21)]. The derivatives are (where b_{jk} is used generically, for c_{jk} as well):

$$\frac{\partial a_3^{(j)}}{\partial b_{jk}} = \frac{ta_1^{(j)} - 2a_3^{(j)}}{a_0^{(j)}} \frac{\partial a_0^{(j)}}{\partial b_{jk}} \equiv a_5^{(j)} \frac{\partial a_0^{(j)}}{\partial b_{jk}}$$

$$\frac{\partial a_4^{(j)}}{\partial b_{jk}} = \frac{a_2^{(j)} - 2a_4^{(j)}}{a_0^{(j)}} \frac{\partial a_0^{(j)}}{\partial b_{jk}} \equiv a_6^{(j)} \frac{\partial a_0^{(j)}}{\partial b_{jk}}$$

For the next derivatives, I will define three new quantities by adding 2 to each subscript: $a_{43}^{(jk)}$, $a_{44}^{(jk)}$, and $a_{45}^{(jk)}$.

$$\frac{\partial a_{21}^{(jk)}}{\partial b_{jk}} = \frac{ta_1^{(j)} - a_{21}^{(jk)}}{a_0^{(j)} - a_0^{(k)}} \frac{\partial a_0^{(j)}}{\partial b_{jk}} \equiv a_{43}^{(jk)} \frac{\partial a_0^{(j)}}{\partial b_{jk}}$$

$$\frac{\partial a_{22}^{(jk)}}{\partial b_{jk}} = \frac{ta_3^{(j)} - a_{22}^{(jk)}}{a_0^{(j)} - a_0^{(k)}} \frac{\partial a_0^{(j)}}{\partial b_{jk}} \equiv a_{44}^{(jk)} \frac{\partial a_0^{(j)}}{\partial b_{jk}}$$

$$\frac{\partial a_{23}^{(jk)}}{\partial b_{jk}} = -\frac{ta_6^{(j)} + a_{23}^{(jk)}}{a_0^{(j)} - a_0^{(k)}} \frac{\partial a_0^{(j)}}{\partial b_{jk}} \equiv a_{45}^{(jk)} \frac{\partial a_0^{(j)}}{\partial b_{jk}}$$

The first derivative of $p_{ji}(t)$ for all c_{jk} is therefore, from equation (6.64):

$$\frac{\partial p_{ji}(t)}{\partial c_{jk}} = \frac{\partial a_0^{(j)}}{\partial c_{jk}} \left(q_{1\cdot}^{(j)}(0)a_5^{(j)} + q_{1\cdot}^{(j)}(t)a_6^{(j)} + x_{ji}(0) \left\{ -ta_1^{(j)} + \sum_k b_{jk}b_{kj}[a_{44}^{(jk)} \right. \right.$$

$$\left. - a_{45}^{(jk)}/t] \right\} + \sum_k b_{jk}\{x_{ki}(0)a_{43}^{(jk)} + q_{1\cdot}^{(k)}(0)a_{44}^{(jk)} + \Delta q_{1\cdot}^{(k)}(t)a_{45}^{(jk)}/t\}$$

$$+ p_{ji}(t) \sum_k b_{jk}b_{kj}a_{45}^{(jk)} \right) \Big/ \left[1 - \sum_k b_{jk}b_{kj}a_{23}^{(jk)}/t \right]. \qquad (6.68)$$

For the derivative with respect to b_{jk} where k is exogenous $(k > m)$, there are in addition quantities involving derivatives of $q_{1\cdot}^{(j)}(0)$ and $q_{1\cdot}^{(j)}(t)$. These derivatives are $\partial q_{1\cdot}^{(j)}(0)/\partial b_{jk} = x_k(0)$, and $\partial q_{1\cdot}^{(j)}(t)/\partial b_{jk} = x_k(t)$. Thus the quantity to be added to the above is

$$\frac{\partial p_{ji}(t)}{\partial b_{jk}} = [68] + \frac{x_k(0)a_3^{(j)} + x_{ki}(t)a_4^{(j)}}{1 - \sum\limits_k b_{jk}b_{kj}a_{23}^{(jk)}/t} \qquad (6.69)$$

where [68] refers to the right-hand side of equation (6.68). Obviously also $\partial a_0^{(j)}/\partial c_{jk}$ in equation (6.68) becomes $\partial a_0^{(j)}/\partial b_{jk}$.

For the derivative with respect to b_{jk} where k is endogenous $(k \leq m)$, the derivative of b_{jk} with respect to b_{jk} is one [although b_{jk} when k is endogenous are excluded from $q_{1\cdot}^{(j)}(0)$ and $q_{1\cdot}^{(j)}(t)$] so that there is, in addition to the right-hand side of equation (6.68), a term for each endogenous attribute:

$$\frac{\partial p_{ji}(t)}{\partial b_{jk}} = [68] + [x_{ji}(0)b_{kj}(a_{22}^{(jk)} - a_{23}^{(jk)}/t) + x_{ki}(0)a_{21}^{(jk)}$$

$$+ q_{1*}^{(k)}(0)a_{22}^{(jk)} + q_{1*}^{(k)}(t)a_{23}^{(jk)}/t + p_{ji}(t)b_{kj}a_{23}^{(jk)}/t]/$$

$$\left[1 - \sum_k b_{jk}b_{kj}a_{23}^{(jk)}/t \right]. \qquad (6.70)$$

One final point remains for the first derivatives: the derivative of $a_0^{(j)}$ with respect to c_{jk} or b_{jk}. There are two cases: (a) $c_{jk} = -b_{jk}$ for all j and k (effects in opposite directions equal in magnitude with reversed signs). In this case, there is a great simplification. Since $a_0^{(j)}$ is equal in this case to $b_{j0} + c_{j0}$, it is constant across individuals and over time, and therefore $\partial a_0^{(j)}/$

259

$\partial b_{jk} = \partial a_0^{(j)}/\partial c_{jk} = 0$ for all $k \geq 1$. Thus the right-hand side of equation (6.68) is zero for $k \geq 1$, and the first derivatives with respect to b_{jk} for exogenous and endogenous attributes respectively are given by the quantities shown on the right-hand sides of equations (6.69) and (6.70), without [68].

(b) $c_{jk} \neq -b_{jk}$. In this case the integration carried out to go from equation (4.17) to equation (4.18) and finally to equation (4.21) is not correct; it is only an approximation. While the integration can be carried out as shown in equations (4.18)–(4.21) for the case where $c_{jk} = -b_{jk}$ and for the case when $c_{jk} \neq b_{jk}$ but x_k is constant or can be assumed to vary linearly with time between $x_k(0)$ and $x_k(t)$ (as is reasonable for exogenous variables in the absence of other information), it is not correct when x_k varies nonlinearly over time, as it will ordinarily do when x_k is endogenous.[5]

It is difficult to know how much damage this approximation through assuming linear change in endogenous k does to the estimation. Extensive comparison of the error in estimates for data generated by systems in which $c_{jk} \neq -b_{jk}$ is necessary to get some idea of the sensitivity of the estimates to this approximation.

Despite the unknown effects of this approximation, I will assume that this approach may be useful in estimation where we do not assume that $c_{jk} = -b_{jk}$, and I will therefore continue to include in the derivatives the component [equation (6.68)] that is zero when $c_{jk} = -b_{jk}$. The derivative of $a_0^{(j)}$ with respect to b_{jk} and c_{jk} is the same:

For constant x_k:

$$\frac{\partial a_0^{(j)}}{\partial b_{jk}} = \frac{\partial a_0^{(j)}}{\partial c_{jk}} = x_k.$$

For x_k changing linearly over time, with mean $\bar{x}_k$,

$$\frac{\partial a_0^{(j)}}{\partial b_{jk}} = \frac{\partial a_0^{(j)}}{\partial c_{jk}} = \bar{x}_k.$$

This, together with equations (6.68), (6.69), and (6.70), gives the first derivatives.

Second derivatives are facilitated by first defining further quantities: Following section 3.9 of this chapter, we have

---

[5] There are minor modifications from the case of constant x_k to the case where x_k varies linearly with time, but this involves using only $[x_k(0) + x_k(t)]/2$ for x_k in the estimation equations. The form of the integration remains the same.

260

$$\frac{\partial a_5^{(j)}}{\partial b_{jk}} = a_7^{(j)} \frac{\partial a_0^{(j)}}{\partial b_{jk}}$$

$$\frac{\partial a_6^{(j)}}{\partial b_{jk}} = a_8^{(j)} \frac{\partial a_0^{(j)}}{\partial b_{jk}}$$

And analogously to the first derivatives:

$$\frac{\partial a_{43}^{(jk)}}{\partial b_{jk}} = -\frac{t^2 a_1^{(j)} + 2 a_{43}^{(jk)}}{a_0^{(j)} - a_0^{(k)}} \frac{\partial a_0^{(j)}}{\partial b_{jk}} \equiv a_{65}^{(jk)} \frac{\partial a_0^{(j)}}{\partial b_{jk}}$$

$$\frac{\partial a_{44}^{(jk)}}{\partial b_{jk}} = \frac{t a_5^{(j)} - 2 a_{44}^{(jk)}}{a_0^{(j)} - a_0^{(k)}} \frac{\partial a_0^{(j)}}{\partial b_{jk}} \equiv a_{66}^{(jk)} \frac{\partial a_0^{(j)}}{\partial b_{jk}}$$

$$\frac{\partial a_{45}^{(jk)}}{\partial b_{jk}} = -\frac{t a_8^{(j)} + a_{45}^{(jk)}}{a_0^{(j)} - a_0^{(k)}} \frac{\partial a_0^{(j)}}{\partial b_{jk}} \equiv a_{67}^{(jk)} \frac{\partial a_0^{(j)}}{\partial b_{jk}}.$$

The various cases of the second derivative follow.

(1) c_{jk}, c_{jl} [the derivative of equation (6.68) with respect to c_{jl}]:

$$\frac{\partial^2 p_{ji}(t)}{\partial c_{jk} \partial c_{jl}} = \frac{\partial a_0^{(j)}}{\partial c_{jk}} \frac{\partial a_0^{(j)}}{\partial c_{jl}} \left\{ q_{1\cdot}^{(j)}(0) a_7^{(j)} + q_1^{(j)}(t) a_8^{(j)} \right.$$

$$+ x_{ji}(0) \left[t^2 a_1^{(j)} + \sum_k b_{jk} b_{kj} a_{68}^{(jk)} - a_{67}^{(jk)}/t \right] \right\} + \sum_k b_{jk} \{ x_k(0) a_{65}^{(jk)}$$

$$+ q_{1*}^{(k)}(0) a_{66}^{(jk)} + \Delta q_{1*}^{(k)} a_{67}^{(jk)}/t \} + \sum_k b_{jk} b_{kj} \{ p_{ji}(t) a_{67}^{(jk)}$$

$$+ [\partial p_{ji}(t)/dc_{jk} + \partial p_{ji}(t)/dc_{jl}] a_{45}^{(jk)} \}/$$

$$\left(1 - \sum_k b_{jk} b_{kj} a_{23}^{(jk)}/t \right) \tag{6.71}$$

(2) c_{jk}, b_{jl} (l exogenous):

$$\frac{\partial^2 p_{ji}(t)}{\partial c_{jk} \partial b_{jl}} = [71] + \frac{\partial a_0^{(j)}}{\partial b_{jl}} \frac{\partial a^{(j)}}{\partial c_{jk}} \frac{x_{li}(0) a_5^{(j)} + x_{li}(t) a_6^{(j)}}{1 - \sum_k b_{jk} b_{kj} a_{23}^{(jk)}/t} \tag{6.72}$$

[where c_{jl} in equation (6.71) is replaced by b_{jl}]

(3) c_{jk}, b_{jl} (l endogenous):

$$\frac{\partial^2 p_{ji}(t)}{\partial c_{jk}\partial b_{jl}} = [71] + \frac{\partial a_0^{(j)}}{\partial b_{jl}}\frac{\partial a_0^{(j)}}{\partial c_{jk}}\left[x_{ji}(0)b_{1j}(a_{44}^{(jl)}- a_{45}^{(jl)}/t) + x_{1i}(0)a_{43}^{(jl)}\right.$$

$$+ q_{1*}^{(l)}(0)a_{44}^{(jl)}+ \Delta q_{1*}^{(l)}(t)a_{45}^{(jl)}/t + b_{1j}p_{ji}(t)a_{45}^{(jl)}$$

$$\left.+ \frac{\partial p_{ji}(t)}{\partial c_{jk}}\, b_{1j}a_{23}^{(jl)}/t\right]\left(1 - \sum_h b_{jh}b_{hj}a_{23}^{(jl)}/t\right) \qquad (6.73)$$

[where c_{jl} in equation (6.71) is replaced by b_{jl}]
(4) b_{jk}, b_{jl} (k, l exogenous):

$$\frac{\partial^2 p_{ji}(t)}{\partial b_{jk}\partial b_{jl}} = [71] + \frac{\partial a_0^{(j)}}{\partial b_{jk}}\frac{\partial a_0^{(j)}}{\partial b_{jl}}[\{x_{ki}(0) + x_{1i}(0)\}a_5^{(j)}+ \{x_{ki}(t)$$

$$+ x_{1i}(t)\}a_6^{(j)}]/\left(1 - \sum b_{jk}b_{kj}a_{23}^{(jk)}/t\right) \qquad (6.74)$$

(where c_{jk} and c_{jl} are replaced by b_{jk} and b_{jl})

(5) b_{jk}, b_{jl} (k exogenous, l endogenous):

$$\frac{\partial^2 p_{ji}(t)}{\partial b_{jk}\partial b_{jl}} = [71] + [73] + \frac{\partial a_0^{(j)}}{\partial b_{jk}}\frac{\partial a_0^{(j)}}{\partial b_{jl}}\frac{x_{ki}(0)a_5^{(j)}+ x_{ki}(t)a_6^{(j)}}{1 - \sum_k b_{jk}b_{kj}a_{23}^{(jk)}/t} \qquad (6.75)$$

[where c_{jk} and c_{jl} in equation (6.71) are replaced by b_{jk} and b_{jl}; and c_{jk} in equation (6.73) is replaced by b_{jk}. [73] above refers to the explicit portions of the right-hand side of equation (6.73).]
(6) b_{jk} and b_{jl} (k and l endogenous):

$$\frac{\partial^2 p_{ji}(t)}{\partial b_{jk}\partial b_{jl}} = [71] + [73] + [73 \text{ with } l \text{ and } k \text{ interchanged}] \qquad (6.76)$$

[where c_{jk} and c_{jl} in equation (6.71) are replaced by b_{jk} and b_{jl}; and c_{jk} in equation (6.73) is replaced by b_{jk}.]

4.3. EXACT SOLUTION FOR THE TWO-ATTRIBUTE LINEAR CASE WITH $c_k = -b_k$

In chapter 4 the probability of a positive response on attribute 1, where the transition rates are functions of attribute 2 and possibly of exogenous variables as well, is

$$p_1(t) = \frac{p_1(0)(s_1 e^{s_2 t} - s_2 e^{s_1 t})}{s_1 - s_2} + p_{1e}\left\{1 - \frac{s_1 e^{s_2 t} - s_2 e^{s_1 t}}{s_1 - s_2}\right\}$$

$$+ \left[-p_1(0)\sum a_{1j}x_j + \sum b_{1j}x_j + b_{12}p_2(0)\right]\frac{e^{s_1 t} - e^{s_2 t}}{s_1 - s_2} \quad (6.77)$$

where

$$a_{hj} = b_{hj} + c_{hj}$$

$$s_1, s_2 = \tfrac{1}{2}\left\{-\sum_j x_j(a_{1j} + a_{2j}) \pm \sqrt{\left[\sum_j x_j(a_{1j} - a_{2j})\right]^2 - 4b_{12}b_{21}}\right\}$$

and

$$p_{1e} = \frac{\sum_j b_{1j}x_j \sum a_{2k}x_k + b_{12}\sum_k b_{2k}x_k}{\sum_j a_{1j}x_j \sum a_{2k}x_k - b_{12}b_{21}}.$$

The task of estimation is to use equation (6.77) and the analogous equation for $p_2(t)$ together with observations on $z_1(0)$, $z_2(0)$, $z_1(t)$, and $z_2(t)$ to estimate the parameters, b_{12}, b_{21}, b_{10}, c_{10}, b_{20}, c_{20}, and any effects b_{1k}, and b_{2k}, of exogenous attributes.

The likelihood of observing a particular set of $z_1(t)$ and $z_2(t)$ for a sample of individuals conditional upon the initial observation $z_1(0)$ and $z_2(0)$ is simply an extension to two attributes of the likelihood given in equation (6.22) for panel data with a single dependent attribute:

$$\mathcal{L} = \prod_{j=1}^{2}\prod_{i=1}^{N} p_{ji}(t)^{z_{ji}(t)}(1 - p_{ji}(t))^{1 - z_{ji}(t)}. \quad (6.78)$$

The logarithm of the likelihood and the first and second derivatives of the log likelihood are like those for the single dependent attribute [see equations (6.23) and (6.24)], with the addition of a summation over the two endogenous attributes. Thus all the correspondences used in section 3 to quantities appearing in section 1 remain the same, and the algorithms of equation (6.3) or equation (6.8) may be used, with those correspondences, for estimating parameters. The principal difference lies in the derivatives, because $p_{ji}(t)$ is in this case a much more complex function of the parameters than in the case of the single dependent attribute. These derivatives follow. In the case where the derivative is the same for all parameters, b_{1k}, b_{2k}, c_{10}, and c_{20}, I will

263

write $b.$ to indicate this. I will delete the subscript i for individual i, implying that the equations refer to a given individual.

First, the derivative of $p_1(t)$ [and analogously $p_2(t)$] is

$$\frac{\partial p_i(t)}{\partial b.} = [p_1(0) - p_{1e}] \frac{\partial}{\partial b.} \left\{ \frac{s_1 e^{s_2 t} - s_2 e^{s_1 t}}{s_1 - s_2} \right\} + \left\{ 1 - \frac{s_1 e^{s_2 t} - s_2 e^{s_1 t}}{s_1 - s_2} \right\} \frac{\partial p_{1e}}{\partial b.}$$

$$+ \frac{\partial}{\partial b.} \left\{ \left[b_{1j} x_j + b_{12} p_2(0) - p_1(0) \sum a_{1j} x_j \right] \frac{e^{s_1 t} - e^{s_2 t}}{s_1 - s_2} \right\} \quad (6.79)$$

This leaves various quantities for which the derivatives must be evaluated. These follow.

$$\frac{\partial}{\partial b.} \left\{ \frac{s_1 e^{s_2 t} - s_2 e^{s_1 t}}{s_1 - s_2} \right\}$$

$$= \frac{(e^{s_1 t} - e^{s_2 t}) \left(s_2 \frac{\partial s_1}{\partial b.} - s_1 \frac{\partial s_2}{\partial b.} \right) + t \left(s_1 \frac{\partial s_2}{\partial b.} e^{s_2 t} - s_2 \frac{\partial s_1}{\partial b.} e^{s_1 t} \right)}{(s_1 - s_2)^2}$$

$$\frac{\partial}{\partial b.} \left\{ \frac{e^{s_2 t} - e^{s_1 t}}{s_1 - s_2} \right\} = \frac{(e^{s_1 t} - e^{s_2 t}) \left(\frac{\partial s_2}{\partial b.} - \frac{\partial s_1}{\partial b.} \right)}{(r_1 - r_2)^2} + \frac{t \left(\frac{\partial s_2}{\partial b.} e^{s_2 t} - \frac{\partial s_1}{\partial b.} s_1 t \right)}{r_1 - r_2}$$

$$\frac{\partial s_1}{\partial b_{1j}} = \frac{\partial s_1}{\partial c_{1j}} = \frac{x_j}{2} \left\{ -1 \pm \left(\sum_k x_k a_{1k} - \sum_k x_k a_{2k} \right) \left[\left(\sum_k x_k [a_{1k} - a_{2k}] \right)^2 \right. \right.$$

$$\left. \left. - 4 b_{12} b_{21} \right]^{-1/2} \right\} \quad (j \neq 2) \quad (6.80)$$

The derivative with respect to b_{2j} and c_{2j} is identical to equation (6.80) but with subscripts 1 and 2 interchanged. The derivative of s_2 is the same as that of s_1, except that the second term on the right (everything excluding the -1) is negative rather than positive:

$$\frac{\partial s_1}{\partial b_{12}} = -b_{21} x_k (a_{1k} - a_{2k})^2 - 4 b_{12} b_{21}^{-1/2},$$

$$\frac{\partial s_2}{\partial b_{12}} = \frac{\partial s_1}{\partial b_{12}},$$

$$\frac{\partial s_1}{\partial b_{21}} = \frac{b_{12}}{b_{21}} \frac{\partial s_1}{\partial b_{12}},$$

$$\frac{\partial s_2}{\partial b_{21}} = \frac{b_{12}}{b_{21}} \frac{\partial s_2}{\partial b_{12}}.$$

Define $\psi_1 = -p_1(0)\Sigma a_{1j}x_j + \Sigma b_{1j}x_j + b_{12}p_2(0)$. Then,

$$\frac{\partial\psi_1}{\partial b_{1j}} = x_j[1 - p_1(0)] \qquad j \neq 2,$$

$$\frac{\partial\psi_1}{\partial c_{1j}} = -x_j p_1(0) \qquad j \neq 2,$$

$$\frac{\partial\psi_1}{\partial b_{2j}} = \frac{\partial\psi_1}{\partial c_{2j}} = 0 \qquad j \neq 2,$$

$$\frac{\partial\psi_1}{\partial b_{12}} = p_2(0),$$

$$\frac{\partial\psi_1}{\partial b_{21}} = 0.$$

To obtain the derivatives of p_{1e}, first define the denominator of p_{1i} as $D = \Sigma a_{1j}x_j \Sigma a_{2k}x_k - b_{12}b_{21}$.

$$\frac{\partial p_{1e}}{\partial b_{1j}} = \frac{x_j \Sigma a_{2k}x_k(1 - p_{1e})}{D} \qquad j \neq 2,$$

$$\frac{\partial p_{1e}}{\partial c_{1j}} = \frac{-x_j \Sigma a_{2k}x_k}{D} \qquad j \neq 2,$$

$$\frac{\partial p_{1e}}{\partial b_{2j}} = \frac{x_j(\Sigma b_{1k}x_k + b_{12} - p_{1e}\Sigma a_{1k}x_k)}{D} \qquad j \neq 2,$$

$$\frac{\partial p_{1e}}{\partial c_{2j}} = \frac{x_j(\Sigma b_{1k}x_k - p_{1e}\Sigma a_{1k}x_k)}{D} \qquad j \neq 2,$$

$$\frac{\partial p_{1e}}{\partial b_{12}} = \frac{\Sigma b_{2k}x_k + p_{1e}b_{21}}{D},$$

$$\frac{\partial p_{1e}}{\partial b_{21}} = \frac{p_{1e}b_{12}}{D}.$$

Using all these derivatives, the algorithm described in section 3 can be used to estimate b_1, b_2, c_{10}, and c_{20}.

Second derivatives, for estimating the covariance matrix, are obtained directly from the first derivatives.

4.4. THE EXACT SOLUTION FOR THE m-ATTRIBUTE LINEAR CASE WHERE $c_k = -b_k$ FOR ALL ENDOGENOUS ATTRIBUTES

In the linear case with $c_k = -b_k$ for endogenous attributes, the 2^m-state stochastic process for an endogenous attribute may be written as a set of m equations for the probabilities of being in state 1 on each of the m attributes. This is shown for two attributes in equations (4.7)–(4.9) and is discussed in the general case in chapter 4, section 4. The system of equations for an individual, in matrix notation, is given in equation (4.34) as

$$\mathbf{P}(t) = e^{\mathbf{G}t}\mathbf{P}(0) + (e^{\mathbf{G}t} - \mathbf{I})\mathbf{G}^{-1}\mathbf{s} \tag{6.81}$$

where $\mathbf{G}$ is an $m \times m$ matrix with elements

$$g_{ii} = -\Sigma(b_{ik} + c_{ik})x_k \qquad k = 0, m+1, \ldots, n$$
$$g_{ij} = b_{ij} \qquad i, j = 1, \ldots, m \quad (i \neq j)$$

and s is an $m \times 1$ vector with elements

$$s_j = \Sigma\, b_{jk}x_k \qquad k = 0, m+1, \ldots, n.$$

The likelihood of observing at time t a set of responses $z_{ij}(t)$ for individuals i and endogenous attributes j, given $z_{ij}(0)$ for all i and j, is

$$\mathcal{L} = \prod_{i=1}^{N} \prod_{j=1}^{m} p_{ij}(t)^{z_{ij}(t)} \tag{6.82}$$

where $p_{ij}(t)$ is given by equation (6.81).

The log likelihood is

$$L = \sum_{i=1}^{N} \sum_{j=1}^{m} \sum_{k=1}^{n} z_{ij}(t)\left[r_{ijk}z_{ij}(0) + \sum_{l=1}^{m}(r_{ijl} - \delta_{jl})r_{ijl}^{*}s_k \right] \tag{6.83}$$

where

r_{ijk} is the j, k element of the infinite series matrix, $e^{\mathbf{G}t}$ for individual i,

r_{ilk}^{*} is the l, k element of the inverse of $\mathbf{G}$,

and δ_{jk} is 1 if $l = j$, 0 otherwise,

266

$z_{ij}(0)$ is 1 if individual i is positive on attribute j at time 0, 0 otherwise,
$z_{ij}(t)$ is 1 if individual i is positive on attribute j at time t, 0 otherwise.

Although the summation is over three indices for the first terms of equation (6.83) and four indices for the second term, the first term is nonzero for each individual i only when i is positive on attribute k at time 0 and j at time t. The second term is nonzero only when i is positive on attribute j at time t.

The first derivative of L with respect to b_{hu} is

$$\frac{\partial L}{\partial b_{hu}} = \sum_i^N \sum_j^n \sum_k^m \left[z_{ij}(t)z_{ik}(0) \frac{\partial r_{ijk}}{\partial b_{hu}} + z_{ij}(t) \sum_l \left\{ \frac{\partial r_{ijl}}{\partial b_{hu}} r_{ilk}^* s_k \right. \right.$$
$$\left. \left. + (r_{ijl} - \delta_{jl}) \frac{\partial r_{ilk}^*}{\partial b_{hu}} s_k \right\} \right] + \sum_i \sum_j \sum_l (r_{ijl} - \delta_{jl}) r_{ilh}^* x_u \quad (6.84)$$

where the subscript h refers to an endogenous attribute and the subscript u refers to an endogenous or exogenous attribute. When u is endogenous, the last term, $(r_{ijl} - \delta_{jl})r_{ilh}^* x_u$, vanishes.

The derivatives of the elements r_{ijk} and r_{ilk}^* from a matrix infinite series are obtained as indicated in the next section (4.5), given that one has the derivative of the matrix $\mathbf{G}$ or $\mathbf{G}^{-1}$ that appears in the infinite series.

The derivative of $\mathbf{G}$ with respect to b_{hu} where u is exogenous is the matrix with only one nonzero element, $\partial g_{hh}/\partial b_{hu} = x_u$. (This includes the derivative with respect to b_{ho} and c_{ho}, where $x_0 = 1$, so that the derivative of $\mathbf{G}$ in these cases is 1.) The derivative of $\mathbf{G}$ with respect to b_{hu} where u is endogenous has only one nonzero element, $g_{hu} = 1$. The derivative of $\mathbf{G}^{-1}$ with respect to b_{hu} is

$$-\mathbf{G}^{-1}\mathbf{G}^{-1} \frac{d\mathbf{G}}{db_{hu}}$$

The second derivative of L with respect to b_{hu} and b_{fu} is obtained by differentiating equation (6.84) by b_{fu}. It is

$$\frac{\partial^2 L}{\partial b_{hu} \partial b_{fu}} = \sum_i \sum_j \sum_k z_{ij}(t)z_{ik}(0) \frac{\partial^2 r_{ijk}}{\partial b_{hu} \partial b_{fu}} + z_{ij}(t) \sum_l \frac{\partial^2 r_{ijl}}{\partial b_{hu} \partial b_{fu}} r_{ilk}^* s_k$$
$$+ \left(\frac{\partial r_{ijl}}{\partial b_{hu}} \frac{\partial r_{ilk}^*}{\partial b_{fu}} + \frac{\partial r_{ijl}}{\partial b_{fu}} \frac{\partial r_{ilk}^*}{\partial b_{hu}} \right) s_k + \sum_i \sum_j \sum_l \left(\frac{\partial r_{ijl}}{\partial b_{fu}} r_{ilk}^* \right.$$
$$+ (r_{ijl} - \delta_{jl}) \frac{\partial r_{ilk}^*}{\partial b_{hu}} \right) x_u + \left[\frac{\partial r_{ijl}}{\partial b_{hu}} r_{ilk}^* + (r_{ijl} - \delta_{jl}) \frac{\partial r_{ilk}^*}{\partial b_{fu}} \right] x_u \quad (6.85)$$

The second derivative of G is zero, but this does not mean that the second derivative of $e^{Gt} (=R)$ is zero, since the infinite series contains terms which involve only the first derivative of G.

As indicated, derivation of the first and second derivatives of the infinite series that is equal to the exponent of a matrix is given in the next section. With that information an algorithm corresponding to equation (6.3) can be constructed for estimation of the matrix parameters. This model, like that of the preceding section, is not included in the LONGIT program.

4.5. SIMULTANEOUS EQUATIONS: GENERAL CASE

For the general case with either linear or exponential decomposition of the transition rate, and without a restriction on the parameters of equality between c_{jk} and b_{jk}, it becomes necessary to use the general solution for a set of equations with constant coefficients. This is, from chapter 1,

$$\mathbf{P}(t) = \mathbf{P}(0)e^{\mathbf{Q}t}$$

In the case where each individual is observed at time 0 to be in state j so that $p_j(0) = 1$ and $p_k(0) = 0$ for $k \neq j$, $\mathbf{P}(t)$ becomes merely the j row of the transition matrix $e^{\mathbf{Q}t}$.[6] Thus the (conditional) probabilities of being in state $1, \ldots, m^*$ at time t (given that one was in state h at time 0) are given by this vector (which for a given individual i can be denoted $r_{ih1}, \ldots, r_{ihm^*}$, where m^* is the number of states in the system). Because the attributes are dichotomous $m^* = 2^m$ where m is the number of endogenous attributes.

The observation at time t on the individual is $z_i(t)$, and it can be denoted (as in preceding cases) by 1 if individual i was in state h at time 0 and k at time t, 0 otherwise. We may suppress the subscripts h and k for the origin and destination states of individual i in the subsequent notation, writing simply r_i for the probability of the destination state actually observed for individual i, given the origin state. With this notation, the (conditional) likelihood function can be written:

$$\mathcal{L} = \prod_{i=1}^{N} r_i(t). \tag{6.86}$$

[6] I will not consider here cases in which $\mathbf{P}(0)$ is a vector with more than one nonzero entry. Such cases would exist with data at the aggregate level (where, for example, only the distributions $\mathbf{P}(0)$ and $\mathbf{P}(t)$ were known at times 0 and t, but not the internal changes) or with data at the individual level, in which the state at time 0 was known only probabilistically. The latter case arises in various kinds of latent structure analysis. It would seem to be a fruitful direction of development of the present work. It is not, however, treated here.

If there are N_i persons all with the same origin and destination states and the same values of exogenous variables (the identity of values of endogenous attributes is assured by the identity of origin and destination states), the likelihood function contains N_i occurrences of $r_i(t)$, or $r_i(t)^{N_i}$. Writing the logarithm of the likelihood function in this more general form gives

$$\mathscr{L} = \sum_{i=1}^{N} N_i \log r_i(t). \tag{6.87}$$

The derivative of L with respect to a given parameter b_k is

$$\frac{\partial L}{\partial b_k} = \sum_{i=1}^{n} \frac{N_i}{r_i} \frac{\partial r_i}{\partial b_k} \tag{6.88}$$

By setting each of the equations thus formed (as the partial derivative with respect to each independent variable for each of the endogenous attributes) equal to zero, we have a set of equations that when solved give the maximum likelihood estimates of these parameters. If there are n_l independent variables (some of which may be other endogenous attributes) for the l endogenous attribute, the total number of parameters, and thus the total number of equations like equation (6.88), is n_a where

$$n_a = 2m + 2 \sum_{l=1}^{m} n_l. \tag{6.89}$$

If the effects in the two directions are constrained to be of equal magnitude so that $c_{lk} = -b_{lk}$ for all independent variables $k > 0$, then

$$n_a = 2m + \sum_{l=1}^{m} n_l. \tag{6.90}$$

The problem that has not yet been addressed is that of finding the derivative of r_i, which is an element of the matrix e^{Qt}, itself an infinite series. First, if we have a matrix $\mathbf{Q}$, a little effort will demonstrate that if we define the partial derivative of a matrix $\mathbf{Q}$ with respect to b_k as the element-by-element derivative, then some of the elementary rules of differentiation hold, such as $d(xy)/dz = (dx/dz) y + x (dy/dz)$. But because multiplication by matrices is not commutative, it is necessary to be careful to maintain the correct order in multiplication.[7]

---

[7] For further discussion and additional references see Aleksandrov, Kolmogorov, and Lavrentev, V. 3, (1963), pp. 93–95.

Thus the derivative of a matrix $\mathbf{Q}$ having elements q_{ij} with respect to b_k is defined as the element by element derivative:

$$\frac{\partial \mathbf{Q}}{\partial b_k} = \left\{ \frac{\partial q_{ij}}{\partial b_k} \right\} \tag{6.91}$$

In the remainder of this section, I will write $\mathbf{A}$ in place of $\mathbf{Q}t$ for simplicity. Thus, in place of $e^{\mathbf{Q}t}$ I will write $e^{\mathbf{A}}$, and wherever an element a_{ij} appears, it is to be understood as equal to $q_{ij}t$. I will also denote the partial derivative of $\mathbf{A}$ with respect to b_k as $\mathbf{A}_k$, again for simplicity of notation.

The partial derivative of the infinite series of matrices represented by $e^{\mathbf{A}}$ is

$$\frac{\partial e^{\mathbf{A}}}{\partial b_k} = \frac{\partial}{\partial b_k}\left(I + A + \frac{\mathbf{A}^2}{2!} + \frac{\mathbf{A}^3}{3!} + \cdots \right), \tag{6.92}$$

or

$$\frac{\partial e^{\mathbf{A}}}{\partial b_k} = \mathbf{A}_k + \frac{\mathbf{A}_k\mathbf{A} + \mathbf{A}\mathbf{A}_k}{2!} + \frac{\mathbf{A}_k\mathbf{A}^2 + \mathbf{A}\mathbf{A}_k\mathbf{A} + \mathbf{A}^2\mathbf{A}_k}{3!}$$
$$+ \frac{\mathbf{A}_k\mathbf{A}^3 + \mathbf{A}\mathbf{A}_k\mathbf{A}^2 + \mathbf{A}^2\mathbf{A}_k\mathbf{A} + \mathbf{A}^3\mathbf{A}_k}{4!} + \cdots, \tag{6.93}$$

This infinite series can be written in another way which facilitates computation. If we define a matrix $\mathbf{U}_{ki}$ as

$$\mathbf{U}_{k0} = 0$$
$$\mathbf{U}_{ki} = \frac{\mathbf{A}\mathbf{U}_{k,i-1} + \mathbf{A}_k\mathbf{A}^{i-1}/(i-1)!}{i} \tag{6.94}$$

then

$$\frac{\partial e^{\mathbf{A}}}{\partial b_k} = \sum_{i=1}^{\infty} \mathbf{U}_{ki}. \tag{6.95}$$

Because matrix multiplication is not commutative, this does not reduce to a simpler series. However, since the derivative of $\mathbf{A}$ with respect to each of the parameters b_k is very simple [for element a_{ij} of $\mathbf{A}$ is either zero or $x_k t$ (linear decomposition) or $x_k t q_{ij}$ (exponential decomposition)], equation

(6.94) may be used to find the derivative of e^A with respect to each parameter.

To find an algorithm by which equation (6.88) may be solved, it is possible to proceed in either of two ways. First, multiplying equation (6.88) by r_i/r_i, and then expanding the numerator by a Taylor series gives[8]

$$\frac{\partial L}{\partial b_k} = 0 = \sum_{i=1}^{N} \frac{N_i}{r_i^2} \left\{ r_i - \sum_{j=1}^{na} [b_j^{(v+1)} - b_j^{(v)}] \frac{\partial r_i}{\partial b_j} \right\} \frac{\partial r_i}{\partial b_k} \tag{6.96}$$

This set of m equations becomes

$$0 = \sum_{i=1}^{N} \frac{N_i}{r_i} \frac{\partial r_i}{\partial b_k} + \sum_{i=1}^{N} \sum_{j=1}^{na} \frac{N_i}{r_i^2} b_j^{(v)} \frac{\partial r_i}{\partial b_j} \frac{\partial r_i}{\partial b_k} = \sum_{i=1}^{N} \sum_{j=1}^{na} \frac{N_i}{r_i^2} b_j^{(v+1)} \frac{\partial r_i}{\partial b_j} \frac{\partial r_i}{\partial b_k} \tag{6.97}$$

Assuming for the moment that we can obtain $\partial r_i/\partial b_j$, let us denote $\dfrac{\partial r_i}{r_i \partial b_j}$ as x_{ji}^*. With this new notation, equation (6.97) becomes

$$\sum_{i=1}^{N} N_i x_{ki}^* + \sum_{i=1}^{N} \sum_{j=1}^{m} b_j^{(v)} N_i x_{ji}^* x_{ki}^* = \sum_{i=1}^{N} \sum_{j=1}^{m} b_j^{(v+1)} N_i x_{ji}^* x_{ki}^* \tag{6.98}$$

Using the notation of equations (6.7) and (6.8), and letting the vector $\mathbf{d}^{(v)}$ in equation (6.7) be a vector of ones, equation (6.98) becomes identical to equation (6.7), and solving for $b^{(v+1)}$ gives equation (6.8) for use as an algorithm to estimate b.

The second algorithm that may be used involves the second partial derivative and use of equation (6.3). From equation (6.88), the second derivative of L with respect to b_j and b_k is

$$\frac{\partial^2 L}{\partial b_j \partial b_k} = \sum \frac{N_i}{r_i} \frac{\partial^2 r_i}{\partial b_j \partial b_k} - \sum \frac{N_i}{r_1^2} \frac{\partial r_i}{\partial b_j} \frac{\partial r_i}{\partial b_k} \tag{6.99}$$

This second derivative of L can be used in conjunction with the first derivative from equation (6.88) in equation (6.3) to obtain the algorithm for iteration. The second derivative $\partial^2 r_i/(\partial b_j \partial b_k)$ is an element from the matrix $\partial e^A/(\partial b_j \partial b_k)$. This matrix is the second derivative of the infinite series that defines e^A. This takes the form

---

[8] In doing this, the r_i in the denominator is taken as $r_i^{(v)}$, while that in the numerator is taken as $r_i^{(v+1)}$, for which the Taylor series expansion is substituted.

$$\frac{\partial^2 e^{\mathbf{A}}}{\partial b_k \partial b_j} = \mathbf{A}_{jk} + \frac{\mathbf{A}_{jk}\mathbf{A} + \mathbf{A}_k\mathbf{A}_j + \mathbf{A}_j\mathbf{A}_k + \mathbf{A}\mathbf{A}_{jk}}{2!}$$

$$+ \frac{\mathbf{A}_{jk}\mathbf{A}^2 + \mathbf{A}_k\mathbf{A}_j\mathbf{A} + \mathbf{A}_k\mathbf{A}\mathbf{A}_j + \mathbf{A}_j\mathbf{A}_k\mathbf{A} + \mathbf{A}\mathbf{A}_{jk}\mathbf{A} + \mathbf{A}\mathbf{A}_k\mathbf{A}_j + \mathbf{A}_j\mathbf{A}\mathbf{A}_k + \mathbf{A}\mathbf{A}_j\mathbf{A}_k + \mathbf{A}^2\mathbf{A}_{jk}}{3!}$$

$$+ \cdots \tag{6.100}$$

In the linear decomposition of q, the second derivative, $\mathbf{A}_{jk}$, is zero and the second derivative of $e^{\mathbf{A}}$ becomes somewhat simpler; however, in the exponential decomposition of q, it is nonzero, with elements $x_k x_j t^2 q$. For the linear decomposition, the fact that the second derivative of $\mathbf{A}$ is zero means that the algorithm given by equation (6.3) together with equation (6.88) and equation (6.99) is identical to the first algorithm of equation (6.98) [or equation (6.8)]. For the exponential decomposition the two algorithms differ. This algorithm has the fault of greater computational complexity in the case of exponential decomposition of q, but it also has the virtue of automatically providing the covariance matrix for $\mathbf{b}$, which is the negative of the inverse of the matrix with elements given by equation (6.99). Both algorithms are provided, with an option for choice in the LONGIT program appended in chapter 4.

For computational purposes, equation (6.100) can be written in another form, based on equations (6.94) and (6.95). From these equations,

$$\frac{\partial}{\partial b_j}\left(\frac{\partial e^{\mathbf{A}}}{\partial b_k}\right) = \sum_{i=1}^{\infty} \frac{\partial \mathbf{U}_{ki}}{\partial b_j} \tag{6.101}$$

$$= \sum_{i=1}^{\infty} \frac{\partial}{\partial b_j}\left\{\frac{\mathbf{A}\mathbf{U}_{k,i-1} + \mathbf{A}_k\mathbf{A}^{i-1}/(i-1)!}{i}\right\}. \tag{6.102}$$

If we define $\mathbf{V}_{jki} = \dfrac{\partial \mathbf{U}_{ki}}{\partial b_j} = \dfrac{\partial \mathbf{U}_{ji}}{\partial b_k}$,

then by differentiating equation (6.102),

$$\mathbf{V}_{jki} = \frac{\mathbf{A}\mathbf{V}_{jk,i-1} + \mathbf{A}_j\mathbf{U}_{k,i-1} + \mathbf{A}_k\mathbf{U}_{j,i-1} + \mathbf{A}_{jk}\mathbf{A}^{i-1}/(i-1)!}{i}$$

$$\mathbf{V}_{jk0} = 0$$

and

$$\frac{\partial^2 e^{\mathbf{A}}}{\partial b_j \partial b_k} = \sum_{i=1}^{\infty} \mathbf{V}_{jki}.$$

5. EVENTS

In chapter 5 four different kinds of observations on events were examined: the *number of events* since a particular point in time; the *time* since the last event, the *sequence* of events, and the *full record* or history of events. These are not the only kinds of observations on events possible, but they are the kinds of observations frequently encountered. The first two of these are of considerably less importance and will be treated summarily here as they were in chapter 5. The LONGIT·EVENT programs in the appendix to chapter 5 do not include these first two forms of observation, that is, numbers of events and time since last event.

Because observations on events can take many varied forms, I will not attempt to specify a general form of the likelihood function as I did in the case of cross-sectional or panel states.

5.1. NUMBER OF EVENTS IN A GIVEN TIME PERIOD[9]

As equation (1.29) shows, the probability of n events in a given time period 0 to t for a continuous-time Markov process for person i with constant transition rate q_i is given by

$$Pr(n|q_i,t) = p_i(m) = \frac{e^{-q_it}(q_it)^n}{n!}. \qquad (6.103)$$

The transition rate q_i is a linear or exponential linear function of the independent variables, as before. Thus the likelihood function for the sample is

$$\mathcal{L} = \prod_{i=1}^{N} \frac{e^{-q_it}(q_it)^{n_i}}{n_i!} \qquad (6.104)$$

where n_i is the number of events observed for individual i. If there are N_i individuals with the same values of independent variables and the same number of events observed, the i term in the likelihood function is raised to the power N_i. The logarithm is

$$L = \sum_{i=1}^{N} N_i[-q_it + n_i \log q_it - \log n_i!] \qquad (6.105)$$

---

[9] This section on number of events assumes independent variables that are constant over the time period 0 through t, except for linear interpolation with the linear decomposition of q. As indicated in chapter 5, the latter case is identical to that of constant independent variables, except with the mean of x_{ki} between 0 and t, $\bar{x}_{ki}$, replacing the constant x_{ki}.

and the derivative with respect to b_j, set equal to zero, is

$$\frac{\partial L}{\partial b_j} = \sum_{i=1}^{N} N_i \frac{(n_i - q_i t)}{q_i} \frac{\partial q_i}{\partial b_j} = 0 \cdot \qquad (6.106)$$

Equations of the form of equation (6.106) are the $m + 1$ nonlinear equations that must be solved for the vector **b**. Use of the Newton-Raphson algorithm involves a Taylor series expansion around $q_i^{(v)}$ for the q_i that appears in the numerator of equation (6.106). The expansion is

$$q_i^{(v+1)} = q_i^{(v)} + \sum_{k=0}^{m} [b_k^{(v+1)} - b_k^{(v)}] \frac{\partial q_i^{(v)}}{\partial b_k} \qquad (6.107)$$

and substitution into equation (6.106) [and adding superscripts (v) and $(v + 1)$ where appropriate] gives

$$0 = \sum_{i=1}^{N} \left[\frac{N_i t}{q_i^{(v)}} \left(\frac{n_i}{t} - q_i^{(v)} \right) \frac{\partial q_i^{(v)}}{\partial b_j} - \frac{N_i t}{q_i^{(v)}} \sum_{k=0}^{m} (b_k^{(v+1)} - b_k^{(v)}) \frac{\partial q_i^{(v)}}{\partial b_j} \frac{\partial q_i^{(v)}}{\partial b_k} \right] . \qquad (6.108)$$

Examination of equation (6.108) shows that it has the same form as the basic iteration equation given in equation (6.6) if the following correspondences are made:

Section 1	Section 5.1	
b_j	b_j	
ρ_i	q_i	
w_i	$N_i t/q_i$	
z_i	n_i/t	
m	$m + 1$	(where m is the number of independent variables)

Using these correspondences, equation (6.8) may be used as the algorithm for estimating the vector **b**. However, the matrix **x***, with elements x_{ki}^*, which are the first partial derivatives of q_i with respect to b_k, differ for the linear and exponential decompositions of q_i. The correspondences for the two models are:

Section 1	Section 5.1	
$x_{ki}^* \left(= \dfrac{\partial \rho_i}{\partial b_k} \right)$	$\dfrac{\partial q_i}{\partial b_k} =$	(linear decomposition): x_{ki}
		(exponential decomposition): $x_{ki} q_i$

274

A second algorithm may be used, making use of both the first and second derivatives of L together with equation (6.3). The second derivative of L is found by taking the derivative of equation (6.106) with respect to b_k. This gives

$$\frac{\partial^2 L}{\partial b_j \partial b_k} = \sum_{i=1}^{N} N_i \left[\left(\frac{n_i - q_i t}{q_i} \right) \frac{\partial^2 q_i}{\partial b_j \partial b_k} - \frac{n_i}{q_i^2} \frac{\partial q_i}{\partial b_j} \frac{\partial q_i}{\partial b_k} \right].$$

(6.109)

This equation simplifies, for the two decompositions, to

$$\frac{\partial^2 L}{\partial b_j \partial b_k} = - \sum_{i=1}^{N} N_i \left[\frac{n_i}{q_i^2} x_{ki} x_{ji} \right] \quad \text{(linear decomposition)}$$

$$\frac{\partial^2 L}{\partial b_j \partial b_k} = - \sum_{i=1}^{N} N_i [q_i t x_{ki} x_{ji}] \quad \text{(exponential decomposition)}$$

Using these definitions of $\mathbf{L}''$, together with equation (6.106) and the appropriate definitions of $\partial q_i / \partial b_k$, equation (6.3), which is $\mathbf{b}^{(v+1)} = \mathbf{b}^{(v)} - \mathbf{L}'(\mathbf{L}'')^{-1}$, may be used as an alternative algorithm for estimating $\mathbf{b}$.

5.2. TIME SINCE LAST EVENT

As indicated in chapter 1, a Markov process with evacuation from a single state allows calculation of the probability of leaving the state within the total time period t at exactly time t_i measured from the present, which I will write as $\pi_i(t_i)$ for individual i:

$$\pi_i(t_i) = e^{-\int_0^{t_i} q_i(\tau) d\tau} q_i(t_i).$$

(6.110)

If individual i takes no action through time t, the probability, which I will write as $\pi_i^*(t)$, is

$$\pi_i^*(t) = e^{-\int_0^{t} q_i(\tau) d\tau}.$$

(6.111)

If $\int_0^{t} q_i(\tau) d\tau$ can be written as a constant α_i times t_i, this simplifies to

$$\pi_i(t_i) = e^{-\alpha_i t_i} q_i(t_i).$$

(6.112)

275

As shown in chapter 5, equations (5.10)–(5.13), all four of the cases considered elsewhere in this book (linear or exponential decomposition with constant or changing independent variables, where the independent variables can be assumed to change linearly between times 0 and t_i) meet this condition of a constant α_i times the elasped time, t_i. Thus equation (6.112) can serve for all four of these cases.

The probability $\pi^*(t)$ of no event during the whole time period t is

$$\pi^*(t) = e^{-\alpha_i t_i}. \tag{6.113}$$

The likelihood of a sample of observed times t_i, $i = 1, \ldots, N_1$ for the N_1 persons who had an event at *some* time, and the nonevents for the $N - N_1$ persons who had no event, is

$$
\begin{aligned}
\mathscr{L} &= \prod_{i=1}^{N_1} \pi_i(t_i) \prod_{i=N_1+1}^{N} \pi_i^*(t) \\
&= \prod_{i=1}^{N_1} e^{-\alpha_i t_i} q_i(t_i) \prod_{i=N_1+1}^{N} e^{-\alpha_i t}.
\end{aligned} \tag{6.114}
$$

The logarithm of the likelihood is

$$L = \sum_{i=1}^{N_1} \left[-\alpha_i t_i + \log q_i(t_i) \right] - \sum_{i=N_1+1}^{N} \alpha_i t \tag{6.115}$$

If we define t_i for those who had no event to be equal to the total time period t, equation (6.115) can be written

$$L = \sum_{i=1}^{N_1} \log q_i(t_i) - \sum_{i=1}^{N} \alpha_i t_i \tag{6.116}$$

and the derivative with respect to b_j, set equal to zero, is:

$$\frac{\partial L}{\partial b_j} = 0 = \sum_{i=1}^{N_1} \frac{1}{q_i(t_i)} \frac{\partial q_i(t_i)}{\partial b_j} - \sum_{i=1}^{N} t_i \left(\frac{\partial \alpha_i}{\partial b_j} \right) \tag{6.117}$$

It is useful to set down in a table the first and second derivatives of $q(t_i)$ and α_1 for the four cases of interest. This is given in table 6.1.

276

TABLE 6.1

	Linear, constant x	Linear, changing x	Exponential, constant x	Exponential, changing x
$q_i(t_i)$	$b_j x_{ji}$	$b_j x_{ji}(t_i)$	$e^{b_j x_{ji}}$	$e^{b_j x_{ji}(t_i)}$
$\dfrac{\partial q_i(t_i)}{\partial b_j}$	x_{ji}	$x_{ji}(t_i)$	$x_{ji}q_i$	$x_{ji}(t_i)q_i(t_i)$
$\dfrac{\partial^2 q_i(t_i)}{\partial b_j \partial b_k}$	0	0	$x_{ji}x_{ki}q_i$	$x_{ji}(t_i)x_{ki}(t_i)q_i(t_i)$
α_i	$b_j x_{ji}$	$b_j \bar{x}_{ji}$	$e^{b_j x_{ji}}$	$\dfrac{t_i\Delta q_i}{\Delta\log q_i}$
$\dfrac{\partial \alpha_i}{\partial b_j}$	x_{ji}	$\bar{x}_{ji}$	$x_{ji}q_i$	$t_i\left[\dfrac{\Delta(x_{ki}q_i)}{\Delta\log q} - \dfrac{\Delta q_i\Delta x_{ji}}{(\Delta\log q_i)^2}\right]$
$\dfrac{\partial^2 \alpha_i}{\partial b_j \partial b_k}$	0	0	$x_{ji}x_{ki}q_i$	$t_i\left[\dfrac{\Delta(x_{ji}x_{ki}q_i)}{\Delta\log q_i} - \dfrac{\Delta(x_{ji}q_i)\Delta x_{ki}}{(\Delta\log q_i)^2}\right.$
				$\left.+\dfrac{\Delta(x_{ki}q_i)\Delta x_{ji}}{(\Delta\log q_i)^2} + \dfrac{2\Delta q_i\Delta x_{ji}\Delta x_{ki}}{(\Delta\log q_i)^3}\right]$

(Note: Definitions for Δq_i, $\Delta\log q_i$, Δx_{ji}, $\Delta(x_{ji}q_i)$, $\Delta(x_{ji}x_{ki}q_i)$ are those given in section 3.9.)

In the case of constant independent variables then, if we set $z_i = 1$ for those persons i who had an event and $z_i = 0$ for those who did not, equation (6.117) can be written

$$0 = \sum_{i=1}^{N} \left(\frac{z_i - t_iq_i}{q_i}\right) \frac{\partial q_i}{\partial b_j}. \qquad (6.118)$$

If, as in the preceding section, we allow the greater flexibility that there are N_i persons with the same time t_i of the last event and the same values of independent variables, each term in the sum in equation (6.118) is multiplied by N_i. When this is done, and with z_i in place of n_i and t_i in place of t, equation (6.118) becomes like equation (6.106). Thus all the derivations in section 5.1 following equation (6.106) hold for the cases of constant independent variables here. The correspondences between this section, section 5.1, and equation (6.6) in section 1 are given in table 6.2.

TABLE 6.2

Section 1	Section 5.1	Section 5.2
b_j	b_j	b_j
ρ_i [algorithm of eq. (6.6)]	q_i	q_i
w_i	$N_i t/q_i$	$N_i t_i/q_i$
z_i	n_i/t	z_i/t_i
m	$m+1$	$m+1$
x^*_{ki}	x_{ki} (linear)	x_{ki} (linear)
	$x_{ki}q_i$ (exponential)	$x_{ki}q_i$ (exponential)
L'' [algorithm of equation (6.3)]	$-\sum_{i=1}^{N} N_i\left(\dfrac{n_i}{q_i^2} x_{ki}x_{ji}\right)$ (linear)	$-\sum_{i=1}^{N} N_i\left(\dfrac{z_i}{q_i} x_{ki}x_{ji}\right)$ (linear)
	$-\sum_{i=1}^{N} N_i(q_i t x_{ki}x_{ji})$ (exponential)	$-\sum_{i=1}^{N} N_i(q_i t_i x_{ki}x_{ji})$ (exponential)

Table 6.2, together with equation (6.6) or equation (6.3), provides two alternative algorithms for estimating **b** with observations on time since last event and constant independent variables. For changing independent variables, it is possible to construct an algorithm using the Taylor series expansion around $q_i(t_i)$ by first writing equation (6.117) as

$$\frac{\partial L}{\partial b_j} = 0 = \sum_{i=1}^{N} \frac{1}{q_i(t_i)}\left(z_i \frac{\partial q_i(t_i)}{\partial b_j} - t_i q_i(t_i)\frac{\partial \alpha_i}{\partial b_j}\right). \tag{6.119}$$

I will not write out the details of this algorithm here. For use of the algorithm of equation (6.3), quantities from table 6.1 can be used together with equation (6.117) and the second derivative of L, given in equation (6.120). (For simplifying notation, $q_i(t_i)$ is written as q_i, which can be done without ambiguity.)

$$\frac{\partial^2 L}{\partial b_j \partial b_k} = \sum_{i=1}^{N}\left[\frac{z_i}{q_i^2}\left(q_i \frac{\partial^2 q_i}{\partial b_j \partial b_k} - \frac{\partial q_i}{\partial b_j}\frac{\partial q_i}{\partial b_k}\right) - t_i \frac{\partial^2 \alpha_i}{\partial b_j \partial b_k}\right]. \tag{6.120}$$

5.3. PARTIAL LIKELIHOOD FOR EVENT SEQUENCES

The probability of individual i not acting until time t_i and then acting at time t_i is given by equation (6.110) of the preceding section, or if not acting at all until time t it is given by equation (6.111). Consequently, the likelihood function for a sample of N individuals can be written

$$\mathcal{L} = \prod_{i=1}^{N} e^{-\int_0^{t_i} q_i(\tau)d\tau} [q_i(t_i)]^{z_i} \tag{6.121}$$

where $z_i = 1$ if there was an event for i, 0 otherwise.

If we think of starting everyone at the same point in time and then observing the sequence of events, with N_1 events occurring altogether, we can order the events $i = 1, \ldots, N_1$ such that $t_i > t_{i'}$ if $i > i'$. Then we may consider the probability of no event between time t_{i-1} and t_i, followed by an event at time t_i from individual i, combining the probabilities for all who remained at time t_{i-1}. This probability is

$$p_i^*(t_{i-1}, \ t_i) = e^{\int_{t_{i-1}}^{t_i} q \cdot (\tau) d\tau} \ q_i(t_i) \tag{6.122}$$

where $q \cdot (\tau)$ is the sum of transition rates over all those who remained at time t_{i-1}. Cox terms this the *risk set*, and $q \cdot (\tau)$ is defined as

$$q \cdot (\tau) = \sum_{i \in R_\tau} q_i(\tau) \tag{6.123}$$

where R_τ is the set of individuals at risk at time τ.

The likelihood function equation (6.121) can then be written as the product of the N_1 probabilities of the form of equation (6.122), from $p_1^*(t_0, t)$ to p_N^* (t_{N-1}, t_N). In effect, what Cox (1972) does in forming his partial likelihood (see Efron, 1977, p. 558) is to divide the likelihood function into a portion that can be written like equation (6.122) for the sample if everyone had the *same* transition rate $q(t)$ multiplied by a portion that expresses the conditional probability that i acted, given that someone acted.

To see how this is done, we can write the likelihood function not as a product of probabilities of the form of equation (6.122), but in slightly expanded form:

$$\mathcal{L} = \prod_{i=1}^{N_1} e^{-\int_{t_{i-1}}^{t_i} q \cdot (\tau) d\tau} \ q \cdot (t_i) \frac{q_i(t_i)}{q \cdot (t_i)}. \tag{6.124}$$

Cox's essential point is that in this form all but the last fraction, the conditional probability, expresses the likelihood of a particular rate of action, independently of which person acts, and only the last fraction expresses the likelihood that a particular person rather than another acts. Thus, if we are not interested in the absolute size of the transition rate but only in factors that cause it to be larger or smaller, this last fraction contains such information. In fact,

279

as Efron shows, it is asymptotically efficient, asymptotically containing *all* such information.

It is possible, then, to consider only this last fraction, the conditional probability. Rewriting the single term for the conditional probability that i acts at time t_j, given that someone in the risk set acts at t_j, we define y_{ij}:

$$y_{ij} = \frac{q_i(t_j)}{\sum\limits_{R_j} q_h(t_j)} . \tag{6.125}$$

Cox assumes an exponential decomposition, although as Efron points out, any other positive multiplicative function could also serve (Efron, 1977, p. 563).[10] Thus with this decomposition of $q_i(t)$ we have for this conditional probability[11]

$$y_{ij} = \frac{e^{bx_i}}{\sum\limits_{R_j} e^{bx_h}} \tag{6.126}$$

Note that e^{bx_i} need not be the full transition rate of person j; if there is a multiplicative factor alike for all persons at a given time, though it may vary over time so that $q_i(t) = e^{\alpha t + bx_i}$, then $e^{\alpha t}$ appears in both numerator and denominator as a multiplier, and drops out.[12] This means also that the constant term in equation (6.8) drops out so that b_0 is not estimated. Heuristically this is understandable since the constant term merely specifies the absolute sizes of the rates, while here we examine only their relative sizes.

The product of these conditional probabilities Cox calls the *partial likelihood,* which forms the foundation of a theory of partial likelihood (Cox, 1975).[13] The product is

$$\mathcal{L} = \prod_{i=1}^{N} \frac{e^{bx_i}}{\sum\limits_{h \in R_i} e^{bx_h}} .$$

The logarithm is

[10] I am grateful to Kazuo Yamaguchi for the derivation in equations (6.128)–(6.137) of an iterative procedure for estimating Cox's partial likelihood. Cox himself describes a slightly different procedure (Cox, 1972a, p. 191).

[11] Here I will not write $x_i(t_j)$, but I will suppress t_j for convenience of notation. It is merely necessary, then, to remember that the independent variables may be functions of time.

[12] Note that the linear decomposition, used elsewhere in this book, is not applicable here because the constant term is additive rather than multiplicative.

[13] These conditional probabilities do not form a true conditional likelihood, but rather, as Cox terms it, a partial likelihood. See Cox (1975).

$$L = \sum_{i=1}^{N_1} \left[\mathbf{bx}_i - \log \left(\sum_{h \epsilon R_i} e^{\mathbf{bx}h} \right) \right].$$ (6.128)

Taking the partial derivative with respect to b_k and setting it equal to zero gives the equations that when solved for b_k maximize the likelihood:

$$\frac{\partial L}{\partial b_k} = 0 = \sum_{i=1}^{N_1} \left[x_{ki} - \sum_{h \epsilon R_i} x_{kh} \frac{e^{\mathbf{bx}h}}{\sum_{l \epsilon R_i} e^{\mathbf{bx}l}} \right].$$ (6.129)

But a portion of the last term is just y_{hi}, so the equation can be written

$$\frac{\partial L}{\partial b_k} = 0 = \sum_{i=1}^{N_1} \left[x_{ki} - \sum_{h \epsilon R_i} x_{kh} y_{hi} \right].$$ (6.130)

Again, as in other cases, there are n equations nonlinear in **b**. Thus we carry out a Taylor series expansion of y_{hi} around $y_{hi}^{(v)}$:

$$y_{hi}^{(v+1)} = y_{hi}^{(v)} + \sum_{j=1}^{n} (b_j^{(v+1)} - b_j^{(v)}) \frac{\partial y_{hi}^{(v)}}{\partial b_j^{(v)}}.$$ (6.131)

The partial derivative of y_{hi} with respect to b_j is

$$\frac{\partial y_{hi}}{\partial b_j} = x_{jh} y_{hi} - y_{hi} \sum_{l \epsilon R_i} x_{jl} y_{li}$$ (6.132)

Substituting from equation (6.132) for $\partial y_{hi}^{(v)} / \partial b_j$ in equation (6.131) and then substituting from equation (6.131) for y_{hi} in equation (6.130) for the equations to be used in iteration gives

$$0 = \sum_{i=1}^{N_1} x_{ki} - \sum_{i=1}^{N_1} \sum_{h \epsilon R_i} x_{kh} y_{hi}^{(v)} \left\{ 1 + \sum_{j=1}^{n} \left[b_j^{(v+1)} \right. \right.$$
$$\left. \left. - b_j^{(v)} \right] \left[x_{jh} - \sum_{l \epsilon R_i} x_{jl} y_{li}^{(v)} \right] \right\}$$ (6.133)

To simplify notation, let us define a vector and a matrix:

$$\text{Let } d_k^{(v)} = \sum_{i=1}^{N_1} \left[x_{ki} - \sum_{h \epsilon R_i} x_{kh} y_{hi}^{(v)} \right]$$ (6.134)

281

$$\text{and } \mathbf{d}^{(v)} = \{d_k^{(v)}\}.$$

Then let

$$\psi_{kj}^{(v)} = \sum_{i=1}^{N_1} \left[\sum_{h \in R_i} x_{kh} y_{hi}^{(v)} x_{jh} - \sum_{h \in R_i} x_{kh} y_{hi}^{(v)} \sum_{l \in R_i} x_{jl} y_{li}^{(v)} \right] \qquad (6.135)$$

and define the $(n + 1) \times (n + 1)$ matrix $\boldsymbol{\psi}^{(v)} = \{\psi_{kj}^{(v)}\}$.

Then equation (6.133) can be written

$$\mathbf{d}^{(v)} + \mathbf{b}^{(v)} \boldsymbol{\psi}^{(v)} = \mathbf{b}^{(v+1)} \boldsymbol{\psi}^{(v)} \qquad (6.136)$$

and solving

$$\mathbf{d}^{(v)} \boldsymbol{\psi}^{-1} + \mathbf{b}^{(v)} = \mathbf{b}^{(v+1)}. \qquad (6.137)$$

This provides an iterative algorithm for the maximum likelihood estimate of Cox's partial likelihood.

An alternative approach, using the second derivative and equation (6.3), is obtained by differentiating equation (6.130) with respect to x_{jh} to obtain L''. The derivative is

$$\frac{\partial^2 L}{\partial b_k \partial b_j} = - \sum_{i=1}^{N_1} \left[\sum_{h \in R_i} x_{kh} x_{jh} y_{hi} - \sum_{l \in R_i} x_{kl} y_{li} \sum_{h \in R_i} x_{jh} y_{hi} \right]. \qquad (6.138)$$

This second derivative turns out to be identical to ψ_{kj} as described in equation (6.135). This results in the algorithm of equation (6.3) being identical to that obtained in equation (6.137). Thus the two alternative algorithms outlined in section 1 of this chapter are identical in this case.

5.4 MODELING THE CENSOR AND MULTIPLE EVENT TYPES

If there is a second kind of event (and censoring can be considered a second kind of event rather than being ignored), then, as indicated in chapter 5, the transition rate takes the form

$$q_{i2}(\tau) = e^{\lambda_\tau + \phi_2 + \sum_k b_{k2} x_{ki}}$$

where the independent variables may be the same as those for the first event or different, and the time periods are those terminated by either type of event.

The analysis in this case proceeds just as in the case of a single event. It is now the case that $q\cdot(\tau)$ includes summation over both types of events; and the component $e^{\lambda\tau}$ in the ratio y_{ji} appears in both numerator and denominator because the rate for each event of whatever type contains this component. Thus, if there are N_1 periods terminated by an event of type 1 and N_2 periods terminated by an event of type 2, then there are $N_1 + N_2$ period-specific parameters. In carrying out the calculations, the parameter ϕ_2 (or $\phi_2, \ldots, \phi_m$ for m types of events) is estimated by assuming an additional independent variable that takes on a value of 1 for transition rates of type 2 and a value of 0 for transition rates of type 1.

5.5. PERIOD-SPECIFIC COMPONENTS IN PARTIAL LIKELIHOOD

One may wish to estimate the full transition rate at a given time since the parameters **b** give only the effects of independent variables in expanding or contracting the rate. For example, DiPrete (1981) has used Cox's partial likelihood function for estimating factors affecting moves to and from unemployment, and then, taking these estimates as given, obtained measures for the total transition rate. To do this, it is possible to take **b** from the maximum likelihood estimation of the partial likelihood as given, and to use equation (6.124) to estimate $q(t)$ given **b**.

First of all, since it is impossible to estimate variations in rates during periods in which nothing happens, variations in $q(t)$ can be estimated only between times t_{i-1} and t_i (where the times of action t_i are ordered so that $t_i > t_{i-1}$). This means the integral in equation (6.124) may be replaced by a summation over i of $q\cdot(t_i)(t_i - t_{i-1})$ where $q\cdot(t_i)$ is taken as constant between times t_{i-1} and t_i (where t_0 is the start of observation). With this modification, and calling the last fraction in equation (6.124) d_i for person i, we have for the logarithm of the likelihood:

$$L = -\sum_{i=1}^{N_1} q\cdot(t_i)(t_i - t_{i-1}) + \sum_{i=1}^{N_1} \log[q\cdot(t_i)d_i]. \qquad (6.139)$$

283

We want to get an estimate of λ_i, the period-specific component of the transition rate, which is contained in $q \cdot (t_i)$, from equation (6.123):

$$q \cdot (t_i) = \sum_{h \in R_i} q_h(t_i)$$

$$= e^{\lambda_i} \sum_{h \in R_i} e^{bx h}. \qquad (6.140)$$

What is desired is to maximize L with respect to each of the parameters λ_i. Taking the partial derivative of L with respect to λ_i gives

$$\frac{\partial L}{\partial \lambda_i} = -q \cdot (t_i)[t_i - t_{i-1}] + 1. \qquad (6.141)$$

Since the derivative with respect to λ_i does not involve any other period-specific components λ_i, each equation may be set equal to zero and solved alone to give[14]

$$q \cdot (t_i) = \frac{1}{t_i - t_{i-1}}. \qquad (6.142)$$

Substituting for $q \cdot (t_i)$ from equation (6.140) and solving for λ_i gives

$$\lambda_i = -\log \sum_{h \in R_i} e^{bx h} - \log (t_i - t_{i-1}) \qquad (6.143)$$

Thus, for each interval $t_i = t_{i-1}$ (where the indexes i are ordered so that when $t_i > t_{i'}$, $i > i'$), a value λ_i may be calculated. This means that for each individual h, the transition rate for an event at time t_i is determined by a set of b_k's, which are alike for all persons and constant over time, his

[14] Efron (1977, equation 2.4) gives a slightly different estimate for $h(t)$, which is the continuous analog of $q \cdot (t_i)$, but evaluated precisely at t_i rather than for the interval between t_{i-1} and t_i. His maximum likelihood estimate of $\int_{t_{i-}}^{t_{i+}} h(t)dt$ is

$$\log \left[\frac{q \cdot (t_i)}{q \cdot (t_i) - \bar{\bar{q}} \, (t_i)} \right]$$

where $\bar{q}(t_i)$ is the average transition rate over the whole sample. The quantity $\int_{t_{i-}}^{t_{i+}} h(t)dt$ corresponds to $(t_i - t_{i-1})\bar{q}(t_i)$, and $(t_i - t_{i-1})\bar{q}(t_i)$ equals $\bar{q}(t_i)/q \cdot (t_i)$. This last quantity is very close to $\log[q \cdot (t_i)/\{q \cdot (t_i) - \bar{q}(t_i)\}$ for reasonably small values of $\bar{q}(t_i)/q \cdot (t_i)$.

own values $x_{kh}(t)$ for variables $k = 1, \ldots, n$ (values that may vary over time), and another parameter λ_i, which is alike for all persons at time t_i but may vary over time.

5.5. EVENT HISTORIES: PARTITIONING INTO SMALL TIME PERIODS

As indicated in chapter 5, section 5, a second strategy for treating event histories is to divide the total time interval into short periods of differing lengths, bounded by events or censors. This strategy is especially valuable for the case in which Cox's partial likelihood is least good: the case in which there are a number of ties—a number of events within the same observational period. That is, if there are J distinct times at which events occur, and the total number of events is N, this method is especially useful if N is somewhat larger than J.

For individual i under observation at the beginning of time period (t_{i-1}) the probability of remaining until the next event (t_j) is

$$p_i(t) = e^{-\int_{t_{j-1}}^{t_j} q_i(\tau)d\tau} .$$

This probability may be divided into two parts, a probability of remaining up until the last measured fine unit of time, and a probability of remaining for the last unit.[15] If the length of a fine unit of time is denoted by θ, then the probability can be written

$$p_i(t) = e^{-\int_{t_{j-1}}^{t_j-\theta} q_i(\tau)d\tau} \; e^{-\int_{t_j-\theta}^{t_j} q_i(\tau)d\tau} .$$

Now suppose $q(\tau)$ is composed of a component λ_j specific to time period j but constant over individuals and components b_k due to independent variables $x_{ki}(\tau)$ characterizing individual i. For the moment assume all $x(\tau)$ to be constant over time; I will return later to the case in which x changes regularly over time, and the case in which $q_i(\tau)$ is linearly dependent on τ. Then for exponential decomposition,

$$q_i(\tau) = e^{\lambda_j + \sum b_k x_{ki}} ,$$

[15] A *fine unit* of time is the smallest unit in which time is measured for the data at hand. In the leukemia example of chapter 5, the fine unit of time was one week.

and for linear decomposition,

$$q_i(\tau) = \lambda_j + \Sigma b_k x_{ki}$$

where λ_j is the period-specific component for period j. The integral

$$\int_{t_{j-1}}^{t_j - \theta} q_i(\tau) \, d\tau \text{ equals } e^{\lambda_j + \Sigma b_k x_{ki}}(t_j - \theta - t_{j-1})$$

$$\text{or} \quad (\lambda + \Sigma b_k x_{ki})(t_j - \theta - t_{j-1})$$

Similarly, $\displaystyle\int_{t_j - \theta}^{t_j} q_i(\tau) d\tau$ equals $e^{\lambda_j + \Sigma b_k x_{ki}}\theta$ or $(\lambda_j + \Sigma b_k x_{ki})\theta$.

If we consider all time periods j preceding events ($j = 1, \ldots, J$), then for time period j there is a risk set R_j consisting of all individuals who are present at the beginning of the time period and either remain present through-out the period, jump at the end of the period, or are censored at the end of the period. The event or the censor at that time point is what defines the period by marking its end. This excludes all persons who were not present at the beginning of the time period.

The likelihood of such observations for a given time period j is the product of p_i for all individuals over time $(t_{j-1}, t_j - \theta)$, p_i over time $(t_j - \theta, t_j)$ for those who remained, and $1 - p_i$ over time $(t_j - \theta, t_j)$ for those who jumped. For the period $(t_j - \theta, t_j)$, those who are censored at the end of this period do not appear, for observation of them ends at the last fine unit of time.[16] Thus, as indicated in chapter 5, the likelihood function for individual i in period j consists of a product of $p_i(t_{j-1}, t_j - \theta)$ and one of three terms, $p_i(t_j - \theta, t_j)$, $1 - p_i(t_j - \theta t_j)$, or 1, depending on whether individual i remained, jumped, or was censored.

Over all individuals i and all periods j, the likelihood is the product

$$= \prod_{j=1}^{J} \prod_{i \in R_j} p_i(t_{j-1}, t_j - \theta) p_i(t_j - \theta, t_j)^{z_{ij}}[1 - p_i(t_j - \theta, t_j)]^{u_{ij}}$$

where $z_{ij} = 1$ if i remained present during period j, 0 otherwise; $u_{ij} = 1$ if

---

[16] As indicated in chapter 5, it would be possible alternatively to treat the censor as a second kind of event and to model the transition rate for the censor in something like the same way the transition rate for the event is modeled. However, I will not pursue that alternative here. Modeling of the censor can, of course, be carried out via an independent analysis, and almost nothing is to be gained by analyzing the two types of events simultaneously.

i jumped at the end of period j, 0 otherwise. If i is not censored at the end of j, $z_{ij} + u_{ij} = 1$; if i is censored, $z_{ij} + u_{ij} = 0$. R_j is the risk set at period j.

To simplify notation in what follows, I will denote the first probability over all but the last fine time unit of size θ by p_{ij_1} and the second probability by p_{ij_2}.

The log likelihood is

$$L = \Sigma\Sigma\{[-q_i(t_j)(\Delta t_j - \theta)] + z_{ij} \log p_{ij_2} + u_{ij} \log (1 - p_{ij_2})\}$$

and the partial derivative of L with respect to b_k is

$$\frac{\partial L}{\partial b_k} = \sum_{j=1}^{J} \sum_{i \epsilon R_j} \left\{ -(\Delta t_j - \theta) \frac{\partial q_i(t_j)}{\partial b_k} + \frac{z_{ij} - (z_{ij} + u_{ij})p_{ij_2}}{p_{ij_2}(1 - p_{ij_2})} \frac{\partial p_{ij_2}}{\partial b_k} \right\} \quad (6.144)$$

and the second derivative, analogous to equation (6.13) or equation (6.24), is

$$\frac{\partial^2 L}{\partial b_h \partial b_k} = \sum_{j=1}^{J} \sum_{i \epsilon R_j} \left\{ -(\Delta t_j - \theta) \frac{\partial^2 q_i(t_j)}{\partial b_k \partial b_h} + \phi_{ij} \frac{\partial^2 p_{ij_2}}{\partial b_k \partial b_h} - \phi_{ij}^2 \frac{\partial p_{ij_2}}{\partial b_k} \frac{\partial p_{ij_2}}{\partial b_h} \right\} \quad (6.145)$$

where

$$\phi_{ij} = \frac{z_{ij} - (z_{ij} + u_{ij})p_{ij_2}}{p_{ij_2}(1 - p_{ij_2})}.$$

For the first derivative with respect to the period-specific component of $q_i(t)$, λ_j, the summation over $j = 1$ to J vanishes (because $\partial p_{ij}/\partial \lambda_{j'} = 0$ for $j' \neq j$) as it does for the second derivative $\partial^2 L/(\partial \lambda_j \partial b_k)$, and the second derivative $\partial^2 L/(\partial \lambda_j \partial \lambda_{j'})$ vanishes for $j' \neq j$.

Since we are assuming for the present that $\int_{t_1}^{t_2} q_i(t)dt = (t_2 - t_1)q_i$, then $p_{ij_2} = e^{-q_i(t_j)\theta}$ and the first derivatives are

$$\frac{\partial p_{ij_2}}{\partial b_k} = -\theta p_{ij_2} \frac{\partial q_i(t_j)}{\partial b_k} \quad \text{and}$$

$$\frac{\partial p_{ij_2}}{\partial \lambda_j} = -\theta p_{ij_2} \frac{\partial q_i(t_j)}{\partial \lambda_j}$$

and the second derivatives are

287

$$\frac{\partial^2 p_{ij_2}}{\partial b_k \partial b_h} = \theta p_{ij_2} \left[\theta \frac{\partial q_i}{\partial b_k} \frac{\partial q_i}{\partial b_h} - \frac{\partial^2 q_i}{\partial b_k \partial b_h} \right],$$

$$\frac{\partial^2 p_{ij_2}}{\partial b_k \partial \lambda_j} = \theta p_{ij_2} \left[\theta \frac{\partial q_i}{\partial b_k} \frac{\partial q_i}{\partial \lambda_j} - \frac{\partial^2 q_i}{\partial b_k \partial \lambda_j} \right],$$

$$\frac{\partial^2 p_{ij_2}}{\partial \lambda_j \partial \lambda_j} = \theta p_{ij_2} \left[\theta \left(\frac{\partial q_i}{\partial \lambda_j} \right)^2 - \frac{\partial^2 q_i}{\partial \lambda_j^2} \right],$$

$$\frac{\partial^2 p_{ij_2}}{\partial \lambda_j \partial \lambda_{j'}} = 0 \ (j' \neq j) \cdot$$

Equations (6.144) and (6.145) are necessary for carrying out the analysis. The partial derivatives of $q_i(t_j)$ will differ for the different models, but the general form remains as in equations (6.144) and (6.145).

When the independent variables are not constant, but we can assume they change linearly between two observation points at the beginning and end of each period, then both the linear and exponential models with nonconstant independent variables take the same form as assumed above. That is, $p_i(t) = e^{-qt}$ where t is the length of the period between two events and q is independent of time but depends on the values of x_k at the beginning and end of the period.

For the four different cases (linear or exponential, constant or nonconstant independent variables), the quantity q_i and the first and second partial derivatives of q_i are:

Linear Constant

$$q_i = \lambda_j + \Sigma b_k x_{ki}$$

$$\frac{\partial q_i}{\partial b_k} = x_{ki}$$

$$\frac{\partial q_i}{\partial \lambda_j} = 1$$

As these first derivatives indicate, all second derivatives are zero.

Exponential Constant

$$q_i = e^{\lambda_j + \Sigma b_k x_{ki}}$$

$$\frac{\partial q_i}{\partial b_k} = x_{ki} q_i$$

$$\frac{\partial q_i}{\partial \lambda_j} = q_i$$

$$\frac{\partial^2 q_i}{\partial b_h \partial b_k} = x_{hi} x_{ki} q_i$$

$$\frac{\partial^2 q_i}{\partial b_k \partial \lambda_j} = x_{ki} q_i$$

$$\frac{\partial^2 q_i}{\partial \lambda_j^2} = q_i$$

Linear nonconstant independent variables x_k are assumed measured at the beginning and end of each period j, with $\bar{x}_{kji}$ as the average value of x_k for individual i during the period. In this case,

$$\int_{t_{j-1}}^{t_j - \theta} q_i(\tau) d\tau \approx (\lambda_j + \Sigma b_k \bar{x}_{kji})(t_j - \theta - t_{j-1}) \text{ and}$$

$$\int_{t_j - \theta}^{t_j} q_i(\tau) d\tau \approx (\lambda_j + \Sigma b_k x_{kji})\theta$$

First and second derivatives of q_i are analogous to the case in which x is constant, with $\bar{x}_{kji}$ or x_{kji} replacing x_{ki} in the derivatives.

For exponential decomposition, nonconstant independent variables changing linearly over time,

$$\int_{t_{j-1}}^{t_j - \theta} q_i(\tau) d\tau \approx \frac{\Delta t q_i(t_1)}{b \Delta x} [e^{b \Delta x t_2 / \Delta t} - e^{b \Delta x t_1 / \Delta t}] \qquad (6.146)$$

where

$$t_2 = t_j - \theta$$
$$t_1 = t_{j-i}$$
$$\Delta t = t_2 - t_1$$

t_j is the time at the end of period j

t_{j-1} is the time at the beginning of period j

and

$$\int_{t_j - \theta}^{t_j} q_i(\tau) d\tau \simeq \theta q_i(t_j) = \theta e^{\lambda_j + \Sigma b_k x_{kji}}$$

For q_i in the last fine period of length θ, the first and second derivatives are the same as in the case of constant independent variables since we assume x constant over the small interval of length θ. For the interval $t_j - \theta - t_{j-1}$,

289

which in general is longer, the derivative is obtained by differentiating the right-hand side of equation (6.146). This may be written as $D_2 - D_1$, where

$$D_2 = \frac{\Delta t q_i(t_1)}{\mathbf{b}\Delta\mathbf{x}} e^{\mathbf{b}\Delta\mathbf{x} t_2/\Delta t}$$

$$D_1 = \frac{\Delta t q_i(t_1)}{\mathbf{b}\Delta\mathbf{x}} e^{\mathbf{b}\Delta\mathbf{x} t_1/\Delta t}$$

Then the partial derivative of the right-hand side of equation (6.146) is $\partial D_2/\partial b_k - \partial D_1/\partial b_k$. Differentiating,

$$\frac{\partial D_2}{\partial b_k} = D_2\left[\frac{x_{k2}\Delta t + t_2\Delta x_k}{\Delta t} - \frac{\Delta x_k}{\mathbf{b}\Delta\mathbf{x}}\right],$$

$$\frac{\partial D_2}{\partial\lambda_j} = D_2,$$

and similarly for D_1. The second partial derivatives are

$$\frac{\partial^2 D_2}{\partial b_k\partial b_h} = \frac{1}{D_2}\frac{\partial D_2}{\partial b_k}\frac{\partial D_2}{\partial b_h} + \frac{D_2\Delta x_k\Delta x_h}{\mathbf{b}\Delta\mathbf{x}},$$

$$\frac{\partial^2 D_2}{\partial b_k\partial\lambda_j} = \frac{\partial D_2}{\partial b_k},$$

$$\frac{\partial^2 D_2}{\partial\lambda_j\partial\lambda_j} = D_2,$$

and similarly for D_1. With these first and second derivatives, we may use the same techniques described in equations (6.5)–(6.8) to give an algorithm for finding maximum likelihood estimates of **b**. Alternatively, the algorithm given in equation (6.3), using both first and second derivatives, may be used.

For the algorithm expressed in equation (6.3), the first and second derivatives are as shown. For the other algorithm, a Taylor series expansion of $q_i(t_1)$ in the numerator of equation (6.146) is used to obtain the equation used in iteration.

Whichever algorithm is used, the second derivatives, in conjunction with equation (6.9), are used to find the covariance matrix after convergence is achieved.

Thus, this method follows very closely the lines of the methods developed for cross-sectional and panel data. The first and second derivatives are different (and much simpler than in the case of panel data), and the form in which the data are organized is somewhat different. But the general equations for estimating **b** and the covariance matrix are the same.

290

References

Aleksandrov, A. D., Kolmogorov, A. N. and Lavrentev, M. A. *Mathematics: Its Content, Methods, and Meaning.* Cambridge, Mass: M.I.T. Press, 1963.

Baltes, Paul B, Cornelius, Steven W., and Nesselroade, John R. "Cohort Effects in Developmental Psychology," chapter 3 in John R. Nesselroade and Paul B. Baltes, eds., *Longitudinal Research in the Study of Behavior and Development.* New York: Academic Press, 1979.

Berelson, Bernard, Lazarfeld, Paul F., and McPhee, William. *Voting.* Chicago: University of Chicago Press, 1954.

Bliss, C. I. *Statistics in Biology.* Vol. 1. New York: McGraw-Hill, 1967.

Breslow, N. "Covariance Analysis of Censored Data," *Biometrics* 30 (1974): 89–99.

Burns, Lawton R. "The Adoption and Diffusion of Decentralized Management in Hospitals," Ph.D diss. The University of Chicago, 1981.

Campbell, D. T. and Clayton, K. N. "Avoiding Regression Effects in Panel Studies of Communication Impact," *Studies in Public Communication* 3 (1961): 99–118.

Clark, Kenneth B., and Clark, Mamie F. "Racial Identification and Preference in Negro Children," in *Readings in Social Psychology,* E. Maccoby, T. Newcomb, and E. Hartley, eds., New York: Holt, 1958, pp. 602–11.

Cohen, Joel and Singer, Burton. "Malaria in Nigeria: Constrained Continuous-Time Markov Models for Discrete-Time Longitudinal Data on Human Mixed-Species Infections," *Lectures on Mathematics in the Life Sciences,* Vol. 12, S. Levin, ed. Providence: American Mathematical Society, 1979, pp. 69–133.

Coleman, James S. *Introduction to Mathematical Sociology.* New York: The Free Press, 1964a.

———. *Models of Change and Response Uncertainty.* Englewood Cliffs, N.J.: Prentice-Hall, 1964b.

———. "The Mathematical Study of Change," in *Methodology in Social Research,* Hubert M. and Ann B. Blalock, eds., New York: McGraw-Hill, 1968, pp. 428–478.

Coleman, James S., Katz, Elihu, and Menzel, Herbert. *Medical Innovation.* Indianapolis: Bobbs Merrill, 1966.

Cox, D. R. "Partial Likelihood," *Biometrika* 62 (1975): 269–276.

———. "Regression Models and Life Tables," *Journal of the Royal Statistical Society* Series B. 34 (1972a): 187–202.

———. "The Statistical Analysis of Dependencies in Point Processes," in *Stochastic Point Processes: Statistical Analysis Theory, and Applications,* P. A. W. Lewis, ed., New York: Wiley, 1972b, pp. 55–66.

Crowley, John, and Hu, Marie. "Covariance Analysis of Heart Transplant Survival Data," *Journal of the American Statistical Association* 72, no. 357 (March 1977): 27–36.

DiPrete, Thomas. "Unemployment over the Life Cycle: Probability Models of Turnover," Ph.D. diss. Columbia University, 1979.

———. "Unemployment Over the Life Cycle: Racial Differences and the Effect of Changing Economic Conditions," *American Journal of Sociology* 87, no. 2 (September 1981): 286–307.

Efron, B. "The Efficiency of Cox's Likelihood Function for Censored Data," *Journal of American Statistical Association* 72 (1977): 557–565.

291

References

Fienberg, Stephen E. *The Analysis of Cross-Classified Categorical Data.* Cambridge, Mass.: MIT Press, 1977.

Flinn, Christopher, and Heckman, James. "Models for the Analysis of Labor Force Dynamics," Chicago: University of Chicago mimeograph, April 1980.

Glasstone, Samuel. *Textbook of Physical Chemistry.* 2nd. ed., New York: Van Nostrand, 1946.

Goodman, Leo A. "Causal Analysis of Data from Panel Studies and Other Kinds of Surveys," *American Journal of Sociology* 78 (1973): 1135–91.

Grizzle, James E. C., Starmer, Frank, and Koch, Gary G. "Analysis of Categorical Data By Linear Models," *Biometrics,* 25 (1969): 137–156.

Haberman, S. J. *The Analysis of Frequency Data.* Chicago: University of Chicago Press, 1974.

Hannan, Michael T., Tuma, Nancy Brandon, and Groeneveld, Lyle P. "Income and Independence Effects on Marital Dissolution: Results from the Seattle and Denver Income-Maintenance Experiments," *American Journal of Sociology* 84 no. 3. (November 1978): 611–633.

――――. "Income and Marital Events: Evidence from An Income-Maintenance Experiment," *The American Journal of Sociology* 82 no. 6 (May 1977): 1186–1211.

Hannan, Michael T., and Carroll, Glenn R. "Dynamics of Formal Political Structure: An Event-History Analysis," *American Sociological Review* 46 (February 1981): 19–35.

Heckman, J. "Simple Statistical Models for Discrete Panel Data Developed and Applied to Test the Hypothesis of True State Dependence," *Annales de l'insee* 30–31 (April/Sept 1978): 227–70.

Heckman, J. J. and Willis, R. J. "A Beta-logistic Model for the Analysis of Sequential Labor Force Participation by Married Women," *Journal of Political Economy,* 85 (1977): 27–58.

Hollingshead, August. *Elmtown's Youth.* New York: Wiley, 1949.

Hovland, Carl I., Lumsdaine, Arthur A., and Sheffield, Fred D. *Experiments on Mass Communication.* Princeton, New Jersey: Princeton University Press, 1949.

Hummon, Norman P., Doreian, Patrick and Teuter, Klaus. "A Structural Control Model of Organizational Change," *American Sociological Review* 40 (December 1975) 813–824.

Inbar, Michael. *The Vulnerable Age Phenomenon.* New York: Russell Sage, 1976.

Inbar, Michael, and Adler, Chaim. *Ethnic Integration in Israel.* New Brunswick, N.J.: Transaction Books, 1977.

Jahoda, Marie, Lazarfeld, Paul F., and Zeisel, Hans. *Marienthal: The Sociography of An Unemployed Community* (trans. from the German original), Chicago: Aldine, Atherton, 1971.

Kalbfleisch, J. and Prentice, R. "Marginal Likelihoods Based on Cox's Regression and Life Model," *Biometrika* 60 (1975): 267–279.

――――. "Some Efficiency Calculations for Survival Distributions," *Biometrika* 61 (1974): 31–38.

Kalbfleisch, J. D., and Sprott, D. A. "Application of Likelihood Methods to Models Involving Large Numbers of Parameters," *Journal of the Royal Statistical Society* Series B, 32 (1970): 175–208.

Kaplan, E. L. and Meier, P. "Nonparametric Estimation from Incomplete Observations," *Journal of the American Statistical Association* 53 (1958): 457–481.

Katz, Elihu and Lazarsfeld, Paul F. *Personal Influence.* Glencoe, Ill.: The Free Press, 1955.

Lazarsfeld, P. F. "Mutual Relations Over Time of Two Attributes: A Review and Integration of Various Approaches," in *Psychopathology,* M. Hammer, K. Salzinger and S. Sutton, eds., New York: Wiley, 1972.

――――. "Panel Studies," *Public Opinion Quarterly* 4 (1940): 122–128.

――――. "Some Episodes in the History of Panel Analysis," in *Longitudinal Research on Drug Use,* Denise Kandel, ed., New York: Wiley, 1978, pp. 249–65.

Lazarsfeld, Paul F., Berelson, Bernard, and Gaulet, Hazel. *The People's Choice.* New York: Duell, Sloan and Pierce, 1944.

Lipset, Seymour M., Trow, Martin, and Coleman, James. *Union Democracy.* New York: The Free Press, 1956.

Lynd, Robert S., and Lynd, Helen W. *Middletown.* New York: Harcourt Brace, 1929.

McDill, Edward L. and Coleman, James S. "High School Social Status, College Plans and Interest in Academic Achievement: A Panel Analysis," *American Sociological Review.* 28, no. 6 (December 1963): 905–918.

McFadden, Daniel. "A Comment on Discriminant Analysis 'Versus' Logit Analysis," *Annals of Economic and Social Measurement* 5 (1976): 511–23.

———. "Conditional Logit Analysis of Qualitative Choice Behavior," in *Frontiers in Econometrics.* P. Zarembka, ed., New York: Academic Press, 1974.

———. "Quantal Choice Analysis: A Survey," *Annals of Economic and Social Measurement* 5 (1976): 363–90.

McGinnis, R. "A Stochastic Model of Social Mobility," *American Sociological Review* 33 (October 1968): 712–722.

Nelder, J. A. and Wedderburn, R. W. M. "Generalized Linear Models," *J. Roy. Statist. Soc. Ser. A.,* 135 (1972): 370–384.

Nerlove, Marc and Press, S. James. *Multivariate Log-Linear Probability Models for the Analysis of Qualitative Data.* Evanston, Illinois: Northwestern University, 1976.

Pelz, D. C., and Andrews, F. M. "Detecting Causal Priorities in Panel Study Data," *American Sociological Review* 29 (1964): 836–848.

Peto, Richard. "Discussion of Cox's Paper," in *Cox* (1972a): 205–207.

Porter, Judith D. R. *Black Child, White Child: The Development of Racial Attitudes.* Cambridge, Mass.: Harvard University Press, 1971.

Prentice, Ross L., and Kalbfleisch, J. D. "Hazard Rate Models with Covariates," *Biometrics* 35 (March 1979): 25–39.

Simon, Rita James, and Alstein, Howard. *Transracial Adoption.* New York: Wiley, 1977.

Singer, Burton and Spilerman, S. "Social Mobility Models for Heterogeneous Populations," in *Sociological Methodology,* by H. L. Costner, ed., San Francisco: Jossey-Bass, Inc., 1973–1974, pp. 356–401.

———. "Some Methodological Issues in the Analysis of Longitudinal Surveys," *Annals of Economic and Social Measurement* 5 (1976a): 447–475.

———. "Trace Inequalities for Mixtures of Markov Chains," *Advances in Applied Probability* 9, no. 4 (December 1977): 747–764.

———. "The Representation of Social Processes by Markov Models," *American Journal of Sociology* 82 (July 1976b): 1–54.

Sorensen, A. B. "Estimating Rates From Retrospective Questions," in *Sociological Methodology,* D. Heise, ed., San Francisco: Jossey-Bass, 1977, pp. 209–223.

Spilerman, Seymour. "The Analysis of Mobility Processes by the Introduction of Independent Variables into a Markov Chain," *American Sociological Review* 37 (June 1972): 277–294.

Theil, Henri. "On the Estimation of Relationships Involving Qualitative Variables," *American Journal of Sociology* 76 (July 1970): 103–154.

Tuma, Nancy. "Rewards, Resources and the Rate of Mobility: A Nonstationary Multivariate Stochastic Model," *American Sociological Review,* 41 (1976): 338–360.

Tuma, Nancy, and Hannan, Michael. *Social Dynamics: Models and Methods,* Academic Press, forthcoming.

Tuma, Nancy, Hannan, Michael, and Groeneveld, Lyle. "Dynamic Analysis of Event Histories," *American Journal of Sociology* 84 (January 1979): 820–854.

Wakeley, P. C. "Planting the Southern Pines," *U.S. Department of Agriculture Forest Service Agricultural Monograph,* 18 (1954): 1–233.

Warner, W. Lloyd, and Lunt, Pearl S. *The Social Life of A Modern Community.* New Haven: Yale University Press, 1941.

Wiggins, Lee M. *Panel Analysis—Latent Probability Models for Attitude and Behavior Processes.* San Francisco: Jossey-Bass, 1973.

Index

DATE DUE

DEMCO 38-297